European

European Integration and Industrial Relations

Multi-Level Governance in the Making

Paul Marginson and Keith Sisson

with the collaboration of James Arrowsmith

Foreword by Harry C. Katz

© Paul Marginson and Keith Sisson 2004, 2006
Foreword © Harry C. Katz 2006

First published in hardback in 2004
First published in paperback in 2006 by
PALGRAVE MACMILLAN
Houndmills, Basingstoke, Hampshire RG21 6XS and
175 Fifth Avenue, New York, N.Y. 10010
Companies and representatives throughout the world

PALGRAVE MACMILLAN is the global academic imprint of the Palgrave
Macmillan division of St. Martin's Press, LLC and of Palgrave Macmillan Ltd.
Macmillan® is a registered trademark in the United States, United Kingdom
and other countries. Palgrave is a registered trademark in the European
Union and other countries.

ISBN-13: 978–0–333–96866–6 hardback
ISBN-10: 0–333–96866–2   hardback
ISBN-13: 978–0–230–00191–6 paperback
ISBN-10: 0–230–00191–2   paperback

This book is printed on paper suitable for recycling and made from fully
managed and sustained forest sources. Logging, pulping and manufacturing
processes are expected to conform to the environmental regulations of the
country of origin.

A catalogue record for this book is available from the British Library.

The Library of Congress has catalogued the hardcover edition as follows:
     European integration and industrial relations : multi-level governance in
     the making / Paul Marginson and Keith Sisson; with the collaboration of
     James Arrowsmith
          p. cm.
     Includes bibliographical references and index.
     ISBN 0–333–96866–2 (cloth) – ISBN 0–230–00191–2 (pbk)
          1. Industrial relations – European Union countries. 2. Europe –
     Economic integration. I. Marginson, Paul. II. Sisson, Keith. III. Arrowsmith,
     James, 1968–
HD8376.5.E933 2004
337.1′42—dc22   2004043854

Printed and bound in Great Britain by
CPI Antony Rowe, Chippenham and Eastbourne

To Keith for almost twenty years of stimulating collaboration – and without whose prompting this (ad)venture would never have got under way

Contents

List of Figures

List of Tables

List of Abbreviations

AFTA	ASEAN Free Trade Area
Amicus-AEEU	Amalgamated Engineering and Electrical Union section of Britain's Amicus trade union
BDA	Bundesvereinigung der Deutschen Arbeitgeberverbände (Confederation of German Employers)
BWK	Bundeskammer der gewerblichen Wirtschaft (Austrian Federal Chamber of Business)
CEC	Commission of the European Communities
CEE	Central eastern Europe
CGIL-FIOM	Confederazione Generale Italiana del Lavoro – Federazione Impiegati Operai Mettalurgici (Metalworking trade union of Italy's largest trade union confederation)
DAG	Deutsche Angestellengewerkschaft (German white-collar trade union, now part of Ver.di)
DGB	Deutscher Gewerkschaftsbund (German Trade Union Confederation)
ECB	European Central Bank
ECJ	European Court of Justice
ECU	European Currency Unit
EEA	European Economic Area
EEF	Engineering Employers' Federation
EFBWW	European Federation of Building and Woodworkers
EFJ	European Federation of Journalists
EIF	European Industry Federation (of trade unions)
EIRO	European Industrial Relations Observatory
EMF	European Metalworkers' Federation
EMU	Economic and Monetary Union
EPSU	European Federation of Public Service Unions
ERT	European Round Table of Industrialists
ETF	European Transport Workers' Federation
ETUC	European Trade Union Confederation
ETUF-TCL	European Trade Union Federation – Textiles, Clothing and Leather

EU	European Union
EU-15	The 15 member states of the European Union prior to the 2004 enlargement
EWC	European Works Council
GDP	Gross Domestic Product
HBV	Gewerkschaft Handel, Banken und Versicherungen (German finance and commerce trade union, now part of Ver.di)
HRM	Human Resource Management
ICT	Information and Communication Technology
IG-BAU	Industriegewerkschaft Bauen-Agrar-Umwelt (German construction trade union)
IG-Metall	Industriegewerkschaft Metall (German metalworking trade union)
ILO	International Labour Office
IMF	International Monetary Fund
IT	Information Technology
LO	Landsorganisationen (DK, S) (Danish/Swedish Trade Union Confederation)
MNC	Multinational Company
NAFTA	North American Free Trade Agreement
NAP	National Action Plan
NGO	Non-governmental Organization
OECD	Organisation for Economic Co-operation and Development
ÖGB	Österreichischer Gewerkschaftsbund (Austrian Trade Union Confederation)
OMC	Open Method of Coordination
OT	'Ohne Tarif' (without collective bargaining) employers' association (Germany)
PEC	Pact for Employment and Competitiveness
R&D	Research and Development
SME	Small and Medium Sized Enterprise
SSCD	Sector Social Dialogue Committee
ULC	Unit Labour Costs
UNICE	Union of Industrial and Employers' Confederations of Europe
UNI-Europa	Union Network International – Europe
Ver.di	Vereinte Dienstleistungsgewerkschaft (German private and public services trade union)
WEM	The Employers' Organization of the Metal Trades in Europe

Foreword

Some books and articles get known for the bold and extreme nature of their arguments, arguments that more often than not are unsupported and simplistic. This book gets it right by doing just the opposite. With a fine attention to detail, Marginson and Sisson describe the complex nature of the evolution of industrial relations in integrated Europe. Their method is institutional industrial relations at its best. The data derive from a series of thorough company- and sector-level studies conducted through a number of projects and with the help of various teams of researchers. A 'governance' perspective is used to analyze how industrial relations are evolving at workplace, company, multi-company, sectoral, national, and European-wide levels.

Given the wealth of information and subtle analysis the authors provide, I am tempted to stop here and merely state that to know what is going on in European industrial relations you should read this book. But even if you are not particularly curious about Europe you should read this book as it provides a rich generic understanding of regional and national labor politics. For example, one of Marginson and Sisson's insights concerns the utility of analyzing the interaction of regional, national and local level activities. While they illustrate the value of this perspective through analysis of European developments, this perspective provides insights into developments in North America and other regions.

Recognition of the contribution Marginson and Sisson bring to the debate about the future of Europe thus reveals the more general applicability of their method. On one side of the great debate regarding Europeanization are those claiming that European industrial relations are in the death-grip of an Americanization involving de-unionization, decentralization and the fatal weakening of union power and social democratic regulation (what might be called the Euro-pessimist position). On the other side are those who see a movement toward, or at least still hope for the possibility of, a leveling-up to a social Europe through the emergence of an active and social democratic European level of social regulation and industrial relations (the Euro-optimist position). Marginson and Sisson see developments in both directions, and what is most striking is that the seemingly contradictory tendencies are shown not to be inconsistent. Marginson and Sisson clarify, for example, how it could be that while on the one hand there is a spread of decentralized collective bargaining, replacing previous multi-company or sectoral forms, there has also been a spread of social pacts and meaningful European-level initiatives, such as European Works Councils. To see how both centralization and decentralization can be occurring at the same time and in a manner that is not contradictory, you will have to read the book.

Marginson and Sisson also argue that how changes are occurring is as important as the outcomes of change, both because the process of adjustment matters for its own sake and because choices made by the parties regarding process ultimately affect outcomes. One way the authors make room for process in their analysis is by adopting a governance perspective in which industrial relations is viewed as a multi-level system involving mixed motives (that is, shaped by both distributive and integrative interests).

In addition to analyzing various levels of industrial relations, Marginson and Sisson focus on the role of multi-national corporations (MNCs). They see MNCs as a key force promoting diversity in workplace employment practices and corporate industrial relations strategies. Developments at MNCs also matter because it is those firms that are bound by the European Works Council Directive, and that have thus become (in the authors' words) a 'focal point for the Europeanization of industrial relations' and (in my words) in some ways also a centralizing force, even though they are simultaneously bringing more variation to industrial relations practices within countries. Here again Marginson and Sisson provide a coherent logic to explain what might at first glance appear to be contradictory and inconsistent tendencies.

While the process of change in labor-management-government interactions matters, Marginson and Sisson are attentive to employment outcomes as well. They focus in particular on wage developments and observe a movement toward 'convergence without coordination'.

I cannot emphasize enough the wealth of insight provided by Marginson and Sisson. They provide a truly comparative analysis organized around thematic issues rather than the much too common country comparisons. Anyone interested in what is going on in European industrial relations – indeed, anyone who wishes to learn how to study industrial relations anywhere – should read this book.

HARRY C. KATZ

Dean

School of Industrial and Labor Relations

Cornell University

Preface

There are three reasons for writing this book. The first is to establish whether the process of European integration is making any practical difference to industrial relations. Is European integration bringing about greater convergence in the existing nationally-based patterns of regulation and, if so, what are the key processes? Is it having a bigger impact on some countries, sectors and companies than others? Where do the supranational institutions, such as the Maastricht social policy process, fit in? Is it mainly a question of adding another tier of governance or is the supranational re-shaping or even taking over from the national? What effect is the much-changed economic policy context associated with economic and monetary union (EMU) having on existing industrial relations processes and their outcomes in terms of wages and hours of work? Is EMU threatening the extensive legal regulation and inclusive structure of collective bargaining associated with the 'European social model'? Is it significantly changing the behaviour of wage bargainers? Above all, is a new model of industrial relations emerging and, if so, what shape and form is it taking?

There is never an ideal time to try to answer such questions. Writing during 2002 and 2003 came after the introduction in January 1999 of the third and critical stage of economic and monetary union (EMU) involving the single currency – circulated as Euro notes and coins from January 2002. Repercussions for industrial relations anticipated EMU, have been augmented since its introduction, but are far from having run their course. In 2000, the European Commission published its first report on industrial relations to be followed in 2002 by a major review by a High Level Group of experts, signalling the 'coming of age' of the area in the EU-level policy arena. The book will appear as the EU is enlarged to 25 member states from 1 May 2004. The accession of eight central eastern European states, most of which have industrial relations systems which are pale reflections of those associated with the 'European social model', is unleashing further dynamics the consequences of which for European integration and for industrial relations are difficult to predict.

The second reason for writing the book is theoretical. In recent years there has been something of a loss of focus among industrial relations scholars. As the policy context has changed, reflecting the decline in industrial conflict and in trade union membership in many countries, the subject has tended to become fragmented, with the traditional disciplines reasserting their influence. For economists, the attraction has been the link between institutions and economic performance; for political scientists, the development of national-level 'social pacts'; and for social policy analysts, concerns for poverty and exclusion. The result is that the established focus of industrial relations – the regulation or governance of the employment relationship – has tended to be squeezed out.

Making matters worse is that the 'governance' focus has also come in for criticism closer to home. For some, it is the association of regulation with rules, conflicts of interest and negotiation that has led to a shift of emphasis to managerial strategies or human resource management (HRM), the seeming decline of institutional industrial relations, with which regulation has been most linked, being the immediate reason (Purcell, 1993; Kaufmann, 2001). For others, ironically, a 'governance' focus smacks too much of a managerialist agenda. Kelly (1998), for example, argues that, instead of the employer's need for control and cooperation to secure work performance, analytical endeavour should start from injustice and focus on the mobilization of workers to redress this.

Paradoxically, however, the coming of the EU has not only meant greater opportunities for the traditional disciplines, but also emphasized the need for the governance perspective associated with industrial relations analysis. Economists, political scientists and social policy specialists tend to see things from a 'top-down' national systems perspective. The key players are political actors. Even where private interest groups are involved, they tend to be viewed as adjuncts to the political process, rather than engaged in a largely private system of governance with the potential to promote its own forms of cross-national integration. Fundamentally important is that the workplace is regarded as a 'black box' where those involved react predictably to external stimuli. On the face of it, HRM passes this test much better, being concerned with the workplace and managerial strategies. Yet it is dominated by concerns with the 'universal' and 'unitary' rather than the 'contingent' and 'pluralist', with the issues of conflict of interest, uncertainty and negotiation that are involved in the management of the employment relationship being rarely addressed (Edwards, 2003).

In reasserting the virtues of a governance perspective, the following main benefits can be identified:

- *It is inclusive or encompassing in its coverage.* It can accommodate the variety of forms of governance such as unilateral management regulation (including HRM), joint regulation or collective bargaining and state regulation and, perhaps most importantly, the interface between them.
- *It is relatively impartial.* The term 'governance' certainly denotes a measure of order and stability. At the same time, however, these rules are also rights with links to issues of quality of working life, citizenship and industrial democracy.
- *It offers a balance between parsimony and complexity.* If focusing on HRM or collective bargaining is too narrow, the opposite is to suggest that 'employment systems' (Rubery and Grimshaw, 2002) or 'labour politics' (Thelen, 2001) offers a coherent alternative. The danger is not just that too much ground has to be covered – industrial relations as it is defined here, employment policy and social protection – but that one aspect, along with its ideas and frameworks, tends to dominate the others. In the case of 'employment systems', it is labour markets and institutional economic analysis. In the case of 'labour politics', it is varieties of capitalism and the discourse of political economy. In both cases, there is a tendency to downplay considerations of industrial relations and/or see them through an oblique lens.
- *It is multi-disciplinary or 'post-disciplinary'.* That industrial relations is eclectic in its approach to theory is sometimes seen as a weakness. Yet, as Flanders (1970: 85) insisted many years ago, the problem with the traditional disciplines is that they 'tear the subject apart by concentrating attention on some of its aspects to the exclusion or comparative neglect of others … a partial view of anything, accurate as it may be within its limits, must of necessity be a distorted one'.
- *It is relevant at many levels* – international, national, sector, company and workplace. Indeed, it is the scope for probing the links between levels and for cross-national comparisons that this focus allows that is one of its great methodological assets.
- *It is an intervening as well as a dependent variable.* A focus on governance does not just solve the dependent variable problem. How the employment relationship is regulated carries a wide range of political,

social and economic implications, as well as having a significant bearing on the life experience of many millions of workers and the functioning of all kinds of employing organizations. A governance focus is fundamentally important not just for reasons of theory but also practice and policy.

From this perspective, the study of industrial relations analysis has some close parallels with political analysis (see Hay, 2002c). Industrial relations, like political inquiry, is concerned with 'the identification and interrogation of the distribution, exercise and consequences of power' (Leftwich, 1984). But there are some distinctive features, reflecting the subject's very different arena. Superficially, the subject matter involves a mix of substantive and procedural matters, but underpinning this is the employment relationship, which involves two parties of unequal power. It may be massively influenced from outside, but it is a matter that is internal to the organization. It is also fundamentally uncertain terrain, where cooperation and conflict are ever present; where outcomes are negotiated – not necessarily formally; and where notions of fairness and legitimacy are profoundly important. The forms of governance are also markedly different. There is a mix of public and private arrangements and of unilateral, joint, state and tripartite forms – with the balance between them being central.

European integration raises novel problems for a governance perspective. The EU is widely seen as a *sui generis* institution – it is difficult to establish precisely of what it is an instance, comparisons with either a superstate or an international organization hardly capturing its essence (Rosamond, 2000). European integration also offers a unique opportunity to explore wider issues. Prominent, following Dunlop (1958: 94–7), is the importance of the locus and distribution of power in the wider society as opposed to technological and market considerations, raising issues such as convergence and divergence, structure and agency and the role of 'path dependency' as opposed to market forces. In particular, it offers an opportunity to test the proposition, first enunciated by Commons (1909/1968) almost a century ago and which perhaps comes closest to a 'law' in industrial relations, namely that industrial relations systems follow the market. Are industrial relations systems developing supranational features with the coming of EMU, just as they assumed regional and national ones as local markets expanded? And if European integration is bringing a supranational dimension, how are national actors dealing with the collective action problem and what are the key processes involved?

This brings us to the third reason for writing the book, which lies in the policy realm. In contemplating the impact of European integration, the main preoccupation of industrial relations commentators has been with the 'end-point' rather than the governance arrangements that are actually emerging. Moreover, a widely held view has emerged that there are only two ways forward for industrial relations in EU member countries. Put starkly, the choice is seen as being between centralization and decentralization. Either the EU establishes a vertically integrated system that is comparable to existing national systems – a social union to accompany economic union. Or existing systems of national industrial relations must fragment leading to the break-up of the inclusive structure of collective bargaining and the dilution of the extensive legal regulation seen as integral elements of the European social model. Perhaps not surprisingly, given the immense policy implications, analytical concerns and normative positions have become inextricably intertwined. For some, a vertically integrated system is essential to protecting the model, while for others it stands in the way of much-needed reform of existing arrangements. An article in the *Financial Times* on 15 September 2000 by Otmar Issing, the European Central Bank's chief economist, captures the tone. Issing suggests that tackling problems such as unemployment

> does not call for supranational, 'European' solutions such as Social Union to complement Economic and Monetary Union…Giving in to such demands would result in higher unemployment and tensions between countries and regions; ultimately, the survival of monetary union would be at risk. Rather than harmonising social standards at the most generous levels in the Euro-zone and imposing uniform wage agreements throughout Europe, wages need to take account of sectoral and regional differences in productivity and local labour market conditions. This is all the more important because labour market mobility is likely to play a smaller role than it does in the US and there is no comparable system of fiscal transfers within the Euro-zone.

Our view is that it is misleading to see the choices in such stark terms. As social affairs Commissioner Anna Diamantopolou responded, in a letter published in the *Financial Times* on 18 September 2000, to pose the choices in terms of 'two extremes of a social union versus a completely de-regulated free-for-all' is to 'conjure up' a 'caricature … of the EU's current approach' which entails the elaboration and strengthening of a multi-level system of governance and attempts to modernize the European social model. Such polarization is also dangerous. It risks distracting attention from what should be the main aim, namely developing a system of industrial relations governance that is capable of achieving the laudable aims set by the EU's Lisbon Summit in 2000, of becoming the 'most competitive and dynamic knowledge economy in the world, capable of durable economic growth, of higher employment levels and jobs of a better quality and of improved social cohesion' (EIRO, 2000). Concurring with Weiss (1998), such a system is most likely to be achieved through the development and adaptation of arrangements that are sensitive to institutional and cultural specificities rather than through the cathartic change that radical forms of decentralization would entail.

The approach of the book can claim to be distinctive in several key respects. Being grounded in the industrial relations tradition, it puts institutions centre stage, holding that they matter not because, as many economists would see them, they constitute 'imperfections' in the smooth working of markets. Institutions matter because markets do not exist in a vacuum – they need institutions to give them shape and direction and it is the choices that social actors make about these institutions that are critical. It is primarily concerned with the governance arrangements that are emerging rather than the extent to which the EU is being, can be or should be integrated. By providing an integrated treatment of industrial relations at, respectively, the EU community, sector and company levels it addresses a 'weakness of industrial relations research that these central components are, generally speaking, discussed independently of one another' (Hoffmann *et al.*, 2002: 47). In this respect it can claim to go further than Keller and Platzer's (2003) welcome edited volume. It also goes beyond much of the literature on EU-level industrial relations in treating developments at national level in the light of the pressures and processes of European integration, as well as those at EU level, and in exploring the interaction between the national and European levels – an area where Keller and Platzer (2003: 163) conclude that there is 'a lack of comprehensive comparative research'. It is multi-disciplinary, which means that the particular frameworks or concerns of any one individual discipline do not limit it. It is empirically as well as theoretically grounded, drawing on the authors' experience of a number of cross-national inquiries in areas including the structure of collective bargaining, the role of multinational companies, changes in work organization, organizational restructuring, the implications of European Works Councils (EWCs) and the impact of EMU itself. It is genuinely cross-national in that it integrates the material theme by theme rather than country by country. It is concerned with policy *and* practice: it deals not only with macro-level policy, but also the repercussions on existing governance arrangements. Its approach is 'bottom-up' as well as 'top-down', paying particular attention to much-neglected developments at sector and company levels.

A work such as this incurs many debts of gratitude. Most evidently there are the many employers' organization and trade union officials, senior company managers and employee representatives throughout Western Europe who gave their valuable time to be interviewed under the various studies from which the book draws its material. The principal projects comprise the study of 'Emerging Boundaries of European Collective Bargaining at Sector and Enterprise Levels' funded under the UK Economic and Social Science Research Council's (ESRC) 'One Europe or Several?' (OEOS) programme; and cross-national investigations into so-called 'pacts for employment and competitiveness' (Sisson and Artiles, 2000) and the impact of EMU on sector- and company-level industrial relations (Sisson and Marginson, 2000) for the European Foundation for the Improvement of Living and Working Conditions. Further details of these three projects are provided in the Appendix. Also drawn upon are findings from studies of EWCs funded by the European Foundation (Marginson *et al.*, 1998; Carley and Marginson, 2000) and ESRC under the research programme of the Centre for the Internationalisation of the Employment Relationship at the University of Warwick (Hall *et al.*, 2003; Marginson *et al.*, 2004).

The field research under the ESRC OEOS programme project was realized with the collaboration and support of, respectively, IST at the Université Catholique de Louvain, Belgium, IAAEG in Trier, Germany and IRES Lombardia in Milan, Italy. Special thanks are due to Evelyne Léonard, Ida Regalia, Dieter Sadowski, Hanna Lehmann, Marco Trentini and Pierre Walthèry for their involvement in the project and the programme of interviews. We are also indebted to the practitioners who gave us the benefit of their advice and insights as members of the project's Advisory Committee: Len Aspell (HSBC plc), Ann Denvir (formerly of Unifi), Richard Fulham (AEEU-Amicus until early 2002) and David Yeandle (Engineering Employers' Federation). Val Jephcott, IRRU's Research Secretary, provided much-appreciated administrative and technical support throughout the three main projects and has tackled the unenviable task of ironing-out the word-processing inconsistencies between the two authors as well as checking the referencing and laying out the figures and tables.

Three further individuals deserve a special mention. In alphabetical order, the first is Jim Arrowsmith, who worked with us on the ESRC's OEOS programme project and was involved in both the European Foundation studies. Jim not only did half of the OEOS interviews, helping to shape the thrust of the project in the process, but also made many pertinent comments on the manuscript, which is perhaps the most demanding task to be asked of a colleague. Next is Hubert Krieger of the European Foundation for the Improvement of Living and Working Conditions. Hubert can be a demanding person to work with, as he would be the first to acknowledge. But for his drive and enthusiasm, however, one of the main projects from which the book draws its ideas and data would never have happened. His firm commitment to the integration of the results of cross-national research on a thematic rather than country-by-country basis has also been an important influence on us. The third person to whom thanks are due is Helen Wallace, formerly director of ESRC's 'One Europe or Several?' programme and now Director of the Robert Schuman Centre for Advanced Studies at the European University Institute. It was not just her encouragement and support of the 'lone' industrial relations project that was important. Involvement in the 'One Europe or Several?' programme exposed us to a literature and frameworks that neither of us would have investigated of our own accord. Its emphasis on 'governance' in general and 'multi-level governance' in particular was especially helpful, as was the refinements of such concepts as 'spillover' and 'path dependency'. Beyond this was the confirmation of the importance of institutional analysis, which seemed to have been lost sight of in industrial relations in recent years. If nothing else, therefore, the hope is that this book will go some way towards restoring such an approach to its rightful place at the core of industrial relations studies.

PAUL MARGINSON
KEITH SISSON

1
Introduction: Contested Terrain

In recent years, the term 'European social model' has acquired widespread currency. Although few have been prepared to spell out what they mean by the term, most would probably agree with Visser and Hemerijck (1997: 13–14), that it is predicated upon upholding fundamental principles in three particular policy domains. These are the right to work, including commitments to full employment and active employment policies; the right to social protection, involving encompassing basic social security cover for the non-working population; and the right to civilized standards in the workplace, covering issues of employment governance or regulation. Kittel (2002: 3), citing Ferrera *et al.* (2000: 13), adds two further common traits: a relatively egalitarian wage and income distribution, which relates to all three domains, and a high degree of interest organization on the part of employers and workers together with coordinated wage bargaining, which relates to the third. In each case, the above rights exist not just for the benefit of workers – they are the 'rules of the game, and like all such rules, they constrain in order to enable' (Marsden, 1999: 5).

It is with the third of these areas, commonly known as industrial relations, that this study is concerned. At its heart is the employment relationship and how it is regulated or governed. Both substantive and procedural issues are involved. The first covers the 'what' (for example, recruitment and selection arrangements, the grading system, the type of wage system and the level of wages, the working time arrangements, the training provisions, the disciplinary arrangements) and the second the 'how' (the extent to which the substantive issues are determined unilaterally by management or jointly in consultation and negotiation with workers and/or their representatives and/or are the result of legal regulation).

The intrinsic importance of employment governance hardly needs emphasizing. Almost half the population of the EU is in some form of paid work or employment, around 168 million people (European Commission, 2002c: 173), and is thus directly a party to an employment relationship. For these many millions, work is one of the biggest influences on life experience, with both individual dignity and the opportunity for personal development being involved as well as the material standard of life which the wages earned support. For policy makers, there is a wide range of political, social and economic implications. At EU level, for example, industrial relations is seen as integral to pushing forward the ambitious strategy for economic and social modernization launched at the 2000 Lisbon Summit.

In practice, with the widespread shift of emphasis of macroeconomic policy from the demand to the supply side, it is industrial relations' link with competitiveness that has tended to dominate policy discourse. In Bordogna and Cella's words (1999: 25), industrial relations has become the 'villain of the piece', the European model being unfavourably compared to the US equivalent. At the risk of caricature, key features of the former are seen as an emphasis on employee rights introduced by collective bargaining and/or legal enactment, leading to security of employment and relatively high levels of wages and conditions. The downside, it is argued, is inflexibility, a lack of competitiveness and high levels of unemployment. The US model is deemed to be the opposite. There may be considerable insecurity, lower levels of wages and poorer working conditions for many, reflecting weak employee protection and 'hire-and-fire' practice. Management is much freer of the restrictions of collective bargaining and legal regulation, however, supposedly leading to greater flexibility, improved competitiveness and a much lower rate of unemployment than in Europe.

The study's specific focus is on the impact of European integration both on the institutions of industrial relations and their outcomes in terms of wages and working time. The progress of European integration has profound practical and policy implications for national systems of industrial relations and for the emerging EU-level framework. It also raises fundamental and challenging issues in theorizing industrial relations. Above all, in highlighting the relationship between markets, states and institutions, it raises questions of the importance of the levels of analysis, the implications for institutional diversity and the nature and extent of the choice available to actors. Indeed, it is not going too far to suggest that it is one of the rare occasions in social science that come close to laboratory experiment.

Of particular interest is the connection between industrial relations and the nature and extent of markets. In a subject not noted for its 'laws', one of the propositions that comes pretty close, first enunciated by Commons (1909/1968) nearly a century ago, is that industrial relations systems follow the market. Accordingly, the development of Economic and Monetary Union (EMU) in particular has led to considerable reflection about the prospects for the 'Europeanization' of industrial relations and the different forms this might take (Kauppinen, 1998; Sisson *et al.*, 1999). Yet, it has also fuelled debate about the implications of increasingly globalized competition. Indeed, one issue is whether EMU is little more than a cipher for 'globalization', reflecting the dominant neo-liberal, monetarist paradigm of a 'banker's Europe' (Milner, 2002). From this has emerged an alternative scenario. Far from encouraging the development of a coherent European system, EMU might lead to the fragmentation and eventual 'Americanization' of industrial relations, involving deregulation and marketization, a reduction in social protection and the break-up of the dominant model of multi-employer bargaining (Martin, 1999).

This chapter has four main tasks. The first is to consider how commentators expect EMU to affect the context of industrial relations. The second is to elaborate the competing hypotheses about this impact. The third is to raise some wider considerations. The fourth is to set out the book's argument and outline its structure.

EMU and its implications – threats and opportunities?

The economic nature of the political project underlying the construction and enlargement of the EU is well established. EMU, broadly defined, is a process of economic integration which has evolved through two key stages: first, the programme – launched in 1985 – to create the single European market by the end of 1992: second, monetary union involving, from 1999, the adoption of a single currency and the establishment of the European Central Bank with the authority to set a common interest rate. It is helpful to begin by distinguishing between the potential micro and macro implications of EMU for industrial relations. The first reflect the pressures of stronger competition and restructuring. The second result from the much-changed economic policy context that EMU entails.

More competition ... and more restructuring?

The programme to create the single market was expressly aimed at promoting the rationalization and restructuring of European industry, so as to enhance its competitive position in global markets. Further impetus was given by the dynamics of monetary union. Both encourage European companies to organize their production and their market servicing on a continental European basis, as Chapter 2 elaborates. Paradoxically, the dynamic is underlined by the extent to which international companies based outside Europe, concerned to consolidate their presence within a key global market, have also been players in the twin processes of restructuring and rationalization within the EU (Ramsay, 1995). In addition, the European Commission has pursued industrial policies to facilitate the rationalization and restructuring of particular industrial sectors, such as steel, and competition policies aimed at opening up previously closed markets to European-wide competition, as in energy, telecommunications and airlines.

Proponents and opponents of EMU alike agree that, as well as savings on transaction costs, the main benefits of monetary union potentially lie in the efficiency gains coming from elevating the single market from a 'formal to a real event' (Münchau, 1998). The single currency, it is argued, will be an important catalyst for change with competition being the keynote. In promoting the case for EMU, the European Commission juxtaposes arguments about the value a single monetary policy will bring in combating unemployment, in terms of low inflation and a stable macroeconomic environment, with extolling EMU's virtues in encouraging greater efficiency and competition. The Euro, says the Commission (1998a: 12–13), will 'improve the transparency of trade, sharpen competition and enable customers to purchase goods at better prices and firms to become more competitive'.

The Commission (1998a: 13–14) also emphasizes that

> The creation of a large Euro capital market in 1999 will radically alter financial markets for the benefit of firms and households through increased competition and improvement in the quality of service ... All economic agents will ultimately benefit from the availability of loans or borrowings in one or the same currency on a larger or more liquid market and under conditions of transparency, equality of access and cost that are similar to those that are prevailing for the US dollar.

The key advantage, stresses Cardani (1998: 118), is the reduction of the exchange rate risk, i.e. that investment in another market could be undermined by devaluation.

Extensive 'external' and 'internal' restructuring results as these developments reinforce the establishment of a single European market. The external aspect takes the form of mergers and acquisitions, joint ventures and strategic alliances, as companies aim to establish and/or consolidate a presence across the single European market. The internal dimension represents significant reorganization of operations in response to competitive challenges, which EMU intensifies. Both dimensions entail an increasingly significant cross-border element bringing additional implications for industrial relations.

A recurring theme is that a single capital market, driven by global stock market considerations, will accelerate changes in the dominant model of business organization, boosting the significance of a so-called 'super league' of European multinational companies (MNCs) and in the process providing further impetus to competition (P. Martin, 1998). Ownership is expected to become more internationalized as foreign direct investment both in the form of new operations and the buying of a significant stake in existing businesses increases. Further, it is anticipated that the 'Anglo-Saxon' model of corporate governance, in which shareholder value predominates, will threaten the 'Rhineland' model, in which social considerations conjoin with economic ones, and the *Colbertist* model under which the state gives strategic direction and resources to enterprises.

Whilst single capital and product markets are progressively emerging, commentators largely concur that a single European labour market seems unlikely in the near future. As Obstfeld and Peri (1998: 243) point out, workers theoretically have full freedom of movement in post-Schengen Europe. But the factors limiting intra-national migration apply even more to international migration, where there are also the barriers of language and custom. Instead, as EMU cements the establishment of single capital and product markets, national labour markets have increasingly been set in competition with each other, with profound implications for industrial relations.

A much-changed economic policy context?

Much economic and industrial relations literature focuses on the possible implications of the much-changed economic policy context that EMU brings (Sisson *et al.*, 1999). A first cause of concern is the perceived incomplete nature of EMU's architecture. EMU is seen as lacking some essential features of other currency unions, such as a common taxation policy and the fiscal resources to secure adjustment through transferring sizeable funds from one region (country) to another. Some would add a negligible social dimension. The Euro zone is not, in Mundell's (1961) terms, an 'optimum currency area'. This matters because in the face of an asymmetric shock affecting one part of the Euro zone some of the adjustment mechanisms found in existing currency zones are absent.

A second feature is the institutional arrangements of EMU. The 1991 Maastricht Treaty set out the timetable for the launch of a single currency by 1999. It also provided for the establishment of the European Central Bank, with responsibility for setting a single monetary policy across the member states joining the single currency. It is the definition of this responsibility that deserves emphasis. The ECB's remit is primarily concerned with price stability, and not with economic growth also. Moreover, its inflation target is asymmetric – unlike the case of the Bank of England – encouraging the ECB towards a monetary policy which under- rather than overshoots the target. The arrangements agreed at Maastricht were subsequently augmented by the Stability and Growth Pact, which severely restricts the fiscal freedom of manoeuvre of individual governments. The Pact calls for fiscal positions to be balanced or in surplus in normal times so that automatic economic stabilisers can operate and establishes a 3 per cent ceiling for public deficits. It clarifies the conditions under which participants will be allowed to exceed the 3 per cent ceiling without it being determined an 'excessive' deficit and therefore in breach of its terms. Countries found to have an excessive deficit are to be subjected to sanctions, involving mandatory deposits that are transformed into fines if the fiscal excess is not eliminated within two years (Eichengreen and Wyplosz, 1998: 67–71).

In these circumstances, the over-riding concern is that EMU will deliver not a 'dream' but a 'nightmare' (Bouget, 1998); that the European Central Bank, in seeking to fulfil its remit to maintain price stability, might set an unduly restrictive monetary policy thereby triggering deflation. If so, the burden of the subsequent adjustment will fall on the labour market (wages and employment) and social protection systems. The same holds in the face of asymmetric shocks, given the absence under EMU of other adjustment mechanisms available in currency zones. Governments will have to squeeze public expenditure, including that on social protection, and employers and trade unions will come under pressure to agree real wage reductions and other measures to reduce labour costs in exchange for active intervention to sustain employment. The nightmare, evoked by Streeck's (1992) term, is also of damaging 'regime competition' between member states.

'Economic Europe' as a means of promoting 'social Europe'

What has been described as the 'fundamental asymmetry' (Scharpf, 2002: 665) between the economic and the social dimensions of European integration has itself been the subject of controversy, under-lining the contested nature of the terrain. Following Pakashlati (1998: 48–56), there are two main views. One sees the asymmetry as flowing from the essentially economic nature of European integration: the implication is that the social dimension is of secondary importance. The economic aspects were *de rigueur*, whereas the social were *au choix* (Atkinson, 1996: 297) or, in Jacques Delors's words (quoted in Venturini, 1998: 115), '*L'Europe de la nécessité*' rather than '*L'Europe de l'idéal*'.

A second view contends that economic integration is 'deliberately underdeveloped' (Pochet, 1998: 69). This explanation for the imbalance is couched in terms of the *importance* rather than *unimportance* of the social dimension. In a survey of perceptions of EMU amongst social partner representatives, leading economists and central bankers in France, Germany and the UK, Verdun (1996: 75) found that 'all actors, including trade unions' expected that fiscal and social policies would undergo a process of market-led harmonization. For the monetary authorities and employers' organizations this was precisely what was attractive about EMU's construction: it would be impossible as well as undesirable to regulate social policies at the supranational level. To remain competitive, however, countries would have to restructure their domestic economies in order to get rid of inefficiencies in their national welfare states and labour markets. At best, therefore, 'market making' (economic Europe) has no necessary implication for 'market correcting' (social Europe) (Streeck, 1995: 40) and at worst is a means of unravelling the European social model.

So why, it might be asked, have trade unions tended to support the EMU project? Alongside interests in the economic benefits, Foden (1998) identifies two main considerations. One might be labelled 'the Europeanization of economic policy making'. Individually, Euro-zone countries will find it difficult to take action to promote the expansion of their domestic economies to create jobs – Keynesianism is no longer possible in one country, whereas the prospects increase if Europe is taken as a single entity. The other lies in the possibility that EMU brings of exerting influence over the wider political agenda: 'In essence, the ETUC has been a supporter of, and in part, an actor in, the strategy of building "economic Europe" as a means of promoting "political Europe", and in particular, "social Europe" ' (Foden, 1998: 92). Pressures for a 'social

Europe' arising from the restructuring at both micro and macro levels which EMU has unleashed, has enabled the ETUC to secure new social rights, such as those on employee information and consultation, which would not otherwise have been possible.

EMU and industrial relations – competing perspectives?

In considering the interactions between the convergent and divergent trends that European integration is promoting, Teague (1999a: 12) talks in terms of there being 'no agreed theoretical framework'; 'the absence of robust theoretical foundations'; and 'a murky theoretical background that tends to produce analytical incompleteness, or at least arguments with loose ends'. The first statement is incontestable. Further, much of the debate has been reduced to a choice between centralization and decentralization in which normative positions have become inter-twined with analysis. For some, a vertically integrated system is essential to protecting the European social model, while for others the imperative is much-needed reform of existing national arrangements. The theoretical cupboard is not, however, quite as bare as Teague suggests. There are a number of threads which can be knit together. Some come from the theoretical perspectives used to understand European integration itself – for example, the concepts of 'spillover' from neo-functionalism and 'isomorphism' from new institutionalist analysis. Others herald from an earlier era – the logic of different levels of governance, for example. There are also three seemingly competing perspectives to be interrogated, that the impact of EMU on industrial relations will result in, respectively, 'Europeanization', 'Americanization' or 're-nationalization'.

EMU = 'Europeanization'

The term 'Europeanization' tends to be used in two ways. The first is to describe an end-state, which takes the form of a vertically integrated system equivalent to that which exists at national levels – the implicit benchmark being the 'Rhineland' or 'Nordic' models discussed in Chapter 2. The other is to describe a tendency or trend in which there is discernible movement with common policies leading to common outcomes achieved by common processes.

A case of 'declining domestic governability'

The grounds for thinking that EMU might create inexorable pressures for a system equivalent to those at national level stem from Commons'

(1909/1968) proposition that industrial relations systems follow developments in the market. With European integration, though, it is the product market rather than the labour market that is important. The establishment of an integrated market for products and services has, as noted above, set industrial relations systems in competition with each other. At the macro level regime competition is, in the eyes of some (Rhodes, 1998; Schulten, 2002), being intensified by national 'social pacts'. At the micro level, ongoing restructuring is pushing management and employees' representatives into new forms of 'productivity coalition' (Windolf, 1989) to reduce the organization's costs and improve its capacities to meet changing market conditions, thereby giving competitive advantage over market rivals and, increasingly, other units within the same company.

For some commentators, it is axiomatic in these circumstances that industrial relations must be 'Europeanized': 'If the model of a socially controlled market economy is to be preserved, it will have to be Europeanized. Social policy must follow the market, which has now become denationalized' (Jacobi, 1998: 2).

Streeck and Vitols (1993: 2–3) provide a simplified account of the model of supranational institution building envisaged. In a first phase, EMU would lead to the creation of an integrated labour market requiring member states to allow cross-border mobility, with responsibility for enforcement given to supranational agencies. In a second, market integration would cause a steady increase in transnational activities, especially of MNCs, leading to 'declining domestic governability', i.e. a mismatch between an internationalized economy and nationally based institutions. In a third phase, governments and trade unions would resort to supranational agencies at EU level to close the 'governance gap' and bolster their 'sovereignty':

[The] continuing progress of economic integration; growing strength of supra-national institutions in charge of imposing compatibility and regulating competition and transnational actors; as well as increasingly successful, and federally encouraged, articulation of interests in equalisation of rules and living conditions, will set in motion a movement towards harmonisation of national regimes, resulting in less and less variation between national systems due to supra-national, federal creation of common standards or, at least, of a meaningful common floor. In this way, institutional changes that were originally meant to defend the sovereignty of national systems under interdependence are expected to result in a gradual conversion of national systems into sub-systems of a federal regime that more or less narrowly circumscribes their autonomy.

The argument is a variant of 'neo-functionalist' reasoning, in which social and political union are seen as 'spillover' effects of economic union. 'Spillover' refers to a situation where 'policies made in carrying out an initial task and grant of power can be made real only if the task itself is expanded' (Falkner, 1998: 8 citing Haas, 1964: 111). Falkner explains that several dimensions have developed over time:

- *functional spillover*, in which action in one area begets action in another one due to the interdependence between sectors or issues;
- *political spillover*, reflecting either shifts in political expectations and loyalties or to an increased decision capacity for the supranational level; and
- *geographical spillover*, when ever more states want to join the integration area.

Partly as a result, the EU has developed a framework for a European industrial relations system. Chapter 4 establishes, however, that this does not amount to a vertically integrated system comparable to national ones. Indeed, the very concept has effectively been rejected with the triumph of the 'subsidiarity' principle embedded in the Maastricht Treaty, leaving many earlier proponents deeply disillusioned (e.g. Streeck, 1995; Keller, 2000, 2001).

A case of isomorphism?

The second way in which the term 'Europeanization' is used is to describe a tendency or trend. We ourselves have referred to a twin process of 'virtual' collective bargaining, in which negotiations continue to take place through existing sector and company structures in individual countries but are increasingly influenced by cross-national developments (Marginson and Sisson, 1998). One of these is the conclusion of 'framework agreements' at EU cross-sector, sector and Euro-company levels establishing parameters and objectives within which negotiators at subsidiary levels in individual countries are incited or required to operate. The other, to use a phrase coined by Batstone (1978), is 'arms length' bargaining, in which employers and union representatives do not negotiate face to face at European level, but the outcomes are coordinated across countries.

Underpinning comes from new institutionalist analysis, in which sectors and the companies comprising them are seen as types of 'organizational field', with pressures to adopt similar or common solutions in the same situation. These derive from the two types of 'isomorphism' – 'institutional' and 'competitive' – proposed by DiMaggio and Powell (1983). Institutional isomorphism involves three essentially political, formal or informal, mechanisms: 'coercive' pressures placed on actors; 'mimetic', in which actors respond to uncertainty by copying others; and 'normative', associated with the professionalization of practice. Applied to management, for example, in the first instance managers may find themselves constrained to adopt standard arrangements as a result of 'coercive comparisons' applied by corporate headquarters. In the second, managers may be encouraged to benchmark 'best practice' both to improve performance and to legitimize the need for change. In the third, managers may feel expected to adopt those solutions that are incorporated into the prescriptions of consultancy and professional organizations, thereby attaining normative status.

The concepts can also be applied to trade unions and employee representatives. As Brown and Sisson (1975) contend, fairness plays a key role in shaping employee expectations and fairness depends on comparisons. Runciman's (1966) three types of reference groups, 'membership', 'comparative' and 'normative', which are helpful in understanding the varying intensity of comparisons, bear a remarkable similarity to DiMaggio and Powell's three types of institutional isomorphism. Furthermore, the term 'orbits of coercive comparison' was originally coined by Ross (1948) in order to emphasize the importance of institutions in wage determination.

The second type, 'competitive isomorphism', is informal and assumes a system of economic rationality presupposing market competition. As McWilliams (1992: 6) notes, within internationally integrated sectors and companies there will a tendency towards convergence in labour costs in the single European market even in the absence of labour mobility or any explicit coordination. This is because increased trade in goods will create pressures for the prices of inputs that go into their manufacture to equalize, while capital mobility will mean that investors can more easily invest/disinvest so as to produce goods in low/high labour cost countries.

There are two advantages in adopting the perspective of 'Europeanization' as tendency. The first is analytical: it requires account to be taken of developments at several levels – not just the Community level or national systems, but also the sector and, most importantly, the company. Second, it offers a more realistic appreciation of the likely scenarios. 'Europeanization' as tendency may not result in 'Europeanization' as end-point. It could coexist with other possible tendencies of 'Americanization' and/or 're-nationalization'.

EMU = 'Americanization'

The second perspective suggests that, far from encouraging the development of a coherent European system, EMU will lead to the 'Americanization' of industrial relations, involving deregulation, the break-up of inclusive structures of multi-bargaining and the weakening of trade unions (Martin, 1999). Again, the term can be used to describe an end-state or a tendency. Here the interest is in the different pathways that might be involved, reflecting the macro and micro distinction noted earlier.

A restrictive macroeconomic policy encourages fragmentation?

At macro level, one starting point is the highly restrictive economic policy regime that EMU's design institutionalizes. The central thrust is that unemployment can only be reduced by supply-side changes, with the management of demand having little, if any, role to play. Indeed, suggests Martin (2001) in a nice touch of irony, EMU's policy regime is far more restrictive than its US counterpart. Whereas the Federal Reserve Bank is charged with maintaining price stability *and* growth, the ECB's remit is primarily concerned with price stability. Moreover, its asymmetric inflation target builds in a deflationary bias which is reinforced by the terms of the Stability and Growth Pact. This economic policy stance is a double source of pressure on the labour market. Indirectly, it keeps unemployment higher than it would otherwise be since, argues Martin, supply-side reforms alone cannot significantly reduce unemployment – there has to be sufficient demand. Directly, it explicitly identifies changes in 'labour regimes', including industrial relations, along with other supply-side measures as the only legitimate target of policy.

Amongst possible 'labour regime' changes, influential economic opinion directs its attention towards the sector-based, multi-employer structures of collective bargaining which characterize most of the pre-enlargement EU member states, hereafter the EU-15. Following Calmfors and Driffill (1988), the consensus has been that the relationship between wage-setting institutions and economic performance is non-linear or 'hump-shaped'. Both highly centralized and highly decentralized bargaining structures are held to outperform those intermediate between these two poles. Calmfors and Driffill cite the Nordic countries (at the time) and Japan and the US, respectively, as examples of the two extremes. Where bargaining is centralized, negotiators are said to take account of the wider economic consequences of their actions. Where it is fully decentralized to firm level, negotiators are held to take account of the impact of settlements on the firm's competitiveness. Either way, wage moderation and therefore low inflation is secured at lower levels of unemployment and higher rates of economic growth than in the intermediate cases. Under bargaining structures which are neither centralized nor fully decentralized, such as the sector-based systems common amongst the EU-15, the wider economic consequences of a decision by wage negotiators in any one sector to increase wages, in terms of higher costs and unemployment, are – it is argued – largely externalized to other sectors.

If the Calmfors and Driffill (1988) model were valid, the creation of the Euro zone transforms even those bargaining arrangements which are centralized at national level into the intermediate range (Martin, 1999). From the perspective of macroeconomic performance, the result would be the worst of all possible worlds, leading to pressures for change in the direction of either centralization or decentralization. A centralized, European-level structure of collective bargaining seems, as noted above, unrealizable. Change towards full decentralization appears more plausible, given the competitive dynamics of negative market integration which further augment extant employer pressure for movement in this direction (see below).

It is a big 'if', however, as the Calmfors–Driffill model has been the subject of substantial criticism. Soskice (1990) highlighted the confusion between centralization and coordination. Once the cross-sector coordination which characterizes many of Western Europe's sector-based bargaining structures is taken into account, the hump-shaped relationship breaks down and countries with coordinated bargaining arrangements appear to outperform those with uncoordinated, decentralized structures. Subsequent criticism emphasized that the model neglects the role of other actors, notably the state and central banks (Iversen, 1999): the economic effects of bargaining are contingent on the monetary regime, which means there is no necessary relationship between bargaining structure and performance.

The most extensive critique comes from Traxler *et al.* (2001), who focus on the nature of the link between collective bargaining arrangements and economic performance as well as identifying the key institutional parameters of collective bargaining which impinge on any relationship. On the first, they persuasively establish that the key link is between collective bargaining and the immediate outcomes of labour and unit labour costs. Any impact on standard measures of macroeconomic performance is mediated through this key link, and therefore more diffuse. On the second, they confirm that coordination rather than centralization of collective bargaining is the key concept, but emphasize the importance of its *vertical* as well as *horizontal* dimension. A critical factor in securing wage moderation is the nature and extent of 'bargaining governability', i.e. the effectiveness of mechanisms of vertical coordination which ensure that lower levels comply with the terms of higher-level agreements. This depends on the provisions for legal enforceability, notably extension arrangements, of collective agreements.

Their finding (Traxler *et al.*, 2001: 253) that, during the 1990s, the links between the rate of increase in wages and unit labour costs and the coordination of collective bargaining broke down is also pertinent. The implication for present concerns is that insofar as different wage bargaining arrangements deliver functionally equivalent labour cost outcomes, the Calmfors–Driffill model becomes emptied of much of its prescriptive force.

Nationally based unions unable to limit competition?

A second set of reasons for thinking that European integration will lead to 'Americanization' are to be found in the work of Reder and Ulman (1993). Their proposition is that 'union organization or its span of control must be at least as broad as the product market. Otherwise, non-unionised firms would be able to sell goods for lower prices than unionised firms, resulting in loss of union jobs and declining membership' (p. 16). On the basis of US experience, they argue that the organizational decline of unions may occur under either of two conditions:

> First, when product markets become spatially extended or further integrated, *unless* (their emphasis) union organization expands with the market, or union decision making becomes more centralized. Second, when organization shrinks within existing market boundaries, *unless* (their emphasis) negotiated wage increases cause non-union workers to join unions or regulations or other arrangements bar non-union entry or operation. (Reder and Ulman, 1993: 16)

The ability of trade unions to take various terms of employment out of competition within national borders also depends upon the framework of public policy. States can provide some protection against external competition by tariff and non-tariff barriers. Where there are floating exchange rates, they can also devalue the currency. Under EMU, however, national states, which could already no longer set tariff barriers, become further deprived of their capacity to establish non-tariff ones and the possibility of devaluation disappears. The combined effects of EU economic integration therefore considerably weaken national trade unions' ability to influence terms of employment. The challenge they pose to trade unions throughout the EU is rather chilling:

> The elimination or attenuation of this power could beset European unions with the same dilemma US unions have faced: either to create more highly centralised structures able to cope with unified markets (as US unions were able to do in the nineteenth century and again in the 1930s) or, lacking that capability, to suffer decentralisation and organisational loss (as happened to US unions in the 1970s and 1980s under the impact of legal deregulation and intensified international competition). (Reder and Ulman, 1993: 38)

Multi-employer bargaining loses its appeal?

A third pathway starts from the employers' perspective. As Chapter 2 establishes, a distinguishing feature of industrial relations in Western Europe has been the prevalence of multi-employer structures of collective bargaining. In recent years, however, for large employers in particular the advantages of multi-employer as compared to single-employer bargaining have been declining (Katz, 1993; Marginson and Sisson, 1996) for reasons which are elaborated in Chapter 6. As a result of the changing economic and political context, many of the benefits which management traditionally perceived multi-employer bargaining to have offered no longer appear as persuasive. Management feels less need of the protection from trade union pressure to shape the wage–effort bargain within the workplace. At the same time, the pressure not to increase costs has increased significantly as competition intensifies. Furthermore, the opening up of international markets means that, for many medium as well as large employers, multi-employer bargaining within the nation state no longer provides a floor taking labour costs out of competition. The result has been growing pressure for decentralization towards company level, either within the framework of multi-employer agreements or by abandoning them in favour of single-employer arrangements.

EMU intensifies these pressures on multi-employer agreements, raising further doubts about their long-term viability. Considered in depth in Chapters 6 and 7, two particular challenges are evident. The first concerns the further pressure towards decentralization prompted by the need to handle ongoing restructuring and the consequent reorientation of the bargaining agenda towards questions of competitiveness, adaptability and employment. The second is that, by internationalizing the scope of the product market, EMU further undermines the role of multi-employer bargaining at national level in taking wages out of competition within the relevant market. The balance of advantage has shifted further away from multi-employer bargaining as EMU has progressed. As Chapters 6 and 7 show, it is primarily the support that some countries' legal framework gives to multi-employer bargaining, together with the continuing strength of trade union organization in key sectors in some countries, that is the prime consideration in its persistence.

EMU = re-nationalization?

A third possibility is that the dominant direction of change in response to EMU may be towards neither 'Europeanization' nor 'Americanization'. Rather there will be a tendency to seek to reinforce national systems. 'Rather than being eroded by competitive forces intensified by the move to a single currency ... national industrial relations institutions might be reinvigorated to cope with those competitive forces' (Martin, 1999: 26).

At first sight, the claim that integration strengthens the nation state appears paradoxical. Yet, as Rosamond (2000: 136–40) concludes, there is considerable support for the idea among political scientists. One line of argument is that national policy makers exploit international agencies to help resolve their domestic problems (Moravcsik, 1993), but remain controlling agents interested only in degrees of integration. Another is that, far from leading to a demand for supranational development, the integration process reinforces existing national institutions, reflecting the so-called 'joint decision trap' (Scharpf, 1988) whereby once a joint decision-making competence is established retreat or reverse becomes impossible. Faced with common problems and yet the difficulties of reaching common agreement, in other words, there is a tendency to fall back on 'familiar and predictable national institutions' (Streeck, 1999: 5), making supranational solutions even more difficult to achieve.

Recent developments in several of the EU-15 offer some support for this analysis. Accompanying the decentralization of collective bargaining towards company level, there has also been 're-centralization' expressed in the negotiation of so-called 'social pacts' by governments, employers' organizations and trade unions at national level. These aim to secure adaption to the new competitive and fiscal pressures arising under EMU. Involving wage moderation, they also include measures introducing greater labour market flexibility and reform of social protection systems. Complicating matters, however, as Chapter 5 discusses, is that the negotiation of 'social pacts' admits of two interpretations. The dominant view is to see them as a form of 'competitive corporatism' (Rhodes, 1998; Schulten, 2002) in which government, employers' organizations and trade unions are being driven to pursue a national 'beggar-thy-neighbour' logic aimed at achieving competitive advantage at the expense of other EU countries. Yet, if 're-nationalization' simply reflects a 'beggar-thy-neighbour' logic, implies Martin (1999: 28), it is hardly sustainable. A vicious circle of 'competitive internal depreciations or labour cost dumping' is likely to give way to 'processes of decentralization and fragmentation' leading to 'Americanization'.

The alternative view is to see 'social pacts' as involving both 're-nationalization' *and* 'Europeanization' (Goetschy, 2000; Dølvik, 2001b). As Chapter 5 shows, there is remarkable similarity in the negotiating processes, agenda and outcomes of the social pacts concluded by distinct sets of national actors across several countries. They seem to be a prime example of 'mimetic' isomorphism or, in Teague's (2001: 23) more accessible terms, 'Europe learning from Europe'. For this reason, and since national-level coordination might be regarded as a prerequisite of any EU-wide coordination, Dølvik contends that they can also be viewed as a form of 'regime collaboration' rather than 'regime competition'.

A further complication is that whilst 're-nationalization' seemingly accommodates the macro pressures flowing from EMU, it does nothing to address the micro-level pressures stimulated by the intensified competition and restructuring which EMU also unleashes. Hence it is also likely to be accompanied by the decentralization pressures towards company level outlined above. The role of the sector level, which links the central (cross-sector) to the company level, is threatened with corrosion from above as well as below. 'Social pacts', in other words, are taking authority away from sector negotiators at precisely the same time as they are under growing pressure to devolve more responsibility to company level in the interests of flexibility. As end-state, re-nationalization represents a potentially unstable accommodation; as tendency it entails multiple dynamics which are taken up in Chapters 5 and 6.

Wider considerations

The impact of European integration raises wider issues which are the subject of continuing controversy across social science. Of particular relevance to our arguments are debates around three: convergence and divergence; the relationship between 'globalization' and 'Europeanization'; and the nature and extent of the choice available to actors. Our approach to each needs to be made explicit if the book's argument is to be fully appreciated.

Convergence and diversity?

A recurring theme in comparative industrial relations analysis is the balance between institutional similarities and differences – whether countries develop a set of common features, resulting from the impact of economic forces, or whether they are characterized by essentially idiosyncratic arrangements, reflecting different historical development, patterns of industrialization and business systems. Earlier work, associated with Kerr *et al.* (1960), tended to be concerned with the similarities. The main drivers of convergence were held to be markets and technology leading to one 'best' way of doing things. In industrial relations, the presumption was of convergence towards the American model, based on internal labour markets and company-based collective contracts. The second view, generally seen as a form of 'societal contingency' but also termed the 'diversity approach' (Teague, 1999a: 8), grew up in opposition, motivated by concerns with the determinism of the convergence approach. One variant is the 'societal approach' of Maurice *et al.* (1986): here national differences result from the structural interdependencies peculiar to each society, involving interactions between the training, production and industrial relations systems. The other is the 'national business systems' approach, which argues that persistent differences in capitalist organization reflect distinctive national development paths (Lane, 1989; Whitley, 1992). Both variants share the view that institutions are generated by the interaction of social actors at critical historical junctures and persist over time, creating 'path dependency'.

Most recently, the so-called 'dual' or 'co-convergence' thesis has become prominent (Hall and Soskice, 2001), reflecting Strange's (1997: 183) stinging criticism that most comparative work in the social sciences was 'misnamed; they do not compare nearly as much as they contrast'. Under the dual convergence approach, analysis is at the level of clusters or varieties of national models as well as cross-country. Hall and Soskice distinguish two main types of regime: *liberal market economies* and *coordinated market economies*, with convergence within each type being accompanied by divergence between them. One implication, recalling debate around the connections between bargaining structure and economic performance, is that there might be functionally equivalent modes of (capitalist) societal organization capable of delivering similar outcomes in terms of economic performance. Another is that alternative forms of societal organization deliver qualitatively different economic outcomes, but in a manner which is mutually complementary within a broader international division of labour.

Traxler (2003) arrives at a not dissimilar position. His main thesis is that the

> way in which industrial relations systems accommodate to external changes is self-referential in that the prevalent bargaining mode and its interaction with procedural state regulation guide the direction of adaption by defining the possibilities for renewing the compromise between capital and labour under changed conditions. (p. 141)

Path dependency, rather than convergence, is the dominant force. On this basis, a fundamental distinction is to be drawn between the countries with multi-employer bargaining and legal frameworks supportive of collective bargaining (which roughly correspond with *coordinated market economies*) and those with single-employer bargaining and less supportive frameworks (which fit the *liberal market economy* category).

Much depends upon the focus and the level of analysis. Concerning focus, Hay (2000) argues that most commentators fail to distinguish between four senses in which the term convergence can be used: convergence in the pressures and constraints placed upon a particular economy (*input convergence*); convergence in policies or the paradigms informing policies (*policy convergence*); convergence in the consequences, outcomes and effects (*output convergence*); and convergence in the processes sustaining developmental trajectories (*process convergence*). 'What is perhaps most significant about such a series of distinctions is that input convergence need not imply policy convergence; policy convergence need not imply output convergence; and output convergence need not imply process convergence' (Hay, 2000: 514). Translated into our domain, *input* convergence in the macroeconomic sphere under EMU may, but not necessarily will, have an impact in three main areas: on *policy*, of governments and also trade unions and employers' organizations; on *outcomes* (for example, wage increases and levels); and on the *processes* by which these outcomes are achieved (for instance, legal enactment, collective bargaining and the different forms of coordination). Conceivably, European integration could lead to similar policies and outcomes across countries even in the absence of significant changes in processes. There could also be similar developments in processes with little change in formal organizations and institutions.

The level of analysis is especially important. Much comparative industrial relations analysis is 'top-down' in its approach. There is a strong tendency to focus on national-level institutions and processes at the expense of arrangements at sector and company levels. Yet the cross-national diversity so evident at national level can hide significant similarities at sector and company level, reflecting the need to confront common problems as Dunlop (1958: 20) argued nearly half a century ago. In their study of the automotive and telecommunications sectors, Katz and Darbishire (2000) show how convergence is occurring amongst the major companies across different countries, around a limited reper-toire of models of business structure, product strategy, production organ-ization and working practice within each sector. Such convergence processes extend to inter-firm relations cross-cutting national bound-aries. These may not necessarily result in identical arrangements from unit to unit, let alone country to country. Nonetheless, the outcomes are more similar because of these pressures, resulting in what Katz and Darbishire call 'converging divergencies'. Since industrial relations systems reflect the articulation between developments at the macro, meso and micro levels, a 'bottom-up' perspective is as essential as a 'top-down' one if the dynamics of change are to be understood.

Combining a 'bottom-up' with a 'top-down' perspective enables the relative importance of the different levels to be explored and the analyt-ical premise of the diversity approach, 'that many of the most important institutional structures...depend on the presence of regulatory regimes that are the preserve to the nation-state' (Hall and Soskice, 2001: 4), to be interrogated. Reviewing the outcome of a set of comparative sector stud-ies, Hollingsworth and Streeck (1994) conclude that whilst important sec-tor and country differences in broader regimes of economic governance are both evident, the latter clearly dominate the former. Whether the sec-ond part of their conclusion still holds good is a question of central rele-vance to this study. Furthemore, adding a 'bottom-up' perspective opens up a richer set of possible trajectories. It becomes plausible to think in terms of a range, rather than competing alternatives. Depending on the features of particular countries, sectors and companies, differing combi-nations of 'Europeanization', 'Americanization' and 're-nationalization' are possible. The tendency towards 'Europeanization' might be 'multi-speed', reflecting differences between sectors, variations between com-panies within any given sector and sub-regional differences between groups of countries within Europe.

The strand of comparative analysis which the book aims to extend underlines the *interdependency* inherent to the processes of convergence and divergence (Katz and Darbishire, 2000; Locke, 1995; MacDuffie, 1995), reflecting differences in the speed, form and spatial 'reach' of developments at the various levels. It is not a question of convergence *or* diversity, but of both convergence *and* diversity. Growing international integration may prompt convergent developments within sectors, and in particular within MNCs, *across* national systems, which may result in increased diversity between sectors and companies *within* national systems. Surveying developments across 17 European countries in the 1990s, Ferner and Hyman (1998) conclude that: 'the (somewhat paradoxical) picture that emerges is one of increasing diversity within national systems but of increasing convergence between them' (p. xiv).

'Globalization' or 'Europeanization'?

The second consideration involves the relationship between 'globalization' and 'Europeanization'. The belief that globalization is the most important driver of structural and economic change is a given for many in the convergence–divergence debate. Accordingly, processes of regional economic integration are mere ciphers for the wider phenomenon. Much, however, depends upon how the terms globalization and regionalization are understood (Hay, 2000: 522–3):

> If, for instance, globalisation is merely taken to connote the emergence, development and deepening of processes which transcend the national … then globalisation and regionalisation might be seen as synonymous, or at least as mutually reinforcing. If, on the other hand … economic globalisation is taken to refer to a genuinely global (and not merely selectively transnational) condition of (economic) integration between formerly national economies then regionalisation and globalisation are likely to be seen as opposed.

Similar to the alternative meanings of 'Europeanization' introduced above, Hay goes on to note that there are also differences between those who regard globalization as an end-point – i.e. as a condition of economic integration – and those who view it as a process. Under the second view there are again differences as to whether globalization as process is undermining or augmenting regionalization. The relationship between globalization and Europeanization, Hay (2000: 524) concludes, is best considered a contingent one, open to empirical investigation.

Useful also is to distinguish trends that are integral to economic globalization from those which may be global in incidence (Sarfati, 2001). Treated as process, economic globalization comprises five main developments. The removal of trade barriers and the consequent expansion of international markets for products; the spatial extension of international competition as new market economies, such as China and central and eastern Europe, emerge; the sectoral extension of international competition as, through market deregulation, privatization and/or marketization economic activities previously conducted within national boundaries and/or on a non-market basis are opened up; the liberalization of financial markets and the development of a worldwide capital market; and the internationalization of production and market servicing through the operations of MNCs that the other developments have encouraged.

The main instances of the second type of global trend are threefold (Sisson, 2001b). First, the new technologies and revolution in information processing facilities made possible by the microchip and associated software developments, which are leading to the creation of new economic activity and affecting the way operations are performed and products delivered in existing activities. Second, is the inexorable rise of the service sector, a trend which is universal amongst the industrialized economies. Both developments are changing the face of the labour market, with significant implications for the occupational and gender composition of the workforce, the nature of employment contracts and trade union membership (Dølvik, 2001a). Many of the emerging new economic and service activities are also outwith the established structures of collective bargaining. Third are demographic changes, which also primarily affect the industrialized countries. Key trends affecting the labour market are low birth rates and a decline in the working life – reflecting a fall in youth participation rates and an increase in the proportion of older workers withdrawing from the workforce before the official retirement age.

Important though these developments are, there are strong grounds for focusing on the impact of the 'regionalization' that European integration is bringing about. As Chapter 2 argues, it is a 'Triad' of regional economies, comprising Europe, North America and Japan and its economic dependencies, that is emerging rather than a single, undifferentiated international economy. MNCs display a distinct and differentiable European dimension in their management structures and international organization of production. Moreover, the structures and institutions of the EU are creating a political, social and economic space whose character and dynamic are distinctive when set against wider, global, developments or those in other regions (Hay, 2000, 2002b). These structures and institutions are having a significant mediating influence on the changes associated with the globalization processes and the global trends identified above. More specifically, many policy makers see European integration as offering new opportunities to deal with the multiple challenges confronting existing industrial relations systems. This helps to explain why the EU has developed a social policy competence that includes a European industrial relations framework. From 'bottom-up' the activities of MNCs and responses from trade unions are generating common developments in industrial relations processes and practices which transcend national borders, at both company and sector levels. These in turn are encouraging a process of 'multi-speed Europeanization', in which differences in the pace, form and spatial reach of developments are bringing about the convergence *and* divergence discussed above.

Structure and agency

A third consideration that European integration raises is the nature and extent of choice available to policy makers and practitioners. Convergence tends to be associated with determinism and diversity with choice. In practice, however, there is a strong element of determinism involved in both. In the first, the source of the determinism is markets and technology: the 'natural selection of market forces' (Traxler *et al.*, 2001: 5) leads to one 'best' way of doing things. In the second, it is 'path dependency' whereby past decisions set actors on a particular course and give some a particular position of privilege and strength to block change. In discussing the importance of existing arrangements for social protection, for example, Scharpf (2000a: 224) talks in terms of the 'path-dependent constraints of existing policy legacies' and the 'institutional constraints of existing veto positions'.

Two main strands of theorizing about 'institutionalism' bear on the determinism associated with 'path dependency': 'rational-choice' and 'sociological' (Scharpf, 2000b). In the first, institutional rules are understood as 'external constraints and incentives structuring the purposeful choices of self-interested rational actors'. Actors are assumed to have standardized and stable preferences defined by their personal or organizational self-interest. They are also assumed to be rational: their perceptions can be taken to be correct representations of the objective situation; and they have sufficient cognitive capabilities to identify the consequences of available options for their self-interest. Scharpf quotes Tsebelis (1999: 4) to emphasize the outcome: 'Since institutions determine the choices of actors, the sequence of moves, as well as the information they control, different institutional structures will produce different strategies of the actors, and different outcomes of their interactions.' Under 'sociological institutionalism', by contrast,

> institutions are defined very broadly, so as to include not only exter- nally imposed and sanctioned rules, but also unquestioned routines and standard operating procedures and, more importantly, socially constructed and culturally taken-for-granted world views and shared normative notions of 'appropriateness'. The implication is that 'insti- tutions will define not only what actors can do, but also their per- ceptions and preferences – and thus what they will want to do'. (Scharpf, 2000b: 5)

'Path dependency' does not necessarily imply an 'iron cage', however (Marsden, 1999: 27). The key to understanding how change takes place, suggests Scharpf (2000b: 5), is to 'treat actor orientations (i.e., their preferences and perceptions) as a theoretically distinct category – influenced, but not determined by the institutional framework within which interactions occur'. Using such an 'actor-centred' institutionalist approach, Visser and Hemerijck's (1997) analysis of the transformation of Dutch labour market management shows how actors are able to adapt and change notwithstanding the constraints of path dependency. They highlight the role of three contributory processes. In the first, 'patching up', additional rules and procedures are grafted onto existing institutions and processes. In the second, 'transposition', institutions established for a particular purpose are put to different uses. The third involves the processes of social learning: they emphasize the role of the Netherlands' social dialogue arrangements, which oblige the partici- pants 'to explain, give reasons for and take responsibility for their deci- sions and strategies to each other and the rank and file, but at times also with respect to the public at large' (Visser and Hemerijck, 1997: 67). Crucial in breaking with the constraints of the past is that the actors have been required to redefine their strategies in a 'public regarding way'.

Multi-level governance in the making?

Summarizing the book's main argument, although there has been much debate about the impact of European integration on industrial relations, there has been a less than objective appreciation of the governance arrangements actually emerging. A vertically integrated European sys- tem of industrial relations similar to those at national level has not emerged nor does it appear likely. Meanwhile, although EMU has increasingly set industrial relations systems in competition with each other, at the national, the sector and the company levels, the dominant pattern of multi-employer bargaining remains largely intact. Indeed, there has apparently been little change in the formal institutions of national systems. Even so, there have been significant 'Europeanizing' developments at each of the main levels – Community or cross-sector, sector and Euro-company – with noticeable effects on national systems. It is difficult to disagree with the conclusion of Social Affairs Commissioner Diamantopoulou: it is something of a 'caricature' to see things in terms of the 'two extremes of social union versus a completely deregulated free-for-all' (letter to the *Financial Times*, 18 February 2000). Just as a 'multi-level system of governance' is the most appropriate metaphor for the emerging EU polity, so too is it for European industrial relations.

Like the multi-level governance system of the EU polity, this multi-level industrial relations framework reflects a history of informal and gradual development as well as deliberate institution building. It has developed, and continues to develop, relatively autonomously rather than by design, as a range of actors seek to exploit the available means to grapple with the implications of the 'regime competition' that EMU is promoting. It cannot simply be defined in hierarchical terms, with a Community level added on top of national systems and decisions cascading down. Developments have been 'bottom-up' as well as 'top-down'; cross-national (horizontal) influences mix with national (vertical) ones and involve the EU sector and Euro-company levels as well as the Community level. There is a great deal of 'hybridization' and 'cross-fertilization'.

A multi-level system of industrial relations is more than a descriptive metaphor, however. The emerging system is, in formal terms, an intervening as well as dependent variable, making it possible to draw conclusions of wider analytical importance. European integration is a *cause* of the multi-level framework in as much as it is contributing to the collective action problem that policy makers and practitioners have to deal with. Application of the 'subsidiarity' principle is a common response, leading to both further decentralization and new forms of centralization within national systems. The *effects* of the system's evolving patterns of regulation, 'policy networks' and opportunities for mutual learning are evident not just in changes in the levels of governance, but also its scope, form and output. The supranational nature of the EU is also encouraging the development of a cross-border dimension at the cross-sector, sector and above all company levels. In bringing about a measure of convergence *within* companies and sectors *between* national systems, the multi-level framework is simultaneously promoting greater diversity *between* companies and sectors *within* national systems.

The drivers of these developments are not only the so-called traditional methods of legal enactment and collective bargaining, but increasingly also newer regulatory processes. These include the coordination and benchmarking which are integral to the 'open method of coordination' (OMC). The result is a shift in regulatory output from 'hard' to 'soft' forms. Also important are the informal processes associated with 'coercive', 'mimetic', 'normative' and 'competitive' isomorphism (DiMaggio and Powell, 1983).

Like the EU polity's multi-level governance system, the trajectory of the multi-level industrial relations framework is uncertain. It is by definition a system 'in the making' and there is no pre-assumed end-point for developments. Talk of 'betweenness' is also misplaced. Just as the EU cannot be placed on a continuum between 'loose inter-governmentalism' and the 'superstate' (Rosamond, 2000: 176), so too it would be wrong to situate the industrial relations framework between 'Europeanization' and 'Americanization'. Complexity, uncertainty and instability look set to be the defining characteristics for the foreseeable future, with considerable scope for policy makers and practitioners to exert influence on future directions. Amongst the more imponderable ingredients is the impact of EU enlargement. It could mean more of the same or, if central eastern Europe should prove to be the 'trojan horse' for Americanization (Meardi, 2002), an unravelling of the multi-level balance.

The rest of the book explains how these conclusions are arrived at, highlighting both the causes and effects of the multi-level framework that European integration is bringing about. Chapter 2 puts the issues in their wider context; it draws attention to the increasing interconnection of European economies, emphasizes the importance of the EU's political dimension and outlines the main features and variants of the national industrial relations systems that constitute a key dimension of the European social model. Chapter 3 introduces and clarifies developments in the main processes of industrial relations underpinning the development of multi-level governance. Chapter 4 considers developments at the EU Community and sector levels. The aim is to understand why there have been considerable moves in the direction of 'Europeanization', even though a vertically integrated system has not emerged. The following three chapters are concerned with developments within national systems. Chapter 5 examines the development of national-level concertation and the conclusion of 'social pacts'. Chapter 6 addresses the nature and extent of the changes being made to sector agreements in the light of the many challenges they face. To illustrate in greater depth, Chapter 7 reviews the changing relationship between sector and company bargaining in two sectors, metalworking and banking, and four countries, Belgium, Germany, Italy and the UK. Chapter 8 focuses on the MNCs that are the source of many of the pressures for Europeanization from the 'bottom-up'. Chapters 9 and 10 deal with outcomes in terms of wages and working time. Chapter 11 reviews the study's findings and Chapter 12 explores their main implications. The research base on which the book draws, embracing a series of projects undertaken by the authors culminating in a study funded under ESRC's 'One Europe or Several?' programme, is summarized in the Appendix.

2
The Starting Point: Three Key Dimensions

The opening chapter made some crucial assumptions about the three key dimensions of the EU – the economic, political and social – as well as taking for granted the wider context. These assumptions need to be substantiated and in the process the context filled in. The first assumption is that 'Europeanization' rather than 'globalization' is the key reference point – that 'Europeanization', in other words, is not just a cipher for 'globalization'. The second is that it is meaningful to characterize the EU polity as a 'multi-level system of governance' with a capability to exercise a significant influence on industrial relations developments. The third is that it is possible to identify the main contours of a 'European industrial relations model' as a constituent element of the European social model, even though the EU framework is skeletal and there are many points of difference between the systems of the member countries.

The economic dimension – a regional bloc within a global economy

As Chapter 1 contended, there are strong grounds for suggesting that the main pressures for policy, output and process convergence stem not so much from 'globalization' as from 'Europeanization'. The economic nature of the political project underlying the construction and enlargement of the EU is well established. The distinctiveness of the resulting European economic space within the global economy is sharpened by parallel developments in the other advanced industrialized regions. More recent and less far-reaching than the EU, NAFTA (North American Free Trade Area) currently embraces the economies of North America; enlargement into central and Latin America is foreseen. Although as yet only in the process of establishing a free trade area, AFTA (ASEAN Free Trade Area) groups the industrialized and industrializing economies of East and South-East Asia. The result is the emergence of a tri-polar international economy, the 'Triad', comprising Europe, North America and Japan and its economic satellites, in which economic exchanges (amongst the countries) within each of these poles are significantly more intense than those between the three poles (Dicken, 1998; Rugman, 2000).

Trade and investment flows

The first of these grounds involves trade and investment flows. Commencing with trade, all of the economies of EU member states have experienced a secular trend towards greater openness. But the geography of this trend is selective, involving a 'consistent and ongoing de-globalisation and attendant Europeanisation (more accurately, an EU-isation) of their trading relations over the past forty years' (Hay, 2002a: 31–2). In 1997, intra-EU trade accounted for 61 per cent of EU exports and a further 13 per cent of EU exports went to non-EU European countries (Rugman, 2000).

Data on foreign direct investment similarly supports the salience of Europeanization. By far the greatest proportion of inward investment into EU member states originates in other EU countries; likewise the greatest proportion of outwards investment from EU countries goes elsewhere in the EU (Kozul-Wright and Rowthorn, 1998). Hay (2002b) shows that the proportion of outward investment going elsewhere in the EU has been growing for France, Germany and the UK, which is indicative of the more general trend. Figures on the distribution of assets and sales further confirm the extent to which European MNCs are regional in the scope of their activities. Hirst and Thompson's (1996, 1999) analysis of the geographical distribution of assets and sales of MNCs headquartered in France, Germany, the Netherlands and the UK shows significant regional concentration on both counts. Van Tulder *et al.* (2001: 63), analysing 200 of the world's largest firms, echoes these findings: in 1997 Europe accounted for some 70 per cent of both assets and sales for European-based companies. Differences between 'home' countries are evident too: both Hirst and Thompson (1996, 1999) and van Tulder *et al.* (2001) find French- and German-based MNCs to be more home, and less extra-European, focused than their Dutch and British counterparts. For British-based MNCs in particular, the US is an important destination for outward investment. Even so, Pain (1997) reports that since 1990 UK-based MNCs have oriented overseas direct investment more towards Europe and less towards the US.

In the case of financial investment flows, the evidence for Europeanization is less compelling. Equally, although restrictions on movements of capital have been eroded, the full integration of global financial markets remains some way off (Hay, 2002a). As the discussions surrounding the EU's March 2000 Lisbon Council demonstrated, 'even where the political will may exist, there are a series of largely intractable institutional problems that render even the integration of European financial markets unthinkable' (ibid., 33). An *Economist* editorial (cited in Hay, 2002a: 34) noted in the midst of the struggle for the takeover of the London Stock Exchange that capital markets are the last bastion of national monopolies. Moreover, of all publicly-traded companies, only some 10 per cent enjoy a listing on more than one market.

The organization of business operations – towards the 'Euro-company'?

The second grounds for suggesting that the main pressures for different forms of convergence stem from 'Europeanization' involve MNCs. The emergence of what we have termed the 'Euro-company' (Marginson and Sisson, 1994; Marginson, 2000a) reflects two developments. One involves the response of MNCs to the economic, political and regulatory space that is being created from above, leading to distinct European dimensions to their forms of (management) organization and coordination of production and market servicing. The other reflects developments from below. Although they continue to bear many of the traces of their national origins, MNCs are more than the extension of national companies beyond their borders. The Euro-company also coheres around characteristics transcending national borders. These comprise the diverse, but overlapping, forms of enterprise found in many national economies and the sector- and organization-specific transnational management practices being forged by MNCs. The Euro-company, in other words, is a plural rather than uniform construct. The European Company Statute, finally adopted by the EU's Nice summit in 2001 some thirty years after being originally proposed, gives legal expression to the salience of these developments.

The Euro-company differentiated from wider global developments

Within the context of regional economic integration, MNCs have invested considerable resources in establishing market servicing and production operations on a pan-European basis. This was reflected in an initial wave of mergers and acquisitions from the mid-1980s in anticipation of the single market, which peaked in 1990, a growing proportion of which were cross-border in scope (Buiges, 1993). The prospect of deeper integration through EMU reinvigorated the process. Cross-border mergers and acquisitions in the EU surged again from 1994, accelerating towards a new peak in 2000 – at which point they accounted for virtually one-half of all mergers (United Nations, 2000, 2002; Macaire and Rehfeldt, 2001). Economic and market integration has also led to the creation of new European-scale companies through joint ventures and, more tentatively, strategic alliances. Importantly, these developments have been far from limited to European-based companies: MNCs headquartered in the other two poles of the Triad have participated in these consolidations (Ramsay, 1995; van Tulder *et al.*, 2001), in the process creating distinct European regional units. Integrating the resulting combinations and securing a coordinated approach to the market and/or to the organization of production at European level is, however, contingent on the strengthening of European-level management structures within MNCs.

More generally, as Edwards (2004) demonstrates, the internationalization of markets and of production has stimulated the deepening of international forms of management coordination and organization within MNCs. Such deepening has also taken on an expressly European dimension, evidenced for example in the creation of European regional management structures, which effectively downgrade the role of national subsidiaries and/or assume a coordination role that might otherwise be exercised by global headquarters. This European dimension is more evident in some sectors than others. Mendez (1994) provides a detailed study of the progressive deepening of Groupe Danone's management structures at European level. Coller (1996) identifies the distinctive coordinating role of the European management structure of the European foods business of a globally-spread European MNC. A regional dimension to the management organization of the European operations of MNCs headquartered outside Europe is also evident. In the automotive sector, Hancké (2000) underlines the coordinating role of the European management organizations in the regionally integrated operations of North American MNCs.

Despite the evident regional concentration of stocks and flows of international investment by MNCs, taxonomies in the international business literature typically locate sectors and companies within a matrix which accounts for the relative strength of global and local (i.e. national) pressures (Bartlett and Ghoshal, 1992). Porter's (1986) distinction between companies operating in 'multi-domestic' industries, where competition is nationally bounded, and those which are 'global' in scope has been particularly influential. Such taxonomies can be refined to incorporate the salience of regional economic influences for marketing strategies and production organization (Marginson, 2000a). In a rare empirical investigation of ten industries in France, Atamer (1993) found that firms differed according to sector in their perceptions of the impact of the single European market. Respondents in agro-chemicals and food manufacturing anticipated a strong impact, and hence the need to develop European-level marketing and production; those in paper, printing and plastics, currently perceived as essentially national markets, anticipated little impact; in machine tools, already perceived as European in scope, little further impact was anticipated. The process of constructing a European economy is driving sectors towards European-level production and/or marketing strategies at varying speed. In some industries the 'domestic' market and the 'domestic' scale of production are now regional: Europe is the new domestic context. But neither are such sectors and enterprises necessarily becoming global. Ruigrok and van Tulder (1995) reach a similar conclusion, finding that during the 1990s regionally focused internationalization strategies dominated global ones.

European company characteristics that transcend national borders

From below, an important source of differentiation between European MNCs is the variety of national institutional forms within which they are located. The societal contingency approaches outlined in Chapter 1 (Maurice *et al.*, 1986; Lane, 1989; Whitley, 1992) insist that enterprises are primarily shaped by these nationally specific features. Yet national economies across Europe are far from homogenous: they continue to support a diversity of forms of organization, some of which transcend national borders. As Mayer and Whittington (1996: 88) observe, 'national economies in Europe seem both to be more internally diverse and to have more in common than most societal-contingency accounts can explain'. They propose instead a 'societal choice' approach, which recognizes that business organization within Europe is simultaneously overlapping and fragmented. Institutional environments contain actors – the state, entrepreneurs, families – that may prefer, and have the resources to support, forms of enterprise organization which do not conform to the dominant model. The approach remains sensitive to dominant patterns of business organization, but is also alert to forms that cross-cut national boundaries.

Enterprise forms cutting across European countries include family-owned companies, which are a persistent feature of France, Germany, Italy and the Walloon region of Belgium. The challenges posed by internationalization do not appear to be insuperable for such companies; some have extended their reach across European markets by acquiring firms in other countries. Until recent privatization initiatives, state-owned enterprise has also been a prominent feature, notably in Austria, France, Italy and Spain, operating within different parameters and ful-filling important roles as 'social buffers' to maintain employment (Ferner, 1994: 57). Also, state-influenced strategic direction and massive state financing have underpinned the internationalization strategies of some public companies, particularly in France.

Turning to enterprise structure, notwithstanding the spread of the multi-divisional form – widely regarded as possessing superior eco-nomic properties – the loosely-structured holding company continues to survive in most EU countries, including Britain. In part, this struc-tural form survives for institutional reasons: the holding company pro-vides a way of mobilizing capital resources (through minority stakes, for example) in the absence of supportive capital markets. It also protects the component businesses from demands from external markets to pri-oritize short-run returns (Mayer and Whittington, 1996). Conversely, the multi-divisional form, which is the prevalent form of large enter-prise structure in the Anglo-Saxon economies, is spreading more widely across countries with 'insider' systems of corporate governance (see below). Internationalization strategies appear to be an important trigger (Ferner and Quintanilla, 1998; Lilja and Tainio, 1996).

Moreover, in becoming international, MNCs partially escape the national institutional configurations in which they were previously embedded. In the words of Morgan *et al.* (2001), such companies con-stitute a form of 'transnational social space'. MNCs are distinctive from national firms in that their organizational boundaries cross national institutional contexts. Unlike nationally based firms, they do not oper-ate in a unified institutional context that reinforces and reproduces par-ticular practices, but in multiple institutional contexts, each of which has distinctive 'rules of the game' as to how economic activities and firms are to be coordinated. MNCs play an active role in determining how they bridge these multiple national environments (Mueller, 1994). In response to economic pressures that stretch beyond national bound-aries, and in the context of limited forms of supranational regulation, MNCs are developing organization-specific transnational practices as well as structures, reflecting the 'institutional' forms of isomorphism referred to in Chapter 1. These 'organization effects' draw upon a wider range of institutions and practices than those found in the home coun-try, including practices drawn from the host economies of overseas operations, through processes of 'reverse diffusion' (Edwards, 1998). Indeed, similar developments in structure and control systems are evident amongst MNCs embedded within different national business systems within Europe. A process of 'Anglo-Saxonization' is occurring along several dimensions, albeit one that entails distinctive national variations (Ferner and Quintanilla, 1998).

In sum, Europe exists as a distinct economic space at the level of cross-border flows of goods and investment and for a growing number of sectors and companies. Variation is evident between sectors and companies, and also between countries. It is analytically useful to differentiate the Euro-company from the global corporation. Empirically this can be more readily discerned in some sectors than in others, and is more apparent in the organization of the business operations and management practice of some firms than in others.

The political dimension – a developed political space

Our second assumption starts from the recognition that, unlike other regional blocs such as the NAFTA, the EU has a developed political dimension. 'Political institutions have been created which have a capacity to control the process of international economic integration that is greater than in any other region' (Martin, 1996: 6). The EU does not just have a Council of Ministers and a secretariat. It also has many of the hallmarks of a national polity including an administration, with in this instance the right of legislative initiation – the European Commission, an elected parliament – the European Parliament, and a judicial authority – the European Court of Justice.

'Multi-level governance'

Capturing the essence of the EU's political dimension has proved a major challenge. According to former Commission President Delors (quoted in Olsen, 2001: 329), the EU is an *'object politique non-identifié'*: it is not merely an intergovernmental organization, but neither is it a superstate; even to conceive of it as 'something in-between' misses the mark, because relations between the EU and the member states cannot adequately be defined in hierarchical terms. As the focus of attention in political science's study of the EU has moved from integration to governance, however, the 'defining metaphor of the EU polity' has become 'multi-level governance' (Rosamond, 2000: 75). The metaphor is also increasingly accepted by policy makers: the European Commission's 2001 *White Paper on Governance* characterizes the EU as being 'based on multi-level governance in which each actor contributes in line with his or her capabilities or knowledge to the success of the overall exercise' (European Commission, 2001c: 34–5). According to Olsen (2001: 329):

> The current institutional configuration is complex, ambiguous and changing. It is multi-levelled, multi-structured and multi-centred, characterized by networks across territorial levels of governance, institutions of government, and public–private institutions.

As Olsen (2001: 335) stresses, the EU's configuration is the result of a history of 'informal and gradual institutional evolution' as well as 'founding acts and deliberate institution building'. Indeed, the present form can be seen as a path-dependent consequence of institutional and policy trajectories set long ago. The original Monnet–Schuman method of integration was designed to yield long-term political union out of economic cooperation largely through the process of 'spillover':

> Integration in modest but strategically significant sectors would create the pressures for the integration of cognate sectors, which – egged on by the High Authority – would be accompanied by the shift in the loyalties of key producer groups away from national authorities. Their instrumental rationality would ensure that shifts in the locus of authority quickly became significant. As they came to operate within an integrating transnational economy, so they would increasingly demand more supranational rules – something that only supranational authorities could supply effectively. (Rosamond, 2001: 71)

In reality, the process has been far from straightforward. 'It is a history where desired policy outcomes and preferred institutional development have not necessarily coincided' (Olsen, 2001: 335). At each step, developments have been highly contested and the outcome is best imagined as the complex consequence of the acts of multiple political and economic agents with differing views about the speed and direction of development and also the destination. There is 'no shared vision of a future Europe and how the EU should be governed ... There is no shared understanding of the institutional requirements and possibilities, and no single central reorganisation authority' (Olsen, 2001: 337). As Hay and Rosamond (2000) argue, the absence of shared understandings or visions is refracted in the way in which the discourse of 'globalization' has been deployed by different interest groups each seeking to mobilize its potential in support of differing political aims. For some globalization has been used to justify the EU adopting a neo-liberal approach to macroeconomic policy, and to advance the case for fundamental reform of the European social model. Whereas for others, given its presumed debilitating consequences, globalization is the reason for developing a social as well as economic union. In the event, such is the nature of the EU political process that it has produced *both* a neo-liberal economic regime *and* a framework for a European industrial relations system.

The 'market making' process of economic integration

Three sets of decisions are particularly relevant to the project of economic integration which has always lain at the heart of the EU's political construction and enlargement. One is the form of the process of economic integration. Following Tinbergen (1965), the creation of the single European market has essentially been a 'negative' process, involving 'market-making' rather than 'market correcting' measures (Streeck, 1995: 34–40). Rather than being concerned with the modification of existing institutions and the creation of new ones and/or with intervention aimed at redistribution, the process mainly took the form of the removal of tarriff and then non-tarriff restrictions on movements in goods, services, capital and labour and regulation aimed at enhancing economic efficiency. 'Market making' began with the creation of the European Economic Community (EEC) in 1956. It was only in the mid-1980s, however, that the process of creating a genuine single market commenced in earnest. In 1985, the Council endorsed the Commission's White Paper on the Single Market, specifying over 300 legislative acts need to 'complete' the single market and setting a deadline for the end of 1992 for implementing all related decisions. The Single European Act, which established the political competence deemed necessary for the EU to complete the single market, was ratified in 1987.

The second and third features relate to the macroeconomic framework which EMU embeds and were outlined in Chapter 1: the incomplete architecture of EMU and its particular institutional arrangements. EMU's incomplete architecture entails the absence of some key features associated with an 'optimum currency area' (Mundell, 1961), notably a common taxation policy and fiscal competence to transfer sizeable funds from one region (country) to another as a tool of economic adjustment. The absence of such mechanisms means that the brunt of any shocks, symmetric or asymmetric, will fall primarily upon the labour market. Key features of EMU's institutional arrangements, including the European Central Bank's remit to focus primarily on price stability (and not also on growth) and its asymmetric inflation target together with the parameters of the Stability and Growth Pact aimed at containing public expenditure deficits, build in a deflationary bias. The result is what has often been described as a 'banker's Europe' (Milner, 2002). As one critic has put it, thinking of the motives of those such as Delors who promoted the single market:

> A project which was, from its inception, inherently social and political in nature has tended, through a slow process of attrition, to mutate into little more than a charter of economic liberalisation and marketisation. As such, it threatens to become the altar upon which the European social model is ultimately sacrificed. (Hay, 2000: 521)

The social dimension – a mix of EU framework and national systems

The EU has nonetheless developed a social policy competence, which includes a framework for a European industrial relations system. The 1997 Amsterdam Treaty sets out the main aims of European social policy in Article 136:

> the promotion of employment, improved living and working conditions, so as to make possible their harmonisation while the improvement is being maintained, proper social protection, dialogue between management and labour, the development of human resources with a view to lasting employment and the combating of exclusion.

Updating Rhodes (1997: 69–70), there are five areas where EU policy might be conceived of as social: the social security and distributive aspects of the Common Agricultural Policy providing subsidy and income-maintenance programmes for farmers; the various funds (regional, social and cohesion), which are addressed at the disparities between different EU regions; regulations on environment, product safety and consumer protection, including the harmonization of health and safety standards at work; regulatory policies for the labour market, which embrace workers' rights, the promotion of social dialogue and collective bargaining; and the employment strategy, which promotes improvement in the rates, quality, adaptability and equality of employment. Our concern is primarily with the fourth of these, although elements of the third – insofar as working time regulation comes under health and safety – and the fifth are also relevant.

A framework for a European industrial relations system

Ever since the founding Treaty of Rome, core industrial relations matters, including the right to association, the right to engage in industrial action (strikes and lock-outs) and wage determination have been excluded from the EU's competence, remaining the province of the member states. Reflecting the emphasis on 'market making' rather than 'market correcting' measures, social policy in the industrial relations sphere has in large part developed through the process of 'spillover' from economic integration. A prime example is the 'social dimension' of the single European market, crystallized in the series of measures proposed in the 1989 Social Charter, initiated to offset the potentially deleterious social and employment effects of the rationalization and restructuring that the single market programme entailed.

Nonetheless, the EU has evolved an industrial relations framework, which, although much criticized, can lay claim to principles, procedures and substantive outcomes. The principles are set out in the Social Affairs Commissioner's foreword to the Commission's first ever report on industrial relations and reflect the conviction that economic and social progress must go hand-in-hand: 'respect for fundamental social rights in a frontier-free Europe; workers' rights to information and consultation on company operations; social dialogue as a mainstay of good governance and a means of involving citizens in the European venture' (European Commission, 2000).

In addition to the original Community procedures for adopting legally based directives and regulations, three processes are prominent. The first is social dialogue, which in its present form was launched at a summit conference involving the Commission and the social partners at Val Duchesse in 1985. Social dialogue encompasses bipartite exchanges between the social partners, with the aim of reaching common positions or even agreement, and which are sometimes directed at – or under tripartite exchanges involve – the public authorities. It also embraces consultation of the social partners under the social policy process outlined below. The intention is to accord employers' organizations and trade unions an enhanced voice, and therefore influence, over issues and developments of common concern arising from the single market programme. In addition to the cross-sector social dialogue there are a series of sector social dialogues, as Chapter 4 elaborates.

Second are procedures relating to consultation and collective bargaining under the social policy process adopted by 11 of the then 12 member states (the UK excluding itself) under the 1991 Maastricht

Treaty. Subsequently incorporated in the social chapter of the Amsterdam Treaty, the process places the Commission under an obligation to consult with the social partners across a range of fields and provides for the conclusion of EU-level collective agreements as a mode of binding regulation. Specifically, Article 137 requires the Commission to consult the social partners in advance of adopting legislative proposals in the following fields: improvement of the working environment to protect workers' health and safety; working conditions; information and consultation of workers; equality of opportunities and treatment at work between men and women; integration of persons excluded from the labour market; social security and social protection of workers; protection of workers where their employment contract is terminated; representation and collective defence of the interests of workers and employers; conditions of employment for third-country nationals residing in the EU; and financial contributions for the promotion of employment and job creation. Article 138 of the Treaty requires the Commission to consult the social partners in two stages: (a) on the need for and the possible direction of Community action; and (b) on its content. At the end of this consultation process, the social partner organizations can present an opinion to the Commission or inform it of their intention to open negotiations on the subject. In this case, the social partners have an initial period of nine months to reach an agreement. Where the social partners do not take the initiative, or do not reach agreement, the Commission resumes its active role.

The third procedure involves the so-called 'open method of co-ordination' (OMC) originally associated with the EU's employment strategy. According to the Commission (European Commission, 2002c: 7):

> The open method of co-ordination means that all countries fix common objectives in a given policy area, prepare national actions plans, examine each other's performance with Commission guidance and learn from their successes and failures. It is a new way of working together in the EU – no longer only through legislation, but through a flexible yet structured co-operation among Member States.

The EU's extraordinary summit in Lisbon in 2000 formally adopted the OMC as a regulatory method. It also saw agreement to attempt to coordinate the so-called 'Luxembourg' and 'Cologne' coordination processes dealing, respectively, with the development and implementation of national action plans for employment and 'macro-economic dialogue' addressing wage policy inter alia involving the European Central Bank, the European Commission and the social partners.

The outcomes include legislative measures in a range of areas: freedom of movement of workers; equal opportunities for women and men; health and safety; collective redundancy; transfer of undertakings; working time; employee information and consultation; pregnant worker, maternity and parental leave rights; rights of posted, part-time and temporary workers; and discrimination at work. In three instances, legislative measures derive from collective agreements between the social partners. Further topics have been addressed in voluntary collective agreements, at cross-sector and sector levels, which are not binding. In addition, a substantial body of joint texts – which are advisory in nature – has emerged from the social dialogue. A further substantive result is an employment policy, giving rise to a series of actions. Completing the picture, there have also been landmark decisions from the European Court of Justice, notably in the area of equality.

Key features of national industrial relations systems

In as much as industrial relations is deemed to be a core responsibility of individual member states, substantiating our third assumption also means a focus on national systems. As Chapter 1 observed, much comparative industrial relations analysis is characterized by the 'diversity approach' (Teague, 1999a: 8) which tends to privilege the enduring specific features of different national industrial relations systems at the expense of their common features. Much, however, depends upon the level of analysis: 'From afar, when we compare the European welfare states with the advanced market economies of North America and Asia, we can recognise Europe's shared distinctiveness, whereas, when we look closer, we perceive intra-European, cross-national diversity' (Ebbinghaus, 1999: 1).

Three common features are prominent when comparing the industrial relations systems of most EU member states with those of the US or Japan. The first is the high degree of interest organization amongst both employers and workers in the countries of Western Europe. Employers' organizations barely feature in the US; their membership density and degree of centralization in Japan are at the bottom end of the European range. Levels of union membership density are substantially higher in all but two of the EU-15 (France and Spain) than in the US or Japan. In most countries too, peak-level union organizations command more authority over their constituent unions than in the US in particular (Traxler *et al.*, 2001; EIRO, 2002e). This high degree of interest organization is reflected in the institutional role that employers' organizations and trade unions have secured in economic, social welfare and labour market policy in many EU countries.

The second is the nature and extent of the legal intervention on behalf of the weaker party to the employment relationship, that is workers. This has established rights in substantive areas (such as minimum wages, hours of work, equality of opportunities, health and safety, dismissal and redundancy). The extensive rights to employee 'voice' in respect of representation, information and consultation, and collective bargaining found amongst EU countries also stand out. These embrace not only the higher levels of the sector and in several instances the economy, but also the company and the workplace. Traxler *et al.* (2001: 292), surveying the situation across the OECD countries, conclude that 'the key criterion that divides national labour relations according to their ability to tackle market-driven opportunism is the (non-)existence of legally based support for collective action'.

The third is the structure of collective bargaining. All of the EU-15 have historically been characterized by an inclusive structure of multi-employer bargaining and, with the exception of the UK, continue to be so. Buttressed in several countries by statutory extension provisions, this means that the benefits of employer association–trade union negotiations are extended throughout a sector or across a country and are not just the preserve of the well organized. The result is that around 80 per cent of the workforce of the EU-15 is covered by a collective agreement (EIRO, 2002e). Such a structure also enables the participation of employers' organizations and trade unions in macro-level social dialogue over economic, social welfare and labour market policy, and in several instances the management of schemes relating to the second and third. The universal rights to representation and to coverage that these provide are the basis for comprehensive substantive provision (in terms of wages and working time) that is the industrial relations equivalent of the welfare state.

The origins of these features have been studied extensively and it suffices to note here that they are deeply rooted. Thus, compared to the US, the state has played a substantially more active role in employment and social policy in EU countries (Crouch, 1993). As Scharpf (2000: 192) remarks, all EU countries are 'capitalist in the sense that the private ownership of the means of production was accepted in principle, and all had in practice come to depend on profit-oriented private enterprise and market interactions for the creation of mass incomes and public revenue through economic growth'. Yet at the same time, he continues, they all relied on the 'state's newly increased capacity for market-correcting action to develop an inter-related employment relations and social protection system'.

The structure of multi-employer bargaining reflects the compromises struck at times of great political and social, as well as economic, crisis, such as those occurring at the end of both world wars (Sisson, 1987). These compromises invariably involved the state as well as employers and trade unions. Multi-employer bargaining made it possible for trade unions to establish what the Webbs (1902) called the 'common rule', thereby preventing undercutting in the labour market. For employers, the common rule brought about a measure of *market control*, putting a floor under competition for labour and in some industries taking wages out of competition altogether. Multi-employer bargaining maximized the bargaining power of employers as well as trade unions – in some countries the threat of the lock-out was a powerful weapon in dealing with trade unions. For employers too, it helped to neutralize the workplace, obliging trade unions de facto to recognize the employer's right to manage and setting limits to the role they could play there. For the state it achieved the widespread institutionalization of industrial conflict, not least because common rules were also perceived to be legitimate.

Variations on a theme

From the perspective of individual countries, the devil is in the detail. Recent analyses of the social protection dimension of the European social model have distinguished several clusters amongst west European countries, each with its own variant of social welfare regime (Esping-Andersen, 1990; Scharpf, 2000). Explanations of the resulting typologies mostly revolve around the significance of state tradition and/or national business system; they also emphasize embeddedness or path dependency. Four main clusters have been identified, which relate also to industrial relations (Ebbinghaus, 1999; Supiot, 2000), although sometimes the first two are combined into a single 'Continental' model:

- the 'Rhineland', embracing Austria, Germany and the Benelux countries;
- the 'Latin' including France, Italy, Portugal and Spain (and also Greece);
- the 'Nordic' comprising Denmark, Finland, Norway and Sweden; and
- the 'Anglo-Irish', i.e. Ireland and the UK.

In surveying the variations between, and also within, the industrial relations systems of these four clusters our focus is on the second and third of the common features described above. It is the extensive rights to employee 'voice' in respect of representation, information and consultation, and collective bargaining found amongst the EU-15 and the prevailing multi-employer structure of collective bargaining amongst all but the UK which most closely bear on the governance arrangements which are of central to concern to this study.

The significance of the role of the state

State tradition is fundamental for the balance between legal enactment and collective bargaining. In the 'Latin' countries, legal enactment has been prior and collective bargaining secondary, reflecting the pervasive role of the state in economic and social affairs. In the 'Rhineland' countries, there is an extensive legal framework, but this includes significant guarantees of autonomy for employers and trade unions to conduct their affairs on the basis of collective agreements. In the 'Nordic' countries, collective bargaining is primary and legal enactment secondary. The industrial relations framework predominantly results from national-level agreements between the employers' and trade union confederations. The 'Anglo-Irish' model is different again, being characterized by 'voluntarism' or 'legal abstentionism'. Industrial relations was removed from the field of the common law and responsibility for regulation delegated to the parties themselves through collective bargaining. It meant a minimal auxiliary framework in support of collective bargaining and, historically, a limited role in regulating the individual employment relationship. Many features of industrial relations systems are affected, including the membership density, structure and organization of trade unions (Ebbinghaus and Visser, 2000) and employers' associations (Sadowski and Jacobi, 1991; Traxler, 2000a) which comprise the first common feature identified above.

Considering the implications for the main features of the governance arrangements for employment, the first is the role of the state in wage bargaining, which also has implications for the degree of centralization of trade unions and employers' organizations. Heterogeneity within country groups is now almost as marked as that between them, with earlier distinctive patterns fracturing over recent years. Following Traxler *et al.* (2001: 174–81), the 'Rhineland' countries fall into two groups. In Austria and Germany, the role of the state has largely been one of 'non-interference' in which the collective bargaining autonomy of employers and trade unions is upheld. In Belgium and Netherlands (since the early 1980s), by contrast, the state has been actively engaged with the social partners in a form of 'tripartitism without authoritative implementation', this giving way to 'state imposition' in Belgium in some periods. Two of the 'Latin' countries, Spain and Portugal, provide examples of state 'non-interference' in wage bargaining; a third, Italy, in the 1970s and 1980s was a further instance, but since 1990 has become a case of 'tripartitism'. France is the exception, with 'state imposition' through the influence of adjustments to the minimum wage and 'public sector pace setting'. Historically, the 'Nordic' countries were all instances of 'bipartitism'. In Denmark and Sweden in recent years, however, the state has adopted the position of 'conciliator' when bipartite negotiations (threaten to) break down. Finally, the UK is largely a case of 'non-interference', as was Ireland until the mid-1980s after which it embraced 'tripartitism'.

The second feature is the status of collective agreements. In effect, in the 'Rhineland', 'Latin' and 'Nordic' countries, multi-employer agreements are compulsory contracts: the terms and conditions are binding on the signatory organizations and their members. In Ireland and the UK, by contrast, collective agreements are voluntary agreements binding in honour only – they are not deemed to be legally enforceable unless the parties agree to making them so. One major difference amongst the first three clusters involves the 'peace obligation' implicit or explicit in the negotiation of collective agreements, under which the parties must refrain from industrial action over issues covered by the contract for its duration. In the 'Nordic' countries, the peace obligation is extremely strong, whereas in the 'Latin' countries it is weak, largely because the constitutional right to strike overrides it. The 'Rhineland' countries divide into three: the situation in Austria and Germany is very similar to that in the 'Nordic' countries, whereas Belgium is closer to the 'Latin' and the Netherlands in between. In Ireland and the UK, although collective agreements are generally not deemed to be legally binding, a key rationale for voluntarism has been that the parties would be more likely to respect the agreements they willingly entered into.

Another difference is provisions for the legal extension of the terms of collective agreements to employers who are not members of an employers' association, and are therefore not covered. In the 'Rhineland' and 'Latin' countries, collective agreements are not just compulsory contracts but also compulsory codes, whose effect it is possible to extend. Traxler *et al.* (2001: 182–5) report that in Austria and Belgium in the first group and in France, Portugal and Spain in the second, collective agreements are regularly extended to non-affiliated employers and employees. In the Netherlands and Germany, extension is used only occasionally, but nevertheless 'on a notable scale'. In Italy, extension practice is widespread, underpinned not by a law but by the courts' interpretation of an article of the constitution. In the 'Nordic' countries, there are no extension provisions in Denmark and Sweden, and although provisions have existed in Norway since 1993 they have been rarely used. Comprehensive coverage of collective agreements in all three is secured as a result of high levels of union and employers' association membership (Traxler, 1998a). Finland is the exception, with collective agreements being regularly extended. In the UK and Ireland extension practice is effectively absent. A number of devices for extending the terms of collective agreements in the UK were discontinued in the 1980s. In Ireland, the possibility exists but has been rarely used.

A key implication of the combination of multi-employer bargaining, legal enforceability and extension practice, as Table 2.1 shows, is that there is little or no correlation between trade union membership and collective bargaining coverage. The most extreme case is France, where trade union membership is around 10 per cent whilst collective bargaining coverage, supported by extension of legally enforceable multi-employer agreements, is over 90 per cent. Employer solidarity is also affected. Other things being equal, the greater the legal priority given to collective bargaining, the greater the requirement for employers to cohere. Thus employer solidarity is stronger in the 'Nordic' and 'Rhineland' countries than it is in the 'Latin' or 'Anglo-Irish'.

The third distinguishing feature is the nature and extent of employee workplace representation. Such representation may be trade union or

Table 2.1 The relationship between trade union membership density and collective bargaining coverage in thirteen EEA countries

Trade union density	Collective bargaining coverage	
	High	Low
High	S (92,88) FIN (83,78) DK (69,78)	
Medium	A (99,43) B (96,50) I (>90,38) N (70,58)	
Low	F (95,10) P (92,27) D (84,29) E (83,19) NL (82,16)	UK (37,32)

Notes: Collective bargaining coverage is for 1996; union density is for 1995. Figures in brackets are collective bargaining coverage followed by union density. For union density 33% and 66% are the split points between the three categories; for collective bargaining coverage, the single split point is 50%.

Source: Derived from Traxler *et al.* (2001: Tables II.11 and III.15).

employee based; its institutionalization may be voluntary or statutory, depending upon whether union constitution, collective agreement or legislation is the basis; and it may be independent of management or incorporated into a joint committee embracing management as well as employee representatives (Rogers and Streeck, 1995; Traxler *et al.*, 2001: 119–22). The first two dimensions give rise to two alternative systems: the 'single channel' of union representation within and beyond the company and the 'dual channel' of works councils within the company and trade unions beyond, that is, for collective bargaining with employers' associations. Complicating matters, though, is the intersection between trade unions and works councils which is found in several countries in which union delegations at company level have certain rights, usually of negotiation, and/or trade unions have certain rights of nomination in respect of works council membership. Even where neither is the case, unions have established a strong presence in formally independent works councils – as in Germany.

The basic contrasts are shown in Figure 2.1. In the 'Rhineland' countries independent (employee) works councils are, with the exception of Belgium, the main vehicle and result from legislation. In Belgium, legislatively-established joint committees (works councils) coexist alongside union delegations which derive from a central collective agreement. In this respect, Belgium resembles three of the four 'Latin' countries: France,

Workplace representation

TUs		Italy Finland Sweden	Denmark Norway	Ireland UK
TUs/Works councils	France Greece	Belgium Portugal Spain		
Works councils	Austria Germany Luxembourg Netherlands			
	Legislation	Central agreements/ Legislation	Central agreements	Voluntarism

Regulatory basis

Figure 2.1 Workplace representation in the EU-15 plus Norway

Source: Based on Regalia (1995) and Traxler *et al.* (2001: Table III.2).

Spain and Portugal also provide for legislatively-based works councils (joint committees in France, employee-only in Spain and Portugal) which coexist with union delegations where such exist. The latter result from legislation in France, and a combination of collective agreement and legislation in the other two countries. The exception is Italy, where the *Statuto del lavoro* of 1970 de facto supports local trade union representation. In the 'Nordic' countries, workplace representation is also through local trade union representatives, but results from multi-industry agreements. In the UK and Ireland, the situation differs from workplace to workplace, there being no general right to representation until the EU's 2002 information and consultation directive comes into force from 2005. Predominantly, though, it has been based on single channel trade union representatives with works councils-type arrangements being rare.

Employee representatives' rights and responsibilities differ *within* as well as *between* the two main forms. Generally, the responsibilities of works councils differ from trade union representation insofar as they include the obligation to cooperate with management and take into account the organization's well-being. The three main areas in which there are differences are information, consultation and co-determination, the scope to negotiate issues which are the subject of collective agreement and the right to strike.

The most extensive rights to information, consultation and co-determination are to be found in the 'Rhineland' and 'Nordic' countries. Works councils in Austria and Germany in particular enjoy co-decision powers over a range of issues, including working-time schedules and wage system rules. This applies to a lesser extent in the Netherlands; in Belgium there are no co-determination rights. By contrast, their role in matters that are the subject of higher-level collective agreements is relatively limited. In particular, their role in wage bargaining is formally restricted to those instances where higher-level agreements empower local bargaining to apply standard provisions flexibly to a company's situation. There is no right to strike action. In Belgium, the union delegates' right to bargain is similarly fixed. In the 'Nordic' countries, the powers of local trade union representatives historically came from national-level agreements, but in Finland and Sweden have been placed on a legal footing with the passage of Co-determination Acts in 1979 and 1976 respectively. There is an obligation on management to negotiate over a broad range of issues, though not necessarily to reach an agreement (except on training and work rules). As for wages, union representatives are authorized to negotiate under the terms of the peace obligation laid down by higher-level agreements.

In the 'Latin' countries, rights to information, consultation and co-determination are less extensive than in the 'Rhineland' and 'Nordic' countries. Set against this, however, is that, with the exception of Portugal, representatives are formally entitled both to negotiate wages and call strikes, these rights being endorsed by statute. In France, Italy and Spain these rights are vested in union delegates. In Ireland and the UK, workplace representatives only began to gain legal rights to information and consultation with accession to the EU and the passage of the directives on collective redundancies (1975), transfers of undertakings (1977), working time (1993), European Works Councils (1994) and national-level information and consultation (2002). Historically, the main source of formalization has been the union constitution. In theory, local union representatives have had the right to negotiate over wages, but have not been entitled to call strikes. In practice, their actual power has depended upon circumstances, with 'unofficial' action in support of local wage demands being widespread in the 1960s and 1970s. With the passage of a succession of national-level agreements, the position of local union representatives in Ireland has moved closer to that of the 'Rhineland' countries model in respect of wages bargaining – that is, a limited mandate within the framework of higher-level agreements.

The fourth feature involves the links between the institutions of industrial relations and social protection. Here the so-called 'Ghent' system of unemployment insurance found in three of the four 'Nordic' countries – Norway being the exception – and Belgium is important. This takes the form of a state-subsidized system run by trade unions. Such involvement not only adds to the legitimacy of trade unions, reinforcing their role in multi-employer bargaining and macro-level social dialogue more generally, but also helps to explain the continued high membership levels in these countries (Traxler *et al.*, 2001: 85).

The significance of corporate governance arrangements

Reinforcing these differences is the influence of national business systems on the strategies and behaviour of enterprises (Whitley, 1992, 1996; Hall and Soskice, 2001). Particularly salient for industrial relations are corporate governance structures. Whitley (1996) underlines the contrast between the 'insider' systems found in the 'coordinated market economies' (Hall and Soskice, 2001) of the continental European countries and the 'outsider' system characteristic of the 'liberal market economies' of the Anglo-Saxon countries. Insider systems, of which the French and German (also Swedish) are examples of the two main 'state-led' and 'collaborative' or 'consensus' variants, respectively, are distinguished by interlinked networks of corporate, institutional or family shareholdings, a financial system based on long-term bank credit, less-developed stock markets and constraints on hostile takeover. Enterprises are embedded in networks of relationships in which the ability to act independently is restricted by ties of mutual obligation to and dependence on various stakeholder groups, including employees. Amongst countries within this group, Whitley emphasizes interdependencies with non-industrial actors, such as the state (France), banks (Germany) or investment foundations (Sweden), and with other industrial actors, such as suppliers or employee representatives. In contrast, outsider systems are characterized by dispersed networks of shareholdings, greater reliance on internal sources of finance, highly developed stock markets and an active market for corporate control. In the first instance, companies' ability to act independently is restricted by ties of mutual obligation to and dependence upon various stakeholder groups, including employees; in the second, they are largely discrete economic actors – 'islands of planned co-ordination in a sea of market relations' (Richardson, 1972: 883) – primarily accountable to shareholders.

In terms of behaviour, enterprises embedded in insider systems are likely to emphasize longer-run performance, and to pursue investment strategies which involve long-term commitments to product and process innovation and associated skill development. In contrast, enterprises embedded in outsider systems place more emphasis upon short-run financial performance, and adopt investment strategies which are driven by purely financial criteria. Edwards (1999) suggests that such differences shape the implicit contracts, comprising informal understandings on issues that are difficult to contract for formally, reached between the parties. Combined with mandatory forms of representation and 'voice', which protect the interests of employee stakeholders, the basis exists under insider systems for generating and sustaining the trust necessary to support wide-ranging implicit contracts. There are incentives both for managers to invest in skill development and for employees to acquire skills. Employees are likely to be regarded as enduring assets who form a potential source of competitive advantage. In contrast, taken together with the absence of employee stakeholder rights, outsider systems do not encourage the development of high trust relationships and the implicit contracts which depend on them. Neither managers nor employees can be confident that their investments will be protected, hence incentives for training are weaker. Employees are likely to be regarded as disposable liabilities and to be the focus of short-run cost minimization by management.

Differences in corporate governance arrangements are refracted onto arrangements for industrial relations governance in two significant ways. First, the universal rights to representation for the purposes of employee information, consultation and, in several countries, co-determination, which are a distinguishing feature of the industrial relations systems of countries with insider systems when compared to those based in outsider systems, reflect the formal voice rights accorded to employees as stakeholders. Works councils or equivalent trade union bodies have, for example, the right to be informed of – and in most cases consulted over – major changes to the company. There are two principal channels through which employee representatives in insider countries actually influence such instances of restructuring (Edwards, 2002). The first is through rights to co-determination or social concertation, expressed in the rights of works councils to negotiate a social plan to deal with the consequences of restructuring found in the Rhineland countries and the board-level rights of co-determination found in the Rhineland (excepting Belgium) and Nordic countries. The second is primarily through trade unions' ability to negotiate social plans, and is found in the 'Latin' countries. Under the 'outsider systems' found in Ireland and the UK the influence of employees over company restructuring largely depends upon the strength of unions at firm level.

Second, along with the nature and extent of the legal framework discussed above, corporate governance structure is a key variable shaping employer solidarity. The interlinked networks of corporate, institutional or family shareholdings characteristic of insider systems makes for considerable solidarity. By contrast, the presumption in outsider systems that companies are largely discrete economic actors primarily accountable to shareholders encourages independence, above all in the absence of encouragement from the state as in the UK. This in turn relates to employer support for multi-employer structures of collective bargaining, which has been notably weaker in the UK than amongst their counterparts in the insider systems of Continental Europe. Arguably where companies are largely discrete economic actors, they exhibit the stronger interest in developing organization-specific employment systems as well as the weaker interest in combining with other employers. In addition to the differences in the legal framework discussed earlier, this helps to account for the different trajectories of 'disorganized' and 'organized' decentralization (Traxler, 1995) evident in the UK and Continental Europe, respectively.

Cautionary notes

Four caveats need emphasizing in closing this survey of national industrial relations systems. The first is that, analytically useful though it is to discern 'clusters' of countries, there are differences within each. For example, France is noticeable by its absence among the 'Latin' countries negotiating 'social pacts' and prominent in the extent to which industrial relations remains state-led. Italy is distinctive in the exclusive rights to representation at workplace and company level accorded to trade unions. Amongst the 'Rhineland' countries, the Netherlands differs from Germany both in the nature of the powers of works councils and the nature and extent of its macro-social dialogue. In the 'Nordic' countries, Sweden and Denmark have seen considerable decentralization in recent years, whereas Finland and Norway remain highly centralized. The two 'Anglo-Irish' countries have also grown apart considerably. The UK continues to be characterized by the absence of macro-level social dialogue, whereas in Ireland the decline of sector bargaining has been accompanied by the development of far-reaching multi-employer bargaining at the national level.

The second is the diversity that exists within national systems. In the case of national business systems, the coexistence of diverse enterprise forms within particular national boundaries has already been noted. In industrial relations there are significant differences between sectors, both at the level of broad aggregation – public versus private, production versus service – and at individual sector level, in collective bargaining arrangements and the incidence and strength of employee interest representation at workplace and company level. The contours and effects of sector differences are explored in Chapters 4 and 7 in particular. There are also substantial territorial differences within countries which, although not elaborated in this study, also caution against the assumption that national systems are undifferentiated entities. Examples include those between the east and west of Germany, the south and north of Italy and Flanders and Wallonia in Belgium.

Third, the cross-national portrait presented above is not static, but changing. Some changes, such as declining trade union and employers' association membership in many countries, may be weakening the hold of the organized system of industrial relations, but leave the comparative picture relatively untouched. Other changes, such as those which have occurred since the 1970s in the mode of cross-sector bargaining coordination in some countries (Traxler *et al.*, 2001: 149–57), tangibly alter the comparative canvas. Further changes impact upon the sharpness of the contrasts evident between groups of countries. For example, the evidence of a trend towards 'Anglo-Saxonization' in corporate governance arrangements in some of the countries with insider systems appears to be reflected amongst some of these in a weakening of the impact of employee influence through social concertation under restructuring, making them more closely resemble the UK (Edwards, 2002).

Fourth, while state traditions and business systems are important, industrial relations also has a degree of autonomy in which the interaction between the parties comes into its own. This is best understood in terms of the strategies and tactics of the negotiating process where structures shape but do not determine behaviour and outcomes. It is impossible, for example, to understand the differing form and status of collective agreements across countries without reference to the patterns of interaction between the parties, which in turn reflected differences in context arising from the timing and pace of industrialization (Sisson, 1987). Many institutional arrangements are also more adaptable than is commonly supposed – sector-level multi-employer bargaining is an obvious case, as Chapters 6 and 7 testify. If anything, the degree of autonomy of some parties, notably large employers, has increased in recent years. MNCs have growing space in which to develop their own approaches, which can be a hybrid of different national systems. Arguably too, similar scope to mesh distinctive traits of different country systems is open to European-level trade union organizations as well as the public authorities.

Summary and conclusion

Conceptually, the relationship between 'globalization' and 'Europeanization' is best viewed as a contingent one. Empirically, it is difficult if not impossible to fully disentangle the effects of the one from those of the other. There are compelling reasons, however, for adopting 'Europeanization' as the present reference point. The economic, political and social dynamics of the construction and enlargement of the EU are distinct and differentiable from those of globalization. The precise forms that European integration has taken are fundamentally important in their own right. Significant are the process of negative integration, EMU's incomplete architecture and key features of EMU's apparatus which build in a deflationary bias. Each of these has implications for industrial relations.

Unlike other regional blocs, the EU also has a developed political dimension under which a unique form of multi-level governance has emerged. This means that while the EU is not yet a polity with the same powers of the nation state, it has nonetheless developed, and continues to develop, mechanisms to promote a steady accretion of social policy measures. That the arrangements are multi-level and combine elements of the superstate and the subsidiarity of nation states goes a long way to understanding the emergence of a multi-level system of industrial relations.

This chapter has also established that it is possible to identify the main contours of a 'European industrial relations model', notwithstanding that the EU framework is skeletal and that there are many points of difference between the systems of the member countries. Most of the EU-15 have three features in common: a high degree of interest organization on the part of both employers and workers; a framework of individual employment rights covering key issues of substance (e.g. minimum wages, hours of work, equality of opportunities, health and safety) and procedure (e.g. information and consultation, representation and collective bargaining); and an inclusive structure of collective bargaining (i.e. multi-employer rather than single-employer). The UK, and to a lesser extent Ireland, are the exceptions. Both have been characterized by 'voluntarism' so far as legal regulation is concerned. In the UK, multi-employer bargaining has all but vanished, whereas in Ireland it remains, albeit in the form of cross-sector national agreements. The survival or demise of this third key feature of the 'European industrial relations model' is one of the underlying concerns of the book.

3
Multi-Level Governance in the Making: Introducing the Key Processes

The multi-level system that European integration is prompting involves both formal and informal processes. Significant developments are taking place in these processes, and in the balance between them, which are integral to the system's dynamics. This chapter seeks to clarify what is involved. The initial focus is on collective bargaining, which, together with legal enactment, represent the two traditional methods of industrial relations regulation. Despite multiple challenges, collective bargaining appears to be not only surviving, but also gaining ground (Spyropoulos, 2002: 395). As well as assuming some of the functions traditionally performed by legal enactment, it appears to be taking on fresh roles. These developments are not restricted to the supranational level, but also feature within national systems, irrespective of different legal traditions. In the process a distinct shift from 'hard' to 'soft' forms of regulation is apparent.

Attention then turns to seemingly 'new' processes – coordinated bargaining, benchmarking and the 'open method of coordination' (OMC) – which are more directly associated with European integration. A key issue is whether such processes will take over from the so-called 'Community methods' of legal enactment and collective bargaining inherited from national systems. Finally, the chapter discusses the significance of the 'informal' processes of industrial relations. Coping with the common constraints that European integration brings means that the various forms of 'isomorphism' introduced in Chapter 1 are playing an increasingly important role. Indeed, it is difficult to understand some major developments, such as the convergence in the rates of change of wages across EU member states without reference to these processes.

The formal processes

- legal enactment
- collective bargaining
- coordination
  - joint (e.g. the OMC)
  - unilateral (e.g. MNCs' 'coercive comparisons'; EMF's bargaining 'rules')

The informal processes

- 'competitive isomorphism' ('convergence without coordination')
- 'mimetic isomorphism' (e.g. 'unintended pattern bargaining'; 'Europe learning from Europe')
- 'normative isomorphism' (e.g. 'best practice')

Figure 3.1   The main processes of employment regulation

Figure 3.1 summarizes the main formal and informal regulatory processes involved.

Collective bargaining – traditional process in a state of flux?

It is collective bargaining that 'distinguishes and gives strong identity to the EU, which is not found in the other similarly developed regions' (European Commission, 2002a: 2). Collective bargaining, though, is a complex process with many dimensions. The main variations along the principal dimensions, between and within countries, are summarized in Figure 3.2. Collective bargaining also admits of a wide range of meanings, reflecting the different traditions discussed in Chapter 2. Our operationalization of the term embraces these main variations, and is therefore broader than that of some other authors (for example, Visser, 1999: 87). In terms of level, collective bargaining can be single-employer or multi-employer; single-employer bargaining can also be single or multi-establishment and multi-employer bargaining single-industry or multi-industry. In terms of agents, it can be restricted to trade unions or extended to cover other collective forms of employee representation including works councils or even work groups. In terms of subject, it can emphasize matters of substance or procedure. Following Walton and McKersie (1965), it can also deal with issues of distribution, such as wages, where one party's loss is another's gain, or integration, such as restructuring, where the parties may have complementary interests that agreement

---

Level – national/regional – company/business unit/workplace

Agency – company managers/employers' organizations – trade union representatives/works councillors

Coverage in terms of employers – multi-employer/single-employer – sector / multi-sector – extendable/non-extendable

Coverage in terms of employees – comprehensive/partial (blue-collar/white-collar) – extendable/non-extendable

Scope of subject matter – substantive/procedural – broad/narrow

Types of substantive rule – minimum/standard – complete/incomplete

Form of rules – voluntary/legally-enforceable – compulsory/permissive – formal/informal

Depth or application – agreement making/agreement making and administration

Enforcement/monitoring/disputes resolution – private/public

Figure 3.2   The key dimensions of the structure of collective bargaining

helps to promote. In terms of activity, it can be viewed as a rule-making process leading to employment regulation or as a negotiating process, whose logic is as much about shaping ongoing relationships as it is about resolving particular issues. Collective bargaining also involves a vertical as well as horizontal collective action problem: the parties have to reach some accommodation among themselves (the vertical dimension) before they are able to deal effectively with the other (the horizontal dimension).

Changing roles for collective bargaining

In discussions of recent developments in collective bargaining, most attention has focused on changes in the level, where the dominant trend across Western Europe has been towards greater decentralization of collective bargaining structures, from the multi-sector to the sector, and the sector to the company level. Such decentralization varies in extent and form the most important distinction being between 'organized' and 'disorganized' forms (Traxler, 1995). The dominant tendency amongst the EU-15 has been towards 'organized' or 'centrally coordinated' (Ferner and Hyman, 1992: xxxvi) decentralization. These changes in level are closely associated with fundamental changes in the functions of collective bargaining. The authoritative Supiot report (1999: 140–7) provides a useful framework for understanding the emerging trends. First, collective bargaining is taking over some of the legislative function of the state that has long been associated with the Nordic and (historically) the Anglo-Irish models. Collective bargaining is being given responsibility for determining the content of legislation, leading to so-called 'negotiated law' (*lois négociée*). This is nowhere more apparent than at EU level where the Maastricht Treaty's social policy protocol – subsequently Articles 137 and 138 of the Treaty – gives the social partners scope to negotiate and reach agreement on issues within a specified range of fields on which the Commission proposes to bring forward legislative proposals. Such agreements, which in late 2003 numbered those on parental leave, part-time working, temporary, fixed-term contracts and teleworking, may then be accorded legal force as directives. Although the Commission retains the right of initiation, effectively the thrust of the legislative process has shifted from legal enactment to collective agreement. Mirroring EU-level developments, there have been changes in collective bargaining and its relationship with legal enactment at national level too. This primarily affects countries under the Latin model, where collective bargaining has traditionally been seen as a means of improving on the legal status of employees.

A second trend is closely related. Collective bargaining is also acquiring greater responsibility for implementing legal provisions (that is, a regulatory function). At EU-level, the 1993 Working Time directive and 1994 European Works Council directives established a new pattern, the first by providing scope for negotiated arrangements to supersede statutory provision on a range of specific matters and the second by giving precedence to arrangements negotiated between the parties over the statutory model of last resort. At national level, a major example is the '*lois Aubry*' in France introducing the 35-hour week which provide for implementation via collective agreement. The result has been an upsurge of negotiations at sector and, above all, company levels (EIRO, 2002a). The *lois* specify a central regulatory framework (with public financial incitements), which sets out the principles governing the contents and the rules of procedure at the lower levels. Through collective bargaining at sector and company levels, detailed substantive rules are agreed and applied within the central principles (Chouraqui and O'Kelly, 2001).

The third and fourth trends are more general. Collective bargaining, which has primarily been seen as dealing with the terms and conditions of employment, has also assumed a flexibility function and a management function. The third reflects growing use of collective bargaining as an instrument of adaptability as the bargaining agenda is oriented towards questions of competitiveness and employment. Although such a shift is evident across all levels, it is fuelling the pressure for decentralization. Léonard (2001: 30) contends that 'bargaining on employment reflects the development of a "different paradigm" of industrial relations, characterised by greater decentralization, higher interdependency of social actors in the regulation of production processes, leading to agreements specifying contractural arrangements at the local level'.

On the fourth, as Chapter 5 discusses, many national governments have responded to the adjustment pressures under EMU by seeking national-level agreements with the social partners – so-called 'social pacts' – embracing wage moderation, greater labour market flexibility and the reform of social protection systems. Collective bargaining has (re)assumed a key role in macroeconomic management. At company level, as Chapter 6 describes, the negotiation of 'pacts for employment and competitiveness' (PECs) has, in some instances, involved employee representatives in business planning and investment decisions. Many PECs also involve procedures for ongoing monitoring and administration of the terms of the agreement, recalling an earlier emphasis in the study of industrial relations on collective bargaining as a form of 'industrial government' (Dunlop, 1958; Flanders, 1970).

From compulsory rigid systems to flexible frameworks?

Paralleling the changing roles of collective bargaining has been a shift in emphasis from 'hard' to 'soft' regulation (Supiot, 1999: 145–6). More issues are being decided by collective bargaining, with the resulting tendency that laws are becoming divested of substantive rules, which tend to be 'hard' in form, in favour of rules of procedure – specifying the parameters of subsequent negotiations – which tend to be 'soft'. 'Proceduralization' has also been affecting collective bargaining in ways which are elaborated below.

There is no easy dividing line between 'hard' and 'soft' regulation, as legal analysts such as Kenner (1995) and Biagi (2000) have recognized. There are nonetheless a number of inter-related contrasts, which help us to understand the distinctions involved:

- 'soft' regulation tends to deal with general *principles*, whereas 'hard' regulation is concerned with specific *rights* and *obligations*;
- 'soft' regulation, where it deals with rights and obligations, tends to be concerned with *minimum* provisions, whereas equivalent 'hard' regulation involves *standard* ones;

- 'soft' regulation often provides for further negotiation at lower levels, whereas 'hard' regulation tends to assume the process is finished – following French usage, 'hard' regulation might be described as *parfait* or *complete* and 'soft' regulation as *imparfait* or *incomplete* (UIMM, 1968: 94);
- 'soft' regulation, in as much as it takes the form of 'recommendations', might be described as *permissive*, whereas 'hard' regulation is almost invariably *compulsory*;
- 'soft' regulation tends to be concerned with *soft* issues such as equal opportunities or training and development, whereas 'hard' regulation deals with *hard* ones such as wages and working time.

The difference between 'hard' and 'soft' regulation is a question of degree. Different forms of regulation are best thought of as being arrayed on a continuum running from 'soft' to 'hard'.

Streeck (1995: 45) rightly observes that: 'what really distinguishes the emerging European social policy regime from traditional national ones is its low capacity to impose binding obligations on market participants, and the high degree to which it depends on various kinds of voluntarism'. 'Soft' regulation, however, is not the exclusive province of the EU level. It is true that most employment regulation in national systems, be it in the form of laws or collective agreements, has historically been of the 'hard' variety. For example, the *standard* or *minimum* provisions dealing with pay or working time in the multi-employer agreements of most EU member states have been characterized as specific, automatic in their effect and compulsory. Yet many rules in these agreements have always had a soft dimension in their application. For example, in the areas of payment by results or training, multi-employer agreements have typically made provision for further negotiation in the workplace. Indeed, it was to capture this distinction that the terms *parfait* and *imparfait* referred to above were coined more than 30 years ago. Even softer have been the rules of *principle*, such as a statement of the employers' right to manage or a commitment on the part of trade unions and their members to improve productivity. The intention is that something should happen in the workplace. The rule of principle, however, is not specific in its application and not easy to enforce.

The prevailing trend towards 'organized decentralization' (Traxler, 1995) which characterizes most of the EU-15 suggests significant growth in the extent of 'soft' regulation within national systems. Typically, the higher the level at which a collective agreement is reached, the more likely it is to take the form of a framework agreement or *accord cadre*, wherein much of the regulation is of the 'soft' or *incomplete* variety. A key rationale of much of the higher-level activity – indeed, it is the essence of 'organized decentralization' – is to pave the way for more detailed negotiations at lower levels that can embrace 'hard' regulation, tailor-made to specific circumstances. Most social pacts between national social partners take the form of 'framework agreements' (Pochet and Fajertag, 2001). An important feature of recent sector bargaining, discussed in Chapters 6 and 7, is provisions giving individual employers greater flexibility in applying the collectively agreed standards at company level.

Coping with complexity – between heteronomy and autonomy

The glib explanation for the emergence of 'soft' regulation is that employers will not accede to trade union demands for the 'hard' equivalent. Above all at EU level, employers are reluctant to contemplate such regulation. Yet this is neither a sufficient nor a complete explanation. A major consideration in the growth of 'soft' regulation is the growing complexity of the economic and social issues policy makers and practitioners have to deal with, stemming from growing differentiation and deepening interdependency. As Chouraqui (1998) insists, the development of 'dynamic complexity' is not a temporary phenomenon involving a transition from one fixed state to another, but a permanent one, with significant destabilizing effects for traditional patterns of regulation. Put simply, many of the 'new' issues that industrial relations practitioners have to confront do not lend themselves to 'hard' regulation in the same way that wages and working time do. Consider, for example, the use of collective bargaining to link employment and competitiveness, which the Supiot report (1999) highlights. Some matters can be the subjects of 'hard' regulation, such as new working time arrangements. Other issues are much more difficult to specify, such as commitments to flexibility and continuous improvement or employee representative involvement in the organization's future planning. In these instances, collectively agreed provisions are 'soft' in their definition. Achieving 'hard' outcomes from such provisions requires delegating responsibility for implementation to lower levels, not only from sector to company, but also within the company itself. Coping with increasing complexity reinforces the tendency towards devolution.

Drawing on Walton and McKersie's (1965) typology, handling complexity also frequently involves a mix of both integrative and distributive bargaining, augmented by changes in the negotiation process, which they term 'attitudinal structuring'. Reaching agreement involves complicated trade-offs and also forging a culture of on-going problem solving. Thus, the 'soft' regulation of an initial collective agreement can encourage a process of ongoing collective bargaining embodying a commitment to the principles of partnership, flexibility and employment security. The process may or may not give rise to written agreements, but produces tangible results reflecting the influence of employee representatives.

Contributing to this complexity is the spread of what has been termed a 'contract culture' (Supiot, 2000: 321), reflecting the growing importance of market principles in policy making. The liberalization and privatization that have dominated policy making since the 1980s have helped to change the role of the state. The result, however, has not been 'deregulation': if anything, the amount of regulation has increased. 'The last fifteen years have been a period less of deregulation than of intense regulatory reform, where the latter term is used to denote the apparently paradoxical combination of deregulation and reregulation' (Majone, 1996: 2). Public/private networks of diverse kinds have multiplied at every level, with decision making involving regulatory agencies as well as representative institutions; formal authority has also been dispersed both upwards to supranational institutions and downwards to sub-national governments (Hooghe and Marks, 2002). In Supiot's (2000: 341) words,

> In face of the commercial contract, which is becoming internationalised, we then have to accommodate the entire contractual panoply which has accompanied decentralization, regional development policy, agricultural policy and employment policy. In labour law this evolution has meant a decentralization of the sources of law: from statute law to collective agreement, from industry-level agreement to company-level agreement to individual contract of employment.

Also influential is the example of the divisionalization, budgetary devolution and marketization that characterize large companies. As Ferner and Hyman (1998: xvi) perceptively recognize, the decentralization of collective bargaining has 'strong parallels – possibly not altogether accidental – with the widespread pattern of coordinated devolution of managerial responsibilities that has taken place within large corporations in recent years'. The large corporation is decentralized operationally, but centralized strategically – helping to strike a balance between heteronomy and autonomy, i.e. central regulation and local responsibility.

The 'managed autonomy' that we have (Marginson and Sisson, 1996: 177) suggested sums up the way the modern corporation is run has strong parallels with the 'regulated autonomy' to be found in theories of so-called 'reflexive law'. In discussing 'reflexive law', Barnard and Deakin (2000: 341) more or less place our argument within a legal discourse:

> The essence of reflexive law is the acknowledgement that regulatory interventions are most likely to be successful when they seek to achieve their ends not by direct prescription, but by inducing 'second-order effects' on the part of social actors. In other words, this approach aims to 'couple' external regulation with self-regulatory processes. Reflexive law therefore has a *procedural orientation*. What this means, in the context of economic regulation, is that the preferred mode of intervention is for the law to underpin and encourage autonomous processes of adjustment, in particular by supporting mechanisms of group representation and participation, rather than to intervene by imposing particular distributive outcomes.

Barnard and Deakin (2000: 341) go on to observe that the regulatory process initiated by the Maastricht Treaty is 'reflexive harmonisation writ large', citing the framework directives as examples of 'negotiated law'. Collective bargaining, as already indicated, is being affected as well as legal enactment.

Considerations of heteronomy and autonomy also return us to Walton and McKersie's (1965) framework. In any social relationship where collective action is an issue the negotiating process assumes considerable significance in understanding the outcomes that emerge. Two main dimensions of such collective action may be identified. In the case of two individuals, it is simply the horizontal that is involved – A has to reach some accommodation with B and vice versa. In the case of relationships where A and B involve more than two individuals, however, there is a vertical as well as a horizontal relationship: the groups comprising A and B have to reach some accommodation among themselves about how they are going to deal with the other group. The greater the complexity on either dimension, the greater the collective action problem.

'Soft' regulation has distinct advantages in dealing with both the horizontal and vertical dimensions. It makes it possible for the principals to set a sense of direction and yet to avoid failures to agree over the details that often bedevil negotiations on the horizontal dimension. At the same time, by delegating responsibilities to representatives at lower levels to tailor solutions to their immediate situation, it helps to relieve the collective action problem on the vertical dimension. Important to note, though, is that the degree of 'softness' can vary, with significant implications for the effectiveness of implementation. There is considerable difference between framework agreements elaborating a set of principles but having no further consequences for representatives at local levels and those whose express intention is to 'incite' negotiations at these levels and which also establish mechanisms to monitor implementation. The contrast is even greater with a framework agreement establishing a set of principles or minimum standards, which are binding on the parties at other levels, but within which these parties have scope to fashion their own solutions. In effect, the last outcome combines a 'hard' with a 'soft' dimension.

Coordinated bargaining – not necessarily second best?

Many commentators see coordinated bargaining, in which parallel sets of negotiators attempt to achieve the same or related outcome in separate negotiations, as one of the main likely vehicles for the 'Europeanization' of industrial relations (Sisson and Marginson, 2002). Coordinated bargaining is also playing an increasingly important role within national systems, as policy makers and practitioners grapple with the pressures to build greater flexibility into their relationships. Explaining its growing appeal, Traxler and Mermet (2003: 231) distinguish between the 'economic' and 'social' functions of coordinated bargaining. The first refers to its potential in aligning bargaining outcomes with macroeconomic objectives of price stability and employment; the second to its role in containing the effects of coercive comparisons across increasingly interdependent bargaining units.

A basic framework

Coordinated bargaining has long been a feature of national industrial relations systems, being found at different levels and in countries with varying institutional arrangements. As Sako (1997) suggests, it is a multi-dimensional concept. Although it shares many similarities with collective bargaining there are also significant differences. In Sako's (1997: 40) words,

> Co-ordination is certainly a more nebulous concept than bargaining structures or bargaining levels because it is about the process of information exchange, consultation, negotiation, decision-making and the exercise of sanctions over those who break any joint agreement ... Operationalising the concept ... involves tracking both the

Levels

Coverage

- single-employer
  - division
  - group

- multi-employer
  - single-sector
  - multi-sector

Agency

- associational
- non-associational
- trade unions
- works councils

Geographical reach

- sub-national
- national
- cross-border

Forms

- unilateral
- joint
  - bi-partite
  - tri-partite
- state imposed

Processes

- information exchange
- benchmarking
- target setting
- pattern bargaining
- synchronized bargaining

Depth

- subject matter
- enforcement

Figure 3.3 Coordinated bargaining: a basic framework

formal and informal occasions for information exchange and decision making.

As with collective bargaining, a fundamental distinction can be drawn between single-employer and multi-employer coordination. The first involves a vertical dimension and covers bargaining units at different levels where there is a dependency relationship and where outcomes at the subordinate level conform to parameters set at higher level. The second involves both a horizontal and a vertical dimension, i.e. the coordination covers independent bargaining units at the same level as well as different levels internally within each of the participating organizations. Further variation involves the levels at which coordinated bargaining occurs, the forms it takes, the processes involved and its depth, i.e. the range of issues covered and the extent to which coordination can be enforced. Figure 3.3 maps these dimensions.

Focusing first on the forms, three main types can be distinguished. Germany provides an example of *unilateral coordination* on the multi-employer dimension. The 'peak' confederations, the BDA and the DGB, are not bargaining agents. More unusually, there is no national-level sector agreement in metalworking and most other sectors, the negotiations taking place at *Land* level. In practice, however, these negotiations have been independently coordinated on both sides for nearly half a century, the leading role of metalworking cementing the 'pattern bargaining' described below. The UK offers contemporary examples of unilateral coordination on the single-employer dimension. There is substantial evidence of widespread management coordination of supposedly decentralized workplace bargaining (Marginson *et al.*, 1993; Cully *et al.*, 1999). In a third example, trade unions are the driving force in the initiatives towards unilateral, cross-border bargaining coordination at cross-sector and sector levels which are considered in Chapter 4.

There are two sub-forms of *joint coordination*: bipartite and tripartite. Austria provides an example of the former. As Traxler (1998b) explains, since the early 1980s, Austria has undergone a step-wise shift to lower bargaining levels, while retaining macroeconomic coordination. While the Parity Commission provides the formal opportunity for regular dialogue, the 'peak' organizations (the BWK and ÖGB respectively) have themselves assumed responsibility for coordination. The vehicle is not a formal agreement between the 'peak' confederations, however, but sector-level 'pattern bargaining' based on metalworking. The second sub-form, *tripartite coordination*, involves government as well as employers' organizations and trade unions. The Netherlands is an example. Since the Wassenar Agreement of 1982, there have been some 70 agreements, understandings and joint opinions emanating from the Foundation for Labour responsible for cross-sector social dialogue (Visser, 1998: 300–1). Two main features characterize this output (Huiskamp and Looise, 2000). The first is the wide range of substantive issues covered – it is much more than a matter of wages. The second is the process of implementation. Much of the output takes the form of recommendations to negotiators at sector and company levels, who can adapt them to their particular circumstances.

Belgium, which has a long-standing tradition of bipartite multi-sector agreements, provides an instance of *state-imposed* coordination. In 1996, following the failure to achieve a tripartite agreement, the government unilaterally introduced three framework laws covering the main points of the negotiations. One established a range within which wage increases should be negotiated for the coming two years: the lower limit was set by index-linked cost of living and incremental rises and the upper by the weighted average of expected pay rises in its main trading partners,

France, Germany, and the Netherlands (Vilrokx and Van Leemput, 1998).

As Figure 3.3 further indicates, coordinated bargaining involves a range of processes. *Information exchange* seemingly speaks for itself. The management of MNCs, employers' organizations and trade unions have routinely collected information from their subsidiaries/members about levels of and changes in pay and conditions, which they have deployed to their advantage in negotiations. However, coordinated bargaining involves more than a question of 'good quality information provided rapidly to those who need it. It also requires a high level of mutual understanding of what is possible in the different circumstances' (Euro-FIET/LRD, 1999).

Benchmarking, which is considered in detail below, involves identification of best or preferred practice, which actors are encouraged to follow. In practice, the dividing line between benchmarking and *target setting* is blurred. Target setting tends to be more specific. For example, EMF's working time charter embodies the target of a maximum of 1,750 hours annually. Another example, which might be described as 'avoidance' target setting, is the so-called '*tabu katalog*' of the German employers' confederation, the BDA. This sets out minimum or maximum standards on issues such as the basic working week from which members are not to depart (Sisson, 1987).

Pattern bargaining entails achieving a set target in one negotiation, which becomes the 'key' or 'pilot' agreement for negotiators elsewhere to emulate. Long associated with the US automotive and steel industries (Seltzer, 1951; Levinson, 1966), pattern bargaining is a widespread phenomenon. In Germany there is in effect a double process. A 'pilot' agreement in metalworking in one of the *Land* (often Baden-Württemberg) sets the pattern, which is spread across metalworking and then other sectors. *Synchronized bargaining* refers to negotiations in a number of companies and/or sectors taking place more or less simultaneously around a common platform. The most celebrated case is that of the *Shunto* or 'Spring offensive' in Japan described by Sako (1997).

The depth of coordinated bargaining is reflected in two considerations: the range of issues covered and the extent to which coordination can be enforced. Coordinated bargaining deals mainly but not exclusively with wages and working time. As mentioned above, the Netherlands' cross-sector dialogue encompasses qualitative issues as well as pay (Huiskamp and Looise, 2000). In addition to its working time charter and bargaining coordination rule covering wage increases, described in Chapter 4, EMF adopted a target on the provision of life-long learning in 2001.

Turning to enforcement, first there is a significant difference between management's practice of unilateral coordination in large companies and other contexts, which is mirrored in the discussion of benchmarking below. Large companies have a range of controls, formal and informal, to ensure local managers follow the line: coordination is, in the final analysis, 'coercive'. Arguably too, much traditional pattern bargaining within countries has rested on the ability of trade unions to mount effective coercive pressure. In other situations, especially where sovereign bodies are involved, the considerations involved in securing compliance in 'traditional' collective bargaining or principal-agent relationships play a relatively limited role. They may be important in specific cases, for example Austria, where Traxler (1998b: 252–3) reminds us that membership of the Federal Chamber of Business, the BWK, is compulsory and the trade union confederation, ÖGB, 'exercises control over the entire system of union finances'. Generally speaking, however, sanctions must be exercised sparingly for fear of undermining the project altogether. All this implies a considerable asymmetry in enforcement potential between the coordination activities of MNCs, on the one hand, and the ETUC's industry federations – considered in Chapter 4 – on the other.

Second, considerable effort seems to go into the process of 'attitudinal structuring' (Walton and McKersie, 1965). Regular meetings help, along with monitoring and review. The first allow personal contact and face-to-face discussion which deepens understanding of each other's perspectives and priorities. The second invoke peer pressure and the threat of 'naming and shaming'. Presence at one another's negotiations is another option, being a feature of the inter-regional coordination of bargaining of the metalworking unions from Belgium, the Netherlands and Germany's Nordrhein Westfalen region (Gollbach and Schulten, 2000).

The circumstances in which coordinated bargaining is practised

Coordinated bargaining takes place in one of two main types of situation. The first, the unilateral form, is where one or other of the parties is opposed to collective bargaining at that level and/or believes it unnecessary. The second, the joint form, is where the parties develop an understanding, which may be implicit rather than explicit, that coordinated bargaining is likely to open up options not available under established collective bargaining arrangements. In both cases, there is a need to understand employer and trade union motives and to appreciate the significance of specific economic and institutional structures.

The motives for engaging in coordinated bargaining are inextricably linked to the negotiating process, with considerations of intra-organizational bargaining being to the fore particularly for unilateral forms of coordination. In German metalworking, for example, it was trade unions who halted a trend towards national negotiations. In the late 1960s, the leadership of IG-Metall was criticized by its members for its excessive centralization and involvement in national-level 'concerted action'. In 1969 widespread unofficial industrial action followed membership rejection of a wage settlement, forcing union negotiators to go back to the employers. IG-Metall decided to press for regional negotiations: as well as meeting demands for more membership participation, they allowed pursuit of a more active policy – achieving a breakthrough in more profitable regions and/or those where IG-Metall membership was strong, which could then be spread to other regions. For their part, although reluctant the employers went along with regional negotiations because, as well as encouraging their own membership participation, they reduced the scope for workplace bargaining (Sisson, 1987: 89–90).

Different considerations apply in the case of *joint coordination*. The common thread linking instances of such coordination is the complexity of the agenda and levels involved, referred to earlier when considering collective bargaining. For example, national cross-sector 'social pacts' based on tripartite coordination can cover employment policy and social protection arrangements as well as wage moderation. In these circumstances, the decentralization that coordination is premised upon enables representatives at lower levels to tailor solutions to their immediate situation, thereby relieving the collective action problem on the vertical dimension. As argued above, it also enables the principals at central level to avoid failures to agree over the details that often bedevil negotiations.

Turning to the specific economic and institutional structures associated with coordinated bargaining, a common feature under unilateral coordination is that similar economic activities are involved. Most multi-employer forms of unilateral coordination involve bargaining units in the same industry. In the absence of the strong state support for multi-employer bargaining found in Europe, US and Japanese employers in highly concentrated industries such as automotive manufacturing were able to resist trade union pressures to enforce the common rule through multi-employer bargaining. Trade unions were obliged to resort to 'pattern bargaining', subsequently leading to 'synchronized bargaining' in Japan. In highly competitive industries such as clothing and printing, however, employers were willing to join with trade unions to enforce

Table 3.1 Types of wage bargaining coordination

Type of wage regulation	1991–93	1994–96	1997–98
State-imposed coordination	F	B, F	B, DK (1998), F
State-sponsored (tripartite) coordination	B, DK, FIN, I, IRL, N, NL, P, S	DK, I, IRL, N, NL	DK (1997), FIN, I, IRL, N, NL
Intra-associational coordination	E	E, P	E, P
Pattern bargaining	A, D	A, D	A, D S (1998)
No coordination	UK	FIN, S, UK	S (1997), UK

Source: Adapted from Traxler, Blaschke and Kittel (2001: 150).

the common rule through multi-employer bargaining in the interests of both market and managerial regulation (Sisson, 1987; Ulman, 1974).

At national cross-sector level, commentators have identified a connection between coordination and small country size, citing examples such as Austria, Finland, Ireland and the Netherlands (Kauppinen, 1998; Fajertag and Pochet, 1997). Yet the experience of Germany and Japan suggests such coordination is not the preserve of small countries. Of arguably greater importance is the role of the state, which helps explain the contrast between two of the EU's large economies, Italy and the UK. As Traxler *et al.* (2001: 164) establish, it is the form of the coordination that tends to differ according to country size, reflecting the nature of the collective action problem. Table 3.1 indicates that state-sponsored and intra-associational coordination are more likely to be found in smaller countries, whereas 'pattern bargaining' features more often in the larger ones. Large countries lack the 'institutional preconditions' for peak-level macro coordination since associational centralization 'significantly decreases with country size' (Traxler *et al.*, 2001: 170).

Reaching an assessment of the potential for bargaining coordination as a regulatory process at European level requires two alternative scenarios to be kept in mind: supranational collective bargaining and uncoordinated bargaining, in which there is neither horizontal nor vertical coordination. The establishment of supranational collective bargaining arrangements at either cross-sector or sector levels is distinctly unlikely (Keller and Platzer, 2003; Marginson and Sisson, 1998; Traxler, 1999). At first glance uncoordinated bargaining at European level appears more likely. As Traxler (1999) observes, some of the factors standing in the way of supranational collective bargaining apply with similar force to coordinated bargaining. Yet it is possible to identify economic, political and social factors under present circumstances which might favour the development of European-level coordinated bargaining. The macroeconomic dialogue prompted by EMU, and outlined in Chapter 4, which involves the ECB, the Commission and the social partners in ongoing deliberations about the links between prices, pay, employment and economic performance, is stimulating interest in the economic function of coordinated bargaining. Politically, coordinated bargaining is consistent with the subsidiarity so important to government and non-governmental national organizations. Socially, trade unions fear the consequences of the downward spiral in terms and conditions that competition between bargaining regimes under uncoordinated bargaining promises to unleash.

Moreover, successful coordination does not necessarily rest on the willingness of both parties to collaborate. Cross-border coordination can emerge on a unilateral basis, as the trade union initiatives described in Chapter 4 confirm. Importantly too, pattern bargaining – which Traxler and Mermet (2003) consider to be the most feasible prospect – rarely rests on an inclusive process at national level. Indeed, the size of the pattern setting group may be relatively small. Thus in Austria, Japan and Germany, the share of the pattern setting industry in the total number of employees was, respectively, no more than 12.3 per cent (1997), 13.3 per cent (1995) and 10.4 per cent (1995) (Traxler *et al.*, 2001: 171). The implication is that effective bargaining coordination at EU level may be built around sub-group coalitions of trade unions and/ or employers' organizations and MNCs in particular countries and/or sectors which come to be accepted as pattern setters.

The rise of benchmarking

The rise of benchmarking from management tool to regulatory instrument has been one of the most striking recent developments. Benchmarking is now at the heart of the EU's approach to coordinating economic and social policy within and across the member states. It is the integrative driver of the 'open method of coordination' (OMC) which, in contrast to the traditional, top-down Community methods, is based on mutual learning, identification and transfer of best practice, monitoring and peer review. It appears at various levels (company, sector and cross-sector, national and transnational) and is widely used to promote delivery of the economic goals of competitiveness and growth and the social goals of cohesion and improved quality and quantity of employment. In the EU, it seems, benchmarking is everywhere.

From management tool to regulatory process

Benchmarking started life as a management tool to increase competitive performance. There is no universally accepted definition: IRS (1999: 15) suggest it is a broad term 'encompassing the simplest comparison of performance data to complex strategic exercises examining how the world's best companies are run'. Three main types, of varying complexity, have evolved (Sisson *et al.*, 2003). First is 'performance benchmarking', involving quantitative comparisons of input and/or output measures. Second is 'process benchmarking', covering detailed scrutiny of the efficiency of particular business processes and activities, plus arrangements such as quality standards accreditation. Third, is 'strategic benchmarking', which is closely associated with the concepts of the 'learning organization'. This involves comparing the driving forces behind successful organizations, including leadership and the management of change, to identify possible alternative ways forward. By the mid 1990s almost four out of five companies in Europe, North America and South East Asia were reported to be using benchmarking (Hastings, 1997).

The appeal of benchmarking rests on two foundations. The first is the connection with learning, which many commentators see as key to developing competitive advantage in a rapidly changing environment. The skills of the workforce, it is argued, form the organization's core competencies and, potentially, its unique competitive advantage. In order to develop and enhance these competencies, training needs to go beyond individual learning to organizational learning. Through systematic learning, the organization can continuously improve its performance (Keep and Rainbird, 2000). Benchmarking offers organizations a practical tool around which to structure such organizational learning through dynamic comparisons with others.

The second source of benchmarking's appeal, which may not sit easily with the first, lies in its use as a means of control, especially in large companies. MNCs in particular have put in place management systems and structures to establish and diffuse 'best practices' across locations (Coller, 1996; Martin and Beaumont, 1998). Methods include the regular convening of meetings of managers from different countries, rotation of managerial personnel from one location to another, compilation of manuals of best practice and the setting up of taskforces and/or nomination of 'lead' operations with responsibility for directing change.

Important in encouraging such developments in Europe has been the adoption of the continent-wide production and market-servicing strategies described in Chapter 2. Benchmarking enables senior management to withdraw from the 'murky plain of overwhelming detail' (Neave, 1988: 12), but to maintain 'control at a distance' through the use of comparisons and target setting. It supposedly avoids senior managers having to impose particular solutions from above. Instead, local managers are encouraged to find their own paths to continuous improvement. Benchmarking helps strike a balance between heteronomy and autonomy.

The logic underlying managers' pursuit of benchmarking reflects DiMaggio and Powell's (1983) 'mimetic' and 'coercive' forms of isomorphism, introduced in Chapter 1. Moreover, the designation 'best practice' gives solutions greater legitimacy akin to 'normative' status. Such legitimacy can be important in helping to persuade employee representatives of the course of action being proposed, but also in winning over uncertain managers. The widespread promotion of Japanese 'lean production' methods is an example of the use of benchmarking to justify change to both managers and employees and their representatives (Delbridge *et al.*, 1995).

Taking their cue from business organizations, national governments increasingly resorted to benchmarking throughout the 1990s. They did so internally as deregulation and marketization led them to apply private sector management methods to the operation of public services. Externally, two kinds of development were involved. First several governments encouraged negotiators to refer to developments in other countries as the basis for wages policy, the most notable examples being Italy's 1993 Social Pact and Belgium's 1996 competitiveness law. Here, benchmarking's control aspect is to the fore. Second, was the emergence of benchmarking of so-called 'framework conditions' related to tax systems, labour market regulations and infrastructure more generally. This form of benchmarking, which aims to promote convergence towards best practice through an emphasis on learning, is associated with the OECD's promotion of policy transfer: its *Job Study* (OECD, 1994) was a catalyst for subsequent EU developments.

Since the mid-1990s, benchmarking has rapidly acquired prominence as a regulatory tool across a range of EU policy fields, leading European Commission President Jacques Santer to suggest that 'We are all benchmarkers now' (quoted in Richardson 2000: 22). As well as the Community institutions and member states, trade unions have also embraced benchmarking as a means of underpinning the cross-border bargaining coordination initiatives described in Chapter 4.

Two main phases may be identified (Arrowsmith *et al.*, 2004). Until the late 1990s, benchmarking was still largely seen as a management tool that policy makers could utilize to promote improved competitiveness. By the turn of the decade it had become something more ambitious: a central plank of policy development and implementation across a range of strategic activities. According to its former Secretary General (Richardson, 2000), it was the European Round Table (ERT), which groups major MNCs, that came up with the solution. Anxious to avoid further social regulation, and yet keep labour market reform on the agenda, it enthusiastically promoted the idea of benchmarking to policy makers as 'more than simply number-crunching'. 'It was a communication tool of enormous value' which, crucially, 'would help them work together towards common goals without jeopardising their freedom to take their own decisions in the light of their own circumstances' (Richardson, 2000: 4).

As an EU policy tool, benchmarking began to gather momentum with the approach of EMU. As Chapter 4 elaborates, it was in the area of employment policy that benchmarking came to prominence and the OMC developed, involving the setting of common objectives, the preparation of national action plans and peer group review (Goetschy, 2003). The 1994 Essen European Council asked member states to establish employment programmes and to report annually to the Commission on their implementation. The 1997 Amsterdam Treaty institutionalized this procedure and, as Teague (1999a: 196) underlines, introduced a Treaty basis for benchmarking. Article 118 stipulates that the Council can 'encourage the member states to adopt initiatives aimed at improving knowledge, developing exchange of information and best practice, promoting innovative approaches and evaluating experiences in order to combat social exclusion'. Subsequently the 2000 Lisbon Summit explicitly confirmed the OMC as a governance method. According to Wallace, quoted in Hodson and Maher (2001: 721), this confirmed the shift of the OMC from a 'transitional mechanism' used as a technique to develop 'light co-operation and co-ordination in order to make the case for direct policy powers' to 'a policy mode in its own right'.

It is not difficult to understand the appeal to EU policy makers. Benchmarking helps to deal with both the horizontal and vertical dimensions of the EU's collective action problem. A broad direction can be set, minimizing the scope for disagreement over detail on the horizontal dimension. At the same time, deference to the principle of 'subsidiarity' helps to relieve the collective action problem on the vertical dimension.

Benchmarking and the OMC have a 'logic of appropriateness' (Wallace, 2001: 592) promising greater democratic legitimacy *and* effectiveness in policy development and implementation. The centre adopts the role of policy entrepreneur, but consults and involves the member states, social partners and other interested parties such as NGOs in decisions on strategy. Involvement of national actors means that interventions may be more appropriate, and therefore more likely to be put into practice. Rather than being tied down with 'institutional harmonization', EU policy makers can take a problem-solving approach with a longer-term focus that is flexible enough to adapt to changing circumstances and extend itself to new areas. The iterative cycle of benchmarking also means that the policy process becomes less opaque (and therefore more legitimate) with the elaboration of clear goals and targets, the identification of best practice and member state and social partner scrutiny. Benchmarking helps ensure the value of the OMC as a coherent policy mode, and one that acknowledges democratic principles of voluntarism and subsidiarity (Borrás and Jacobsson, 2003; Goetschy, 2003).

The two faces of benchmarking: coercion and consensus

There are similarities in the practice of benchmarking at the different levels, including the emphases on learning, identifying 'best practice' and target setting. Some of the issues that benchmarking raises also appear to be similar, but there are also marked differences. Much attention has focused on technical problems. A common refrain is that meaningful benchmarking is more difficult than it seems (Delbridge *et al.*, 1995; Tronti, 1998; Arrowsmith and Sisson, 2001). Defining 'best practice' is no easy matter, especially when there are potentially conflicting policy goals. Data have to be collected and collated in comparable terms, and where benchmarking is external, reaching agreement on the most appropriate bases can be difficult. All this is to be resolved before the implementation of findings can be addressed. In practice, performance benchmarking rarely becomes process benchmarking, let alone strategic benchmarking. Instead, it tends to be concerned exclusively with quantitative measures. 'Focusing on the numbers', as Elmuti and Kathawala (1997: 236) put it, is so much easier than analysing the reasons for the differences behind them. At company level, it can mean attention to the costs and flexibility of labour rather than adaptability in its widest sense. At national and EU levels, it can mean an obsession with placings in 'league tables' to the detriment of the quality of outcomes.

Yet the technology of benchmarking is not the only source of problems; so too is the political nature of the process involved. The elevation of benchmarking to the macro level has not only underlined its potential, but also exposed weaknesses. Depending upon the level, the balance between the internal and external dimensions of benchmarking is very different, with profound implications for the choice of comparisons and for implementation. At the micro level, benchmarking takes place within the vertical or hierarchical structure that typifies the business organization. As industrial relations analysis has long recognized, benchmarking within MNCs is not so much used to identify 'best practice' externally but internally (Coller, 1996; Coller and Marginson, 1998; Mueller and Purcell, 1992). Moreover, it plays a key role in the operation of management control systems, being inextricably linked with the use of 'coercive comparisons' to help discipline the behaviour of local management as well as local workforces. The collection and analysis of data on practices and performance outcomes is used to exert pressure on business unit management within the context of an internal 'market' for investment.

At (inter)governmental and EU levels, the balance between the internal and external dimensions is significantly different. Benchmarking is essentially a consensual rather than coercive process, with profound implications for the choices of comparisons and for implementation. Governments, and trade unions also, are democratic organizations, which complicates internal compliance. Even more problematic is that the external dimension involves sovereign bodies. This is particularly acute given the heterogeneity of contexts and institutions and level of abstraction involved in benchmarking framework conditions across member states. The choice of comparator and the focus of comparison are complex and potentially controversial issues, involving immensely political as well as practical issues of identification (deciding what to measure), measurement (how to standardize criteria and data collection) and transferability (how to take account of specific context). Topping these is the problem of enforcement: benchmarking between sovereign bodies, be they governments or trade unions, relies on voluntary mechanisms of enforcement through regular monitoring, peer review and even 'naming and shaming'. In its essence, the relationship is horizontal and so the controls available in vertical structures are of little avail.

Coping with common constraints: the informal processes of 'isomorphism'

Informal processes are also integral to understanding the impact of European integration, as Chapter 1 explained. 'Competitive isomorphism' suggests that market forces will encourage actors to adopt similar solutions when confronted by common constraints, regardless of institutional processes. Several lines of reasoning can be found (Traxler *et al.*, 2001: 5–6). The view of Dunlop (1958) and Kerr *et al.* (1960) holds that using similar technology is the main driver. By contrast, the 'efficiency view' associated with transaction cost analysis (Williamson, 1986) suggests that there is a process of 'social Darwinism' at work, in which the 'natural selection of market forces weeds out inferior institutions' (Traxler *et al.*, 2001: 5). A third view emphasizes 'market-led opportunism'. Implicit in the notion of 'regime competition', for example, is that negotiators will come under pressure to make sacrifices, which will then set in motion a downward spiral of emulation elsewhere.

Underpinning 'competitive isomorphism' is the 'rational choice' approach introduced in Chapter 1. A specific application concerns wage determination. A fundamental premise of a non-accommodating monetary policy is that negotiators will adjust their behaviour to take into account the constraints such policy brings. If they do not, they risk unemployment as a result of the central bank adjusting interest rates. As Scharpf (2000b: 11) observes, 'rational-choice institutionalism tells us that the centralization or fragmentation of wage-setting institutions should not matter. Large or small unions alike should find it in their organizational self-interest to save the jobs of their members through wage restraint.' Convergence in the rates of change of wages and in unit labour costs across EU member states in recent years would appear to bear this out, previous relationships between institutional arrangements and measures of economic performance, considered in Chapter 1, seemingly breaking down under the spread of non-accommodating monetary policy and the prospect and subsequent reality of EMU (Traxler *et al.*, 2001: 253).

'Mimetic isomorphism' recognizes that there is a strong tendency for actors faced with common constraints to copy one another. Again, wage determination provides an illustration. As Traxler *et al.* (2001: 147–8) observe, much coordination in the form of 'pattern bargaining' does not involve formal organization. It results from negotiators emulating the level of settlement reached elsewhere. Such 'unintended pattern bargaining' helps to explain Hancké's (2002) contention that 'convergence without coordination' in the rates of change of wages has taken place across EU member states. Traxler *et al.* suggest that this emulative behaviour follows from 'differential union power across sectors, such that one particular union sets the pace simply because the other unions are too weak to go beyond this standard' (p. 253). This underestimates the wider significance of the resort to comparisons, however. As Ross (1948: 52) observed many years ago, following the 'pattern' enables employers and trade unions to reconcile the former's competitive constraints with the latter's need to achieve fairness:

> The ready-made settlement provides an answer, a solution, a formula. It is mutually face-saving … it is the one settlement which permits both parties to believe that they have done a proper job, the one settlement which has the best chance of being 'sold' to the company's board of directors and the union's rank and file.

Similar ways of doing things can become accepted and established, even in the absence of any formal processes of coordination, reflecting the third process of 'normative isomorphism'. Marsden (1999: 269) puts it like this:

> Employment systems are institutional frameworks which enable firms and workers to organise their collaboration while protecting both parties from certain kinds of opportunistic behaviour … even in sectors from which collective representation is absent, the pressure on firms to conform to the prevailing methods of contracting are very powerful. In this sense, even though each decision by a firm and its workers may be taken individually, there are strong pressures to conformity … These pressures do not necessarily arise from direct constraints on the parties, but … from the benefits that stem from using commonly applied rules. It is important that people trust the rules by which they bind themselves … As they diffuse across an economy, the transaction rules are transformed from being techniques for solving the problem of opportunism in employer–employee relations into a social institution.

Marsden adds the important rider that an employment rule may be adopted 'even though it may not be the one best suited to a particular type of service, because people prefer a rule with which they are familiar and which they trust' (p. 269). Industrial relations behaviour is better understood in terms of 'sociological' rather than 'rational choice' institutionalism.

Underpinning mimetic and normative processes is information and learning. The nation state plays a key role in setting the parameters to these processes, but so too do the sector and company. Both are organizational fields comprising more than a set of 'objective conditions', such as market structures and technology. They are 'cognitive arenas', where ideas about 'accepted' and 'best' practice are generated. They are 'collaborative networks', offering a wide range of opportunities, formal and informal, to acquire and diffuse the information and experience going to make up shared understandings (Smith *et al.*, 1990; Arrowsmith and Sisson, 1999). In establishing a single market with a common currency the EU constitutes an important catalyst to these informal processes, by extending the range of reference groups with which comparisons are made and widening the opportunities for learning. Furthermore, as Teague (2000: 439) concludes, 'Active engagement with EU-level policy deliberations not only introduces national actors to new ideas, routines and practices, but it also, on occasions, encourages them to pursue regulatory or collaborative solutions to integration problems that are more ambitious than first considered necessary.' He cites two major studies of how this 'deliberative supranationalist' process has had a significant impact: Eichener's (1997) on health and safety, where the *acquis communautaire* is now considerable; and Dølvik's (1997) on the role of the ETUC, where the European social dialogue pushed trade unions to rethink the objectives they should pursue in engaging at EU-level. A key informal process, in other words, is 'Europe learning from Europe' (Teague, 2001: 23).

Conclusion: complementary rather than alternative processes?

Significant developments are taking place in industrial relations governance in the light of European integration. One is the changing balance between legal enactment and collective bargaining, reflecting two common developments: the growing complexity of the issues that the regulatory processes are having to deal with; and the spread of a 'contract culture' (Supiot, 2000: 321). More and more issues are being delegated to collective bargaining as policy makers seek to balance heteronomy with local responsibility. For collective bargaining, 'organized decentralization' (Traxler, 1995) is the prevailing trend as negotiators likewise try to combine providing a central steer with the scope for flexibility that increasingly differentiated local circumstances require. The overall effect is a significant shift in emphasis from 'hard' to 'soft' regulation both in legislation and collective agreements, raising fundamental questions about future directions. Admittedly, European integration is not the only consideration, but it is fundamentally important in as much as it is adding considerably to complexity.

Seemingly new processes have also made their entry. Thus, as well as the tendency towards framework directives and agreements, there is coordinated bargaining, benchmarking and the OMC. Such processes are not altogether new, however, and are integral to national industrial relations systems as well. One way of viewing growing emphasis on coordinated bargaining and benchmarking is as institutional expressions of the processes of isomorphism that European integration is encouraging. Reflecting the strong tendency for actors faced with common constraints to adopt similar solutions, these include the informal processes of 'competitive', 'mimetic' and 'normative' isomorphism. A further reason why coordinated bargaining and benchmarking have become prominent lies in the nature of the collective action problem policy makers and practitioners are faced with. At EU levels in particular, given the non-appearance of a vertically integrated system, they offer the inestimable advantage of apparently helping to resolve both the horizontal and vertical dimensions of the collective action problem. They also resonate with the subsidiarity principle.

Chapters 11 and 12 return to the issues raised. There is one, however, which merits attention at this stage. It is whether the new processes represent a 'durable alternative' to the traditional EU political mode (Hodson and Maher, 2001: 739); whether they will lead to the 'slow death' of the traditional methods of legal enactment and collective bargaining (Goetschy, 2001). The barriers to 'hard' regulation, above all at EU levels, will remain formidable. Employers, if anything, are becoming even more resolute in their opposition to further binding regulation. Moreover, the barriers will grow with EU enlargement since the increase in the number of member states and the further institutional diversity that they bring will exacerbate both the horizontal and vertical dimensions of the collective action problem. Seemingly the OMC provides a viable alternative for managing and regulating such diversity and the more it does so, the less likely will be the prospects for the 'harder' forms of regulation.

Even so, despite their obvious attractions, coordinated bargaining and benchmarking do not resolve the problems associated with the traditional methods. There are fundamental differences in practice between business organizations, on the one hand, and employers' organizations, trade unions and governments, on the other. In the former, the processes are essentially coercive, whereas in the other instances they are voluntary, requiring agreement between sovereign bodies. There are also strong grounds for doubting whether, in these instances, the new processes can exist in a vacuum, that is in the absence of the harder, more traditional forms. Following Wedderburn (1997: 11), the effectiveness of voluntary processes – and the social dialogue to which we turn in Chapter 4 – depends upon a 'fundament' of 'hard' regulation, giving employee representatives the sense of security that is necessary to engage in voluntary processes as well as legitimizing them in the eyes of employers.

4
Industrial Relations at EU Community and Sector Levels: a Glass Half Full as Well as Half Empty?

For many commentators, the story of industrial relations at the EU Community and sector levels is one of a failure to develop a vertically integrated system equivalent to those of most national systems. The reasons have been exhaustively analysed (see Falkner, 1998; Hay, 2000; Keller, 2000; Streeck, 1995; 1998). They include the sustained opposition of employers, the preoccupation of trade unions with specific national problems, differences amongst governments about the role of social policy and the immensely practical difficulties of overcoming the collective action problem of multiple sovereign bodies reaching agreement. In addition, they extend to considerations intrinsic to the process of 'negative' rather than 'positive' integration, whereby obstacles to a single market were removed rather than measures being put in place to control its operation. Crucially, although the EU has developed a far more extensive political dimension than the NAFTA, a 'highly developed state protagonist' (Traxler, 1996: 289) has not emerged with sufficient authority to sponsor the creation of a vertically integrated system. Indeed, instead of responding with greater EU regulation to the 'declining domestic governability' referred to in Chapter 1, the commitment to subsidiarity means that member states have confirmed the sovereignty of national systems. In Streeck's (1996: 313) striking words, the European nation-state appears 'obsolete and alive at the same time: obsolete as the wielder of effective sovereignty over "its" economy, and powerfully alive as the most effective opponent of the recreation of internal sovereignty at the international level'. More pragmatically, 'Because the EC is a "latecomer" which co-exists with historically grown and differentiated social and labour law systems it would be questionable to expect it to simply replace or copy them' (Falkner, 1998: 153–4).

Even so, as Chapter 2 emphasized, the EU has produced an industrial relations framework that can lay claim to principles (including 'social dialogue as a mainstay of good governance' (European Commission, 2000)); procedures (the Maastricht social policy process providing for 'negotiated law' and the Cologne and Luxembourg coordination processes dealing with wages and employment); and substantive outcomes (including an *acquis communautaire* affecting important areas of the employment relationship). At the sector level, the principle of social dialogue as a central component of good governance and the procedures of the Maastricht social policy process also apply. In addition, trade union initiatives in developing procedures and common 'rules' to coordinate national collective bargaining are prominent. Substantive outcomes are, however, more meagre.

Chapters 1 and 3 introduced the concepts associated with these developments. Our concern here is to put developments into their specific contexts and consider the questions they raise about the evolving character of EU-level industrial relations, namely:

- the nature and extent of industrial relations processes at the EU Community and sector levels;
- the changing forms of regulation and the reasons for this;
- the strengths and weaknesses of the new regulatory developments;
- the likely development of industrial relations activity at the two levels.

The chapter starts with the EU Community level, examining the nature and form of the developing *acquis communautaire* in industrial relations and recent developments in coordination of policy on wages and employment. It then moves to the sector-level focusing on the twin tracks giving rise to 'virtual' forms of collective bargaining at European level (Marginson and Sisson, 1998): sector social dialogue, which has recently given rise to several European framework agreements, and cross-border coordination of bargaining by trade unions.

The *acquis communautaire*

Evolution – limits to the Maastricht policy process?

A mix of 'hard' and 'soft' regulation is evident at EU Community level. In terms of legislation, the *acquis communautaire* affects key areas of industrial relations and social protection. These include measures on freedom of movement of workers; equal opportunities for women and men; health and safety; collective redundancy; transfer of undertakings; working time; employee information and consultation; pregnant worker, maternity and parental leave rights; rights of posted, part-time and temporary workers; and discrimination at work. The Commission suggests that the development of this legislation may be divided into six periods (European Commission, 2000: 24), details of which will be found in Figure 4.1. The adoption of the 1989 Social Charter and the Maastricht Treaty's social policy protocol gave, respectively, substantive and procedural impetus to the legislative process during the fourth and fifth periods.

The European Court of Justice has also had a strong influence on the *acquis communautaire* through its responsibilities in interpreting Treaty titles and thereby establishing case law. There have, for example, been significant developments in equal rights for women workers, including those working part-time, as a result of the Court's judgments.

As for the outcome of the cross-sector social dialogue, 'soft' regulation is the order of the day, the new possibilities of negotiation envisaged by the Maastricht Treaty notwithstanding. By the end of 2002, the Commission (2000; EIRO, 2003d) recorded that there had been 40 'joint texts' since the start of the so-called Val Duchesse process in 1985, addressing a wide range of issues. By late 2003, a further three had been concluded. Of these joint texts, only five have been designated as either 'agreements' or 'framework agreements' – the 1991 agreement on the role of the social partners in framing regulation on social policy matters which underpinned the Maastricht social policy protocol, three framework agreements on parental leave, part-time working and fixed-term temporary employment – which were subsequently given legal effect as directives – and the 2002 agreement on teleworking. The bulk of the texts were either '(joint) declarations' or 'joint opinions' (7 and 17 instances respectively) ranging across aspects of EU policy on economic growth and competitiveness, employment and unemployment, the labour market, training and qualification, equality at work and restructuring and change.

Although innovatory in nature, the limited scale of the development of negotiated legislation – amounting to just three framework agreements by late 2003 – suggest that the post-Maastricht era has hardly ushered in the qualitative shift towards harder forms of regulation implied by the Commission's (2000: 8) assessment that 'The "joint opinions" period has thus gradually given way to the negotiation of European framework agreements.' If anything, joint opinions have themselves proliferated over the same period, with three-quarters of the total being concluded since the social partners' 1991 agreement.

Stage 1: the 1960s and early 1970s

The instruments establishing and reinforcing freedom of movement for workers, and the co-ordination of social security schemes for migrant workers, occupied the attention of the European social legislature until the early 1970s. The Treaty of Rome contained a chapter on freedom of movement for workers, Articles 48 ff. (new article 39 ff) for freedom of movement, and Article 51 (new article 42) for social security for migrant workers. In 1972, the basic legal framework for achieving these aims was in place. It was subsequently to be considerably developed and reinforced by the case law of the Court of Justice of the European Communities. It also included a social chapter (Articles 119 ff.) which made no provision for legislative interventions.

Stage 2: the second half of the 1970s

This period is characterized by the adoption of the first directives on labour law,
equal opportunities for women and men, and health and safety at work. The institutional framework has remained unchanged, but a number of events led the European legislature to act: for example, the oil crisis and the first major industrial restructuring exercises (the first labour law directive deals with collective redundancies) and the discovery of the carcinogenic effects of vinyl chloride monomer, a substance used in the plastics industry. These provisions were based on Article 100 of the Treaty, which enabled the Council to adopt unanimously directives for the approximation of such national provisions as affect the establishment or functioning of the Common market, and on Article 235 for equal Opportunities for women and men.

Stage 3: the 1980s

This period enabled the progress achieved in relation to equal opportunities for women and men and health and safety at work to be consolidated.
A framework directive adopted in 1980, defining a strategy for dealing with all physical, chemical and biological agents at work, was followed by a series of specific directives. The Single European Act strengthened the legal basis for health and safety provisions. The first indent of Article 137(1) (ex Article 118a of the EC Treaty) enabled the adoption by qualified maturity of directives laying down minimum requirements for safety and health at work. The other significant legal innovation in the Single Act in the social field was that the social dialogue was recognized at European level (Article 118b – new Article 139).

Stage 4: 1990–93

The signing in 1989 of the Community Charter of the Fundamental Social Rights of Workers was a milestone in the development of social policy. A number of initiatives followed, some of them legislative. The action programme based on

Figure 4.1 Main developments in EU industrial relations regulation

the charter led to the adoption of 15 health and safety directives, one equal opportunities directive and four labour law directives. However, the experience of this second action programme showed the need for a stronger legal basis for social policy. The entry into force of the Maastricht Treaty and, in particular, its social protocol (currently Articles 136 ff.) extended the use of qualified majority voting beyond health and safety and defined the role of the social partners at Community level.

Stage 5: 1994–99

The social protocol attached to the Maastricht Treaty provides an active role for collective bargaining. It enables the social partners to make a direct contribution to the production of Community social legislation. On three occasions, (parental leave, part-time work and fixed-term contracts), the directives have implemented agreements between the social partners at European level. The European Works Council Directive was adopted in 1994, after a failure to agree by the social partners. The protocol also establishes a more favourable political, institutional and legal context and enables proposals pending for the action programme linked to the Social Charter to be followed up

Stage 6: since 1999

The Treaty of Amsterdam consolidates and significantly reinforces the institutional framework and instruments of Community social policy. It ends the UK opt-out and moves Europe forward in four areas: employment, combating discrimination, equal opportunities for men and women, and the role of the social partners (Articles 3, 13, employment chapter, 137, 138 and 141). It also signals a shift towards new, 'softer' regulatory mechanisms, including benchmarking (Article 118) and the OMC, subsequently endorsed by the 2000 Lisbon summit. In 2002 the EU social partners conclude the first agreement, on teleworking, to be implemented through collective agreements within member states. Adoption in 2002 of the directive on national information and consultation largely completes the action programme linked to the Social Charter.

Figure 4.1   Continued

Source: Based on European Commission (2000: 25).

The subject matter – more than a question of 'spillover'?

In trying to make sense of these patterns, it is helpful to draw a distinction between the subject matter and its form. As Hall (1994: 281) reminds us, the EU's role in social policy has been 'highly sensitive to shifts in prevailing political and economic context'. The subject matter of much of the legislative regulation can be understood in terms of the 'spillover' process discussed in Chapter 1, together with the changing logic of social policy. Some measures were deemed to be essential to integration, such as freedom of movement. Concerns about 'social dumping' led to measures dealing with health and safety, which were subsequently extended to working time. The directives dealing with employee information and consultation stemmed from pressure to put a 'human face' on the restructuring that creating the single market and EMU have unleashed. Recent emphasis reflects the ambitious employment targets agreed at the 2000 Lisbon Summit and the commitment to improve the quality of industrial relations.

The impact of 'spillover' has not been automatic, however. In seeking to explain the evolution of EU social policy – and in particular the genesis of the Maastricht social policy protocol – Falkner (1998: Ch. 6) persuasively argues for a multi-perspective or 'syncratic' approach, emphasizing the importance of 'ideas, interests and identities'. Thus the establishment of the ETUC in 1973 and its development into an articulate voice was a major consideration. The 'policy entrepreneurship' of Delors and his team at the Commission provided 'indispensable impetus' (p. 200), while 'ideas and communicative action' (p. 202) played a key role in shaping the views of most member governments. By the time of the Maastricht Treaty, she argues, an effective 'corporatist policy network' was in place: 'the *EC social dimension* with a view to backing the "European social model"... had already been accepted as a principled idea with high normative validity' (p. 202).

Changes in 'ideas, interests and identities' were also a factor in the marked switch in emphasis from 'hard' to 'soft' regulation discussed below. Important in this process was the Commission's embrace of a 'catalytic' role 'to complement and reinforce the legislative activity which has formed the backbone of the social dimension in the past' (European Commission 1995: 9, quoted in Wendon, 2000). The Commission should become 'a catalyst in promoting joint discussion, exchange of experience, and concerted action on a transnational basis in responding to common problems'. A priority, as the Commission's 1997 Green Paper, *Partnership for a new organization of work* confirms, was the promotion of the so-called 'high road' European model, involving the modernization of labour markets and work organization. In these circumstances, it was not so much heavily prescriptive methods that were required, but open-ended and flexible ones (Teague, 2001: 23).

The form – from 'hard' to 'soft' regulation?

As is widely recognized (Sciarra, 1995; Dølvik, 2000; Keller, 2000; Wendon, 2000), there has been a marked switch in emphasis in the last three of Figure 4.1's periods from 'hard' to 'soft' regulation. In its Green Paper (European Commission, 1997: 14–15), the Commission talks approvingly of 'the likely development of labour law and industrial relations from rigid and compulsory systems of statutory regulations to more open and flexible legal frameworks'.

Five main types of EU regulation may be identified, whose relative importance has changed over time (see Figure 4.1). The first, 'hard' regulation, takes the form of 'one-size-fits-all' legislation such as the 'daughter' directives dealing with specific aspects of health and safety, and is reserved for the earlier periods. The second type combines a 'hard' and a 'soft' dimension. Examples include the European Works Councils (EWCs) and Working Time directives, both of which allow flexibility in implementation through collective agreements. Legislation of this type has been a feature since Maastricht. With the third type, 'framework agreements', the balance shifts further in the direction of 'softness'. 'Framework agreements' establish a broad principle whose purpose is to incite negotiations and/or legislation at national and/or lower levels. Binding in honour only, they are accompanied by mechanisms aimed at monitoring and reviewing their implementation. These are the most recent: the 2002 teleworking agreement is an example. The fourth category is softer still, and comprises the 'joint declarations' and 'joint opinions' which characterize much of the output of the cross-sectoral social dialogue. These are at best advisory and implementation is not addressed. As noted above, this fourth category has proliferated in the two most recent periods. The fifth type is also softer than the first and second, but represents a different point of departure. It takes the form of the 'open method of coordination' (OMC) of the EU's employment strategy, and involves putting national policies to the test of cross-country comparison, targets to be reached within a specified timeframe and benchmarking and peer review. This fifth development, examined below, is also a feature of the current period.

The logic of this shift towards softer forms of regulation, and the 'proceduralization' involved in the Maastricht social policy process in particular, was elaborated in Chapter 3. The premise is that regulation will enjoy greater legitimacy if those most directly affected take responsibility for it. This means not only 'decentralisation of the sources of law' (Supiot, 2000: 341) from legal enactment to collective bargaining, but also the delegation of responsibility to representatives at lower levels for detailed implementation. In seemingly resolving one problem, however, the Maastricht social policy process created another. Falkner (1998: 83) provides the vital clue in suggesting that the social policy protocol involved a form of 'double subsidiarity'. Action at community level is justified only 'if and in so far as the objectives of the proposed action cannot be sufficiently achieved by the member states (Article 3b, ECT)'. In addition, collective agreements have priority over legislation. 'Traditional legislation is only envisaged if the social partners do not open collective negotiations, if the negotiations fail, or (implicitly) if the agreement's provisions are deemed insufficient by the Commission and the Council' (Falkner, 1998: 83–4).

It is far from clear that the hurdles to be overcome in order to secure the adoption of regulation are lower than they were before Maastricht. By extending the scope of qualified majority voting within the social policy sphere, the Maastricht Treaty has facilitated the passage of important elements of the 1989 Social Charter into Community legislation (Hall, 1994). But because the new regulatory possibilities via collective agreement involve more actors, decision making has become more complex and the collective action problem greater. In the absence of a social partner agreement, the Commission can proceed, as in the case of the European- and national-level employee information and consultation directives. The pressures not to do so, however, and/or to dilute proposals are considerable because of the logic of the process.

The problem is that employers have consistently been reluctant to negotiate. The European Commission does not possess the authority, and trade unions lack the power resources, to induce them to do so. The reason for employer reluctance, as a former senior official of UNICE has candidly acknowledged, is that current arrangements provide little incentive (Hornung-Draus, 2001). The Treaty stipulates that negotiations can only cover *minimum* or *equivalent* standards on employment conditions as defined in Article 137. From the point of view of employers, therefore, entering negotiations invites the imposition of additional burdens without any opportunity to make trade-offs as in the case of sector or company negotiations within national systems:

> Therefore the only motivation for employers' organisations to take up negotiations is the threat of even more restrictive regulation, if it is left to the Commission and the [European Parliament]. However, this negative motivation is rather weak and becomes less and less credible as a basis for the development of negotiating practice at EU-level from the employers' perspective. (Hornung-Draus, 2001: 9)

Moreover, national business interests have kept UNICE weak in terms of both decision-making mandate and resources precisely in order to forestall incorporation into the Maastricht process (Rhodes, 1995). The 'power relationship between the EU social partners and their affiliates' (Hoffman *et al.*, 2002: 58) has been identified as a central source of weakness on the union side too, involving problems of central authority, internal cohesion and lack of resources on the part of ETUC (Dølvik, 1999). According to Hoffman *et al.* (2002: 58), such problems extend to 'fundamental political differences on European integration' and 'divergent perceptions of the purpose of social dialogue and the prospects for collective agreements at European level'. These weaknesses are all the more salient for trade unions because of a crucial asymmetry: 'employers are able to refuse to negotiate with few adverse consequences whereas the trade union movement requires the dialogue to pursue its demands' (Hoffman *et al.*, 2002: 58).

Further, the 'rather weak' negative motivation for employers to negotiate is itself weakening since the 'stream of legislative proposals [deriving from the 1989 Social Charter] is declining' (Falkner, 2003: 24). The Commission has identified few fresh areas of industrial relations in which it intends to bring forward proposals for legislation. Accordingly the 'shadow of the law' is, in Falkner's words, 'fading'. In this context, the cross-sectoral social dialogue appears to have taken a new turn with the social partner's joint contribution to the Laeken European Council in December 2001. This committed them to developing a more autonomous social dialogue around a work programme to be implemented through their own national procedures (EIRO, 2003d). Subsequently, in November 2002, the social partners adopted a work programme for 2003–05 covering a range of actions under three main themes – employment, EU enlargement and mobility – to be implemented through a range of instruments: exchange of good practices and information, such as the compilation of compendiums, and production of opinions, recommendations and declarations; benchmarking by means of charters, codes of conduct and frameworks of actions; and production of standards by means of agreements which are either voluntary or transposed in the form of a directive (EIRO, 2003d).

Consistent with this new, more autonomous, approach are the 2002 agreement on teleworking and the 2002 framework of actions on life-long earning. As noted earlier, the teleworking agreement is to be implemented by the parties themselves in accordance with the 'procedures and practices specific to management and labour in the Member States'. Implementation will be monitored by the social partners in keeping with the OMC. The life-long learning framework, which is non-binding, is also subject to annual monitoring to be followed by an assessment of its impact on companies and workers (EIRO, 2003d). A 2003 joint statement on managing change and its social consequences sets out good practice in handling restructuring, but falls short of joint recommendations (EIRO, 2003g). Such developments seem to confirm the shift from 'hard' to 'soft' regulation.

Assessing the impact – more than meets the eye?

It is easy to criticize the EU's *acquis*, along with the Maastricht social policy process, particularly if the benchmark is the integrated systems found in most member states. It deals with minimum provisions, which means that its contents can be rather limited in comparison with existing national regulation. The bulk of the social dialogue's output is 'not binding for the signatory parties' (Keller, 2000: 38). It is therefore more difficult to enforce than collective agreements commonly associated with national systems of collective bargaining – the Commission has 'no institutions or instruments of its own to implement existing regulation' (Keller, 2000: 42). It does not cover 'hard' issues such as wages, the right of association, the right to strike and the right to lockout, all of which are expressly excluded from the scope of EU social policy under the Treaty.

Arguably, the national system is not a helpful benchmark, especially if it is an idealized picture. Keller and Sörries (1999: 119) contend that an 'implicit prerequisite' for voluntary agreements to have effect is centralized or highly co-ordinated bargaining structures with a high degree of coverage, and note its absence in several member states. Hoffmann *et al.* (2002: 61) point, however, to the alternative benchmark – consistent with subsidiarity – used by Jacobs and Ojeda Avilés (1999) that European agreements receive equivalent treatment to those concluded at national level. Nor does it follow that because an agreement is a legal contract it is more likely to be implemented. Non-compliance, it seems, is no more a problem in Ireland and the UK, which are characterized by 'voluntarism', than in other countries where collective agreements are legally enforceable. Even in Germany, whose tradition of 'hard' regulation providing for standard provisions is often the implicit benchmark, not all companies comply with the key wages and working time provisions of sector agreements (Hassel and Schulten, 1998: 505–7).

Furthermore, implementation does not necessarily rely on the presence of traditional regulatory instruments. Take for example the process under the Dutch Wassenar Agreement of 1982. As Visser (1998) explains, the central accords concluded in the cross-sector social dialogue do not take the form of instructions which must be applied, but of guidance to lower-level negotiators which carry considerable 'moral weight' (p. 306). Also relevant are the new forms of enforcement based on benchmarking and peer review which feature in the EU's employments strategy and the trade union cross-border bargaining coordination initiatives addressed later in the chapter. And 'soft' forms of regulation can deal with hard issues, as developments in national collective agreements at the cross-sector and sector levels, explored in Chapters 5, 6 and 7, also testify.

Neither has the *acquis* been without impact. 'Soft' regulation has made it possible to extend collective agreement to issues not widely dealt with at national level, such as equal opportunities and health and safety. And, as Leisink (2002: 103) observes, 'soft' regulation can lead to hard results:

> The social dialogue on minimum standards for 'soft' issues also possesses a hard side, directly or indirectly: for instance the costs of health and safety arrangements or the impact of vocational training qualifications for job requirements and wage ladders.

Most importantly, having a minimum framework in place has enabled the European Court of Justice (ECJ) to use case law to extend employee rights beyond the provisions of existing national regulation. Teague (2001: 11) cites the Court's ruling in the 'Barber' case which brought pension entitlements within the competence of the Treaty and continues: 'Such rulings have had important consequences for national legal regimes in such areas as equal treatment, part-time work and affirmative action'.

In the two countries characterized by 'voluntarism', the UK and Ireland, the *acquis* has had a substantial effect, with much 'soft' regulation being tantamount to 'hard' in its impact. In the UK, virtually every area of the *acquis* has been involved – from health and safety and working time, through equality of treatment, to information and consultation (Bach and Sisson, 2000: 32–3). Even in other countries, where its direct effect may have been more limited, the *acquis* has had an indirect impact on 'domestic opportunity structures' (Knill and Lehmkuhl, 1999). EU regulatory initiatives have had knock-on effects within national systems leading to the passage of new and/or the revision of existing regulation. Spain's national agreement dealing with the shift from temporary to permanent jobs provides an example.

More generally, the Maastricht social policy process has had a significant impact on the wider context of industrial relations in member states. Most importantly, it has helped to legitimize social dialogue and collective bargaining as the vehicles for handling change. It thereby helps to explain the upsurge in concertation discussed in Chapters 5 and 6 – both at the national level, in the form of 'social pacts', and at company level, in the form of 'pacts for employment and competitiveness'.

Wages, employment and 'open coordination' – benchmarking towards 'Europeanization'?

In recent years, the EU has acquired considerable powers of coordination involving identification of 'best practice' and target-setting based on benchmarking. As Chapter 3 emphasized, the attraction for EU policy makers is that coordination and benchmarking help to resolve the collective action problem associated with legal enactment and collective bargaining. Common goals can be identified and their achievement encouraged, but countries retain autonomy to decide means of implementation appropriate to their own circumstances.

Striking, given that the Treaty expressly recognizes wage determination to be the province of member states, is that coordination has emerged in the area of wages, as well as employment. In accounting for this development, much of Falkner's (1998) explanation for the emergence of social policy outlined earlier in the chapter holds true. The coordination of wages and employment is a 'spillover' from the coordination of macroeconomic policy, but not an automatic outcome. The policy 'entrepreneurship' of the Commission, and in this context the Council of Ministers also, has been crucial, the prevailing wisdom being that

> Within the current paradigm of sound money and sound finance, national responses in the framework of commonly agreed parameters to this issue [of factor and product market flexibility] are deemed superior to either uncoordinated national action or action via the traditional and more legally structured Community method. (Hodson and Maher, 2001: 721)

The case of wages

The rationale for the coordination of wages 'stems from the *asymmetric relationship* between the three main determinants of macro-economic policy under EMU – *monetary, fiscal and wage policies*' (Dølvik, 2000: 40). Prior to EMU, all three policy levers were controlled by interacting agencies at the national level. Under EMU responsibilities are diffuse: monetary policy is set by the European Central Bank (ECB); fiscal policy remains the responsibility of national governments; and wage bargaining that of national actors. There is an 'inherent risk that policies will pull in different, if not contradictory, directions, leading to sub-optimal outcomes' (Dølvik, 2000: 12). The main purpose of European-level coordination therefore is to enhance *predictability* and means of *communication* between wage bargainers and the ECB – 'thereby allowing for more expansionary monetary policies, a better attuned interplay between the different pillars of economic policy, and thus higher employment growth than would otherwise be the case' (Dølvik, 2000: 12).

Accordingly, wage bargaining has to meet two challenges which map onto the 'economic' and 'social functions', respectively, of wage coordination identified by Traxler and Mermet (2003: 231). The first is the need to avoid conflict between the three components of the macroeconomic policy mix. Wage settlements that could jeopardize price stability might force the European Central Bank to tighten monetary policy, which in turn could trigger recession. The second is a recognition on the part of national wage bargainers that any attempt to exceed the level of settlements elsewhere in the Euro zone will have an adverse effect on competitiveness and employment. This is because exchange rate movements will no longer be able to compensate for divergent wage trends. Conversely, this has heightened trade union concerns about competitive wage moderation whereby the social partners in one country try to secure competitive advantage through undercutting the level of settlements elsewhere.

The key messages were taken up in the broad economic policy guidelines adopted by the Council on 6 July 1998 and updated in subsequent years (European Commission, 2003a: 75). In particular, the Council invited the social partners in member states to conclude wage agreements in accordance with four general rules: (i) aggregate nominal wage increases consistent with price stability; (ii) increases in real wages which safeguard the profitability of capacity-enhancing and employment-creating investment; (iii) taking better into account differentials in productivity levels according to qualifications, skills and geographical areas; and (iv) avoidance of wage imitation effects. Subsequent guidelines added a fifth aim of reducing de facto gender wage discrimination.

In 1999 the Council of Ministers launched the 'Cologne process' to parallel the so-called 'Luxembourg process', which deals with the development and implementation of national action plans for employment (see below). The 'Cologne process' introduced a macroeconomic dialogue, involving representatives of the ECB, the social partners, the European Commission and national finance and labour ministers. The aim is to improve the interaction between wage development, fiscal policy and monetary policy. Meetings are informal and no negotiation of economic policy co-ordination occurs, the final decisions remaining the prerogative of the member states.

Nonetheless, the Cologne process appears to be pushing at an opening door. The 1990s witnessed considerable 'convergence without co-ordination' (Hancké, 2002: 133) in the rate of increase in both nominal and real wages compared to earlier periods. As Chapter 9 shows, nominal wages have moved in line with price inflation, and there has been little increase in real wages. Insofar as real wages have increased, this has been less than the rate of increase in productivity, reflecting the shift in the 1980s from a 'productivity' to a 'competition oriented' wage policy (Schulten, 2002: 178). Following Hassel (2002b: 165), it seems possible to refer to a new 'European going rate'.

Looking ahead, as Dølvik (2000: 40) contends, much is likely to depend upon the overall economic situation. In his *zero* or *status quo scenario*, there is little incentive for governments or employers to move, given that there is already a 'European going rate'. It would need trade unions to build on the bargaining coordination initiatives of ETUC and its industry federations, discussed below, and develop a viable productivity-based wages policy to change the situation. Under his *vicious-circle* scenario, where the ECB's restrictive monetary approach and the inability of EU members to pursue effective stabilization policies lock the Euro economy into sluggish growth and high levels of unemployment, the prospects look even bleaker. Only if EMU leads to a more *virtuous circle* of rising growth, combined with a more accommodating monetary and fiscal policy stance, would the conditions for the formal 'Europeanization' of wage setting be likely to arise. The prospects of wage inflation and a tightening of monetary policies might just persuade governments and possibly the ECB to change course. Even then, it is not clear what form 'Europeanization' would take. The development, for example, of a European 'social pact' looks rather unlikely, given that the EU institutions lack the formal competence to engage in such a venture.

The case of employment

The genesis of the European employment strategy lies in the European Commission's 1993 White Paper on *Growth, Competitiveness and Employment*. As Chapter 3 explained, it was developed, along with provision for a form of monitoring, by the 1994 Essen European Council, the deliberations leading up to the 1997 Amsterdam Treaty – which added a new title on employment to the Treaty – and the Extraordinary Summit in Lisbon in 2000. Substantively, it involves a rolling programme of yearly planning, monitoring, examination and readjustment based on the four so-called 'pillars' of action, each with its own set of guidelines: improving employability; developing entrepreneurship; encouraging adaptability in businesses and their employees; and strengthening policies for equal opportunities. The Lisbon Summit added sixty specific targets for member states to reach within ten years, including workforce participation rates (70 per cent on average and 60 per cent for women). Procedurally, the strategy involves the OMC whereby national employment policies are put to the test of cross-country comparison, including peer review.

The context was set by concern about Europe's labour market performance, expressed in persistent high levels of unemployment and low rates of job creation, particularly when compared with the US. Although some advocate engaging in more expansionary fiscal and monetary policies, the predominant view has been that the 'Achilles heel' of EMU is the labour market:

> It is in the area of labour markets that the euro area faces its greatest policy challenge. High labour costs and entitlement systems that hamper incentives for job search have depressed employment creation. The flexibility of European labour markets needs to be addressed through structural reform measure across a wide front to safeguard the key principles and objectives of European welfare systems and at the same time lessen distortions and strengthen incentives to work and create jobs. (IMF, 1998: 19–20)

Rather differently, Goetschy (2003) suggests that a commitment to action on employment was important to legitimizing the project of EMU with important political and trade union constituencies, invoking parallels with the earlier pledge of a social dimension to the single market.

The form that the European employment strategy has taken, coordination through benchmarking, is – as Chapter 3 demonstrated – influenced by business practice (Arrowsmith *et al.*, 2004). The method's appeal to the Commission was its apparent potential in helping to overcome the problems that had bedevilled previous social initiatives. It was not the grand 'employment pact' with the substantial investment and further legal regulation that some wanted, but this was hardly feasible in the light of opposition from employers and conflicting positions of national governments. Equally, however, it was more than the negative market integration associated with 'neo-voluntarism' (Streeck, 1995). Employment could be placed firmly on the EU agenda; and the new methods of coordination and benchmarking offered some distinct advantages. In Goetschy's words (2001: 403):

> the fact that the EES is an *iterative process* between EU and national lev-
> els, articulating closely an intra-governmental logic with an EU com-
> munity logic, presents a number of advantages: it enhances Member
> States' political commitment in EU decision-making … placing them in
> a better position to control, accept and implement EU guidelines; it
> should mean decisions which are better adjusted to the national diver-
> sity of institutions and employment policies, and, moreover, decisions
> that are in consequence more realistic and less likely to be 'wish-lists';
> and it enables the involvement of a multitude of economic, social and
> political actors at various levels (supranational, national, regional).

Critics of the employment strategy, such as Keller (2001), have pointed to
the lack of real sanctions; the subordination of employment guidelines to
the broad economic guidelines; and the scarcity of EU financial resources
for active employment policies. There are also concerns that it has had
little impact within its own terms. Keller cites Goetschy (1999: 29), who
suggests that

> most [national action plans] NAPs consist of a mere list of initiatives
> which often are just what countries were carrying out already … and
> the majority of NAPs fail to define precise objectives of a quantitative
> nature, the concrete resources affected to the measures, the timetable
> for implementation and the statistical tool which will enable evalua-
> tion of the outcome.

Even in cases, such as Finland and Ireland, where national concertation
is strong, trade unions have complained of insufficient social partner
involvement (ETUC, 2001). The Commission's five-year evaluation of
the employment strategy confirms such shortcomings (Goetschy, 2003).

Potential and problems

The jury remains out on the overall potential of the OMC as a regulatory
tool. The advantage from the point of view of integration is that the
ongoing and iterative nature of the process helps to keep issues in the
forefront of attention, fuelling the process of 'Europe learning from
Europe' (Teague, 2001: 23). OMC can be extended to other policy fields,
as is already the case with social welfare policy (Atkinson, 2002). In this
vein, the Commission's high-level group on industrial relations proposed

a range of indicators to measure and assess the 'quality of industrial relations' (European Commission, 2002b: 35–6). Conceivably, too, OMC could be the springboard for the application of the traditional methods. As Hodson and Maher (2001: 740) suggest, 'if a "window of opportunity" emerges ... it may result in a shift in belief systems'; coordination could become an instrument of positive integration, with even the transfer of employment policy (including wage policy) to the EU becoming feasible.

One drawback, as Chapter 3 emphasized, is that in its present form the OMC does not wholly resolve the collective action problem associated with the traditional Community methods. Just as it is impossible to make progress with these if there is insufficient consensus among member states, so too with the OMC. Crucially, unlike the business organization, where the process is essentially coercive, benchmarking between governments is voluntary, requiring agreement between sovereign bodies. Then there is the problem of enforcement: unlike in the case of the traditional methods, there is no resort to the ECJ. Another problem is that discourse surrounding the OMC tends to make the crucial assumption that, like the traditional methods, the aim is to improve the position of employees by establishing a floor of rights and/or encouraging 'upwards harmonization'. Equally, however, the OMC could be deployed to introduce 'competitive harmonization' around a neo-liberal agenda (Begg, 2002). In some countries, for example, realizing the Lisbon employment targets might be used to justify attenuating employment rights on the grounds of increasing participation, flexibility and/or mobility.

The key question is whether the OMC can be developed to take account of the criticisms to become a more thoroughgoing instrument of policy coordination. Conceivably, there could be mandatory fines for non-compliance as under the Stability and Growth Pact. This seems hardly plausible, however, with doubts being raised about their feasibility in enforcing the Pact (Eichengreen and Wyplosz, 1998). As Chapter 12 argues, a more realistic way forward would be to establish closer links with the traditional methods of legal enactment and collective bargaining. In this way the OMC, backed by the credible prospect of 'harder' regulation, might better overcome the obstructionism that has seemingly stalled the traditional Community methods and left the field open for softer forms of regulation.

The sector dimension – encountering variable terrain

The sector is the key level of collective bargaining in most of the EU-15. Recalling Chapter 1, it is an organizational field nationally, but also internationally. Most sectors have European-level umbrella organizations to which national trade unions and, to a lesser extent, employers' organizations are affiliated. It might be expected that the EU sector level would be a major focus of industrial relations activity. Yet two features catch the eye: the underdeveloped nature of this activity and the marked variation between sectors, underlining our conclusion that a process of multi-speed Europeanization is under way. In terms of output it is as much a question of the form of Europeanization as it is of the extent. Focusing on collective bargaining, broadly defined as in Chapter 3, a sector-level European dimension is emerging along two main tracks (Marginson and Sisson, 1998). The first, through the sector social dialogue, is the appearance of a limited number of framework agreements and codes of conduct intended to incite further action by the parties within member states. The second, being driven forward by national and European trade union organizations, are cross-border bargaining coordination initiatives built on systematic exchanges of bargaining information and attempts to coordinate the outcomes of sector negotiations across countries. Analysis of this second development equally points to variations between groups of countries in the extent of the Europeanization of sector industrial relations.

Sector social dialogue

From the late 1990s the European Commission has made strenuous efforts to breathe life into the sector social dialogue, which dates back to the 1960s in agriculture and transport. The single market programme launched in 1985 gave impetus to a broadening of the sectors covered and by 1998 formal structures were in place in 18 sectors. Unstructured arrangements operated in a further six (Keller and Bansbach, 2000). From the beginning of 1999, the Commission relaunched the sector social dialogue with the aim of streamlining procedures and thereby increasing the coverage of, and the quantity and quality of output from, the dialogue. The Commission's motivation was twofold. First, a desire to facilitate the new competences to negotiate European agreements acquired by the social partners under the Maastricht social policy protocol, which also apply to the sector level. Second, to shift the sectoral dialogue from a 'tripartite' to a 'bipartite' character (Hoffmann *et al.*, 2002: 62).

Replacing the existing two-type structure came sector social dialogue committees (SSDCs), to be established on the basis of a joint request by sector social partners. The employers and trade union organizations concerned have to meet new Commission criteria as to their 'representativeness' (Keller and Bansbach, 2000: 299). As of late 2003, 28 SSDCs had been established, all but six of which replaced 'old' arrangements. Apparent from Table 4.1, which lists the sectors covered, is that significant parts of

Table 4.1 Sector social dialogue committees

Social dialogue committee established	New dialogue
Agriculture	
Banking	
Civil aviation	
Cleaning	
Commerce	
Construction	
Culture	✓
Electricity	
Fisheries	
Footwear	
Furniture	✓
Inland waterways	
Insurance	
Leather/Tanning	✓
Mining	
Personal services (hairdressing)	
Postal services	✓
Private security	
Railways	
Road transport	
Sea transport	
Sugar	
Shipbuilding	✓
Telecommunications	
Temporary work	✓
Textiles & clothing	
Tourism	
Wood	

Source: Updated from European Commission (2002a).

manufacturing – including metalworking (with the recent exception of shipbuilding) and chemicals – and public services remain uncovered by sector dialogue. Indeed coverage remains at about 40 per cent of the EU-15's workforce (Keller, 2003), which is little different to the level prevailing prior to the Commission's relaunch. Social dialogue remains concentrated in agriculture and fishing; construction; transport and communications and private services.

The output of the sector social dialogue by the end of 2002 amounted to some 230 joint texts (ETUI, 2003), the great majority of which take the form of agreed statements of view. Different from the cross-sector social dialogue, a substantial proportion of these – estimated at around one-half

(European Commission, 2000) – deal with industrial, technical and commercial questions. The other half address social policy matters, ranging through vocational training, employment measures, working time, health and safety, equal opportunities and the working environment. Two main types of joint text are evident: recommendations to a third party, usually the Commission (joint opinions); and reciprocal commitments between the social partners (joint declarations and, more recently, codes of conduct and framework agreements). The sectoral distribution of social policy output is distinctly uneven, being concentrated in agriculture, commerce, transport and communications (European Commission, 2000).

From the late 1990s, there have been signs of a qualitative shift in the outcomes of sector-level dialogue in the shape of 'new generation' texts (Kirton-Darling and Clauwaert, 2003) including codes of conduct, best practice guidelines and framework agreements, embodying a longer-term commitment to implementation. Practically unknown prior to the conclusion of agriculture's framework agreement on annual working time in 1997, there are now a small but growing number of instances, as Table 4.2 indicates. In most instances these codes, guidelines and

Table 4.2 Recent European-level sector codes of conduct, guidelines and framework agreements

Sector (Date)	Text	Implementation
Agriculture (1997)	Framework agreement on employment and working time	Voluntary: collective bargaining in member states
Construction (1997)	Joint agreement on application of directive on posted workers	Voluntary: inciting action by affiliates; monitoring & review of implementation
Textiles and clothing (1997)	Code of conduct on fundamental rights	Voluntary: inciting action by affiliates; monitoring & review of implementation
Maritime transport (1998)	Agreement on organization of working time	Binding: given effect by a Directive
Railways (1998)	Agreement on organization of working time	Binding: given effect by a Directive
Commerce (1999)	Code of conduct on fundamental rights	Voluntary: inciting action by affiliates; monitoring & review of implementation

Table 4.2 Continued

Sector (Date)	Text	Implementation
Civil aviation (2000)	Accord on organization of working time	Binding: given effect by a Directive
Footwear (2000)	Code of conduct on fundamental rights	Voluntary: inciting action by affiliates; monitoring & review of implementation
Leather and tanning (2000)	Code of conduct on employment practice	Voluntary: inciting action by affiliates
Postal services (2000)	Best practice anti-discrimination guidelines	Voluntary: inciting action by affiliates
Telecommunications (2000)	Framework agreement on employment	Voluntary: inciting action by affiliates
Commerce (2001)	Framework agreement on teleworking	Voluntary: inciting action by affiliates; monitoring & review of implementation
Personal services (hairdressing) (2001)	Code of conduct on employment practice	Voluntary: inciting action by affiliates; monitoring & review of implementation
Telecommunications (2001)	Agreement on guidelines regulating teleworking	Voluntary: inciting action by affiliates
Agriculture (2002)	Framework agreement on vocational training	Voluntary: collective bargaining in member states: monitoring and review of implementation
Banking (2002)	Joint declaration on life-long learning	Voluntary: inciting action by affiliates
Commerce (2002)	Guidelines supporting age diversity	Voluntary: inciting action by affiliates
Private security (2003)	Code of conduct aimed at raising industry standards	Voluntary: inciting action by affiliates: monitoring of implementation
Railways (2003)	Agreements on a common European drivers' licence and minimum standards for working conditions	Voluntary: inciting action by affiliates

Sources: European Commission (2000, 2002a), and EIRO 2002 (various) and 2003 (various).

agreements are non-binding on the affiliates of the employer and trade union organizations concerned, aimed at inciting actions by the sector social partners at national level to implement the principles agreed. However, several, including commerce's teleworking and agriculture's vocational training agreements, establish mechanisms to monitor and review the progress of implementation. The two teleworking agreements are ground- breaking in another respect, in that they set the precedent for the subsequent cross-sector agreement. Inasmuch as they are non-binding, the regulatory nature of these 'new generation' texts is to varying degrees 'soft'. In addition, as Table 4.2 shows, there are three instances of 'negotiated legislation' under the Maastricht process, which being implemented as directives are binding and therefore 'hard' in form. These are the agreements on working time in maritime transport, railways and civil aviation, which were amongst the sectors excluded from the scope of the 1993 Working Time Directive. There are, however, few grounds for expecting any more general spread of such sector-specific 'negotiated legislation' (Keller, 2003).

Whether these developments call for a reappraisal of the potential for the sector social dialogue to develop into a significant source of collective regulation has been the subject of diverging views. The Commission detects grounds for optimism, pointing to a doubling over a ten-year period in the number of sectors covered, especially newer service sectors such as personal services and temporary work; an acceleration in the number of joint texts concluded; and the conclusion of the three agreements under the Maastricht procedures and the 'new generation' texts in several sectors (see Table 4.2) (European Commission, 2000: 16–19). Kollewe and Kuhlmann (2003: 273) refer to over 100 joint texts being concluded since the relaunch of the sector dialogue, amounting to a virtual doubling of the total since 1998.

Keller, however, takes a more pessimistic view of sector social dialogue, concluding that there are 'more impasses' than 'new opportunities' (Keller and Sörries, 1999: 300) and that 'the quality of output has not significantly changed' since the 1998 relaunch (Keller, 2003: 37). The nature of the topics addressed continues to be essentially 'soft' and consensual in nature; 'hard' topics, such as pay and standard working time, which are the core of collective regulation at national level, are excluded from the agenda. Insofar as agreements have been concluded in some sectors recently, with the exception of the three working time agreements concluded under the Maastricht procedures, these are neither binding on the parties themselves nor at national level. Moreover, a commitment to implementation through national collective bargaining, as under agriculture's working time agreement, would only be realizable to the extent that collective bargaining coverage is extensive across all member states.

At root, Keller and his colleagues identify a range of structural fault lines underlying the sector social dialogue which are held to impede further development of the process. On the employers' side, the European-level interest organizations in many sectors are trade or business associations whose primary function is to represent the economic interests of firms. They either have no mandate or only limited competence to act as employers' associations. Fragmentation of employers' interest organization into multiple associations is a feature of several sectors. And unlike ETUC, UNICE has no sectoral dimension to its structure. These organizational features reflect a more general reluctance on the part of employers to engage in sector social dialogue, at best questioning its relevance and at worst fearing that by providing trade unions with an institutional platform the process may eventually lead to European-level collective bargaining. Such concern helps explain the absence of dialogue in the metalworking and chemicals sectors. On the trade union side, sectoral organization around the European Industry Federations (EIFs) is well established. But, reflecting the national priorities of their affiliates, these have limited resources and frequently lack a clear mandate from member unions to negotiate on their behalf. For its part, the Commission has few incentives with which to entice employer organizations to engage. The main exceptions are the threat of sector-specific legal regulation on employment questions – unlikely to arise frequently – and the potential to exercise influence over common EU policies – more relevant in some sectors than others (see below).

As in the earlier consideration of the impact of the EU's *acquis* at cross-sector level, much depends on the benchmark. If this is supranational sectoral collective bargaining resulting in binding agreements, then the sector social dialogue remains tantamount to a travesty of the real thing. If, however, the benchmark is regime competition between national labour market systems, then recent outcomes from the sector social dialogue can be viewed as opening up a new dimension of EU-level regulation aimed at coordinating developments at national level. Moreover, several of the counterpoints made in the earlier discussion are relevant to Keller's criticisms. 'Soft' agreements at EU sector level on so-called 'soft' issues can extend collective regulation into areas not widely dealt with at the national level. Implementation of agreements establishing minimum standards on 'soft' issues can entail 'hard' costs for employers. The exclusion of 'hard' issues, especially pay, from the sector dialogue is the result of 'hard' Treaty-based regulation and not shortcomings of the dialogue per se. And non-binding agreements are not necessarily ineffective, not least because successful implementation need not be legally-backed but can rest on the 'moral weight' (Visser, 1998: 306) of jointly agreed principles together with monitoring and benchmarking processes.

Any assessment needs also to recognize and account for the marked variation between sectors as to whether social dialogue structures have been established and, if so, the nature of the output. Identification of the factors underlying such variation is key to understanding future prospects. Conditions favouring the establishment and development of sector dialogues include 'economic, institutional and political factors that may push (a significant degree of economic integration of product markets) or pull (socio-economic policies of the Commission) employers and trade unions towards social dialogue at European level' (Leisink, 2002: 107). There are differences in the degree to which product markets are integrated across the EU, which help to explain the absence of dialogue in the public services, although not differences within the trading sector. Conditions are also more favourable where labour is mobile across borders, as in construction and transport. Implementation of common industry policies of the EU in sectors such as agriculture, coal, steel and transport have provided an important impetus to social dialogue, since both employers and trade unions see advantages in the potential to exercise influence. In other sectors, such as telecommunications and civil aviation, political measures to liberalize markets have stimulated sector dialogue. In construction, the posted workers' directive has been a focus for concerted actions by employers and trade unions through the sector dialogue.

Differences within sectors are a further consideration. Keller (2003: 50) notes that no common definition of 'sector' underpins the existing structures for sector dialogue, which range from large general sectors such as commerce to smaller, more homogenous sub-sectors within a wider and more heterogeneous sector such as transport. Keller and Sörries (1999) point to the varying nature and state of development of the sectoral dialogue across the different transportation sub-sectors. Their conclusion is that a devolution of the sector dialogue in large general sectors to sub-sectors where there is greater homogeneity of circumstances and interests is likely to increase the chances of productive outcomes. Confirmation would appear to come from the metalworking sector where, in the absence of a sector dialogue, employers and unions have come together in the steel and shipbuilding sub-sectors to reach common positions on aspects of restructuring and its consequences for employment (Kollewe and Kuhlmann, 2003).

More generally, since economic integration is proceeding at different speeds and taking different forms between sectors, Leisink's 'push' and 'pull' factors impinge differentially in promoting the establishment and development of sector dialogue. Employers' organizations in sectors such as agriculture, construction and the transport sub-sectors have developed competency and activity on social policy questions. Trade unions in these sectors have provided their respective EIFs with a stronger mandate to act on their behalf than in other sectors. Conversely, it is the absence of common industry policies and sector-specific political measures which explain the absence of dialogue in key manufacturing sectors, such as metalworking and chemicals, as much as employers' fear that the process will open the door to European-level collective bargaining. Identification of areas of common interest in handling restructuring could lead to a change in direction in such sectors.

Coordinated bargaining

Core issues with which collective bargaining deals at national level, especially wages, remain outside the scope of the sector social dialogue. Whilst Commission efforts have focused on promoting dialogue, trade unions' energy has been directed towards cross-border bargaining coordination initiatives aimed at combating downward pressure on wages and conditions that intensification of 'regime competition' under EMU is expected to exacerbate. For some, coordinated bargaining is a means to an end – to revive and ultimately go beyond the sector social dialogue. In Hoffmann's (1998: 145–6) words, the aspiration is that trade unions will be, as they were (sometimes) at national level, the 'midwives of the birth of the European employer federations at sectoral level'. For others, such as Schulten (2003: 113), it has become an end in itself: 'it assumes the continued existence of different national bargaining systems, but seeks to link them so as to limit national competition on pay and labour cost developments'. As Chapter 3 argues, coordinated bargaining holds the promise of the best of both worlds: establishing guidelines and standards that will help prevent undercutting whilst giving negotiators scope to tailor details to their own situations.

Reflecting their clear preference for further decentralization of collective bargaining towards company level, employers' organizations are generally either hostile to or reluctant to engage in sector-level cross-border coordination of bargaining agenda and outcomes. At most, European-level employers' organizations have extended and streamlined their systems for exchange bargaining information and data in response to trade union activity (Marginson and Schulten, 1999). The form of bargaining coordination which is emerging at European level is therefore 'unilateral' in the terms introduced in Chapter 3.

These unilateral initiatives by trade unions comprise a mixture of, and interaction between, 'bottom-up' and 'top-down' developments in which particular national- and European-level trade union organizations have been to the fore. Reflecting the bottom-up dynamics are developments at the inter-regional level, encompassing unions from two or more neighbouring countries. Top-down developments have been driven by several of the EIFs, and by the ETUC. As Table 4.3 confirms, cross-sectoral developments are evident as well those at sector level and by no means all sectors are covered by bargaining coordination initiatives. Noticeable gaps are evident in the private service sectors, where product markets tend to be less internationally exposed and trade union organization is generally weaker.

At inter-regional level, the earliest and most influential development was the cross-sectoral 'Doorn' initiative bringing together trade union confederations and major sectoral unions from the Benelux countries and Germany. The initial move came from the Belgian unions, prompted by the Belgian government's 1996 competitiveness law which tied wage settlements to movements in labour costs in its neighbours. Their 1998 meeting in Doorn adopted a declaration committing the unions to a bargaining coordination rule under which negotiators should aim for settlements consistent with the increase in the cost of living plus that in labour productivity. At subsequent annual meetings, the unions have extended their agenda to elaborate common policies aimed at establishing common (minimum) standards on non-pay matters, beginning in 2002 with life-long learning (Schulten, 2003). In between annual meetings, a small working group of experts meets to facilitate information exchange and progress policy decisions. This information exchange forms the input to a database which enables settlements to be monitored against the bargaining coordination rule and to assess progress on non-wage qualitative issues. These different aspects of the inter-regional and EU-level trade union bargaining coordination initiatives are summarized in, respectively, the second, third, fourth and fifth columns of Table 4.3.

The Doorn initiative was influential in stimulating ETUC towards building cross-border bargaining coordination across the wider EU (Dufresne, 2002). Yet of the inter-regional trade union councils established under ETUC auspicies, only the 'Trois frontières' council embracing Belgium, France and Luxembourg has been active in developing bargaining cooperation (Mermet and Clarke, 2002). Other inter-regional bargaining coordination initiatives are focused at the sector level and, with the

Table 4.3 Trade union bargaining coordination initiatives

Sector (Countries covered)	Settlement coordination rule (inflation + productivity)	Common or minimum standards	Collective bargaining committee/ working group	Information collection & dissemination
Inter-regional				
Metalworking				
– *Germany:* IG-Metall regional networks with neighbouring countries	Yes (under EMF, Doorn)	Yes	Exchanges of observers in some regions	Yes (under EMF)
– *Nordic area*	Yes (under EMF)	Yes	Exchanges of observers	Yes (under EMF)
Construction				
– *Austria, Germany and Switzerland*	No	Yes	Not known	Yes
– *Belgium, Germany, Netherlands*	No	Yes	Annual negotiators' meeting	Yes
– *Nordic area*	No	Yes	Not known	Yes
– *Germany: IG-BAU regional cooperation agreements with Italy, Poland, Portugal*	No	Safeguarding rights of posted workers	No	No
Chemicals				
– *France, Germany*	No	[Yes]*	No	Yes
Cross-sectoral				
– *'Doorn'initiative: Benelux, Germany*	Yes	Yes	Yes	Yes
– *Belgium, France, Luxembourg*	No	Yes	No	[Yes]**
EU-wide				
Metalworking (EMF)	Yes	Yes	Yes	Yes
Construction (EFBWW)	No	Yes	Yes	Yes
Chemicals, Mining and Energy (EMCEF)	Yes	Yes	Yes	Yes
Textiles, Clothing and Leather (ETUF-ELC)	Yes	Yes	Yes	Yes

Table 4.3 Continued

Sector (Countries covered)	Settlement coordination rule (inflation + productivity)	Common or minimum standards	Collective bargaining committee/ working group	Information collection & dissemination
EU-wide				
Food, Agriculture and Tourism (EFFAT)	Yes	No	Yes	No
Transport (ETF)	No	Yes	No	No
Graphical (UNI-Europa Graphical)	Yes	Yes	Yes	Yes
Finance (UNI-Europa Finance)	No	Yes	No	[Yes][***]
Commerce, Personal Services, Post, Private Security Telecomms (other UNI-Europa sectors)	No	No	No	No
Entertainment (EEA)	No	No	No	No
Publishing (EFJ)	No	Yes	No	Yes
Education (ETUCE)	No	No	No	No
Public services (EPSU)	Yes	Yes	Yes	No
Cross-sectoral (ETUC)	Yes	Yes	Yes	Yes

Notes: [*] Commitment to minimum standards implicit in aim of coordinating bargaining policy across the two countries.
[**] Decision in 2002 to establish a database covering Lorraine, Luxembourg and Wallonia.
[***] Sector- and company-level database due to be established by 2004.

Sources: Adapted from Schulten (2003: Table 6.3, p. 126) using information from Dufresne (2002), Leisink (2002), Mermet and Clarke (2002), Schulten (2003), EIRO on-line and authors' own data.

exception of the Franco-German cooperation agreement in chemicals, are concentrated in two sectors: metalworking and construction. They are also largely focused on two regions within the EU: Germany and its neighbours, particularly the Benelux countries, and the Nordic area. Under the aegis of the bargaining coordination initiatives of EMF and EFBWW two German trade unions, IG-Metall and IG-BAU respectively, have established a series of inter-regional networks with unions in neighbouring countries. IG-Metall's initiative links each of its bargaining districts with those in neighbouring countries. There is considerable variation in activity, with the network linking the Nordrhein Westfalen region with Belgium and the Netherlands being the most advanced (Gollbach and Schulten, 2000; Marginson *et al.*, 2003). It embraces regular monitoring of settlements in the three territories against EMF's bargaining coordination rule (see below), exchanges of observers at meetings preparing claims and, where possible, at negotiating sessions, lodging of claims aimed at establishing common standards (e.g. on cross-border work experience) and joint training activities. Other regional networks are 'an information exchange initiative in essence' (IG-Metall official) and more embryonic in character. For example, that bringing together the Lower-Saxony region and the Amicus-AEEU in the UK has to date focused on reciprocal visits, joint seminars and developing bilateral information exchange. Developments amongst the Nordic metalworking unions bear comparison with those in the most advanced IG-Metall networks. The focus of IG-BAU's initiative has been on providing reciprocal rights of representation for members working in other countries, and thereby safeguarding the interests of posted workers. Indeed, as Table 4.3 shows, only two of its inter-regional networks embrace commitments to develop common bargaining aims on specific issues and to collect and monitor data on settlements. Schulten (2003) reports a similar focus on posted workers for the construction unions' network in the Nordic area.

Of the EU-level initiatives summarized in Table 4.3, the EMF's bargaining coordination initiative is the longest-established, the most developed and widely regarded as the pacesetter. Attempts to coordinate bargaining in the metalworking sector date back to the mid-1990s, with the convening of its first collective bargaining conference in 1993 and the separate and successful development of a common template for negotiations establishing European Works Councils (EWCs) with a series of multinational companies (see Chapter 8). Subsequently EMF adopted a bargaining coordination rule for wage negotiations in 1998, specifying that settlements should be equivalent to the cost of living plus a balanced share of economy-wide productivity gains, and a working time charter which lays down a minimum standard of 1,750 hours annual normal working time and an annual maximum of 100 overtime hours. More recently, it has established minimum standards on the scope and quality of training aimed at realizing life-long learning. Its long-standing collective bargaining committee has been envigorated by the creation of a smaller working group which has driven forward these initiatives and, in tandem, EMF has established a comprehensive electronic database of collective bargaining information, aimed at both diffusing information across affiliates and monitoring outcomes of negotiations (Schulten, 2001; 2003). Also important have been the nurturing of 'reflexive mechanisms' (Traxler and Mermet, 2003: 237) such as peer review and an annual summer school through which national negotiators become integrated into the coordination process.

Whilst EMF's initiative has provided a template for developments in other sectors and also for ETUC, there are some noticeable differences as well as similarities amongst the sectors where coordination activity is underway. Some – such as UNI-Europa finance and EPSU – are in their early stages, whilst others – including EMF, EFBWW and ETUF-TCL – are more firmly established. The formal status of initiatives varies. Whilst EMF and others in manufacturing are inclusive of affiliates within the EU-15, UNI-Europa finance's initiative is voluntary: participation is through a supplement to the affiliation fee and not all affiliates have signed up. There is difference too in whether initiatives are single- or double-tier in the bargaining levels embraced. Most, including EMF, are single-tier, focusing on national sector-level negotiations. UNI-Europa finance's initiative is double-tier, embracing the company as well as the sector level, and incorporates EWCs within the major MNCs within its collective agreements database. In a similar vein, EFBWW encompasses the multinational companies involved in 'multi-country' construction projects, such as the trans-Alpine tunnels, within its coordination activity.

Several of the EIFs concerned have elaborated settlement coordination rules which resemble EMF's cost of living plus a balanced share of national productivity gains formula. Some, including EFBWW, UNI-Europa finance and EFJ, have not (yet) adopted a specific formula. EFBWW considers that given the specific features of the economic structure and labour market of the sector a preferable strategy is to progressively intensify bargaining information exchanges across borders and establish common reference standards for key non-wage matters (Dufresne, 2002). Campaigning for and attempting to shape specific legislative measures, notably the posted workers directive, has also been a feature of EFBWW's approach. This applies even more to ETF, which campaigns for a European floor of minimum standards across the sector.

The capacity to implement initiatives and monitor outcomes also varies. Reviewing the situation in 2000, Hoffmann and Mermet (2001) noted the absence of structures to support bargaining coordination in many EIFs. Just four had collective bargaining committees and a further two had established working groups. Table 4.3 indicates that there has been little subsequent change. There are also differences in the extent of information collection on bargaining matters and its dissemination. In some instances, such as publishing, this takes the form of issue-specific comparative surveys. At the other end of the spectrum are those EIFs, including EMF, ETUF-TCL and UNI-Europa graphical, which have developed website databases of the contents of collective agreements and key wage and working time parameters. Open to union representatives across the sector, they also provide the basis for systematic peer review processes of outcomes in respect of settlement coordination rules and common policy standards. The bargaining coordination initiatives in the metalworking, clothing, footwear and leather and graphical sectors involve a rather harder form of self-regulation than in other sectors.

Straddling the EU-level sector initiatives is ETUC's cross-sectoral bargaining coordination activity. A 1999 Congress resolution resulted in the establishment of ETUC's own collective bargaining committee, comprised of representatives of the EIFs as well as national confederations. In December 2000, ETUC adopted its own European guideline for coordinating collective bargaining. Similar to those adopted under the Doorn declaration and by EMF, it calls for wage settlements equivalent to cost of living increases plus a proportion of productivity gains sufficient to redress the declining share of wages in GDP. The remainder of the productivity margin should be used for (quantifiable) improvements in qualitative aspects of work. Subsequently, ETUC has added substantive aims to narrow the gender wage gap and reduce numbers of low paid workers (Schulten, 2003). Progress is reviewed in an annual benchmarking exercise of settlement outcomes and economic data (Mermet, 2001; Mermet and Clarke, 2002).

A range of issues and problems surround the elaboration and implementation of these various bargaining coordination initiatives. Some of them relate to securing consensus on the standards to be targeted. For example, our field research revealed that EMF's seemingly straightforward working time charter was not achieved without difficulty. The process involved heated debate about whether the target should be expressed in the form of a yearly figure or a weekly figure; some affiliates even wanted to specify daily working time. The Belgian, German and French representatives wanted a ban on Sunday working; the Nordic unions demurred, because their agreements give scope for workforces to organize working time on a preferred basis, including Sunday working. The debate did not end, though, once the decision to go for a yearly figure had been taken. Should the figure be the highest, the lowest or 'somewhere in the middle'? In the event, 'somewhere in the middle' was chosen. If it had been the lowest level, then 'the European house would be built from the lowest brick' (EMF official), which was not desirable. The highest level, on the other hand, would have amounted to a demand for the 35-hour week, which would have been unrealizable in some countries.

Further problems, elaborated in assessments of their respective settlement coordination rules by EMF (2001) and ETUC, arise in the interpretation – in the context of cost of living plus a share in productivity gains formulae – to be placed on qualitative improvements which are either non-measurable, such as improved rights and facilities for lay representatives, or whose effect is uncertain, such as entitlement to partial pre-retirement where take-up is difficult to predict. Insofar as the intention of data collection and dissemination is also to monitor progress, such issues of measurement become pressing.

Difficulties also arise from the different bargaining systems found across Europe. A first arises in the case of two-tier bargaining over pay, which occurs in Denmark and Italy, where the value of the overall settlement in a sector is not evident until after a series of company-level negotiations have been concluded. More fundamentally, as Traxler and Mermet (2003) recognize, is the issue of vertical coordination which entails how far pay bargaining at company level results in outcomes which are consistent with terms of higher-level agreements. A second challenge entails meshing systems where bargaining is single-employer-based with sector-level coordination premised on multi-employer agreements. Ireland and the UK, where there are no longer sector agreements, are cases in point: in practice data is drawn from the key company-level settlements (Marginson, 2001). Eastern enlargement of the EU to several countries which, with the exception of Slovenia, have single-employer-based systems will exacerbate the issue.

This links to another problem, which concerns differential engagement with initiatives by unions from different countries. Reflecting the concentration of inter-regional networks in the Nordic countries and amongst Germany and its neighbours, Dufresne (2002) reports that unions from the Nordic and Germanic (Germany, Austria and Benelux) countries tend to drive sector initiatives. This, she argues, is reflected in the forms of coordination envisaged: wage norms in the mould of German trade unions and multilateral benchmarking by union experts, as practised in the Nordic area. Unions from southern Europe (including France), which are less centrally engaged, advocate a different idea of coordination based on realizing common qualitative goals, an orientation which is, however, gaining influence. Finally, those from Ireland and Britain remain relatively detached. Similarly, EMF (2001) report that concrete actions by unions taken in support of pending or actual industrial action in another country are confined to instances between Germany and Benelux, between the Nordic countries and between the Nordic countries and Germany.

Yet probably the most important problem confronting bargaining coordination initiatives is enforceability. As Schulten (2003: 131) underlines, these initiatives are essentially voluntaristic: 'compliance is largely dependent on [trade unions] voluntary commitment to adhere to agreed positions'. The settlement coordination rules and common or minimum standards adopted carry moral force only, whose application can be facilitated but not ensured by the implementation of transparent processes of benchmarking and peer review. Drawing on its database to review its bargaining coordination rule, EMF concluded that in any given year several countries did not achieve settlements consistent with the rule (although settlements below the cost of living were rare) and acknowledged that the rule was far from prominent in the actual negotiating priorities of many affiliates (EMF, 2001). Nevertheless, as Schulten (2003: 124) explains:

> the EMF took a relatively positive view on the political impact of the rule, as it had helped strengthen cross-border union cooperation and was successful in establishing an awareness and 'a moral claim' of a 'shared responsibility' that 'no negotiations are a national issue alone, but that all have implications beyond national borders'. (quotations from EMF, 2001)

Overall, the pace at which coordinated bargaining is developing varies considerably both between and within sectors. Europeanization through coordinated bargaining is occurring at multiple speeds: hardly evident in some sectors, emergent in others and becoming a practical reality in a few. The degree of intensity of coordination within the more advanced sectors also differs between groups of countries, with more intensive activity apparent amongst Germany and the Benelux countries and within the Nordic area than elsewhere. By increasing the number of countries with single-employer-based collective bargaining systems, which hitherto have proved more difficult to integrate into sector-based coordination initiatives, as well as by bringing new players into the coordination process, EU enlargement will augment the multi-speed nature of the process.

From the perspective of EU-level concerns to secure macroeconomic stability, the overall coherence of this patchwork of arrangements as a potential mechanism for underpinning wage coordination is far from being self-evident. Yet, as Traxler and Mermet (2003: 245) argue, what is important is not inclusive coverage of countries and sectors, but effective arrangements which link bargaining units able to constitute a 'critical mass' of sufficient size to influence macroeconomic developments. As Chapter 3 noted, under pattern bargaining the size of the pattern setting group might be relatively small (Traxler, 1999). Pattern bargaining based on a group of countries with Germany, and in particular the metal-working sector, at its core seems the most feasible prospect (Sisson and Marginson, 2002).

Looking ahead, trade union attempts to coordinate bargaining at the sector level seem set also to become further complicated by company-level developments. One reason is the noticeable shift that is occurring in the balance between the sector and company level within national systems; a central concern of Chapters 6 and 7. Not only does the growing importance of the company level in collective bargaining affect the ease with which comparisons can be made across countries within the same sector, but the way in which the objectives of bargaining coordination are implemented at company as well as at national sector level becomes increasingly salient. Effective vertical coordination within national sector agreements constitutes an increasingly important condition of successful horizontal coordination across borders.

A second reason is the asymmetry evident between the focal points of trade union and employer cross-border coordination activity, at sector and company levels respectively. Amongst employers, promotion of a cross-border dimension to collective bargaining is increasingly evident at company level, as Chapter 8 elaborates. In finance, for example, the potentially adverse implications for national sector agreements of the promulgation of cross-border HRM policies by large, multinational groups was central in prompting unions, led by their Dutch colleagues, to embark on the creation of a robust system of cross-border benchmarking and information exchange (UNI-Europa, 2000). The central challenge for trade unions in successfully developing cross-border bargaining coordination will be how to link the sector and company levels.

Different routes towards Europeanization

Although a European dimension to sector-level industrial relations is emerging along two main tracks, the relative prominence of social dialogue and coordinated bargaining differs markedly between sectors. In most private service sectors and agriculture it is social dialogue which is to the fore, whereas in leading manufacturing sectors, including metal-working, chemicals, food manufacturing and graphical, the emphasis is on bargaining coordination. In some sectors, such as construction and finance, developments along both tracks are underway. In construction too, the importance of a third track towards collective regulation at the European level, namely sector-specific legislation, is also apparent. The same applies to transport, where social dialogue is also prominent.

Developments along these different tracks are interdependent, with the nature of the interaction varying between sectors. In construction, legislation on the rights of posted workers was a major focus of union campaigns. It also became the subject of joint opinions through sector dialogue, and, once the legislation was adopted, of joint action towards its implementation. The terms and conditions of posted workers have been a focal point of bargaining coordination activity by EFBWW and its national affiliates. In metalworking, according to an EMF official interviewed in the field research, one objective of the unions' bargaining coordination initiative was to place pressure on employers to 'come to the dialogue table'. This has met with some success. From 2001, informal meetings between EMF and the employers' organization, WEM, have been convened addressing issues of potential common interest, including life-long learning and handling restructuring. Leisink (2002: 111) makes a similar observation on the graphical sector.

The emergence of trade union cross-border coordination initiatives also signifies a crucial shift in the substantive focus of European sector-level industrial relations beyond the softer issues which have dominated sector social dialogue agendas, to embrace the 'hard' issues of pay and working time which are at the core of national sector agreements. Whether trade union bargaining coordination over 'hard' issues can deliver 'hard' outcomes remains to be seen. Coordinated bargaining, and also framework agreements and other 'new generation' texts adopted through sector social dialogue, involve daunting challenges of implementation, relying as they do on the voluntary cooperation, commitment and actions of the European- and national-level actors involved.

Conclusions and implications

The EU may not have developed a vertically integrated system. From the perspective of the development of a multi-level governance system, however, the glass is far from empty. The *acquis communautaire* may be limited by comparison with national systems, but it is wide-ranging, and has had a considerable direct impact in some countries and an indirect impact in others. The Community-level arrangements for social dialogue and negotiation may be criticized for the 'soft' nature of the bulk of its output and the limited results, respectively. They have nonetheless helped to keep the social dimension in play and, perhaps more importantly, served to legitimize the role of social dialogue and collective bargaining in handling restructuring within national systems, which Chapters 5 and 6 explore. The ECJ has effected judicial spillover through interpretations of the Treaty which have extended the purchase of EU-level regulation. In setting up the ECB with responsibility for setting a single monetary policy, EMU has created the focus for ongoing dialogue about the links between prices, wages, employment and economic performance. In the process, as Hoffmann *et al.* (2002: 53) observe, the Treaty-based exclusion of one issue of 'high politics' from the EU's competence, namely wages, is coming under pressure from economic spillover. EMU has similarly given rise to an employment strategy characterized by a novel form of regulation, OMC, based on coordination and benchmarking. And OMC is being extended to a wider range of issues with the prospects of encouraging further 'Europeanization'.

In contrast to most national systems in the EU-15, industrial relations at EU sector level remains underdeveloped. The Commission's promotion of sector social dialogue and European and national trade union initiatives towards cross-border bargaining coordination are contributing to the Europeanization process. Yet, the results of the sectoral social dialogue have been even sparser than those from its cross-sectoral counterpart. And the promise of trade union bargaining coordination initiatives is at present rather greater than their fulfilment. Striking is the variable speed at which Europeanization is proceeding as between sectors and, in the case of coordinated bargaining, also between groups of countries. Nonetheless, the significance of unions' bargaining coordination initiatives is that they too introduce the 'hard' issue of wages into the European-level policy domain. And under both the sector dialogue and trade union bargaining coordination the methods of benchmarking and peer review are taking root.

A marked shift from 'hard' to 'soft' forms of regulation has accompanied these developments. As Falkner (2003: 25) contends, now that the legislative programme deriving from the 1989 Social Charter is almost completed, and with little by way of a subsequent legislative agenda, 'the emerging dominance of non-binding over binding EU social policy can no longer be hidden'. Looking to EU enlargement, the accession countries are unlikely to agree to contemplate further initiatives, given the burden of implementing the existing corpus of regulation. Enlargement will also add considerably to the collective action problem in reaching agreement.

Growing use of social dialogue, coordination and benchmarking makes the prospect of a vertically integrated system ever more remote. This is because these methods not only offer procedural solutions to immediate problems, but do so in ways which embed additional complexity, complicating further the wider collective action problem. Once a joint decision-making competence is established retreat or reverse becomes impossible, invoking Scharpf's (1988) 'joint decision trap'. A way forward might lie in combining coordination and benchmarking with the traditional methods of legal enactment and collective agreement, in the guise of either framework law or agreements. Compounding difficulties of collective action and coordination at Community level might also signal, as Chapter 12 argues, that it is time to recognize the limits and shift the focus to EU sector level.

5
National 'Social Pacts': A Case of 'Re-nationalization' *and* 'Europeanization'?

Developments within national systems have also been integral to the emergence of a multi-level system. Most EU countries are characterized by an inclusive structure of multi-employer bargaining at cross-sector and/or sector level. In the face of growing international competition in general and EMU in particular there are two seemingly contradictory developments. The first, which is the focus of Chapter 6, is a widespread trend towards more decentralized arrangements giving management greater scope to negotiate at company level. In most cases, however, decentralization has seen 'a controlled and co-ordinated devolution of functions from higher to lower levels of the system' (Ferner and Hyman, 1998: xvi–xvii). Or in Traxler's (1995) terms, decentralization in Western Europe has predominantly been 'organized' rather than 'disorganized'; the company bargaining occurs within the framework of higher-level agreements. Only in the UK, reflecting the different form and status of multi-employer agreements referred to in Chapter 2, has decentralization been 'disorganized', with sector agreements disintegrating and being displaced by company-level arrangements. Second, 'organized decentralization' has also involved a strengthening of the national level in many countries. Governments have sought national-level agreements with the social partners – so-called 'social pacts' – on wage moderation, greater labour market flexibility and reform of social protection systems. In Italy and Spain, national-level agreements have also established new procedural rules formalizing the respective competence of the different bargaining levels. Even in Germany, where there has been little or no consensus, the macro-social dialogue has taken a new form. Only France and the UK have not witnessed the emergence or re-emergence of such national-level concertation.

The voluminous literature which social pacts have spawned suggests their development is remarkable for two main reasons. First, developments in national-level social concertation or 'corporatism' supposedly peaked in the 1970s (Schmitter and Grote, 1997). Such concertation, it seemed, was closely associated with a macroeconomic policy regime rooted in Keynesian demand management. The shift in policy emphasis to the supply side in the 1980s, along with the pressures for deregulation and decentralization, were held to render it redundant, with governments turning to new forms of 'steering' such as 'contracts, action plans, contracting out, marketisation' (Jörgensen, 2001: 1). Even in countries such as Denmark and Sweden, where agreements between the peak-level employer and trade union confederations at national level had been a long-standing feature, the trend towards decentralization appeared to be overwhelming. In Denmark, power shifted throughout the 1980s from the confederations to sector-based employer and union organizations and 'bargaining cartels'. In Sweden, the developments were even more extreme: the period of central wage agreements, which had begun in 1956, came to an end in 1983. In 1990 the employers' confederation SAF closed its collective bargaining department and the following year it withdrew from almost all national tripartite bodies (Swenson and Pontusson, 2000). Only in Austria, Finland and Norway did 'corporatism' appear to survive.

Second, the national-level political exchanges associated with 'corporatism' were supposed to be dependent upon particular 'associational properties' and 'decision making characteristics':

> Under the former rubrique, they [political scientists] looked about for such things as monopoly of representation, hierarchic co-ordination across associations, functional differentiation into non-over-lapping and comprehensive categories, official recognition by state agencies and semi-public status, involuntary or quasi-compulsory membership and some degree of heteronomy with regard to the selection of leaders and the articulation of demands. In terms of decision making the search was for 'concertation', i.e. for contexts in which there was regular interaction in functionally specialised domains, privileged and even exclusive access, consultation prior to legislative deliberation, parity in representation, active and concurrent consent and not just passive acquiescence or majority voting as the usual decision rule, and devolved responsibility for policy implementation. (Grote and Schmitter, 1998: 40)

Traxler *et al.* (2001) shift the focus, contending that it is not so much the organization of employers and trade unions that are key, but the nature and extent of the structure and process of collective bargaining. Whether it is coordinated on the *vertical* as well as the *horizontal* dimension is shown to be crucial. Thus, differences in the ability to secure wage moderation are linked to the role of the legal framework in providing for the extension of collective agreements, imposing a peace obligation and constraining further negotiation at lower levels, as discussed in Chapter 2.

In the event, countries such as Ireland and Italy, which conform to neither of these types of prerequisite, have been at the forefront of the development of 'social pacts' alongside countries which do, such as Denmark, Finland and the Netherlands. Indeed, some analysts have understood the policy process involved in the 1990s in terms quite different from the 'corporatism' of the earlier period, even raising questions about whether 'political exchange' is involved (O'Donnell, 2001).

Our concern is with an issue the literature has addressed only indirectly, yet which is crucial to understanding the development and trajectory of the emerging multi-level system. It is whether social pacts are to be perceived as a case of 're-nationalization' *and/or* 'Europeanization'. Specific questions raised include:

- the extent to which there are common features and a common logic reflecting the impact of EMU;
- the interpretation to be placed on social pacts: whether they are to be seen as 'barriers' ('regime competition') or 'stepping stones' ('regime collaboration') towards the 'Europeanization' of industrial relations;
- the likelihood of national social concertation becoming a permanent feature of the emerging multi-level system; and
- the wider implications of social pacts – in particular, for the sector bargaining that has been the bedrock of most systems.

Key features

France and the UK apart, national-level concertation is found across the EU member states. In many, but not all instances, such concertation has led to the conclusion of successive multi-annual social pacts. The countries concerned include Denmark, Finland, Greece, Ireland, Italy, the Netherlands, Portugal, Spain and Sweden. In Belgium concertation has resulted in failure to conclude (bi-ennial) agreements in some years and success in others. In Germany, an unsuccessful attempt to establish a macro-social dialogue in the mid-1990s was followed by the launch in 1998 of the Bundnis für Arbeit (Alliance for Jobs), which has proved unable to deliver much in the way of substantive outcomes. In Austria and Norway, existing centralized structures have been utilized for concertation. Most recently, the phenomenon has spread to the accession countries, with Hungary concluding a national tripartite agreement on recommendations for wage increases at sector and company levels (EIRO, 2002g) in the context of the economic pressures surrounding accession.

The subject matter

Most attention has focused on pay with, as Table 5.1 confirms, the emphasis being on wage moderation. Social pacts in the majority of countries have involved a form of 'soft' incomes policy with wages guidelines rather than explicit and binding figures (Hassel, 2002b). Also unlike the incomes policies associated with earlier periods of 'corporatism', there is little emphasis on equality through compressing differentials and/or by raising minimum wages: the main concern is with competitiveness. Consequently, a major feature is external benchmarking. In the social pacts in some (larger) countries, including Italy and Spain (and also Finland), the benchmark for the wage formula is expressed in terms of inflation and productivity. In other (smaller) countries, including Belgium, Denmark, Greece, Ireland, the Netherlands, Portugal and Sweden, the benchmark takes the form of explicit comparisons either to the European average or the average of the most important trading partners (Schulten and Stückler, 2000). In the case of Belgium, for example, the reference is to developments in France, Germany, and the Netherlands. Typically, explicit comparisons tend to be used as an upper limit (e.g. Denmark, Sweden and Belgium) or as a target (such as Greece and Portugal) (Mermet, 2001: 41).

As Chapter 9 explains, this external benchmarking is important for two reasons. First, it has helped to achieve a substantial moderation in wage increases. Second, and arguably more important from the point of view of economic integration, it has contributed to the emergence of a 'European going rate' (Hassel, 2002b: 165).

Wages, though, are far from the only topic covered in social pacts. As the summary of their contents in Figure 5.1 indicates, most have 'broader scope than the traditional issues of collective bargaining,

122

Table 5.1 Wage guidelines or recommendations

Country	Agreement	Wage guidelines or recommendations
Belgium	Cross-sectoral bipartite agreements (1998, 2000, 2003)	Defining of a maximum wage increase which should correspond with the average wage increases in France, Germany and the Netherlands
Denmark	National tripartite declaration (1987)	Developments of Danish labour costs should not exceed the development of labour costs in competing countries
Finland	Agreement of the national tripartite incomes policy commission (1995). National two-year incomes policy framework agreements concluded in 2000 and 2002	Wage increases should be in line with the total sum of the target inflation of the Bank of Finland (today the European Central Bank) and the national productivity growth
Germany	Statement of the national tripartite 'Alliance for Jobs' (2000)	Results of collective bargaining should be based on productivity growth and should be primarily used for job-creation measures
Greece	National tripartite 'Confidence Pact' agreement (1997). Two-year 'National General Collective Agreement' concluded for private sector in April 2002	Wages should rise along with inflation, and should also reflect part of national productivity growth
Ireland	National tripartite agreements (1987, 1990, 1994, 1997, 2000, 2003)	Determining of maximum wage increases in line with the 'European Stability Pact'
Italy	National tripartite agreements (1993, 1998)	Nationally agreed wage increases should reflect national and average European inflation, additional wage agreements at company-level should reflect productivity

Netherlands	National bipartite agreements within the Labour Foundation (1982, 1993, 1999). In November 2002 government and social partners reach 'social agreement' for 2003 with 2.5% pay increase limit	Recommendation of moderate wage increases in order to improve overall competitiveness
Norway	National tripartite incomes policy agreements (1992, 1999)	Wage increases should be in line with average wage developments in Norway's main trading partners
Portugal	National tripartite agreement 'employment pact' (1996)	Wage increases should reflect inflation and productivity growth
Spain	Bipartite national pay moderation accord (2001). Pay negotiations during 2002 concluded within framework agreement	Wages should reflect forecast inflation and productivity growth
Sweden	Bipartite agreement for the industry sector (1997)	Recommendation for a 'European norm' according to which Swedish wages should not rise faster than the EU average

Note: Even where collective bargaining takes place at sector level, the original national agreement or understanding or declaration often continues to influence the outcome.

Sources: Based on Schulten and Stückler (2000). Updated using eiro.eurofound.eu.int/2002/03/feature/tn0203103f.html (Comparative overview of industrial relations in Europe in 2001) and eiro.eurofound.eu.int/2003/03/feature/tn0303101f.html (Comparative overview of industrial relations in Europe in 2002).

- **Wage policy**

Wage moderation: Wage agreements in line with productivity increases and inflation, consideration of competitiveness vis-à-vis wage development in neighbouring countries.

Public/private sector pay: De-coupling of public sector wages from private sector wages, caps on public sector wage bill and freezing of public sector wages.

- **Reform of social protection/transfer payments**

Pension schemes: Reducing expenditure for state pensions by cutting benefits and extending the retirement age. Introducing new pension schemes by shifting from 'pay-as-you-go' public schemes towards private funded pensions.

Early retirement: Reversal of policy favouring easy exit from the labour market, closing special exit schemes, limiting early retirement, reducing replacement rates, and a shift towards gradual, part-time retirement.

Unemployment benefits: A cut of unemployment benefits due to cost pressures and in order to increase work incentives (lowering the reservation wage). Experiments with 'workfare' policies and closing off unemployment as an early retirement route.

- **Labour market policies**

Active employment policies: Setting up active employment creation schemes for target groups: youth, long-term unemployed and ethnic minorities.

Employment regulation: Greater flexibility of employment contracts (allowing fixed-term contracts); introduction of temporary work agencies; flexible working time: relaxation of redundancy protection and seniority rights.

Training: Enhancing the employability of unskilled workers and young jobseekers by improving their training.

- **Reform of collective bargaining system**

Especially the rationalization of the hierarchy of bargaining levels, framework agreements on wage growth and decentralization to workplace-level bargaining.

Figure 5.1   The contents of social pacts

Source: Based on Ebbinghaus and Hassel (1998: 69–70).

encompassing tax policy, social security policy or education policy' (European Commission, 2002b: 26). A major aim has been to reduce non-wage costs in the form of pension and social security charges, and a key feature has been the de-coupling of both from wages (Ebbinghaus and Hassel, 2000). Another has been a reduction in the level of benefits in order to coerce or encourage the unemployed back into work. Active employment policies have also been introduced with the same end in mind. Sometimes, there has been a breakthrough in both content and steering arrangements, as in the case of the 1994 labour market reform in Denmark which introduced significant regional decentralization (Jörgensen, 2001).

The drive to reduce labour costs stems from the changed macroeconomic policy environment. EMU's limit on public deficits has inevitably emphasized the importance of the links between social protection arrangements and labour market performance. The problems are especially acute in the 'Rhineland' and 'Latin' countries, which tend to be characterized by an overcommitted transfer system and relatively low rates of employment in the service sector: financing social protection from social insurance contributions rather than general taxation effectively deters employment in private services. As Scharpf (2000a: 221–2) explains:

> The comparatively high dependence of Continental welfare states on social insurance contributions also creates specific vulnerabilities. On the one hand, job losses will, at the same time, reduce the revenue of insurance funds and increase the expenditures for unemployment and other forms of subsidised inactivity. On the other hand, the fact that social security is institutionalised in the form of compulsory insurance programmes tends to create entitlements (or even constitutionally protected property rights) in expected benefits that are resistant to cutbacks or against means-testing than is generally the case of tax-financed benefits.

Finland is a particular case because of its vulnerability to asymmetric shocks, reflecting its dependence on wood, pulp and paper products, resulting in no fewer than 11 devaluations and three revaluations since 1945 (Boldt, 1998). With Euro-zone membership ruling out devaluation and the Stability and Growth Pact restricting the use of fiscal policy, the trade unions insisted on the inclusion of alternative so-called 'buffer funds' to ease adjustment problems under monetary union. These 'buffer funds' involve both pension and social security contributions and the intention is that extra payments are made in 'good' times to help smooth through 'bad' times when they can be drawn down to help deal with any unemployment. Illustrating the potential of cross-border learning, the establishment of similar buffer funds in Sweden was a key condition for trade union support for the government in its 2003 campaign for entry into the Euro zone, a commitment the government refused to accede to (*Financial Times*, 4 November 2002).

Some social pacts, notably those in Italy and Spain, also provide for the reform of the collective bargaining system, involving the procedural rationalization of the hierarchy of bargaining levels and decentralization to company level. In the terms introduced in Chapter 3, 'social pacts' take the form of framework agreements and so can be characterized as a form of 'soft' regulation, but one in which the degree of 'softness' varies across countries. In some, such as Belgium, the framework lays down binding parameters within which sector- and company-level negotiators have to operate, whereas in others, such as the Netherlands, the framework essentially provides recommendations to negotiators at these levels.

The process

The process involved in national-level social concertation has received much less attention than the subject matter. Two issues in particular are in doubt, both of which are important in comprehending the nature of the emerging multi-level system: the role of the state and whether and in what respects it is changing; and the appropriate metaphor to capture the process – whether it is best understood in terms of 'political exchange' or the problem-solving associated with 'deliberative governance'.

The role of the state – 'steering' rather than 'rowing'?

Regardless of whether dialogue has been bipartite or tripartite, the state has been at the heart of the process. In many cases, the initiative has come from government and the threat of direct state intervention has been ever present. In some cases, notably Belgium, Denmark and Sweden, a bipartite process has become a tripartite one, with the government usurping some of the autonomy of the social partners, intervening in a dialogue that had previously been their preserve. Italy, however, has recently moved in the opposite direction, with the conclusion of a bipartite pact following earlier tripartite arrangements (EIRO, 2003i). Government-sponsored committees of experts also play a key role in both determining the agenda and guiding the discussions. Examples include the Central Council for the Economy and the National Labour Council in Belgium, the Labour Foundation in the Netherlands and the Incomes Policy Commission in Finland, with more informal arrangements in Ireland (Hancké, 2002: 140–1).

Most commentators are silent on whether a new role for the state is emerging. Following Majone (1996: 54), however, some talk in terms of paradoxical tendencies – of the state being more interventionist in

Traditional central roles	Arena of problem solving
• allocating	• policy entrepreneurship
• directing	• monitoring (obliging and supporting)
• administering	• facilitating deliberation
• underwriting monopoly representation	• protecting non-statutory organizations
	• supporting interest group formation

Figure 5.2 Traditional and new roles of central government

Source: O'Donnell (2001: 316).

terms of regulation and yet weaker in terms of its ability to pursue the distribution and stabilization functions associated with traditional Keynesianism. Commentators from Denmark (Jörgensen, 2001), Ireland (O'Donnell, 2001) and the Netherlands (Visser and Hemerijck, 1997) suggest that the state undertakes the key role of 'policy entrepreneur', with the 'steering' rather than 'rowing' metaphor being more appropriate. The state is finding it increasingly difficult to operate with a strategy based on a top-down perspective, leading it to delegate authority both to regions and to expert bodies, complemented by policy networks. O'Donnell's (2001) contrast of the 'traditional' and 'new' roles of central government is summarized in Figure 5.2. The 'new' roles do not mean that state is 'neutral' or that it comes to issues 'without an agenda or interests of its own. The state is much more than a referee. Its democratic mandate and resources give it a unique role in the partnership process.' Given the difficulty of directing and administering policy, however, central government is often 'more effective when it provides an arena for problem-solving by others'. A key role therefore is to take responsibility for 'the systematic organisation of deliberation and information-pooling' (O'Donnell, 2001: 315–17).

'Problem solving' rather than 'political exchange'?

The second and related issue turns on the nature of the process involved in the negotiation of 'social pacts'. Early analysis tended to see things in terms of the previous era of 'corporatism'. Social pacts essentially involved a form of 'political exchange' cemented in more or less explicit agreements much as Pizzorno (1978) had suggested more than two decades ago, albeit there was a 'clearly asymmetric slant' (Schulten, 2002: 187). For example, in comparing the reform policies resulting from tripartite concertation with those in countries with strong liberal market traditions, Ebbinghaus and Hassel (1998: 69–70) suggest that

> The difference between the Anglo-Saxon variant of institutional welfare reform and those which are agreed by tripartite concertation lies in the degree of compensation by the government for the detrimental effects of the reforms to the working population. Tripartite agreements on labour market and welfare reforms are generally accompanied by compensatory measures sponsored by the government. For example, a number of those agreements imply that labour costs should be lowered, while the net income of individual employees should be preserved, thus governments can either reduce taxation or top up subsidies for lower incomes. In some cases, policy reforms are exclusively focused on reducing non-wage labour costs, which improves the income position of employees. With regard to flexibility and work incentives, social agreements deriving from tripartite concertation usually combine increased labour market flexibility and cuts in transfer payments with the creation of employment schemes, improved training and other measures which help individuals to adjust to a more flexible and more dynamic labour market.

In recent years, a different interpretation has emerged, particularly in Denmark, Ireland and the Netherlands, in which the very notion of 'political exchange' has been challenged. Social concertation is seen as an ongoing process of problem solving or 'deliberation' and not so much as being about making agreements – be they all-embracing or issue-specific. According to O'Donnell (2001: 312) in the policy reports of Ireland's National Economic and Social Council:

> A definite characteristic … is argumentation or reason-giving … the social partners and others present society not with a *deal*, however good, but with the *reasons* why a certain perspective or policy initiative has commanded their agreement. It is to the *problem-solving* and the *reason-giving* that we should attribute whatever successes these bodies have. This contrasts with the view which attributes their influence to their apparent focus on *'high level strategy'* or *'policy making'*. (emphasis in original)

The European Commission's (2002b: 24) High Level Group lent its weight to this perspective, describing social concertation as engaging the actors in 'a process of "deliberation" which has the potential to shape and reshape both their identity and preferences' and continuing

> Participants are obliged to explain, give reasons and take responsibility for their decisions and strategies to each other, their rank and file, and to the general public. Probably, the most interesting property of concertation lies in the possibility that interest organisations such as trade unions and employers' associations redefine the content of their self-interested strategies in a 'public regarding' way. They must be prepared to assume a wider responsibility that goes far beyond the partial interests that are usually expressed through collective bargaining.

From this perspective, social pacts are to be seen mainly as a procedural mechanism, giving rise to agreements of intent rather than transactional agreements with a relatively precise content. Furthermore, social concertation is gaining ground not 'because the labour market parties fear losing more in not participating ... but because [they] see that bridging their interests and those of a weakened state creates long-term mutual advantages (and because a common orientation towards competitiveness requires co-ordinated action)' (Jörgensen, 2000: 7).

An important implication, also relevant to subsequent discussion about longer-term prospects, is that the prerequisites would appear to be quite different from those involved in 'political exchange'. It is not so much the 'associational properties' and 'decision making characteristics' associated with the earlier period of 'corporatism' that are important. The parties must be placed in situations where their actions – or non-actions – have serious consequences for themselves and society. The state must accord the social partners increased responsibility for policy making and implementation through delegation and participation. In return, employers and trade unions must bind themselves to using the exit option only as a matter of final resort, as occurred in Denmark with the 1998 industry-wide strike (EIRO, 1998b), and commit themselves to a process involving 'give-and-take' agreements.

In practice, as Fajertag and Pochet (2000) suggest, much depends upon the context. In countries where national-level social concertation is relatively recent and there is a lack of trust between the various actors, social pacts would seem to approximate to 'political exchange' rather than 'deliberative governance'. This is the case, for example, in Portugal, where there is debate over the relative merits of the legislative and contractual routes to implementing undertakings. In countries where national-level social concertation is long-standing and wide-ranging, such as Denmark and the Netherlands, or where there is no other level available for trade unions to exercise a measure of influence, as in Ireland, the 'deliberative governance' model may be more appropriate. Arguably, too, returning to the example of Denmark's 1998 industry-wide strike – where the LO union confederation mobilized action in support of further concessions on working time – the *capacity* to engage in political exchange remains a prerequisite for engaging in problem solving. To be effective the 'soft' regulation involved in steering depends on 'hard' regulation, as Chapter 3 concluded. What has emerged is a new alignment of integrative and distributive bargaining.

A common logic?

Input convergence = policy convergence = process convergence?

Negrelli (2000: 102) contends that 'reconstructing the individual countries' stories and the specific strategies of the actors can pinpoint substantial variations in experiences of social pacts, which superficially often appear similar'. Even so, a strong case can be made for a common logic. Recalling Hay's (2000) distinctions introduced in Chapter 1, common pressures and constraints have not only led to convergence of the policies or paradigms informing policies, but also of the processes. In the case of policies, all industrial market economies have been under pressure to undertake structural reforms to labour markets and the system of social protection, reflecting the predominance since the 1980s of the neo-liberal economic paradigm. Central to influential documents such as the 1994 OECD *Jobs Study* cited in Chapter 4 has been an emphasis on achieving supply-side reforms to foster employment growth: labour market flexibility, tax cuts, more wage differentiation and improved work incentives summarizes the main elements of the labour market reform advocated (Hassel, 2002b). Reform of social protection had also become 'a matter of urgency' (Goetschy, 2000: 44).

According to Ebbinghaus and Hassel (1998: 69), from national governments' perspective reducing labour costs, improving work incentives and increasing labour market flexibility serve multiple purposes. Lowering real unit labour costs through wage moderation, for example, has a direct impact on export-oriented industries, but also an equally important moderating effect on the public sector wage bill. Lowering transfer payments reduces the reservation wage and thus creates more work incentives, which has the double effect of decreasing social expenditure and lowering unemployment. Measures such as extending the retirement age or allowing partial pensions increase the employment rate among older workers. These can be powerful instruments for alleviating overburdened pension schemes as they reduce benefit payments and raise contributions. Increasing labour market flexibility serves the adjustment needs of exporting industries but also the necessary transformation towards a service economy.

In the case of the EU-15, the prospects of a single market and a single currency, coupled with Commission-led market liberalization, gave a particular twist to these pressures. As Chapter 4 argued, low rates of employment activity and high levels of unemployment constituted a major social challenge, adding yet another dimension. The process of EMU may not have involved European-wide mechanisms for handling the implications of these developments (Grote and Schmitter, 1998). Yet, they did nonetheless put a figure on the external constraint in the form of the convergence criteria for monetary union, along with a clear timetable for its achievement, both of which sharply focused attention on the need for action. Moreover, even though member states had willingly entered into EMU they were able to present it in the national arena as an 'external constraint' helping to justify far-reaching reform. 'The desire to join EMU is undoubtedly what motivated several national pacts in the nineties and the necessary adjustments to industrial relations systems' (Goetschy, 2000: 42). The European Commission's encouragement of an all-round view of policy making (on wages, employment, social protection, fiscal and macroeconomic policies) also played a part: 'The Member States' joint experience in these areas has been harnessed and exchanged at European level... This pooling of European experience has undoubtedly contributed towards a broader perspective on national views and deeds' (Goetschy, 2000: 47). Crucially, the fact that social pacts were consistent with the approach being advocated at EU level and that they became a cross-national phenomenon, helped give them considerable legitimacy. Social pacts, in other words, are a major instance of 'Europe learning from Europe' (Teague, 2001: 23).

This brings us to the issue of process, where the grounds for suggesting a common logic are even stronger. The European-level 'pooling of experience' Goetschy refers to embraced not only what might needed to be done in terms of policy, but also how it might be done. The 'industrial relations method' of social dialogue and collective bargaining receiving an 'authoritative confirmation of its value at the EU level' (Bordogna and Cella, 1998: 27) signalled by the incorporation of the Maastricht social policy protocol in the Treaty of Amsterdam.

In theory, the desired reforms could have been pursued through government imposition of the 'market', as was the case in New Zealand, the UK and the US. Indeed, it might have been expected that such an approach would have been preferred since it would have helped to minimize the collective action problem. As Traxler (1997: 30) explains:

> agreements committed to market solutions are clearly superior, since they require reaching consensus only on a rather limited number of procedural rules. Among these rules the basic one is to let the market work while any further substantive issue is subject to the principle of laissez faire. This contrasts with joint policy-making within the framework of non-market institutions. They always presuppose dealing with the troublesome task of formulating common substantive goals.

In practice, although the social concertation method might appear both inflexible and sub-optimal, the context was one of extreme uncertainty over the cost–benefit calculation to attach the neo-liberal alternative. The latter would have involved a 'leap in the dark' of massive proportions. The potential exit costs for both governments and employers were too high. By contrast, working with established processes of social dialogue and collective agreement – the 'rediscovery of the potentialities of industrial relations' (Bordogna and Cella, 1998: 27) – supplied a psychologically reassuring familiarity to those operating within them. 'Effective consultation may reduce the uncertainty felt by investors, employers and workers and foster restructuring decisions among the population at large' (Traxler, 1997: 30).

The inclusive structure of multi-employer bargaining at the heart of most west European industrial relations systems, is also in many countries the platform for the deep involvement of both trade unions *and* employers' organizations in other arenas of national-level decision making. These cover such issues as labour market policy, training and social security. Multi- and single-employer bargaining differ markedly in their macroeconomic relevance, with significant implications for the role of the state (Traxler, 2003). Governments can ignore the outcome of single-employer bargaining because none of the numerous agreements has a noticeable impact on macroeconomic outcomes. They cannot ignore the outcome of multi-employer bargaining, so long as it embraces the majority of employees, regardless of whether a demand-side or supply-side policy regime prevails. Bearing in mind the links between wages, social protection arrangements and labour market performance discussed above, the state is under pressure to incorporate organised business and labour into public policy making, even if it may appear at odds with a commitment to deregulation. For their part, few employers wanted to lose what they saw as the advantages of multi-employer bargaining.

Traxler's (1997) discussion of the logic of social pacts helps explain the reasons behind trade union involvement. Compared to the 1970s, the 'political exchange' involved is asymmetric: 'unions are asked to make extensive wage-policy concessions in advance, but only rarely obtain a clearly defined "quid pro quo" ' (Schulten, 2002: 187). Trade unions in most member states nonetheless seem to have recognized that concertation on wages and working conditions at national level represents their best line of defence. Scharpf (2002) underlines the point, comparing the move to the Euro with the adoption of the 'hard' currency regime by Germany in the 1970s. In the latter case, trade unions in Belgium, Denmark and the Netherlands paid little heed to the changed circumstances, leading to inflation and unemployment. Such was the build up to EMU, however, that negotiators across the prospective Euro zone were under no illusion about the significance of the regime being imposed. At the least, involvement in social concertation confirmed the importance of trade unions as an accepted social actor at national level as well as helping to stabilize the national institutions of industrial relations (Streeck, 1999).

Exceptions to test the rule

Important though the social pacts phenomenon has been, it is not all-pervasive. In terms of the processes of social concertation, the most notable absentees have been France and the UK. Germany has seen the attempt to launch a new form of social concertation with the 1998 Bundnis für Arbeit (Alliance for Jobs) even though few of the outcomes envisaged by its government and trade union proponents have materialized.

It seems hardly coincidence that the three EU countries without social pacts are also three of the four largest. While it would be wrong to conclude, in the light of Italian and Spanish experience, that social pacts derive from a 'small-country' effect, the potential complexity of the horizontal and vertical coordination entailed would appear to pose particular difficulties for larger countries. Traxler *et al.* (2001: 170) contend that 'large countries lack the "institutional preconditions" for peak-level macro co-ordination since associational centralisation significantly decreases with country size'. This would be true of Germany and the

UK, but less so of France. More prosaically, there are many more centres of power, which intensifies the problem of reaching a consensus within, let alone between, the parties.

The impact of EMU's macroeconomic regime has, for different reasons in the three countries, weakened the pressure accumulating in other member states for path innovation. In the case of Germany, the economic rules for EMU were to a considerable extent drawn up to conform with, and ensure the continuation of, the economic and monetary orthodoxy of a strong currency, low inflation and fiscal discipline which had prevailed in Europe's largest economy. In order to champion (alongside Germany) the cause of closer European economic integration, France had politically committed itself to the same orthodoxy following the failure of the Socialist experiment of 'Keynesianism in one country' in the early 1980s. Neither Germany nor France presumed that the stringent terms of the Stability and Growth Pact, aimed at less-disciplined economies elsewhere in the EU, would come to haunt them. In the UK the particularity is the decision not to join the single currency, and therefore not to confront directly the monetary, exchange rate and fiscal implications. In each case, pressure for change has been less, enabling 'path dependency' to assert itself.

In industrial relations, Germany has a strong tradition of 'agreement making' as opposed to social dialogue. The Bundnis für Arbeit sought a 'revision of socio-economic institutions that have traditionally represented a certain balance of power relations and have marked in their material substance a particular "distributional compromise" ' (Bispinck and Schulten, 2000: 212). In France, the opposite is the case. Successive initiatives by French governments to promote autonomous governance by employers and trade unions have had relatively little effect. The problem is that the state feels unable to withdraw until the social partners have developed the kind of relations found in other countries, but the partners themselves appear unable to achieve this, not least because they can fall back on the state to intervene (Van Ruysseveldt and Visser, 1996). As for the UK, a path change came in the 1980s as successive Conservative governments rejected not only the less than robust forms of concertation developed during the 1970s but also the principle of collective bargaining and social dialogue as the preferred means of employment governance. By the time the pressures leading for a renewal of concertation elsewhere in Western Europe emerged, path reversal appeared politically impossible, but also undesirable, to the incoming Labour administration in 1997. Labour has consciously set its face against systematic national-level concertation, concerned to demonstrate that it has broken with its own 'corporatist' past. 'Partnership' is seen primarily as an organization-based rather than a national-level activity (Taylor, 1999).

'Regime competition' or 'regime collaboration'?

If some consensus has emerged about the logic of social pacts, there continues to be controversy about their overall significance. The dominant view sees them as a form of 'regime competition' – the reaffirmation of the importance of national systems ('re-nationalization') entailed in the negotiation of social pacts being focused on increasing their attractiveness as an environment for business and investment (Martin, 1999; Schulten, 2002). Thus, Rhodes (1998) refers to a 'transition from "social corporatism" to "competitive corporatism"', while Traxler (2000b) talks of a move from 'demand-side to supply-side corporatism'. As Schulten (2002: 186) remarks:

> the social corporatism of the 1960s and 1970s was an integral part of a policy of Keynesian macro-management and was based on a 'political exchange' in which the unions abandoned a potentially inflationary 'redistributive', *expansionary* wage policy in favour of a *productivity-oriented* wage policy that was 'neutral' in terms of distribution, for which they were compensated by tax benefits, the extension of the welfare state or enhanced social rights of participation and codetermination. By contrast, wage policy in the competitive corporatism of the 1990s is driven by the dictates of national competitiveness. Almost all new social pacts have contained more or less binding wage guidelines which either aim to undercut the average wage increase in the main competitor countries or seek to reduce national labour costs by concluding pay settlements below the growth of productivity. (emphasis in the original)

One of the most problematic aspects of 'competitive corporatism' is that it transfers the microeconomic logic of competition between companies to macro-level regime competition between nation states. While, Schulten continues, such a 'beggar-thy-neighbour' strategy might function well as a niche strategy for smaller countries, it cannot work if all states enter into the race. Under EMU, permanent reductions of labour costs (and taxes and social benefits) are equivalent to real depreciations that might set in motion a deflationary spiral and destabilize the whole macroeconomic system (Flassbeck, 1999). From this perspective, the negotiation of social pacts tends to be seen as a barrier to 'Europeanization'. Governments, trade unions and employers' organizations have opted for 'national strategies which extend beyond class borders' at the expense of 'class policy strategies which extend beyond national borders' (Streeck, 1999: 114).

More recently, an alternative and less manichean interpretation of 'social pacts' has emerged. Rhodes (2003: 129) acknowledges that

> Gradually there has been a shift away from an earlier concern with a 'race-to-the-bottom' in social and labour standards, towards a view that, given the right kind of pan-European regulatory system ... EMU, the single market and 'globalisation' might have much less dramatic consequences than often feared for Europe's social and economic fabric.

Rather than viewing national social pacts as a 'barrier' to Europeanization, this interpretation suggests that they should be seen as 'stepping stones'. In Goetschy's (2000: 43) view, the process of European integration has enabled member states to hold greater collective sway over economic and social policies:

> In essence, the national social pacts of certain countries reflect the national social actors' support – after a slight time-lag – for EMU, a pact signed by the Member States and backed by the European social actors. In our opinion, adjusting the national social order while erecting defences against undesirable 'external' effects demonstrates a real desire to Europeanise industrial relations (*i.e.* to make them obey the new European rules of the game), and does not derive solely from a mere wish to re-nationalise social policies, as some authors have implied.

Elaborating this alternative perspective, Dølvik (2000) makes three key points. First, equating 'social pacts' with a 'beggar-thy-neighbour' strategy is too simplistic – 'social pacts' have essentially been about restructuring, shaped by each country's specific circumstances. Second, the aim of EU coordination is not the regulation or adjustment of relative wage differentials between countries. Rather it is to define 'economically viable criteria for national wage growth', such as an inflation + productivity formula, for which a two-tier model involving cross-national pattern bargaining at sector level and national cross-sector bargaining is appropriate. In this case:

> the persistence of social pacts and/or co-ordination through industrial pattern bargaining within the nation state is not inconsistent with, but a pre-condition for developing the first [i.e. cross-national sector co-ordination] in a way that does not impede social cohesion and growth more generally. By the same token, the development of cross-national sector co-ordination can provide a framework that helps in preventing the pursuit of national concertation from perverting into 'beggar-thy-neighbour' policies or falling part. (Dølvik, 2000: 13)

Most tellingly, Dølvik (2000: 5) argues that, 'if labour solidarity breaks down nationally, it is hard to imagine that it can somehow be reinvented at the European level'.

Whilst it is too early for a definitive judgement, a number of reflections can be offered. As Ebbinghaus and Hassel (1998) recognize, the measures stipulated by social pacts do not easily fit the pure macroeconomic interpretation of lowering labour costs and public debt. Important elements of bi- and tripartite agreements are both moderate wage agreements and a greater degree of flexibility in the labour market. But, in contradiction to cost-saving measures, these agreements often contain an extension of employment creation programmes which are funded by public finances. In addition, they regularly include a commitment by governments to improve education and training, as well as to lower taxation and social security contributions. In general, they involve rather complicated bargains in which governments have to take on quite substantial policy reforms in order to gain the acceptance of the social partners.

As for wages, Schulten (2002) is correct in pointing out that in most countries real wage increases have generally been less than increases in productivity since the 1980s. The shift from a former 'productivity-oriented' towards a 'competition-driven' wage policy has also led to a sustained fall in the wage share of national income with a significant redistribution in favour of profits. Yet this in itself does not necessarily imply a 'beggar-thy-neighbour' approach, as the Dutch case illustrates. Hemerijck *et al.* (2000: 274–5) argue that many observers jumped to the conclusion that employment growth in the Netherlands came at the expense of employment in other countries, reflecting the favourable development of Dutch unit labour costs. Yet the evidence does not support this contention. What commentators missed is that the Netherlands witnessed growth in employment not in internationally-traded manufacturing, but in the service sector, reflecting an increase in labour market participation and growth in the number of part-time jobs.

Future prospects

Commentators subscribing to the 'competitive corporatism' thesis question whether national-level concertation will become a permanent feature. Continuing consensus about the need for wage moderation, they argue, cannot be guaranteed: a trade union policy of wage concessions cannot be pursued indefinitely (Schulten, 2002). The run-up to EMU produced a unique set of circumstances. With the pressure to join the Euro zone removed, and unemployment declining, circumstances have changed considerably (Hancké, 2002). Already there are signs in some countries of growing pressure on wages, while in others trade union coalitions that developed to deal with the implications of EMU are beginning to break down (Pochet and Fajertag, 2001). The end of the EMU qualification period may also make collaboration in social security and pensions reform less compelling.

Others highlight the problems intrinsic to the emerging multi-level governance system. As Rhodes (2003) argues, a major problem in sustaining social pacts stems from problem 'overload'. 'Linkage strength' (cementing the bargain by linking policy initiatives and broadening deals) may give way to 'linkage stress' with the danger of failure in one part of the bargain (most obviously the incomes policy pillar) putting everything else at risk. Another problem concerns the levels of negotiation and internal cohesion of the participating organizations (Waddington, 2001). In principle, suggests Rhodes (2003), agreements in two-level systems allow sector negotiators to strike decentralized deals over productivity, training, and job opportunities within the framework of a longer-term commitment to macroeconomic stability. The more issues, levels and methods, however, the greater the difficulties of resolving the collective action problem on the vertical, as well as horizontal, dimension. The shift of influence from union confederations to sector unions – especially the 'pacesetters' in national wage bargaining rounds – and from sector to company bargaining, is raising doubts about the ability of trade unions to sustain solidarity in wage bargaining (Waddington, 2001: 450).

Linking the various levels also creates its own problems. The difficulty lies in achieving horizontal coordination while also sustaining some order in the process of vertical decentralization. If authority at the higher levels of the system becomes increasingly 'soft', this will have important consequences for union (and also employer) organizations and their capacity for system monitoring and control. If that authority and control is diminished, then they will become less valued partners for governments seeking to steer the system (Hyman, 2001). The more the emphasis shifts from agreement making to social dialogue and from 'hard' to 'soft' regulation, the more important becomes the issue of 'trust'. The problem for several countries is that there is not the background of 'trust' found in the Netherlands or Denmark to sustain concertation.

Even so, there are persuasive grounds for suggesting that, far from being merely a response to crisis, national-level concertation is likely to be a permanent feature of industrial relations for the foreseeable future. The external constraint remains in terms of ensuring compatibility between the outcomes of national wage bargaining and the macroeconomic parameters of EMU. Social protection and labour market reforms are also long-term agenda items. Pension arrangements are especially prominent if the implications of demographic developments are to be aligned with budgetary constraints. As Rhodes (2003: 130) observes:

> macro-economic management and social and labour market policy making under EMU will indeed provide significant functional incentives for sustaining or creating consensus-seeking arrangements in its member countries. European nations remain faced with the difficult choices and trade-offs that they have always had to deal with; but EMU will now discipline the form and substance of those trade-offs, ensuring that the large budgetary imbalances of the past are not repeated.

There are also signs that some of the problems identified are not as insurmountable as seems. Crucially, social pacts do not appear to be taking authority away from sector-level negotiators. As developments in Denmark, Italy, the Netherlands, Portugal and Spain indicate, there are signs of a new division of labour between national, sectoral and local levels. Social pacts tend to deal with issues not currently on the agenda of the sector, such as social protection arrangements. Most do not involve detailed negotiations over pay, taking the form of guidelines. Moreover, the practical reality is that there is a limit to the agreement that can be reached at the central level, recognized in the decentralization of wage bargaining in those countries, such as Denmark and Sweden, where it has historically been centralized. It means, though, the involvement of sector organizations in an unprecedented degree of monitoring and control.

In the last resort, it remains open in many countries for governments to intervene, thereby ensuring the continued importance of the national level. In Belgium, for example, the government unilaterally introduced three framework laws covering the main points of the stalled 1996 inter-sector negotiations (Vilrokx and Van Leemput, 1998). In Denmark, in 1998, government intervention led to the so-called 'climate agreement', renewing pay bargaining coordination among the confederations, followed by the introduction of a new tripartite forum (Lind, 2000). A similar evolution has occurred in Sweden when in 1999, following more than a decade of decentralization in wage bargaining, the social partners failed to agree their own 'pact for growth' and new rules for bargaining. The government stepped in with a new Mediation Authority to help resolve labour conflicts and develop a revised system of pay determination (Dølvik and Martin, 2000).

Perhaps the key issue is whether some form of transnational coordination is essential for social pacts to remain a permanent feature of a multi-level system. On this, proponents of both the 'regime competition' and 'regime collaboration' perspectives concur on the necessity of such a development (Schulten, 2002; Dølvik, 2001b):

> unless national collective bargaining is complemented by transnational coordination, there is…a danger that pro-cyclical wage-inflation during economic upswing and deflationary wage-bidding during recession will inhibit development of accommodating, growth-oriented macro-economic policy at the EU level, and that the EMU thereby will cause higher European unemployment and increased pressures on the national industrial relations systems in the longer term. (Dølvik, 2001b: 7)

As Dølvik (2000: 40) recognizes elsewhere, it is only if a virtuous trajectory of higher growth and accommodating economic policies takes hold that cross-national coordination becomes important to 'prevent inflationary pressures from strangling the upswing and to remove structural obstacles to labour market expansion'. Under other plausible economic scenarios, however, the absence of transnational coordination makes national coordination more rather than less necessary, as Chapter 4 established. Moreover, Scharpf's (1988) 'joint decision trap' suggests that the more successful social pacts are in handling the situation, the less likely are supranational arrangements.

Conclusions and implications

Social pacts have aroused considerable controversy and there is little consensus on their overall significance or their durability. Even so, several implications are clear. Most importantly, social pacts have entailed the addition or re-emergence of a national level in many countries, thereby contributing to the development of a multi-level system. In several countries also, social pacts represent a significant instance of the ability to break with the constraints of 'path dependency'. The phenomenon is also continuing to spread, beyond the frontiers of the EU-15 to the CEE accession countries, signalling the extent to which Europe is indeed learning from Europe. Social pacts have also added legitimacy to several developments discussed elsewhere in the book. In terms of substance, there is the encouragement to negotiators at sector and company levels to focus on competitiveness. In terms of process, there is encouragement of the 'industrial relations method' of collective bargaining and social dialogue, and also further extension of the principle of subsidiarity. Most social pacts have encouraged further decentralization within national systems. In some cases, the vehicle has been 'soft' frameworks; in others, it has been an ongoing process of social dialogue or integrative bargaining.

Clear too is that the development of national-level concertation and European integration are inextricably linked. Although not the only consideration in their emergence, the external constraint of EMU qualification made it possible for policy makers and the social partners to accept positions they might not otherwise have done. Moreover, the 1991 Maastricht social policy agreement, with its emphasis on social dialogue and collective bargaining as the most effective means of handling change, set a steer for the emergence of social pacts. To that extent, European integration has reinforced rather than undermined the inclusive model of multi-employer bargaining at the heart of the 'European industrial relations model'. For social pacts depend on multi-employer bargaining not only at the national level, but also at the sector level, the firm foundations of the latter making it possible to devolve responsibility for handling the issues of detail and implementation that might otherwise make central agreement impossible. This also helps to explain why social pacts have been less of a major threat to sector bargaining than might have been supposed. Indeed, as Traxler (2003) contends, they have created the conditions for a possible new compromise between the state, employers and labour. Procedurally, this is built around organized decentralization and substantively around competitiveness and employment.

There is a strong case for seeing social pacts as both 're-nationalization' *and* 'Europeanization'. They have reaffirmed the importance of national systems. At the same time they have reflected and facilitated a process of 'Europeanization'; coping with common constraints is leading to similar outcomes and similar processes. Moreover, national actors find that the politics of concertation are increasingly penetrated by issues defined at European level (Grote and Schmitter, 1998). Whether social pacts represent a 'stepping stone' towards more formal transnationally coordinated arrangements is more doubtful. They seem likely to become a permanent feature: the national level will continue to be required to play a key role under European integration.

6
National Sector Agreements: The Foundations under Threat?

Recent years have seen significant changes in national systems of industrial relations which, Chapter 5 emphasized, are contributing to the development of a multi-level system. As well as strengthening of the national level through the negotiation of social pacts, there has also been the rise of company bargaining – examined in this and the following chapter. Seemingly contradictory – the one involving centralization, the other decentralization – they represent complementary responses to the twin problems posed by the 'regime competition' that European integration is promoting and the greater adaptability required to handle the widespread restructuring that it has set in train. These twin developments are both a response to the deficiencies, and a challenge to the long-term viability, of the sector multi-employer bargaining that has been the cornerstone of most national systems. The development of social pacts recognizes that national systems are operating within a single market and also that, with the growth of the service economy, sector bargaining no longer has the coverage that it did. The rise of company bargaining reflects the inability of the 'one-size-fits-all' regulation associated with sector agreements to deal with the increasingly diverse business circumstances faced by companies within a sector. Seemingly, a combination of national, cross-sectoral and company bargaining questions the need for sector arrangements – the former can set the overall framework and the latter fill in the details.

Yet, sector multi-employer bargaining continues to survive. Many large companies, including the MNCs which have been to the fore in the rise of company bargaining, remain committed players. Indeed in some cases, large companies have been responsible for a revival of sector bargaining. In banking in Belgium, for example, the large banks such as Fortis and BBL have played a leading role in reviving the dormant sector agreements dealing with wages and working time (Marginson *et al.*, 2003). In Spain, the AXA Group helped to develop the new sector agreement for insurance (Sisson and Marginson, 2000). Echoing Ferner and Hyman's (1998: xvi) assessment when reviewing developments in 17 west European countries, reform rather than abolition appears to be the main objective.

Our concern in this chapter is with a set of issues that are crucial to understanding the development and trajectory of the emerging multi-level system; the role of path dependency and the conditions which promote change; and patterns of convergence and divergence between countries and sectors:

- the reasons why sector bargaining has attracted substantial criticism in recent years;
- the particular challenges that EMU, and also the emergence of new business activities, pose for sector bargaining;
- the nature and extent of the changes being made to sector agreements in the light of these and other challenges;
- the reasons why, despite the mounting pressures, sector bargaining nonetheless continues to enjoy widespread support;
- the future prospects for sector bargaining – whether sector agreements are likely to remain a permanent feature of the emerging multi-level system or give way to company bargaining or a combination of national and company bargaining.

In view of the relative neglect of the issues, Chapter 7 considers in more detail the shifting balance between sector- and company-level bargaining in two major sectors, metalworking and banking, and four EU countries, Belgium, Germany, Italy and the UK, highlighting the significance of both country and sector influences.

A contested logic?

As Chapter 2 established, although there were considerable variations from one country to another, sector multi-employer bargaining had a common logic (Sisson, 1987; Traxler *et al.*, 2001). The universalization of standard terms and conditions across the sector appealed to trade unions, both establishing the common rule and providing comprehensive regulation of the labour market. So too did the opportunity to husband scarce resources by focusing on a single set of negotiations.

The economies in transactions costs involved, a significant consideration in less concentrated industries, was also attractive to employers. For employers, multi-employer bargaining brought further benefits, in terms of both 'market' and 'managerial' regulation. It provided a degree of market control by putting a floor under competition on wages and working time. It pooled their strength vis-à-vis organized labour and could perform an important coordinating function in the face of trade union 'whipsawing' tactics. And it could neutralize the activities of the union in the workplace by exhausting the scope for negotiations and/or limiting the role that unions could play there. The state tended to look favourably on sector agreements as a means of institutionalizing and containing industrial conflict, along with delivering other key policy goals, ranging from employment standards to price control. Depending on the legal framework, multi-employer agreements can be compulsory codes whose provisions can be extended throughout entire sectors. They ensured a measure of stability through the legitimacy that comes with consistency of treatment.

There was never as much consensus as it has come to be assumed, however, and in recent years employers in particular have increasingly called the logic into question. The precise form of the initial compromise between employers and trade unions, usually facilitated by the state, which established sector multi-employer bargaining was just that – a compromise contingent on particular circumstances. Changing management imperatives have led to employer reappraisal of both the 'market' and 'managerial' functions of sector bargaining, with the coming of EMU fuelling further long–standing criticisms of the first of these functions.

Changing management imperatives

While trade unions and employers' organizations might have had a common interest in using sector bargaining to achieve a measure of market regulation, their positions on its implications for managerial regulation always differed. For trade unions, the sector agreement was the beginning of the process of seeking influence over the employment relationship; for many employers it was the end – the neutralization of the workplace involved helped to uphold managerial prerogative. Thus, for several decades after the historical compromise mentioned in Chapter 2, it was trade unions, notably in Britain, France and Italy, who pushed for a greater role for workplace negotiations, with management resisting (Sisson, 1987). In recent years, there has been something of a role reversal. It is management that has been the main proponent of decentralization while trade unions have sought to maintain the status quo. Several considerations, some bearing on managerial and others on market regulation, appear to underpin this shift in employers' position, which has been driven by large, multinational companies across Western Europe (Katz, 1993; Marginson and Sisson, 1996; Thörnqvist, 1999).

Managerial regulation

First, reflecting intensified competitive pressures and greater market uncertainty, is employers' need of greater flexibility to negotiate organization-specific arrangements suited to the particular requirements of individual companies and their constituent businesses. Sector agreements, argue employer critics, emphasize standardization and rigidity at the expense of the flexibility and adaptability increasingly required; much-needed changes in wages systems, working practices or training are difficult to bring about with the result that the industry moves at the pace of the slowest. At best sector agreements can provide a framework within which further negotiations can take place at company level to secure changes to working practice: they cannot prescribe the detailed changes to practice to be applied within companies. Moreover, management may be concerned to legitimate such changes in practice amongst its own workforce by consulting or negotiating with employee representatives, either trade union or works council, at company level. Further, employers differ in their capacity to develop organization-specific arrangements, as between larger and smaller companies, and therefore in their preparedness to meet trade union substantive demands in sector negotiations in return for the concessions in working practice that they are seeking.

Second, multi-employer agreements run contrary to the logic of devolved budgetary responsibility associated with the multi-divisional form of corporate organization, referred to in Chapter 2, which is now widespread amongst large employers. The purpose of devolving operational and financial responsibility is to transmit the competitive pressures on companies to the individual units and, in making them more responsive to these pressures, to enhance the adaptive capability of the wider company to changing market circumstances. Unit-level management should, as far as possible, be in a position to determine their own costs – including labour costs – and revenue. Multi-employer agreements, in which the determination of labour costs is located beyond both the business unit and the wider company, runs counter to this logic. Accompanying it has been a shift in emphasis from administrative to performance control, which cover not only measures of financial and market performance, but extend to indicators of labour performance as well. Corporate management is able to compare the performance of workforces at different locations, within and across countries, and use the information to exert pressure on management in the individual businesses and on local workforces for performance improvements. These internal mechanisms for exercising discipline over the workplace are making management in large companies increasingly confident of engaging with employee representatives at company level on its own terms, thereby tending to render the role of multi-employer agreements in neutralizing the workplace redundant.

Fuelling these criticisms have been new ways of thinking about managing the employment relationship associated with 'human resource management' (HRM). HRM has been variously interpreted as encouraging a more strategic approach towards managing employees and/or as more effectively utilising the workforce through new instruments of performance control (Storey, 1992). Controversy continues to surround the 'rhetoric' and 'reality' of HRM (Legge, 1995), but definitions usually embrace a number of common elements (Bach and Sisson, 2000: 11–16): the view that employees are a strategic resource for achieving competitive advantage; emphasis on the coherence of personnel policies and their integration with business strategy; an approach to managing employees which is proactive rather than reactive; a shift in emphasis from management–trade union to management–employee relations; stress on commitment of and exercise of initiative by employees; and elaboration of group- and individual-based mechanisms of performance control. From an HRM perspective, if employees really are an asset crucial to securing competitive advantage, it becomes difficult to justify relinquishing control of wages and major conditions to an external agent, i.e. employers' organizations through multi-employer negotiations.

Market regulation

The challenge to the market regulation previously secured by multi-employer agreements flows from the intense change over the past quarter century in the 'external face' of business organization amongst large companies in particular. Three developments are relevant: diversification of business activities, the growing importance of non-price dimensions to competition and internationalization of markets for products and services.

Diversification of business activities intensified from the 1970s onwards across major European economies, including France, Germany and the UK (Whittington and Mayer, 2000: 144). In the 1970s many companies embarked on substantial programmes of diversification in order to spread the risk of their investment. In the 1980s the fashion changed, largely as a result of the realization that it could be problematic to transfer particular management skills from one set of activities to another. Many drew back as substantially as they had expanded to concentrate on their 'core' activities or businesses ('sticking to their knitting', as Peters and Waterman (1982) recommended). Movement around this axis has been more or less continuous ever since with the recent period characterized by streamlining of portfolios around fewer lines of business as companies have sought to extend their geographical reach across markets. In effect, 'breadth' across business activities has been traded for increased geographical reach across established international markets and those in rapidly emerging economies (van Tulder *et al.*, 2001).

Such developments confirm the company as the centre of gravity. But diversification across established sector boundaries also means a growing mismatch between the constituencies of employers' associations and the activities of large companies. Provisions of agreements that may be appropriate in one sector may prove damaging to operations in others in which the company is involved. Alternatively, in blurring existing boundaries between sectors, these developments are placing a question mark over the continued viability of established sector structures. An example is the emergence of so-called *bancassurance* groups in financial services, which cut across traditional boundaries between banking and insurance, each of which has its own sector agreement in most countries.

It has long been established that employers in more concentrated industries, by dint of their greater ability to translate cost increases into price rises, have less need of the market regulation that derives from multi-employer bargaining than their counterparts in sectors with a more fragmented structure (Ulman, 1974). In recent years, growing emphasis on non-price dimensions to competition, such as branding, quality, reliability and service-delivery, amongst larger companies, has further downgraded the prominence of labour costs per se in securing competitive advantage and elevated considerations of labour quality. This is reflected, for example, in the attention paid to employee commitment under HRM.

The internationalization of markets for products and services and the intensification of international competition within given territorial markets means that for growing numbers of medium as well as most large MNCs, multi-employer bargaining within the nation state no longer provides a floor taking wage costs out of competition. Although reaching wider than the EU, this factor is of particular salience under European integration which involves the establishment of a pan-European market for goods and services. In this context sector bargaining at national level might appear increasingly anomalous for some groups of employers.

Fracture lines appear

Consequently, several of the traditional benefits of multi-employer bargaining appear less persuasive, especially to larger employers. Bearing also on employers' calculus in terms of both 'managerial' and 'market' regulation has been the general weakening of trade union organization and capacity for action across Western Europe, brought about by the changed economic and political context of the 1980s and 1990s (Ebbinghaus and Visser, 1999; Frege and Kelly, 2003). Reflecting this shift in bargaining power (Katz, 1993; Marginson and Sisson, 1996), large employers have felt less in need of protection from trade union pressure on the wage-effort bargain within the workplace and more confident in their own ability to reach agreements with representatives of their own workforce which secure competitive advantage. Trade unions, for their part, have increasingly found themselves on the defensive at company level – responding to initiatives tabled by management in local negotiations – and less able to secure improvements in individual large companies which can be subsequently generalized across the sector. Neutralization of the workplace, it would seem, has become less of a consideration for large employers in particular.

The significance of the links between changing business strategies, management structures and HRM practices is graphically illustrated by the decision of the three major Dutch financial services groups, ABN-AMRO, ING and RABO, to withdraw from their sector agreements in banking and insurance in 1999. As representatives of the Dutch unions explained to their colleagues from other countries (UNI-Europa, 2000):

> The three all-finance groups under consideration are all the product of mergers between banks and insurance companies which took place from the late 1980s onward. Within the Netherlands these concerns have worked within the scope of a sector agreement for banking and a sector agreement for insurance until today. The differences between these sectoral agreements have led to complex human resource management situations in the companies. It is fair to say that as a result of the sectoral agreements, an integrated HRM [policy and practice] within the groups has been difficult to develop. One of the most important reasons for the banking and insurance groups to seek their own company agreements therefore, appears to be the increased flexibility within the HRM which can be obtained. According to the

concerns, company agreements will lead to greater co-operation between the different parts of the groups.

Another consideration is a greater willingness on the part of the Dutch groups to compete with one another in the labour market, undermining the principle of market regulation:

> Simply put, the groups are fighting for (the best) employees and HRM is believed a powerful tool to engage in this continuous fight (pulling employees in and binding them). Not surprisingly, on the reward side, employee benefits as part of the integrated HRM play an increasingly important role. The groups all state that they would like to meet the demands of their (potential) employees by offering the individual more flexibility within the package of remuneration. The groups concede that individualisation and differences in the personal situations of the increasingly heterogeneous employee population lead to different wishes.

Such developments are generating important differences between employers within sectors, especially between large companies and their small and medium-sized counterparts, making it more and more difficult for employers' organizations to arrive at a consensus. Differences between larger and smaller companies reflect those in the domain of competition: for many SMEs, competition remains regionally or locally bounded, whereas larger companies increasingly operate within market segments whose horizons are international in scope. For the latter, national, sector bargaining no longer provides a minimum substantive floor. Further, management in larger companies may, as argued above, be concerned to legitimate changes to practice amongst its own workforce by negotiating directly with company employee representatives. Conversely, smaller companies have less incentive, and fewer resources than larger employers, to engage in company negotiations trading-off improvements in substantive terms and conditions in return for concessions in employment and working practices (Sisson, 1991). Indeed, as Hornung-Draus (2001: 7) observes, increasing resort to outsourcing has often intensified such conflicts of interest:

> The big global players which were exposed to international competition were interested above all in avoiding industrial disputes, particularly strikes, which would lead to a loss of international clients for their companies. At the same time they imposed cost reductions on their

small supplier companies, which were sitting at the same negotiating table, and were therefore interested above all in avoiding cost increases imposed by collective agreements. The result of this was a situation of increasing tension on the employers' side with a number of smaller companies either leaving the employer organisations or not respecting contractual obligations arising from the collective agreements.

The result is that smaller companies are displaying growing disillusionment with and, in some cases, withdrawing from membership of employers' organizations. This is nowhere more evident than in Germany. In the key metalworking sector, the membership density of *Gesamtmetall*, the employers' association, has declined steadily since 1980, when it stood at 58 per cent, to 44 per cent in the western part of the country in 1993 and 34 per cent in 1998. In the eastern part of the country, it stood at only 17 per cent in 1998, having fallen from 35 per cent in 1993 (Hassel, 1999: 494; 2002a: 312). The decline in the proportion of the metalworking workforce employed in member companies has, however, been slower and between 1993 and 1998 levelled out, leading Hassel (2002a: 312) to conclude that 'big companies tend to remain members of the employers' associations while small companies tend to resign'.

A further significant development in some industries and regions is the establishment by German employers' associations, under the same roof, of separate 'Ohne-Tarif' ('without collective agreement') organisations. 'OT' members receive the same services from the employers' association, but have considerable flexibility in determining levels of pay and working time, payments systems and working time arrangements. Take-up of 'OT' membership varies widely between industries, for example including all companies in sawmills in the Rhineland Palatinate region – where the practice originated in the late 1980s – but not being on offer at all in some other sectors (EIRO, 2002f). In the key metalworking sector, the practice has spread from *Gesamtmetall*'s regional associations in the east to the west. Transfer to the 'OT' associations was said in our metalworking field interviews to be facilitated by low union density and an accommodating works council.

Multi-employer bargaining – not necessarily a 'public good'?

The view that sector bargaining is a public 'good' is also under challenge, its role in institutionalizing and containing industrial conflict increasingly forgotten as the incidence of strikes has declined. As Schulten (2002: 177–8) emphasizes in considering the concept of a solidaristic wage policy, since the 1980s the 'new ideological hegemony of neo-liberalism' in Europe has meant criticism of the both the goals and institutions associated with 'political correction of market outcomes'. From this viewpoint, any correction leads to 'greater inefficiency' (Hank, 2000: 155): in as much as sector bargaining sets non-market wages, it is held to result in unemployment, thereby generating inequality in the labour market. Rather than being inclusive, too little wage differentiation favours 'insiders' at the expense of 'outsiders'. The role of policy is to ensure that all individuals can hold their own equally in the market, in the sense of 'supply-side egalitarianism' (Streeck, 1999: 5). The criticism, Schulten continues, is usually reinforced by contending that the political and institutional prerequisites for the kind of market-correcting behaviour associated with sector bargaining have largely disappeared with the changing structure of modern capitalism:

> On the one hand, it is asserted that in a globalised world economy the nation state has largely lost its ability to conduct redistributive policies... On the other, it is argued that whereas the innovation-based model underlying the solidaristic wage policy may have been reconcilable with the conditions in which a Fordist industrial society operates, in those of a post-Fordist service society it leads to dysfunctional results.

Debates over the connections between bargaining structure and economic performance are relevant too. Chapter 1 noted that the prevailing consensus amongst economic opinion is that the relationship involved is non-linear (Calmfors and Driffill, 1988). Highly centralized bargaining structures, such as those characterizing the Nordic area at the time, apparently performed better in terms of key economic outcomes, because the scope for externalizing the wider economic effects of wage decisions is minimized, as did highly decentralized ones because they were disciplined by the market. The worst performing structures were those that were neither fully centralized nor decentralized, i.e. those based on the sector. This received economic wisdom has recently been subject to a thoroughgoing reappraisal by Traxler *et al.* (2001), who demonstrate the importance of the particular forms of bargaining coordination, both on the horizontal (across sectors) and vertical (hierarchical relation between cross-sector, sector and company levels) planes, in mediating the relationship between bargaining structure and economic performance. Crucially, Traxler *et al.* identify forms of coordinated sector-level bargaining, including pattern-bargaining as practised in Germany and peak-level coordination with strong discipline over lower levels, as practised in Finland and the Netherlands, which outperform the fully decentralized alternative found in the UK. A reassessment of the public good aspects of sector-based arrangements seems called for.

EMU exacerbates the pressures

The process of EMU is fuelling the strains on sector collective bargaining arrangements. By intensifying competition within the single market and therefore generating further employer pressure for increased scope to negotiate organization-specific arrangements, EMU is accelerating the decentralization trend discussed above. EMU has also unleashed widespread restructuring and rationalization as companies look to service one regional, rather than a series of national, markets. Combined with intensifying competition, handling this restructuring has prompted a reorientation of bargaining agenda towards questions of competitiveness, adaptability and employment security. Because these questions are frequently easier to address at the company than the sector level, decentralization pressures are compounded. Furthermore, in promoting deregulation so as to extend the reach of the single market across a wider range of business activities, EMU has led to the privatization of former state enterprises that are not part of established multi-employer bargaining arrangements. Finally, pressures for a European dimension to national, sector-level collective bargaining are ever more apparent as national arrangements are increasingly set in competition with one another.

Reorientation of the bargaining agenda

The agenda of sector bargaining has increasingly become oriented towards questions of competitiveness, adaptability and employment. From the early 1990s a shift is evident from 'productivity-oriented' to 'competition-oriented' collective bargaining (Schulten, 1998: 209). Sector negotiations are being used to constrain the growth in labour costs, often reflecting the imprint of the national-level developments addressed in Chapter 5. In Belgium, the 1996 law on competitiveness ties wage increases to movements in labour costs in its neighbouring economies, with the cross-sector agreement specifying the wage margin open for negotiation at sector (and company) level. In Italy, the 1993 cross-sector agreement stipulates that the cost-of-living wage increases negotiated at sector level every four years should be tied to anticipated inflation, with an interim adjustment in the light of actual inflation negotiated every two years. Other cost-cutting measures being promoted by employers include the 'opt-out' or 'hardship' clauses discussed below and lower wages for specific groups, sometimes linked to specific guarantees for long-term unemployed or younger workers.

As well as constraining growth in labour costs, measures addressing employment have become prominent on the agenda of sector negotiations (Sisson and Artiles, 2000; Zagelmeyer, 2000). For example, reductions in the working week have been linked to commitments to create new jobs in France (in line with the provisions of the *lois Aubry* establishing the 35-hour week), with the same being true of overtime working in Austria (education, public services, construction and metalworking) and Germany (chemicals). Measures designed to better manage the consequences of the restructuring of business activities include a number of agreements providing for a reduction in employment. Examples include municipalities in Finland (40,000 between 1991 and 1996), steel in Luxembourg (in both the 1980s and 1990s), and coal in Germany (48,000 up to 2005) and Spain (4,000 up to 2001). Early and partial retirement are features of several sector agreements in France under the *Allocation de Remplacement pour l'Emploi* initiative. They also feature in several sectors in Belgium, Germany and the Netherlands. Further agreements introduce arrangements dealing with the temporary placement and training of employees who lose their job as a result of restructuring. Examples include banking in Italy, port transport and confectionery in the Netherlands, winemaking in Spain and Austria's Steyr region covering mainly metalworking. Converting temporary into permanent jobs also features in several Spanish agreements (chemicals, glass and winemaking) and in chemicals in Germany.

Measures designed to increase adaptability are also increasingly widespread in sector agreements (Sisson and Artiles, 2000; Zagelmeyer, 2000). Most prominent are the introduction of more flexible working time arrangements involving shifts, part-time and Saturday working. Also featuring are the promotion of ongoing training and the re-design of job classification and wage payment structures, all of which are designed to enable companies to adjust.

Handling restructuring – a boost to company bargaining

Recognition of the importance of its role in handling restructuring has bolstered collective bargaining at company as well as sector level. Indeed, many of the developments in the scope and process of collective bargaining stemming from the shift to a 'competition' orientation reflect 'bottom-up' rather than 'top-down' innovations. Bargaining over employment and competitiveness signals a qualitative shift, as Chapter 3 argued, reflecting the 'development of a "different paradigm" of industrial relations' (Léonard, 2001: 30). At company level, the restructuring process has both external and internal dimensions. Externally, it involves extensive cross-border mergers and acquisitions which, as Chapter 2 charted, are increasing the number of European-scale operations. Internally it focuses on rationalization of facilities across the single market, involving centralizing the supply of given product lines at fewer locations, shifts in activities between them and closures. The two dimensions are frequently related; consolidating newly merged companies or acquired businesses requires extensive internal reorganization and rationalization.

'Pacts for employment and competitiveness'

Company-level negotiations dealing with restructuring, so-called 'pacts for employment and competitiveness' (PECs), are almost universally found across EU countries, Greece being the apparent exception (Zagelmeyer, 2000). Although the available data do not allow a precise picture to be drawn, the diffusion of such agreements seems widespread. In Germany, for example, in 1997–98, around one in four workplaces with a works council (i.e. about one in ten of all workplaces) reported the negotiation of such an agreement in the recent past. In Spain, in 1997, nearly 10 per cent of collective agreements were found to deal with employment preservation. In France, in 1998, almost 40 per cent of the agreements dealing with reductions in working time also contained measures allowing for adjustments to handle fluctuations in workload (Sisson and Artiles, 2000). The negotiation of these PECs enables us to gain an up-to-date insight into the subject matter and process involved in company bargaining.

Although there is no typical PEC, most have two main objectives: to minimize reductions, preserve and/or stabilize employment; and to reduce the organization's costs and/or improve its ability to adapt, thereby contributing to future conditions for economic growth and job creation (Sisson and Artiles, 2000). Three main ideal-types may be identified depending on the balance of emphasis between short-term cost reductions to safeguard jobs and measures to improve the flexibility and adaptability of the organization in the medium term. In the first, agreements are essentially concerned with the 'survival' of the business or some of its operations. In the second, agreements are intended to aid the process of 'retrenchment' – the situation is not so much one of survival, but of slimming down in the light of changing market conditions. In the third, agreements are designed to help with the 'adaptation' of the business to deal with new situations, for example under market deregulation. Figure 6.1 indicates the contents that can be covered in PECs.

- guarantees of employment and/or no compulsory redundancy (open-ended or specific period)
- investment for particular establishments
- transformation of precarious into more stable jobs
- additional employment for specific groups (e.g. young people, long-term unemployed)
- the relocation of the workforce within the company
- the introduction of 'work foundations' to improve the employment prospects of redundant workers
- reduction in pay levels and associated benefits, lower starter rates for new employees
- commitments to moderate pay demands
- increases linked to key indicators such as prices, productivity, exchange rates
- share ownership
- temporary or long-term reduction in the working week
- greater variability in and extension of working hours without overtime premium
- the increased use of part-time work
- extension of operating hours (e.g. weekend work)
- conditions of use of fixed-term contracts, temporary work and contracting out
- new forms of work organization (e.g. teamwork)
- training and development

Figure 6.1   Possible contents of PECs

Source: Sisson (2001a).

PECs are adding to the pressure for collective bargaining decentralization because the kind of detail involved in their negotiation cannot be dealt with exclusively at sector level. Indeed, sometimes it cannot even be dealt with at the overall company level. Many PECs take the form of framework agreements leaving detailed implementation to individual business units within the company, reflecting also the need to legitimate change with those involved. An example is Air France's 'Accord Pour un Développement Partagé'. Publicized as an agreement trading off a reduction in working time against the creation of 4,000 new jobs – in accordance with the *lois Aubry*, it is in essence a framework agreement (*accord cadre*). Mériaux (1999) reports that the achievement of this objective depends on local agreements in 26 establishments dealing with the flexibility of working time and work organization.

Although PECs might be contributing to the erosion of the universal standards that sector agreements traditionally provided, they do not in most instances openly breach the terms of these. Wages have not generally been traded-off against job security. In some cases, PECs have involved reduction and/or absorption of company-specific payments, but the collectively negotiated wage rates in sector agreements have remained sacrosanct. Insofar as PECs have their origins in higher-level agreements, their precise shape and form reflect these agreements' priorities. Spanish PECs, for example, emphasize the transfer of temporary into permanent jobs – indeed, Artiles and Alós-Moner (1999) suggest that these company agreements might be described as 'improvement pacts' in as much as they go beyond the provisions of higher-level agreements. In France, employment creation rather than reduction or preservation is the key feature. In Austria and the Nordic countries explicit links between employment and competitiveness are less prominent at company level, whereas the establishment of employment 'foundations' is more in evidence (Sisson and Artiles, 2000).

As in the case of national social pacts, a strong element of problem solving and 'quid pro quo' bargaining characterizes the process of negotiating PECs, reminiscent of Walton and McKersie's (1965) integrative bargaining. Many of the mechanisms of integrative bargaining are also to be found, including joint working parties, third-party facilitation and continuous review of progress. As yet, the jury remains out on whether this shift is leading to a fundamental change in relationships between the parties (Sisson, 2001a). Clear, however, is that employee representatives at company and site levels are becoming more involved in the management process. There is also an increase in forms of negotiation that, especially in countries such as Germany with tightly prescribed boundaries between collective bargaining involving trade unions and consultation involving works councils, are deemed to be outwith the traditional framework of collective bargaining.

In this shift, it is management which often initiates the negotiations, coming to the bargaining table with their own negotiating agenda. Two issues are key. One is the need for management to secure greater flexibility in areas such as working time and work organization. The other relates to the issue of recognition. Intensifying competition requires management both to minimize costs and promote the cooperation and commitment of the workforce necessary for continuous improvement. Historically, it was sufficient for management to have the passive or implicit recognition of its right to manage from employee representatives. Given the nature and extent of the restructuring currently taking place, however, this implicit recognition is no longer enough. Management needs the legitimacy that only explicit recognition, through agreement over change, can bring.

A case of 'converging divergences'?

Although PECs are a common, cross-country development, suggesting some convergence of approach across institutionally different collective bargaining systems, there is a strong sector effect. Most PECs are to be found in three main sectors – recently-privatized public corporations in transport, telecommunications and the utilities, manufacturing (automobiles, food and drink, household appliances and some branches of electronics) and banking (Sisson and Artiles, 2000). The examples of former state-owned enterprises negotiating PECs cited below mainly involved the 'adaptation' model. The situations in manufacturing and banking are more complicated. In some manufacturing cases the agreement was about 'survival'. Examples are Philips in Austria, Opel (General Motors) in Germany and Rover and Vauxhall (General Motors) in the UK. Elsewhere, such as Irish Cement in Ireland and Blue Circle Cement in the UK, the 'retrenchment' model more accurately captures the essence of the agreement. Examples of the 'adaptation' model are Bonfiglioli and Zanussi in Italy, Heineken in the Netherlands and Volkswagen in Germany. In banking, cases such as Die Erste Bank in Austria, the FöreningsSparbanken in Sweden and the Co-operative Bank in the UK typify the 'retrenchment' model, whereas the agreement at La Caixa in Spain was essentially about 'adaptation'.

In addition to pressures for extensive restructuring, albeit of varying kinds, some other features are evident which mark out these sectors from others where the incidence of PECs is altogether less marked. There are differences too, helping to explain variation between – and within – the sectors in the type of PEC. Common is an intensification of competition for mature products and services, which in the case of manufacturing derives from the increasing international openness of national and EU markets. This consideration also applies to a varying extent in the hitherto more sheltered transport, telecommunications, utility and banking sectors. Probably of greater significance in these four sectors, however, is deregulation and – for (former) state-owned enterprises – marketization. Second, each of the sectors has relatively well-organized workforces. Union density is high and, in manufacturing especially, workplace trade union organization is also strong, effectively obliging management to legitimize change through negotiation. Third, is the impact of rapid technological change. This is most apparent in banking, where new technologies have had a substantial impact on established banking processes and products, but have also created opportunities for new players to enter the market, for example, in telephone and internet banking. Even in manufacturing, transport and utilities, where the basic technology may appear to be stable, there have been significant changes reflecting the revolution in information and communications technology (ICT).

The result is a twin dynamic with considerable differences between sectors within national boundaries, but also some striking similarities within sectors across national boundaries. Several MNCs, most notably those in automotive manufacturing, have negotiated PECs in a number of countries, leading – in the case of Ford and General Motors, but not Volkswagen – to the adoption of common practices across their subsidiaries. Examples include teamworking, annualized hours and overtime 'corridors' (Sisson and Artiles, 2000). Significant too, as Chapter 8 elaborates, is the context in which these practices had been introduced. Typically, national negotiators had been left in no doubt that a failure to introduce them would lead to the withholding of investment in favour of operations which had in other countries (Hancké, 2000). No such cross-border dimension is evident in the negotiation of PECs within any individual bank. Nonetheless a process of cross-border 'isomorphism' is apparent across organizations within the sector. For example, in the face of major reorganization remarkably similar provisions for retraining and redeployment were evident in PECs concluded at Erste Bank (Austria), Leonia Bank (Finland), FöreningsSparbanken (Sweden) and the Co-operative Bank (UK).

Privatization

In promoting deregulation as part of the drive for a single market, EMU has also led to the privatization or, short of this, 'marketization', of former state-owned enterprises (airlines, railways, telecommunications, utilities) in those EU countries where this had yet to occur. The significance for sector-level bargaining arrangements lies in the emergence of major new companies that are outwith the established structures of multi-employer bargaining. More generally, the accompanying deregulation has significantly reduced, if not eliminated altogether, the market protection that such companies used to enjoy. With full and partial privatization, management has to have regard to the expectations of shareholders in running the business and not just the interests of government. Indeed, a substantial reduction of the cost base involving cuts in employment has often been seen as a necessary preliminary to flotation of shares on stock markets. As a consequence, these companies have been to the fore in the negotiation of the PECs, as noted above, setting a template for their private sector counterparts. Examples include Post und

Telecom (Austria), Belgacom (Belgium), Air France and EDF-GDF (France), Deutsche Bahn and Lufthansa (Germany), the Electricity Supply Board (Ireland), Alitalia and Ferrovio dello Stato (Italy), Telia (Sweden) and Hyder and Scottish Power (UK) (Zagelmeyer, 2000; Sisson and Artiles, 2000).

The cross-border dimension

So far our concern has been with the balance between sector and company levels *within* existing multi-employer structures. EMU also has significant implications for the interface *between* sector bargaining arrangements in different countries, reinforcing the potential for regime competition between national bargaining systems within an integrated economy. As Chapter 1 explained, such pressures stem not so much from the development of a European labour market, which save for some highly skilled groups such as airline pilots and IT specialists there is little sign of, but from the consequences of the further internationalization of production and marketing servicing that EMU promotes. Specifically, the creation of the Euro zone de facto makes national bargaining systems into a set of potentially competing sub-regional ones (Martin, 1999), none of which is able to provide comprehensive regulation of the labour market at a level corresponding to the scope of Europe's single market.

The prospect of such 'bargaining regime' competition translating into a downward spiral in terms and conditions has prompted the various trade union initiatives aimed at coordinating the agenda and outcomes of national, sector-level bargaining across borders described in Chapter 4. To recall, these comprise both EU-level initiatives by the EIFs and inter-regional ones involving unions from two or more countries in different regions of the EU, primarily Germany and its neighbours and the Nordic area. On the part of employers' organizations there is no parallel desire for cross-border bargaining coordination. Indeed, as Chapter 4 established, there is strong opposition: cross-border coordination is seen as tantamount to centralization, which runs counter to employers' decentralizing agenda.

This means that there is a sharp asymmetry in the focal points of cross-border bargaining cooperation and coordination on the trade union and employer sides, further complicating the collective action problem. On the trade union side, the sector level is the focus of cross-border initiatives. At company level, with the exception of some of the large automotive manufacturers, the potential offered by EWCs for employee representatives to coordinate local negotiations appears to remain largely unfulfilled, as Chapter 8 reports. The situation is reversed on the employers' side. Whilst employers' organizations remain opposed to any cross-border coordination of sector negotiations, the management of many of their MNC members are increasingly coordinating bargaining at local company level over working practices, working time arrangements and company-specific pay systems across sites in different countries. As with the trade union bargaining coordination initiatives analysed in Chapter 4, there are significant sector differences which Chapter 8 describes in more detail.

The challenge of unorganized activities

A further challenge to sector agreements comes from the emergence of new business activities that by definition have no established collective bargaining arrangements. A key issue is whether as a result significant 'agreement-free' space is opening up or whether sector agreements are being adapted and extended to provide coverage. These developments embrace new industries, such as the ICT sector, and occupations, but also the reconfiguration of established industries to accommodate technological changes to production processes and modes of product delivery. Such reconfiguration is characterized by extensive internal restructuring within companies in which previously integrated business activities are differentiated and separated out into distinct business streams or units, some of which are then outsourced to other (specialist) companies. Reconfiguration of established industries is blurring existing boundaries between sectors and their agreements. In addition, outsourced activities may be moved to sectors where there are no established multi-employer bargaining arrangements or where the provisions of agreements are less stringent.

To anticipate discussion in Chapter 7, developments in metalworking and financial services illustrate the range of developments involved. In metalworking, a central challenge to existing sector agreements is the burgeoning ICT sector, reflecting both the growth of new companies and the increasing emphasis that established companies are placing on 'systems and solutions' as compared to manufacturing. Established companies are also moving into after-sales service, in which the brand rather than the product is the focus. Either way, there is less emphasis on the actual manufacture of the product amongst large companies, which in some cases is being outsourced altogether. An example is automotive components, where the major, first-tier, suppliers are increasingly becoming providers of components systems, with manufacture of the individual components being outsourced to second-tier suppliers. These new 'systems and solutions' and 'after-sales' activities are neither well-organized by trade unions, nor do they automatically fall under the coverage of existing metalworking agreements.

In financial services, new modes of product delivery via telephone and the internet are a major development affecting both banking and insurance, the former more sharply because of its extensive branch networks. New service providers have emerged, a development facilitated by financial deregulation across the EU, as well as established banks and insurance companies developing new products. Internal restructuring amongst established players has led to the separating out of back-office activities and the growing number of call centres into distinct business units. Direct banking and insurance activities have frequently been established as separate subsidiaries. Separation and transfer out of 'back-office' operations, growth of call centres (frequently employing new labour) and the establishment of new direct banking and insurance operations are all adding to the challenges to existing sector-level collective bargaining arrangements and to unions organizing in the sector.

The extent of the challenge to existing collective bargaining arrangements posed by the growth of outsourcing found across many sectors is encapsulated by a recent comparative study of automotive manufacturing (Caprile and Llorens, 2000), which, given high levels of collective bargaining coverage and a tradition of strong workforce organization and negotiation at company and site levels, might be regarded as a critical instance. Three main outsourcing developments amongst the major manufacturers are identified: progressive withdrawal from manufacture of components, in favour of outsourced supplies; a sharp reduction in the number of first-tier suppliers, which are now required to supply complete systems (see above); and growing outsourcing of services, ranging from labour-intensive activities such as cleaning and catering to, increasingly, higher-value-added activities such as computing and software systems, maintenance of plant and buildings and more routine aspects of administration. Ranging across the EU-15, Caprile and Llorens find that existing collective bargaining arrangements have rarely been extended to the third group of outsourced activities, and only with any pattern of consistency to the first-tier suppliers involved in the first and second types of activity.

The particular implication of privatization and marketization in establishing new companies outside of established sector-based bargaining structures has already been noted. Growing outsourcing of public service activities through compulsory competitive tendering procedures also poses problems for established sector agreements. A more general threat to sector bargaining potentially comes from the changing balance between manufacturing and services as new service activities emerge. The service sectors are far from homogenous in terms of their activities, size of company composition, levels of skills and industrial relations, with levels of union density and collective bargaining coverage varying significantly across different service sectors and also between countries. Overall, however, membership of trade unions and employer associations is generally lower in private services than in manufacturing and public services (Dølvik, 2001a). In many countries, moreover, with the exception of finance, the coverage of collective bargaining is markedly lower also. This observation is less true of those countries where arrangements exist to extend coverage across the workforce, such as Belgium where the 'catch-all' auxiliary agreement provides coverage for all white-collar workers not covered by a specific sector agreement, than it is of the larger number of countries where they do not. Also absent in most countries is the tradition of strong workplace organization and local bargaining associated with manufacturing. The result is that the reach of sector agreements as compulsory codes within national economies is less than it was. One important consideration in the (re)centralization towards the national level discussed in Chapter 5, was the need to influence the development of labour costs in services (Streeck, 1999) which in some countries could no longer be realized through sector bargaining.

Reform, erosion or abolition? A range of responses

Turning to the response to these multiple pressures, most attention has focused on the handling of decentralization. The 'organized' process of most of the EU-15 is contrasted with the 'disorganized' of the UK, where the demise of multi-employer bargaining in all but a few sectors has been accompanied by a marked decline in collective bargaining coverage (Traxler, 1998a; Traxler and Behrens, 2002). Yet developments that are often labelled indiscriminately as 'decentralization' take various forms, which are reshaping the relationship between sector and company in different ways. Neither is the decentralization in the countries where it has been regarded as 'organized' solely a top-down process; autonomous bargaining at company level outwith the scope of sector agreements is also playing an important role.

From compulsory codes to flexible frameworks?

Amongst the countries characterized by organized decentralization, the nature of sector agreements has been changing away from enumerating detailed and universally applicable provisions towards establishing core wages and conditions, such as working time, along with guiding principles for subsequent negotiations at lower levels. A variety of devices have been used to introduce scope for company-level variation within the framework of sector agreements. Recalling the terms introduced in Chapter 3, these vary in the degree of the 'softness' introduced into the regulation provided: they differ in the extent to which they are consistent with the principle of universal standards that sector agreements have traditionally promulgated and in the extent to which the regulation provided is 'complete', i.e. prescribes the parameters of local outcomes.

Some forms of organized decentralization remain consistent with the notion of a universal sector standard insofar as variation between companies is introduced according to a principle of equivalence. The sector agreement remains comprehensive in prescribing the main parameters, but becomes less so in detailing implementation. For example, framework agreements dealing with working time have tended to specify the main parameters such as normal weekly working hours or an annualized equivalent, maximum overtime hours and holiday entitlement, leaving actual working time arrangements to be negotiated at company level within a specified frame. Examples of opening clauses providing for equivalence include those in the German chemical and textiles and clothing sector, which specify working time corridors under which actual working time can fluctuate around the standard working week (EIRO, 1997b).

Other forms of organized decentralization, such as 'hardship' and 'opt-out' clauses, but also some opening clauses, expressly provide for derogation from the universal standard, which nonetheless remains in place. Comprehensiveness in prescribing main parameters is, however, compromised and the universal standard potentially becomes less credible. Examples of hardship clauses where the employer is able to pay less than the collectively agreed rate under special economic circumstances are to be found in construction and metalworking in eastern Germany and chemicals in the west (EIRO, 1997b). An 'opt-out' clause for companies undergoing restructuring exists in Belgium's metalworking agreement (see Chapter 7). So-called 'gradual alignment' and 'discount clauses' have been introduced in the textile and footwear sectors in Italy to encourage SMEs to come within the recognized economy for the payment of wages and social charges (Sisson and Artiles, 2000). Opening clauses permitting derogation from the universal standard include those in Austria (metalworking) and Germany (banking, chemicals and metalworking) whereby companies can make local agreements on short-term working time reduction below the normal weekly level with no wage compensation, but with a guarantee of employment security for the term of the reduction (Zagelmeyer, 2000).

Further forms, such as 'incomplete' framework agreements, effectively mean a departure from universal standards in as much as they encourage substantive variation between companies. The main parameters are no longer prescribed by the now less than comprehensive sector agreement. Even wages and working time, which often provided the core of sector agreements' standards, are being affected. In the case of wages, for example, the amount of the increase may be decided in the sector agreement, but distribution of the settlement and the precise ways in which the money is actually paid may be delegated for decision at the company level. In the case of working time, the same is true of reductions in working hours: the decision as to whether these are to be taken in the form of fewer weekly hours or additional holidays can be left to the parties to decide locally. An example of such developments in determining pay and working time is Belgium's banking sector, described in Chapter 7. The same process is even more marked under a shift from universal to minimum standards, as has become the case with the wage provisions of many French sector agreements.

A different approach has been evident in Italy, where the 1993 inter-sector agreement formally demarcated between the respective bargaining competence of the sector and company level (Regalia and Regini, 1998). In effect, this formalized the extensive bargaining that had developed at company level in sectors such as metalworking. However, whilst company bargaining is supposed to take place within the procedural framework specified in the inter-sector agreement, it is no longer subordinate to sector-level bargaining. Matters dealt with in company-level negotiations are not subject to a substantive framework concluded at sector level. The sector is no longer the lynchpin, but one element of an articulated system in which each level has a prescribed role.

A rough continuum is apparent in the degree of 'softness' introduced into sector agreements under these different mechanisms, with complete opening clauses and framework agreements at one end and incomplete frameworks and specifying minimum standards at the other. The further towards the 'softer' end of this continuum, the more the substantive content of sector agreements tends to become 'hollowed-out' and the more they assume a procedural character.

Developments in Denmark and the Netherlands also suggest that the company level is far from being the end-point of the decentralization process. In Denmark, innovative agreements in the banking, insurance and important slaughterhouse sectors concluded in early 2003 effectively introduced *à la carte* provisions. A proportion of the wage package is left open for individual employees to make annual choices between more money and other items including more time off and (in the case of slaughterhouses) increased occupational pension contributions. In financial services, the choices available will be specified by 'catalogues' to be drawn up between the parties at company level (EIRO, 2003b). In the Netherlands, the Foundation of Labour (the joint body responsible for advising the government on socioeconomic decision making) reached an agreement promoting 'tailored employment conditions' in 1999. Referred to as a 'multiple-choice model' (van der Meer, 2001), the understanding encourages negotiators at lower levels to introduce, within the framework of the collective agreement, scope for greater individual choice with regard to certain employment conditions. There might be a trade-off, for example, between 'time and money' or current and deferred remuneration. By mid-2001, 14 sectors had concluded agreements containing such *à la carte* arrangements and a further 14 had commissioned exploratory studies. Individual companies concluding such agreements included ABN-AMRO and Philips (Fajertag, 2002: 271).

Unauthorized and authorized decentralization

An implication of the prevailing terminology of 'centrally coordinated' and 'organized' is that devolution of bargaining activity is a 'top-down' process, occurring with the prior authority and under the control of higher levels. In practice, however, the articulation of bargaining activity at different levels has also reflected a 'bottom-up' dynamic in which higher-level agreements are periodically adjusted to take account of autonomous developments at company level. Such a dynamic has long been a feature, for example, of the relationship between sector- and company-level bargaining in Italy. It is also becoming apparent in countries where it has been less evident hitherto: Hassel and Rehder (2001) trace the emergence of a powerful bottom-up dynamic in Germany. Recognition that company-level bargaining activity results from bottom-up as well as top-down processes suggests a contrast between 'authorized' and 'unauthorized' decentralization. Under the former, the relationship between the sector and company levels is re-adjusted as increased scope for company-level negotiation is introduced into the sector agreement through one or more of the various means identified above. 'Unauthorized' decentralization embraces two phenomena: company agreements in open breach of sector-level standards and agreements on (new) issues on which the sector agreement is silent.

In Germany, recent economy-wide surveys of works councillors have estimated that some 15 per cent of companies are in breach of at least one major substantive aspect of their respective agreements, including pay in six and working time in four out of every ten of such cases (EIRO,

2001). Such breaches of the terms of sector agreements seem, however, to be much more widespread amongst smaller than large employers. A study focusing on three sectors dominated by SMEs – sawmills, wood and plastics and construction materials – found that 80, 85 and 69 per cent of companies, respectively, reported that they deviated from the terms of their respective sector agreements on working time and/or pay (EIRO, 2002f).

Amongst large companies unauthorized company-level bargaining predominantly takes the form of negotiations on matters on which the sector agreement is silent. PECs are a case in point. Hassel and Rehder (2001) indicate that agreements contravening the terms of the sector agreement whilst not unknown are relatively unusual amongst German large companies: 10 per cent of the 150 plus PECs they analysed did so. The cross-country evidence indicates that insofar as PECs address non-wage issues which fall within the scope of sector agreements, they tend to do so within the 'windows' which provide scope for company-level negotiation. Working time arrangements are an example. However, a range of further issues addressed by PECs, such as work organization and continuing training, are ones on which sector agreements tend to be silent (Sisson and Artiles, 2000). Crucially, the dynamic of many PECs is bottom-up, driven by imperatives at company level. As such, they are contributing to what Hassel and Rehder contend is an inversion of the established relationship between the sector and company levels.

Adapting Sisson's (1987: 41–2) typology of different forms of company bargaining enables us to capture this evolving relationship between the sector and company levels, especially amongst large companies. Under the first type, company bargaining is 'administrative' and essentially concerned with the application of the terms and conditions of the multi-employer agreement. The second, 'supplementary', type involves the negotiation of add-ons or extensions to the sector agreement's terms and conditions within its framework. Under the third 'autonomous' type, pay and major conditions are primarily shaped by company-level negotiations whilst the sector agreement specifies minimum standards which are of no direct consequence. Adding a fourth, 'semi-autonomous' type captures instances where company-level negotiations are more detached from the sector agreement than under the supplementary mode. In this instance the sector no longer provides a complete framework for the range of issues on company-level agenda, but it nonetheless continues to have a tangible impact on the evolution of major terms and conditions. Over time, processes of authorized and unauthorized decentralization can be expected to be reflected in successive movement away from the 'administrative' and 'supplementary' categories and towards the 'semi-autonomous' and even 'autonomous'. The pace at which such movement takes place is nonetheless likely to differ from country to country, reflecting the nature and extent of the legal framework – considered below – and from sector to sector, which Chapter 7's comparison of banking and metalworking makes clear.

Reform rather than abolition – the 'flexible rigidity' of multi-employer agreements

Even though sector agreements face serious challenges, both ideological and practical, reform rather than abolition seems to be the main objective:

> In general, firms have exerted little pressure for radical decentralisation … while employers are anxious to see greater flexibility at corporate level, they wish also to preserve the framework of labour peace provided by a structure of higher-level agreements. (Ferner and Hyman, 1998: xvi)

Path dependency is a major consideration: the tried and tested nature of existing arrangements, it seems, invests them with a high degree of legitimacy in the eyes of both managers and employees. This particularly applies if these arrangements are widely applied in other workplaces with which the actors are most familiar, i.e. those within the sector (Arrowsmith and Sisson, 1999; Marsden, 1999). An element of opportunism is also involved. Companies may not necessarily be greatly committed to the principle of multi-employer bargaining. For some, the sector agreement nonetheless provides a useful framework within which to negotiate restructuring. For others, it offers protection against the development of collective bargaining at the Euro-company level.

Less pragmatically, although neutralization of the workplace is seemingly less of a major incentive for employers, crucial elements of the traditional logic of multi-employer still hold: it continues to set common standards, which help to prevent undercutting and guarantee consistency; it also usually provides some mechanism for resolving disputes and/or 'peace obligation', thereby contributing to social peace. The last point is especially relevant for employers as well as the state. As Chapter 7 shows, even large companies are nervous about becoming the 'target' for trade union attention if they withdraw from their sector agreements. In the 'Rhineland' and 'Nordic' countries in particular the 'peace obligation' enshrined in sector agreements continues to be valued by employers (Traxler *et al.*, 2001: 137). In the wake of IG-Metall's historic defeat in the 2003 conflict over working time in eastern Germany, Gesamtmetall reaffirmed that sector bargaining 'has substantial advantages, one of the most important being the obligation to refrain from industrial action during the period in which regional agreements are valid' (cited in EIRO, 2003f). There are also worries about the implications of pushing too far: unions have countered employer demands for further decentralization in Germany, Sweden and Norway with the threat to push for the right to strike to be given to local employee representatives. Containing, if not neutralizing, the workplace would seem to be a continuing employer priority.

A second possible explanation for continued employer adherence to sector bargaining is that they 'have usually lacked the power to escape multi-employer bargaining ... [which] may be restricted by two factors: associational strength and labour law upholding multi-employer settlements' (Traxler *et al.*, 2001: 135). In practice, associational strength tends either to be underpinned by the second factor or, as in the Nordic countries, by the discipline employers feel they need in the face of extensive union organizational coverage. Apart from the UK and Ireland, multi-employer agreements are not only legally enforceable contracts between the parties, but also compulsory codes – as Chapter 2 established. By a process of extension (for example, in France and Spain) or 'customary law' (for example, Italy and Sweden), multi-employer agreements become de facto a private system of regulation (Sisson, 1987; Traxler, 1998a). In the absence of such agreements, governments would have to intervene directly in the employment relationship with legislation, as British governments are increasingly finding. Consequently, they remain an important instrument through which the state has been able to 'steer' social developments, delegating responsibility for the details to the social partners and thereby increasing the legitimacy of the outcome.

Yet, as has been demonstrated, continuation of multi-employer bargaining has also entailed changes in the nature and content of sector agreements. There are also grounds for contending that the traditional relationship between the sector and company levels has become inverted. This raises wider questions about the conditions under which bargaining systems successfully adapt to new contingencies. Ferner and Hyman (1998: xxiv) discuss this capacity in terms of the 'flexible rigidity' of different national systems: 'developments in several [west European] countries in the last few years suggest that institutional robustness and successful adaptation depend on a peculiar combination of flexibility and rigidity'. Towards elaborating what might distinguish successful from unsuccessful combinations of 'flexible rigidity', Chapter 7 examines developments in three countries where sector-level bargaining remains entrenched.

The prospects for sector agreements

The developments described here, and in particular the changing balance between sector and company bargaining, raise understandable concerns. Trade unions worry about the danger of 'micro-corporatism', increasing diversity and the threat to cohesion and solidarity, the potential for 'concession bargaining' and 'regime competition', and the 'hollowing out' of sector agreements and the fragmentation of the multi-employer bargaining (Hyman, 1994; Streeck, 1998). By contrast, employers' organizations are concerned about securing consensus among their members for any agreement, while many companies complain about the costs and time involved in pursuing negotiations at both sector and company levels (Hornung-Draus, 2001). The collective action problem that both sides are facing is also increasing the likelihood of failure to agree.

This does not necessarily herald the demise of sector agreements, however. The extent to which sector agreements remain entrenched in west European countries is likely to be shaped by two considerations. One, introduced in Chapter 2, is the legal framework. Thus, the incentive to remain involved in sector bargaining is particularly strong in Germany, where agreements are legally binding, imposing a 'peace obligation' on trade unions; where there is an explicit division of responsibilities between trade unions and works councils; and where, although the procedure is rarely used, non-member companies can be obliged to follow the terms of agreements through the statutory provision for extension. It is also strong in the Nordic countries, where the first feature combines with high associational strength. In other countries, such as France or Italy, where the right to engage in industrial action is much less restricted and the division of responsibilities partial or absent, the incentive is not as strong. It was always weakest in the UK, where none of these considerations applied. The possibility that prevailing sector bargaining arrangements disintegrate, as has happened in Britain, hardly seems feasible, given their very different form and status in other countries. Yet much will also depend on employer and trade union preferences, which is the second consideration. If lessons drawn from the UK experience are correct, a critical factor will be the extent to which trade unions continue to seek to transfer benefits won in the larger companies into the sector agreement.

How far can decentralization go without undermining the capacity of sector agreements to set and enforce the common rule? And what is the likelihood of 'disorganized' variants of decentralization emerging within sector-based systems? There are a number of possible directions that sector bargaining might take. A first possibility is that the scope for company-level negotiation is progressively widened as 'organized decentralization' is taken further and sector agreements increasingly become framework agreements, as many employers' organizations have argued. The frameworks specified might introduce variation below company level and introduce different options for individual workers, or à la carte agreements, as has occurred in certain sectors in Denmark and the Netherlands. A variant on this theme would involve the respective roles of the different bargaining levels being redefined, as might re-occur within Italy's multi-tiered structure.

A third possibility is that twin-track arrangements emerge: large employers may abandon sector bargaining and establish their own company agreements, leaving the sector agreement to regulate the terms and conditions for small and medium-sized companies. This could be either by design, which is under consideration in the Danish banking sector, or by default, as has recently occurred in Dutch banking. The fourth possibility is what might be described as the 'Irish' solution: in smaller countries sector bargaining finds itself squeezed between the national and the company level. A variant would be something similar to the 'auxiliary' agreements of Belgium, which apply to white-collar workers outwith the jurisdiction of established sector agreements. Indeed it was national rather than sector employers' organizations that were originally the more prominent in countries such as Sweden, Denmark and even Italy, reflecting the difficulties employers and, to a lesser extent, trade unions experienced in developing organization at sector level (Sisson, 1987).

Some of these possibilities, notably the third, entail a combination of 'organized' and 'disorganized' elements of decentralization under which the longer-term viability of multi-employer bargaining rests on the company-based bargaining amongst large employers continuing to be the subject of a measure of coordination by the sector-level actors. Alternatively, recalling the distinction between 'authorized' and 'unauthorized' decentralization, as well as more company-level bargaining within the scope of sector agreements, there may also be more autonomous bargaining outside the limits specified. Indeed, the very process of 'authorized' decentralization may, by opening up a company-level bargaining agenda, be encouraging 'unauthorized' decentralization as employers become more confident in negotiating with their own workforces. If as a result of continuing employer pressure for decentralization, sector agreements become wholly 'soft' in their content, they run the risk of decline by attrition. As Traxler *et al.* (2001: 134) observe: 'organised decentralisation may prove self-defeating in the long run'.

Conclusions and implications

Sector bargaining faces challenges on many fronts, with its logic increasingly questioned. The rise of company bargaining within existing multi-employer structures has long been a feature reflecting widespread pressure from management for greater scope to negotiate working and employment practices to meet changing market conditions. EMU is adding to the pressure, pushing local management to restructure the organization's costs and capacities. The negotiation of PECs is in turn bringing about considerable changes in the structure, process and agenda of collective bargaining, with significant 'spillover' effects for sector-level agreements. Simultaneously, the progressive creation of a pan-European product market has heightened the interdependence between sector-level arrangements in different countries. Whereas trade unions have been anxious to develop cross-border coordination to contain the potentially detrimental effects of regime competition between countries, employers' organizations remain strongly opposed. A further challenge is not directly connected to EMU. The emergence of new business activities without established collective bargaining arrangements poses a major threat to the comprehensive regulation of the labour market through inclusive multi-employer structures, as well as blurring established boundaries between sectors.

Notwithstanding these challenges, sector-based bargaining systems do not seem about to collapse, for two main reasons: the legal support that the state continues to give; and the benefits to employers in terms of the 'peace obligation' and the restrictions on the activities of local employee representatives. Pressure for further decentralization seems likely to be contained within sector (and cross-sector) frameworks, with the UK remaining as a distinct case of 'disorganized' decentralization. 'Reform rather than revolution' appears to be the order of the day. Sector agreements are increasingly taking a framework form, tending towards 'soft' regulation in the terms introduced in Chapter 3, leaving considerable scope for flexibility at company level. Much of what is happening is better understood in terms of 'pull-down' rather than 'top-down' in which sector agreements are increasingly adjusting to company-level developments rather than mapping out their direction, as occurred previously. Unclear is whether this transformation will ultimately prove corrosive of their basic functions or whether there is likely to be a readjustment around some form of two-tier system, perhaps based on the national level in the case of the smaller countries and the sector in the case of the larger ones.

These developments, and in particular the changing balance between sector and company bargaining, are more or less evident cross-nationally. Often labelled indiscriminately as 'decentralization' they nonetheless take various forms, reflecting the changing character of sector agreements and their relationship to companies. Both country and sector differences are significant. By country, the extent and precise forms reflect above all the legal framework of industrial relations. By sector, it is activities exposed to international competition that are the most affected, with the implications tending to be greater for larger companies than medium and smaller ones. One result of the changing balance between sector and company bargaining is therefore to bring about increased diversity within countries, but – as the review of PECs showed – also convergence within sectors across countries, thereby adding to the complexity of the emerging multi-level system. Chapter 7 develops and illustrates this argument.

7
The Changing Balance between Sector and Company Bargaining: Two Sectors Compared

Chapter 6 established that the sector-level collective bargaining arrangements, which constitute a cornerstone of the industrial relations systems of most west European countries, find themselves under increasing pressure. Of the challenges identified, that posed by the rise of company-level collective bargaining activity is foremost. In the face of growing international competition, there has been a widespread trend towards more decentralized bargaining arrangements giving management greater scope to negotiate working and employment practices appropriate to the circumstances of the company or its constituent units. The process of EMU has served both to unleash extensive restructuring and rationalization and to extend and intensify competition across borders. As Chapter 6 argued, under a context of restructuring pressure for further decentralization is reinforced as the bargaining agenda becomes increasingly oriented towards addressing questions of competitiveness, adaptability and employment. Internationalization of production and market servicing on a pan-European basis makes multi-employer bargaining at national sector level appear increasingly anomalous: in many sectors it can no longer take wages and conditions out of competition within the new spatial boundaries of the relevant product market. Hence the growing cross-border dimension to collective bargaining also has implications for the balance between the sector and company levels. Chapter 6 also underlined the challenge to established sector-based structures coming from the emergence of new industries and new forms of product delivery in existing industries, prompting reconfiguration of activities within and outwith established companies and the blurring of established boundaries between sectors. How sectors and leading companies handle this last challenge can result in step, as distinct from incremental, changes in the balance between collective bargaining at the sector and company levels.

This chapter draws on findings from our in-depth comparative, cross-country and cross-sector study – details of which are provided in the Appendix – of collective bargaining developments at sector and company level in two sectors – metalworking and banking and in four countries – Belgium, Germany, Italy and the UK. It throws more specific light on the shifting balance between collective bargaining at the sector and company levels. Although in the first three countries, multi-employer, sector bargaining remains a fundamental pillar of labour market regulation, in the UK it has largely disappeared: inclusion of the UK provides a point of reference in assessing the continuing robustness of sector-level arrangements elsewhere. In drawing on findings from both the sector and company levels, the analysis is informed by 'top-down' and 'bottom-up' perspectives on the evolution of the relationship between bargaining arrangements at these two levels.

After establishing the rationale for examining the sectors and countries in question, and providing a short economic and industrial relations profile of each, the chapter's assessment of the shifting balance between collective bargaining at the sector and company levels is informed by six sets of questions:

- what forms is the introduction of greater scope for variation at company level within sector agreements taking?
- what are the consequences of the changing bargaining agenda for the balance between sector and company levels?
- what is the extent and nature of any company-level bargaining not expressly authorized by the sector agreement?
- what is the position and role of large, multinational employers in opening up greater space for company-level negotiation and what explains their continued attachment, or otherwise, to multi-employer bargaining?
- are existing sector agreements adapting, or new sector arrangements emerging, to regulate new business activities?; and
- does the growing cross-border dimension to collective bargaining represent an incipient further pressure for decentralization to company level?

The purpose of the chapter is also comparative, between sectors and across countries. It charts the similarities and differences in the handling of the multiple challenges to sector collective bargaining and in the changing balance between the sector and company levels. It finds further evidence of the simultaneous occurrence of processes of convergence and divergence, in the shape of continuing differences between countries which are common across the two sectors within a given country, but also of some striking parallels within each of the two sectors across national boundaries which also represent differences within a given country.

The countries and sectors in focus

The countries reflect differences in size of economy and integration with other EU economies, as well as different systems of industrial relations. Germany, Italy and the UK are all large economies, whilst the Belgian economy is smaller. Belgium, Germany and Italy are part of the Euro zone, whilst the UK has remained outside. As a member of the 'de facto' Deutsche Mark zone preceding monetary union, economic interdependence between Belgium and Germany far exceeds that between either country and Italy. The collective bargaining systems of Belgium, Germany and Italy represent (differing) instances of 'organized decentralization' (Traxler, 1995). The UK, where sector-level collective bargaining has all but disappeared, is the main instance of 'disorganized decentralization' in Western Europe.

There are differences between Belgium, Germany and Italy in the means by which horizontal coordination across sectors occurs and in the extent to which sector agreements are effective in prescribing the scope for company-level bargaining. In Belgium and Italy, cross-sector agreements play an important but differing role, whereas in Germany there is no cross-sector agreement and coordination is secured through pattern bargaining (Traxler *et al.*, 2001). There are legal provisions for extension in Belgium and Germany, more widely used in the first than the second, whilst in Italy extension practice derives from 'customary law'. In what Vilrokx and Van Leemput (1998: 318) describe as 'a highly institutionalised pyramid of negotiation', the cross-sector agreement in Belgium specifies the parameters for the subsequent sector negotiations and can introduce space for company-level negotiations. In the case of failure to agree, the state has on several occasions imposed a settlement. In Italy, the parameters of collective bargaining at sector and company levels are formally governed by the 1993 cross-sector tripartite agreement, which 'specified in detail for the first time the respective competences of the national-sector and company or local bargaining levels' (Regalia and Regini, 1998: 493). Essentially, bargaining over cost-of-living related wage increases is to take place at sector level and bargaining over productivity and performance at company level. 'Bargaining governability', ensuring that company-level bargaining is contained within the parameters established in higher-level agreements, is considered by Traxler *et al.* (2001) to be relatively 'high' in Germany and relatively 'low' in Belgium and Italy, reflecting differences in the legal framework of bargaining and particularly the strength of the peace obligation in Germany as compared with the other two countries. In this one respect Belgium and Italy are closer to the situation which formerly prevailed under multi-employer agreements in the UK.

The logic of competitiveness has been inserted into the bargaining agenda of sector-level negotiations in Belgium, Germany and Italy in different ways. In Belgium, as Chapter 6 noted, the 1996 law on competitiveness ties wage increases to movements in labour costs in its neighbouring economies (France, Germany and the Netherlands) and the cross-sector agreement specifies the wage margin that is open for negotiation at sector (and company) level. In Italy, the 1993 cross-sector agreement stipulates that the cost-of-living wage increases negotiated at sector level every four years are tied to anticipated inflation, with an interim adjustment in the light of actual inflation negotiated every two years. In Germany, wage increases at sector level have not been constrained in such ways by either law or tripartite agreement. Instead, the state tries to shape bargaining outcomes through the provision of detailed economic data and forecasts to the social partners.

The two sectors provide contrasts in terms of market structures, production organization, and institutional structures; the dynamics of the widespread restructuring occurring in each also differ. Metalworking – which accounts for over 5 per cent of the EU-15's total workforce – is a key manufacturing sector in each of the four countries, long open to international competition. Large numbers of SMEs notwithstanding, it is increasingly dominated by MNCs which in some parts of the sector are internationally-integrated manufacturers. Further internationalization is moving in the direction of global integration of operations by the major players. Finance – which represents around 3.5 per cent of the workforce in the EU-15 – is a significant part of the service economy in all four countries. Investment banking is already characterized by globally organized operations and increasingly too commercial banking operations are European or wider in scope. Retail banking, however, remains a largely domestic affair with some sharp contrasts between EU countries in the extent to which domestic markets are dominated by a few players.

Chapter 6 referred to the major changes in business activities, technologies and products underway in both sectors. In metalworking, large companies in Western Europe are moving in one or both of two directions: towards a focus on systems and solutions, in which the emphasis is on R&D and IT activities; and into after-sales service, in which the brand rather than the product is the focus. Accordingly, there is less emphasis on the actual manufacture of the product, which in some cases is being outsourced altogether. In the automotive sub-sector, in which four of our five metalworking company cases are located, the cost and price transparency afforded by EMU combined with overcapacity is intensifying competition further and with it pressure to rationalize capacity and reduce costs. One result is further consolidation of ownership amongst the major vehicle manufacturers reflected in a series of high-profile acquisitions, divestments and strategic alliances. These manufacturers are increasingly sourcing their components on a European, and world-wide, rather than local basis, leading to consolidation amongst the major components suppliers. Increasingly these major suppliers are becoming assemblers of systems, with the individual components being manufactured by second- or third-tier producers (Sisson and Marginson, 2000).

In banking, new modes of product delivery via the telephone and the internet are a major development with important implications for banks' extensive branch networks. Internal restructuring is seeing the creation of separate subsidiaries for direct banking, and in some instances back-office operations. Financial deregulation has resulted in increased competition between financial institutions as new providers move into established markets and new financial products proliferate. A further consequence in some countries is the emergence of new 'bancassurance' organizations combining both banking and insurance activities. An important dimension of the recent wave of mergers and acquisitions is consolidation of banks within national boundaries. In several countries, including Belgium, Germany and Italy, virtually all of the leading banking groups have been involved in within-country consolidation (or attempts at such) in the past few years. In the first instance, at least, EMU would seem to be stimulating the creation of 'national champions' in retail banking better able to compete within the single market. As compared with the degree of national consolidation, cross-border mergers and acquisitions have been less prominent (Sisson and Marginson, 2000).

Turning to collective bargaining arrangements, sector agreements remain influential in metalworking in Belgium, Germany and Italy, although company-level bargaining with either trade unions or works councils is well established within or alongside sector agreements. It is the sole level of bargaining in the UK. In Belgium, metalworking is regarded by both employers' organizations and trade unions as a leading sector in terms of its influence in inter-sector negotiations and as a pace-setter for bargaining innovations in the production sector. Collective bargaining coverage approaches 90 per cent. In Germany, metalworking has long been regarded as the pace-setting sector (Hassel and Schulten, 1998), collective bargaining coverage in western Germany being around 75 per cent. Negotiations are regionally based, but in practice are tightly coordinated by the federal employers' organization, Gesamtmetall, and the IG-Metall trade union. The pilot agreement has traditionally been concluded in Baden-Württemberg, where IG-Metall has a strong position, and generalized to other regions and districts. In Italy, metalworking is also regarded as the lead production sector. There is a single national agreement which under the 1993 cross-sector agreement has provenance over general, cost-of-living-related wage negotiations. Bargaining over pay related to performance at company level should be additional. Collective bargaining coverage approaches 90 per cent. In the UK, up until 1989 a two-tier national system of pay bargaining prevailed in metalworking under which national minimum rates were 'topped up' through local bargaining. In practice, actual levels of pay and conditions were increasingly determined in local negotiations. This was particularly so amongst the major multinational manufacturers, several of which had withdrawn from national bargaining during the course of the 1980s. In 1990, the employers' organization withdrew from the national negotiating arrangements altogether. Subsequently, collective bargaining has been on a single-employer basis and coverage is a little over 30 per cent.

In banking, there are multiple sector agreements covering banking in Belgium, Germany and Italy, whilst in the UK there are no longer any sector agreements. Company-level agreements with trade unions or works councils are more recent in origin than in metalworking, but now constitute the only level of bargaining in the UK and are becoming more widespread amongst large banks in the other three countries. In Belgium, there are different employers' organizations and trade unions covering the respective agreements for private banks and public credit institutions. Collective bargaining coverage approaches 90 per cent. In Germany, there are four separate banking agreements for, respectively, private banks, cooperative banks, state banks and savings banks. In practice, the agreements for the private, cooperative and state banks are very similar. The three employers' associations have an alliance under which they conduct negotiations together. All three sub-sectors were organized by the same main two trade unions, HBV and DAG (both now part of

Ver.di). Savings banks are covered by the public sector agreement. Collective bargaining coverage for banking in western Germany is about 65 per cent. In Italy, collective bargaining in banking has also been fragmented with separate agreements for three different sub-sectors – national banks, cooperative banks and savings banks – and for different occupational groups within these sub-sectors (respectively bank officers and managers). The four agreements in the national and savings banks were combined into a single agreement in 1999, and the cooperative bank agreements are expected to be consolidated into this agreement in the near future. The coverage of collective agreements is almost 90 per cent. In the UK, the national sector agreement in England, which set basic rates of pay and conditions, was terminated in 1987 when the employers' organization – which grouped the major clearing banks – withdrew from national bargaining. The separate sector agreement for Scotland had been terminated a year earlier. Subsequently bargaining over pay and major conditions has been on a single-employer basis. Forty per cent of employees are covered by collective agreements.

The ten company cases (one in each sector in Belgium, Germany and Italy and two in each in the UK – for which summary data are provided in the Appendix) are all large organizations in the country concerned and, simultaneously, MNCs with extensive operations in other European countries. In Belgium, Germany and Italy, the six companies concerned are either the leading or one of a leading group of companies within the employer's association, and therefore influential in shaping developments in their respective sector agreements. In analysing the differential impact of country and sector factors on organizational responses to the existing balance between sector- and company-level bargaining, the nature of the case study companies as large and dominant players allows wider conclusions to be drawn which are relevant to other large firms and therefore the sector. Although company-specific features are important in shaping collective bargaining traditions and current agenda, there are market, transactions cost and power factors common to other large firms that shape a shared sector and country context for decisions. It is this 'firm in sector' (Kenis, 1992; Smith *et al.*, 1990) analytical framework that the analysis draws on.

Further decentralization: the changing role of sector agreements

Dimensions of decentralization

In considering the implications of 'centrally co-ordinated' (Ferner and Hyman, 1998) or 'organised' (Traxler, 1995) decentralization for the balance between sector and company levels, the different *means* by which greater company-level variation is introduced are potentially crucial but, as Chapter 6 observed, have rarely been considered in any detail. Some forms of organized decentralization, such as complete framework agreements and many opening clauses, remain consistent with the notion of a universal sector standard insofar as variation between companies is introduced according to a principle of equivalence. The sector agreement remains comprehensive in prescribing the main parameters, but becomes less so in detailing implementation. Other forms, such as 'hardship' and 'opt-out' clauses, expressly provide for derogation from the universal standard, which nonetheless remains in place. Because comprehensiveness in prescribing main parameters is compromised, the universal standard potentially becomes less credible. Further forms, such as incomplete framework agreements, effectively mean a departure from universal standards in as much as they encourage substantive variation between companies. The main parameters are no longer all prescribed by the sector agreement, which is rendered less than comprehensive. This is even more true of a shift in emphasis from universal to minimum standards. Each of these developments, to a greater or a lesser extent, tend to 'hollow out' the substantive content of sector agreements, with the result that they increasingly assume a more procedural character.

Metalworking

The scope for company-level variation within the metalworking agreements has widened in recent years in Belgium and Germany. In both, the sector agreements remain pretty comprehensive and movement towards a more framework character has been incremental. Yet in Belgium a degree of flexibility in the application of the sector agreement is evident amongst the internationally integrated automotive companies. In Italy, greater formal scope for company-level negotiation was established under the 1993 cross-sector agreement with the sector level becoming less comprehensive in substantive terms. This demarcation between the two levels is increasingly being called into question.

In Belgium, the earliest opening clause deals with working time flexibility. There is also a hardship clause under which companies being restructured can move outside of the terms of the agreement. In recent years further opening clauses have been agreed on supplementary pension schemes, introduction of financial participation schemes at company level and, in 2001, on the distribution of a proportion of the cross-sector pay increase. These clauses establish a framework for subsequent company-level negotiation, the specification of which is a growing feature of sector negotiations. Use of the opening and hardship clauses is regulated by the sector-level parties: trade unions in particular deploy their right to 'sign-off' the resulting company agreements to closely control developments. However, in the case of the large automotive companies, flexibility is evident in the application of the sector agreement. Under formal derogations from the agreement, these tend to fix their own agreements for pay and working time. The process is 'organized': the companies liaise closely with the employers' association over company-specific negotiations, whilst the trade unions acknowledge the rationale for such a flexible approach given the tensions which arise from the internal, cross-country comparisons which the plants concerned are subject to. *Belmetal* is an example: since 1996 it has concluded two three-year agreements dealing with pay and major conditions.

The opening clause on working time flexibility in the German metalworking agreement dates back to 1984. Pressure for further decentralization in the 1990s was significantly augmented by employers' reaction to the harsh economic conditions confronting companies in the eastern *Länder*, prompting the introduction of a hardship clause in the east (1993), subsequently extended to the west (1996). In the west, the 1990s also saw the introduction of opening clauses on working time in the context of safeguarding employment, payments structure and performance pay and, in 2002, a special hardship clause enabling pay reductions for a fixed period and a new framework agreement introducing a single status payments system. Use of opening and hardship clauses is closely regulated by the parties: the hardship clause in particular is strictly policed by IG-Metall. As a result of these clauses, company-level negotiations were said to no longer be solely 'administrative' implementing the terms of agreements but 'creative' – 'there's more space for variation' (union official).

Italy's 1993 cross-sector agreement signalled the formalization of increasing company-level negotiating activity, in which metalworking was prominent (Regalia and Regini, 1998). As explained above, the agreement demarcates the respective roles of the sector and company levels; there has been no recourse to opening clauses. Company-level bargaining over pay related to performance occurs in around 30 per cent of metalworking companies in the Lombardy region, which is traditionally influential in developments within the sector. The demarcation between the two levels has become increasingly contested. The criteria for uprating cost-of-living awards have been the subject of disagreement not only between employers and trade unions but also between unions. Inter-union differences were laid open in 2001 with the conclusion of a sector pay agreement opposed by CGIL-FIOM, the largest metalworking union, a development which recurred when the agreement was renewed in 2003 (EIRO, 2003e). The criteria for measuring performance at company level, to which any pay increases are linked, have also been the subject of ongoing controversy: employers' prefer a profitability, whilst unions favour a productivity, measure.

Banking

The scope for company-level variation within banking agreements has grown over recent years, although there is noticeable variation between countries. In Belgium, the incomplete nature of recent sector agreements on pay and working time leaves considerable scope for company-level negotiation. In Germany, the agreement remains more closed, with a limited number of opening clauses. In Italy, the sector agreement has provided a detailed framework for restructuring within the sector, to be implemented by the parties at the company level.

There are several sector-wide agreements in Belgium dealing with specific issues. On some matters, such as job classification and payments structure, agreements remain detailed and specific. On pay and working time, however, between 1982 and 1997 there were no changes in the agreements. Technically, both remained in force but bargaining activity shifted to company level. Considerable differences, especially over working time, emerged between banks. Reversing the trend, new three-year sector agreements were concluded on pay and working time in 1998 and renewed in 2001. Reflecting the diversity of company-specific arrangements that needed to be bridged, these are incomplete providing for considerable flexibility in application. The pay agreement specifies an annual amount, whose distribution is then the subject of company-level negotiations. On working time, the way of achieving the decrease from 1,780 to 1,620 annual hours specified in the sector agreement is left open to company-level negotiations. Unlike in the case of metalworking, there is no hardship clause. Overall, the sector agreements would appear to be in a phase of flux, evidencing movement towards more open, incomplete framework arrangements.

Under the private banks sector agreement in Germany, openings for company-level negotiations are more recent in origin than in metalworking. The framework agreement giving scope for company-level negotiations on working time arrangements was the earliest. Over the past five years opening clauses have been concluded on working time reductions in the context of employment security and long-term working time accounts. The 2002 agreement signalled a major development with the introduction of a sector opening clause for performance-related variable pay, implementable through company agreements with works councils (EIRO, 2003a). On one further matter the sector agreement is left partially open: the total amount of bonus payments is fixed in the sector negotiations, but its distribution is the subject of company-level negotiations. There is no equivalent of the hardship clause found in the metalworking agreement. The contested nature of the agreement's evolution is underlined by ongoing conflict over flexible working time arrangements, and in particular Saturday working.

The handling of extensive restructuring and consequent large-scale redundancies have dominated negotiations in the recent period in Italy. The issues involved have been dealt with at sector level, thereby enhancing its authority, with the 1999 agreement establishing a framework for implementation at company level covering redundancy provision (including establishing a sector-wide redundancy fund), training and employability, changes in occupational status, job reclassification and outsourcing. Substantive company-level negotiations deal with pay linked to performance. Unlike metalworking, the two-tier system of pay determination was not seen to be problematic by either side. If anything, the authority of the sector agreement has been augmented in recent years through the establishment of the comprehensive framework for addressing restructuring.

Summary and prospects

Overall, although a complex picture emerges one trend is clear: the direction of movement is for agreements to become less comprehensive in content, and more procedural in nature. Also clear is that the agreements in the two German sectors remain the most closed. In practice, if not in form, there appears to be greater 'elasticity' in the application of sector agreements in the two sectors in Belgium. In Italy, substantive negotiation is authorized at company level in both sectors. As between the sectors, the agreements in metalworking tend to be relatively more comprehensive in the range of issues addressed than in banking; in part reflecting this, they also contain more formal openings for negotiations at company level than do those in banking. For instance, the hardship clauses evident in metalworking have no equivalent in banking. If this suggests more 'elasticity' in the metalworking agreements, it is important to note that trade unions in metalworking exercise a greater measure of control over the application of opening clauses than those in banking. Also, the extent of the framework provisions in the banking agreements in Belgium and Italy (albeit taking differing 'incomplete' and 'complete' forms) exceeds anything currently found amongst their metalworking counterparts.

Developments in Italy's banking sector indicate that issues of competitiveness, adaptability and employment can be handled in a comprehensive way at sector level, through developing a common framework. Yet this was the exception rather than the rule across the three countries. In both sectors a key finding, elaborated in the next section, is that employment, adaptability and competitiveness have been prominent issues in the extension of company bargaining into areas on which sector agreements have hitherto been silent. The choices employers are making over the level at which such issues are handled are a crucial consideration in shaping the evolution of sector-based arrangements.

Employers' associations in the two sectors are pressing for reforms which would further augment the scope for company-level differentiation. Those in metalworking and banking in Germany have both adopted reform programmes in recent years. The 1997 'Frankfurt declaration' of Gesamtmetall calls for a reduction in the scope and content of the sector agreement to focus on a few core issues, stipulation of minimum rather than standard provisions, the introduction of a general 'company clause' enabling companies with economic problems to 'opt out' of the agreement for a fixed period and the possibility to do so through an agreement with the works councils and not the trade union. Pressure for such reform is likely to intensify following IG-Metall's defeat in the 2003 dispute over working time in eastern Germany (EIRO, 2003f). The 1998 statement by AGV Banken similarly called for the sector agreement to focus on a few core topics, including time and money, to set minimum rather than standard provisions and to increase the room for company level manoeuvre through more opening and optional clauses. Similar aspirations were expressed by employer counterparts in our field interviews in Belgium and, to a lesser extent, in banking in Italy. In Italian metalworking employer concerns are focused on a reform of the two-tier system for negotiating pay.

Trade union responses to employers' proposals for further scope for company-level negotiations vary. In some instances, as in banking in Germany, future differentiation for sub-activities within the sector agreement was said to be likely. In German metalworking, IG-Metall has countered the employers' 'Frankfurt declaration' with proposals of its own, including specifying a 'menu' of equivalent options in the sector agreement from which company-level agreements could select (EIRO, 1997c) and, more recently, additional recourse to opening clauses and/or company-specific supplementary agreements to enhance differentiation within a centrally specified and controlled framework (EIRO, 2002d). In Italy, there are differences in emphasis between trade unions in both sectors, including disagreement over the relative importance of the sector and company levels in negotiations over pay in metalworking.

Pull-down as well as top-down: the nature and extent of company-level bargaining

Authorized and unauthorized decentralization

An implication of the prevailing terminology of 'centrally coordinated' and 'organized' is, as Chapter 6 contended, that devolution of bargaining activity is a 'top-down' process, occurring with the prior authority and under the control of higher levels. In practice, however, the articulation of bargaining activity at different levels has also reflected a 'bottom-up' dynamic in which higher-level agreements are periodically adjusted to take account of autonomous developments at company level. Recognition that company-level bargaining activity results from bottom-up as well as top-down processes underlies the contrast between 'authorized' and 'unauthorized' decentralization introduced in Chapter 6. Under the former, the relationship between sector and company levels is readjusted as increased scope for company-level negotiation is introduced into the sector agreement through one or more of the various devices identified above. 'Unauthorized' decentralization, which is the focus of this section, embraces two phenomena: company agreements in open breach of sector-level standards; and agreements on (new) issues on which the sector agreement is silent.

Scope and focus of the company bargaining agenda

Amongst the large companies which tend to lead developments in sector agreements, Chapter 6 established that unauthorized company-level bargaining predominantly takes the form of negotiations on matters on which the sector agreement is silent. None of our six case companies in Belgium, Germany and Italy had concluded any agreement that breached sector standards; the leading role of these companies in their respective employers' associations probably makes such a development difficult to contemplate for either side. In general, reflecting established trade union strength within companies, there is more negotiating activity at company level in metalworking than the formal picture charted in the previous section suggests. These autonomous company-level negotiations are more widespread and more extensive in the range of issues addressed than in banking, where our sector-level respondents reported that negotiations rarely went beyond the parameters laid down in the sector agreement. A more extensive company-level bargaining agenda was, however, evident in two of the continental banking case companies as well as in the UK.

Metalworking

There is considerable company-level negotiating activity in Belgian metalworking on matters not covered by sector agreements. Almost all of the major automotive manufacturers have concluded company-level PECs (Zagelmeyer, 2000). The potential scope of the company-level negotiating agenda is indicated by the contents of the second three-year agreement at *Belmetal*. As well as pay and payments systems, for which there was formal derogation from the sector agreement, the agreement covered additional benefits, promotion principles, scheduling of time-off and working time arrangements. In addition, a number of companies (including *Belmetal*) have agreements for a working week which is below the 38 hours specified in the sector agreement.

In Germany, company-level PECs, extending to matters on which the sector agreement is silent, are widespread amongst large metalworking companies (Hassel and Rehder, 2001). Union respondents commented that, as a result, the relationship between wage agreements and company-specific extra payments is changing; company-level negotiations are now tending to qualify the actual sector wage increase – thereby reducing company-specific wage premia – rather than supplementing it, as happened in the past. Such developments, it was observed, can have feedbacks into the sector agreement: 'Opening clauses can also confirm what has already taken place – it's a dynamic relationship' (union official).

In Italy, there is evident discrepancy between the formal system specified in the 1993 agreement and actual practice, in which the role of company-level negotiations is greater than that prescribed. Controversies over pay between and amongst the parties have already been mentioned. Although shift patterns and the use of atypical working should be the subject of national-level negotiation, employers in effect negotiate on these matters at company level in order, it was said, to avoid paying more than once for changes. At *Italmetal*, in addition to group-level negotiations over pay related to performance, there are plant-level negotiations on the distribution of working time and other flexibility-related issues. PECs have been concluded at several of the company's sites, and at other leading metalworking companies (Zagelmeyer, 2000).

The theme of handling the consequences of restructuring found a clear parallel in the negotiating agenda in the UK case study companies. Crucially, the company- or site-level negotiations over pay which are a feature of the UK's metalworking sector are generally taken out of the equation in the trade-offs around restructuring, which like their counterparts elsewhere in Europe are based on exchanges involving (non-wage) cost reduction, flexibility and employment security measures (Arrowsmith and Sisson, 2001; Sisson and Artiles, 2000). At *Britmetal1* job security was a pressing concern for unions, who were keen to intensify discussions with management over alternatives to redundancy such as redeployment, retraining, working time arrangements and work organization. Job security was also important at *Britmetal2*, especially following a recent major site closure, against the context of earlier agreements trading off enhanced flexibility practices for undertakings on employment security. In local-level negotiations the issues being addressed were wide-ranging, including shift working and premia, overtime and transfers, outsourcing, absence control and the conversion of temporary employees to permanent status.

Banking

Although, according to employer and trade union officials, company-level negotiating activity frequently does not go beyond the limits specified by sector agreements, the large banks which comprised our case studies in Belgium and Germany both count as exceptions. An extensive company-level negotiating agenda at *Belbank* has been driven by the need to address the consequences of the 1998 acquisition of one of the country's largest private sector banks and its merger with an ex-public sector bank already owned by the group. Since 1999 substantive agreements have been concluded addressing key aspects of the ongoing restructuring, covering geographical workforce mobility, early retirement and employment security. In mid-2002, negotiations on a new job classification system to underpin a unified salary system were at an advanced stage. Although job structures and payments systems are formally covered by a sector agreement, the proposals under consideration bore little resemblance to these.

A wide-ranging bargaining agenda, addressing several matters beyond the scope of the sector agreement, was also apparent at *Gerbank*. As at *Belbank*, restructuring lies behind developments. During 2000 and 2001 the company and the two main general works councils had concluded a series of agreements covering such matters as employment security (beyond the scope of the sector framework), outsourcing and working time arrangements. A union official described the approach as 'a big patchwork of measures' in which some patches relate to the possibilities available under the sector agreement whereas others derive more from the employer's obligation to propose and agree a social plan with the works councils. A further agreement, covering one of *Gerbank*'s two largest subsidiaries, is suggestive of management's intention to further expand the company-level negotiating agenda: this provides for a new performance-related payments system linked to appraisal, hitherto seen as a 'no go' area in many German companies. In contrast, company-level bargaining at *Italbank* remains focused on the issue of pay related to performance, as specified under the 1993 agreement. Other negotiations deal with the implementation at company level of the sector-level framework for handling restructuring. Indeed it is the presence of this sector framework which underlies the contrast with *Belbank* and *Gerbank*.

As with metalworking, there were clear parallels in the focus of the negotiating agenda in the two UK case study banks, where again company-level pay bargaining was largely taken out of the equation in negotiation and consultation over handling the consequences of restructuring. At *Britbank2* a 1996 employment security agreement had provided the union with extended consultation rights ranging over a wide range of issues flowing from the management of change, including measures to avoid redundancy, changed working patterns and changed management reporting lines. An agreement providing scope for flexible hours contracts, underpinning longer branch opening hours, had been concluded centrally and negotiations were in progress over a group-level framework agreement on work–life balance. A central framework agreement on working time, which provided scope for local level negotiations on flexible working time patterns, was also a feature at *Britbank1*.

The two sectors compared

Although the extent of unauthorized bargaining at company level is greater in metalworking, the similarities in the subject matter of such bargaining amongst large companies across the two sectors are striking. Moreover, these similarities reach across the contrasting contexts of sector-level bargaining in Belgium, Germany and Italy and, setting aside pay, single-employer bargaining in the UK. In both sectors issues of employment and competitiveness have been prominent in the extension of company bargaining into areas on which sector agreements have hitherto been silent.

As noted earlier, developments in Italy's banking sector suggest that such issues can also be addressed at sector level. But there is no automatic process which ensures that sector agreements periodically 'catch-up' with the kind of company-level developments described above. As an illustration from *Gerbank* indicates, much depends upon the preferences and strategies of the parties. The union is keen to introduce some of the company-level provisions negotiated in the context of restructuring into a sector-level agreement, thereby extending such innovations. Management, for their part, see little point in so doing: viewing the arrangements concluded as being advantageous to *Gerbank* in respect of its major competitors. Specific instances such as this, as well as the extension of the company bargaining agenda to matters outwith the sector framework, underline the role of large employers in the shifting balance between sector- and company-level bargaining.

The role of large companies: reform rather than revolution?

Considerations of transactions costs and power relations

Chapter 6 established that amongst employers it is large MNCs that have been to the fore in the pressure for decentralization towards the company level (Marginson and Sisson, 1996). The size of these firms gives them enormous influence in the sector, but increased internationalization and diversification have raised questions about their continuing commitment to national sector arrangements. At its starkest, as experience in the UK underlines, the decision of large companies to remain within or to withdraw from sector bargaining is crucial to its future. All firms face a choice over the degree to which the governance of their industrial relations, as with other activities, should be externalized, as is the case under multi-employer arrangements, or internalized within the firm. This choice is shaped by market characteristics such as homogeneity, stability and competition, and by internal features of the firm such as size, production technologies, skill requirements and the division of labour. State policy and industrial relations systems, as Chapter 6 explained, are also important in shaping firms' choice. As markets and firms have become more differentiated and more international in scope, the calculus behind the respective degrees of internalization and externalization has shifted. In industrial relations, nowhere is this more acute than in the relationship between the operations of MNCs and national sector-based structures of multi-employer bargaining.

The continuation of sector bargaining therefore centres in important respects on the actions of large MNCs. Consideration of transactions costs and power relations helps to inform an analysis of the pressures for internalization relative to externalization within these large firms, throwing crucial light on changing relations between the sector and company levels (Arrowsmith *et al.*, 2003). Transaction costs analysis predicts that increased scale, especially in integrated and standardized systems, leads to pressures for internalization in order to control environmental uncertainty more efficiently (Williamson, 1985). More specifically, increasing firm scale and associated market concentration is likely to bring transactions costs savings in internalizing bargaining arrangements and increase the probability of successful tacit collusion between firms, thereby removing the need for formal organization. Also important is heterogeneity of activities (Schmitt and Sadowski, 2001), which as it increases across companies weakens common interests and makes tacit collusion between employers more difficult.

Power considerations referring to both product and labour markets are also relevant. The structure of the product market, whether concentrated or atomistic, influences the interest and capacity of employers to control their own labour costs and to rely on tacit forms of collusion or on formal collaboration, through multi-employer arrangements, with other employers. Large employers especially in concentrated markets have a greater interest in controlling their own labour costs and opportunities for tacit forms of collusion are greater and less costly. The converse applies to smaller employers and those in more atomistic markets. Turning to the labour market, large companies may be better placed to resist union demands because of their labour market presence, or to accommodate them because of the scope for redistributive bargaining that derives from lower unit costs (Ulman, 1974). The strength of trade unions at different levels makes employers more or less vulnerable to 'going it alone' and unions more or less concerned to extend protection to areas that may be less well organized. A strong trade union can provide an externalization imperative for employers in order to maximize their collective strength, as well as to minimize the resources consumed by domestic collective bargaining.

Transaction cost and power factors also interact: both sets of factors combine to explain the circumstances under which large firms willingly externalize collective bargaining because it is more efficient to confront rationalization and restructuring through coordinated means rather than independently (Kenis, 1992). The internationalization of markets and firms tends to undermine national sector-based, multi-employer bargaining in both transaction costs and power terms: it reduces the relevance and therefore the transaction-cost savings that can be derived from externalizing to the sector and in the context of an internal, cross-country market for investment and product mandates, it may also increase management's power to 'divide and rule' between trade unions organizing in different countries.

The role of the state is also vital, as Chapter 6 explained, shaping the terrain on which transactions cost and power factors play out. In Belgium, Germany and Italy the role of the legal framework is crucial in supporting and sustaining sector-based, multi-employer bargaining arrangements. In the UK, by way of contrast, the legal framework was always less robust in its support. And Conservative administrations of the 1980s and 1990s introduced a series of measures weakening further the capacity of multi-employer bargaining to comprehensively regulate the labour market.

Reach, relationship and trajectory

The commitment of large employers to sector bargaining arrangements can be analysed in terms of the 'reach' of the sector agreement across any given company; the 'relationship' of the company to the sector agreement; and the 'trajectory' of that relationship (Arrowsmith *et al.*, 2003). 'Reach' calibrates the extent to which the relevant agreement is inclusive of the company's workforce. For example, the reach of the sector might be compromised by the development at firm level of new high-technology-based activities, such as direct banking or ICT in metalworking, which do not easily fit the conventional confines of the sector. Or it might reflect a firm's strategic shift of focus, for example from retail banking to investment banking, or from manufacturing to systems and/or after-sales service. 'Relationship' draws on Sisson's (1987: 41) distinction between company-level bargaining which is essentially 'administrative' in respect of the sector agreement, that which is 'supplementary' and that which is 'autonomous', and was introduced in Chapter 6. A fourth, 'semi-autonomous' type was added to reflect instances where company-level negotiations are more detached from the sector agreement than under the supplementary mode but the sector nonetheless continues to have a tangible impact on the evolution of major terms and conditions.

'Trajectory' captures whether large employers remain committed to the sector agreement, and are pressing for either limited or extensive reform, or are loosening their ties with it. 'Limited reform' describes employers keen to see the introduction of further opening or opt-out clauses, but not pressing for radical change in the sector agreement. 'Extensive reform' refers to those looking to effect a qualitative change in the role of the sector agreement – for example, from specifying detailed arrangements to frameworks. 'Loosening ties' is where the future commitment of the company to the sector agreement appears open and attempts have been made to move some activities out from the coverage of the agreement. These are not necessarily mutually exclusive strategies. Different parts of the business could be subject to different pressures for reform, raising the prospect, for example, of new activities serving as a 'lever for change' in the relationship of core parts of the business to the sector arrangements.

Surveying the six case companies in, respectively, Belgium, Germany and Italy, the 'reach' of the sector agreement in terms of the proportion of the workforce covered by the relevant metalworking or banking agreement remains high in five, the exception being *Gerbank*. In terms of the 'relationship' between the companies and their respective agreements, none fell solely into the 'administrative' category. Nor, at the other end of the spectrum, were any of the companies 'autonomous' of the sector agreement. The two German and two Italian companies were, with some variation, closest to the 'supplementary' category, whilst the relationship of the two Belgian companies to their sector agreements is best described as 'semi-autonomous'. Turning to the future trajectory of companies' relationship with the sector agreement, *Gerbank* was distinctive in that it seems to be 'loosening ties' with the sector agreement. The other five companies are each pressing for further reform in the sector agreement to open up additional space for company-level variation, more extensive in nature in the cases of *Italmetal* and *Belbank* than in the remaining three companies. Overall, more pressure for further change was evident amongst the banks than in the metalworking companies.

Metalworking

The sector agreement is comprehensive in its reach across the workforce at *Belmetal*. Since 1996 *Belmetal* has utilized the agreement's opt-out clause in the case of major restructuring to conclude two three-year company agreements covering pay, other benefits and a range of conditions. At the time of field interviews, a pre-agreement for a further three-year deal had been concluded. Its relationship is best described as 'semi-autonomous'. Both management and union representatives remain important players within, respectively, the employers' association and metalworking trade unions. Provisions in the sector (and cross-sector) agreement continue to trigger company-level negotiations and the company-level bargaining agenda is shaped by, and there is close choreography with, developments in the sector agreement. In terms of 'trajectory', management welcomed augmentation of the (limited) scope for differentiation at company level resulting from recent sector agreements, and would like to see further openings. Until then it seems unlikely to revoke its exemption status.

The reach of the sector agreement extends to almost all of the workforce in *Germetal*: 2 per cent, mainly employed in small start-up companies, fall outside its coverage. The company has also concluded a special company agreement with IG-Metall on working time for engineers at its R&D centre. Management pointed to the exceptional character of the circumstances involved. The relationship to the sector agreement is supplementary: negotiations with the central and local works councils focus on matters, such as working time arrangements, over which opening clauses provide scope for company-level variation or on questions on which the sector agreement is silent. Management advocates further reform of the sector agreement: introduction of scope for further differentiation at company level; and procedural reform to increase the scope to conclude agreements with works councils without the need for the trade union to 'sign them off'. Overall, *Germetal* remains strongly committed to the sector agreement, underlining the extent to which the company, as a major automotive supplier, would be exposed to union pressure in its absence. As one senior manager put it, '[*Germetal*] would be lost alone, we need the protection of the sector agreement.'

The reach of the sector agreement is also comprehensive of *Italmetal*'s extensive metalworking activities. Indeed, outsourced activities such as logistics and distribution, which were previously part of its metalworking businesses, continue to be covered by the metalworking agreement. In part this reflected union pressure, but also management reluctance to see a fragmentation of bargaining arrangements at its major locations. In formal terms *Italmetal*'s relationship to the sector agreement remains supplementary, although at the time of the field research it remained unclear as to how the company would respond to the 2001 sector agreement on pay (see above), which continued to be opposed by the largest union organizing in the company. Differences between the company and the trade unions, and also between the unions, have spilled over into company-level negotiations. The 1996 group agreement which expired in 2000 had yet to be renewed: deadlock surrounded the criteria to be used in determining pay related to performance. The current situation is therefore uncertain. In searching for a resolution, *Italmetal* favours extensive reform of the two-tier system: management dislike having two rounds of pay negotiations which it feels adds to costs.

Banking

The reach of the banking sector agreement at *Belbank* is virtually comprehensive for the group's banking operations. Indeed, under a recent company agreement the direct banking subsidiary is being brought back under the coverage of the sector agreement. A further company agreement freezes the proportion of *Belbank*'s retail outlets operated as franchises, a means through which competitor banks have placed much of their retail operation outside of the reach of the sector agreement. Management's desire to handle the consequences of the 1998 merger as expeditiously and smoothly as possible probably explain its willingness to conclude these agreements. The 'semi-autonomous' nature of *Belbank*'s relationship to the sector agreement partly derives from the incomplete nature of the recent sector agreements on pay and working time. In part too, it derives from the extent that innovations at company level are anticipated to drive change in the sector agreements. Negotiations over a new, unified salary classification system across the two former banks provide an example. The shift to a competency-based system envisaged was said to represent a major innovation in the sector, one which both sides anticipated would trigger subsequent change in the sector agreement. More generally, management is pressing for extensive reform: it wants a shift to a set of framework agreements, along the lines of those found in the public banks sector.

The reach of the sector agreement is least comprehensive at *Gerbank*. The bank's internal service and IT operations are outside the coverage of the sector agreement; so too is its direct banking subsidiary. *Gerbank*'s relationship to the sector agreement remains essentially supplementary, utilizing the openings available under the sector framework within an extensive 'domestic' bargaining agenda. Group management advocates more scope for company-level variation: 'we need more and more opening clauses, more windows, more flexibility so as to achieve differentiation' (senior manager). Yet its continued commitment to the sector agreement seems to be in doubt. Management is looking to move more groups within the workforce outside of the sector agreement. As noted above, it is also resistant to union proposals to extend the scope of the sector agreement to deal more comprehensively with restructuring. *Gerbank*'s continued participation in the sector agreement was tacitly acknowledged to be kept under review. It seems to be loosening its ties.

In contrast, in *Italbank* the reach of the sector agreement is comprehensive of the workforce and the company remains committed to the sector agreement. Management has no current agenda for extensive reform, but wishes to ensure scope for greater differentiation between its different business activities. The relationship of the company to the sector remains supplementary; in important respect this is due to the extensive framework which the sector agreement has provided for handling restructuring.

The UK: the imprint of the sector lives on

Evidence from the British case studies also has a bearing on the relationship between sector and company levels. The pursuit of organization-based collective bargaining does not mean that the sector becomes wholly redundant as a reference point (Arrowsmith and Sisson, 1999). It remains important both directly, in terms of the horizontal relationships actively maintained through management and trade union networks, and indirectly, in the emergence of common understandings of basic industry terms and conditions such as a standard or 'going rate' for pay. *Britmetal1*, for example, remains a member of the Engineering Employers' Federation (EEF) which undertakes regular surveys of pay and major conditions amongst its members. Senior union negotiators in the company also referred to the importance of external benchmarks in pay bargaining in particular. A similar situation was also found in banking. Though *Britbank1* was instrumental in the break-up of the London Clearing Banks' Agreement, it too maintains strong informal links with the handful of other major national banks, all of which negotiate with the same trade union. Sector-based structures may decay, but the sector continues to provide parameters which shape company-level developments.

The two sectors compared

Overall, there are noticeable differences between the two sectors, but also between countries. The salience of the external framework provided by the sector agreement for our case companies is greater in metalworking than in banking. Put another way, a company-specific, internal framework looms larger amongst the banks – with the important exception, for the present, of *Italbank*. This relates to the ways in which scope for company-level variation has been introduced into agreements. As shown earlier, the metalworking agreements tend to be relatively more comprehensive in the range of issues addressed and although they have relatively more formal openings these are more closely controlled by more strongly organized trade unions than those in banking. Conversely, the framework arrangements evident in the Belgian and Italian banking sectors provide greater scope for company-level variation than anything in the metalworking agreements. The country dimension is also apparent, with – as established above – greater elasticity being evident in the sector agreements in Italy and Belgium than in Germany. This, in the face of growing differentiation of activities, helps to explain why *Gerbank* has, in seeking greater scope for company-based arrangements, removed emerging parts of the group's activities from the scope of the sector agreement. Country patterns are easier to discern in the 'relationship' between the sector and company levels, whereas sector ones are more evident in 'trajectory'. The banks are more strongly in favour of reform than the metalworking companies, with the exception of the Italian bank, where multi-employer bargaining has evolved to become a more flexible instrument in order to manage the rapid restructuring of the sector.

In order to better understand the dynamics underlying the patterns which emerge, we return to the transactions costs and power considerations introduced above. An indicative summary of the main transactions costs and power factors facing the case study firms, in terms of both prevailing state and change trajectory of relevant sector and company characteristics, is provided in Table 7.1. 'Pluses', (+) [+] respectively for 'state' and 'change', indicate tendencies favouring externalization, whereas 'minuses', (−) [−] respectively for 'state' and 'change', indicate those pointing towards internalization. In terms of sector context, the broad pattern in both sectors, although different in detail, is of a mixture of pluses and minuses in the columns on 'state', reflecting a degree of ambivalence towards sector-level bargaining arrangements by major employers. There are more minuses for 'change' than 'state' in both sectors, indicating the pressures for the reform of the relationship between sector and company levels. This tendency is more pronounced in banking than metalworking. At company level, in metalworking the pattern for 'state' is dominated by minuses except for the crucial factor of trade union strength; the same is true of the pattern for 'change'. In banking, there are more pluses in the 'state' column than for metalworking, although trade union strength is a minus. There are no pluses in the 'change' column, again indicating that whilst pressure for reform towards a greater internalization is evident in both sectors, it is relatively stronger amongst the banks.

Table 7.1's findings do not predict the demise of sector-level bargaining structures, however, because of the weight of some of the remaining 'plus factors' and because the table does not capture the key role played

Table 7.1 Power and transaction costs factors shaping the prevailing state and change trajectory of sector multi-employer bargaining

Sector/product market:	Metalworking	Externalization implication: (state) [change]	Banking	Externalization implication: (state) [change]
Concentration	Still lots of players across sector even if high within market segments	(+) [+]	High except for Germany. Increasing concentration	(−) [−]
Internationalization	Growing international competition and ownership	(−) [−]	Retail banking largely domestic in competition and ownership. Some internationalization of back office	(+) [+/−]
Heterogeneity	High. Increasing due to new technology: new activities, e.g. ICT, and work organization (Cad/cam; JIT). Shift to after-sales and systems and solutions	(−) [−]	Low, but increasing due to new technology: facilitating separation of back office work, call centres, internet and direct banking. 'Bancassurance'	(+) [−]
Trade union strength	High, but generally lower than in past	(+) [+]	Lower than metalworking	(−) [−]

Company

Merger/acquisition	Acquisitions and divestments: tend to reinforce diversification	(−) [−]	Mergers: internalization and centralization to manage integration and rationalization	(−) [−]
Diversification	Wide and growing range of interests and activities	(−) [−]	Focus on core activities, but diversifying to wider financial services	(+) [−]
Internationalization	Increasing cross-border business streams and internal investment markets	(−) [−]	Separate national structures for subsidiaries; but emergence of cross-border business streams	(+) [−]
Trade union strength	Remains high in large firms. Unions principal firm-level bargaining agents in B, I; closely connected with works councils in D	(+) [+]	Lower than metal. In D, works councils may not be closely union controlled	(−) [−]

by the state. In all three countries, the pivotal role of trade union strength in sustaining sector-based bargaining arrangements in metalworking is underpinned by the legal framework which governs the institutional arrangements for employee representation. The unions are legitimate bargaining agents at company level in the Italian and Belgian systems, and the reality for the larger companies is that they must be faced whether the firm remains in or out of the sector agreement. In Germany works councils are accorded significant bargaining responsibility, but again the reality is that these have close links to the trade unions, especially in larger metalworking companies. Moreover, only trade unions have the legal right to conclude binding collective agreements with employers' associations or, if they choose, individual employers. The reality for the larger companies is the same as for their counterparts in Belgium and Italy.

Handling new and reconfigured business activities: a choice point

Developments at the boundaries of existing sector arrangements are, as Chapter 6 explained, further perturbing the prevailing equilibrium between sector- and company-level bargaining. Industries are being reconfigured as a result of the development of new business activities, technological changes to production processes and modes of product delivery. Such reconfiguration includes extensive internal restructuring within companies in which previously integrated business activities are differentiated and separated out into distinct business units, some of which are then outsourced altogether. Existing boundaries between sectors become blurred, placing a question mark over the continued application of established sector arrangements. More striking is the emergence of new business activities, such as ICT, on the boundaries of existing sectors that, by definition, have no established collective bargaining arrangements. The regulation of these new and reconfigured activities represents a choice point for employers and trade unions alike: are sector agreements being adapted and extended to provide coverage? or are new single-employer, company-based agreements being concluded? and/or is significant 'agreement-free' space opening up?

A range of responses

Metalworking

A central challenge to metalworking sector agreements in the three countries is the burgeoning ICT sector. The extent to which ICT operations are 'agreement free' varies between the countries. In Belgium, new companies in ICT come under the jurisdiction of the agreement of the auxiliary joint committee for white-collar staff, a 'catch-all' agreement for employers not covered by a specific (white-collar) sector agreement. Terms and conditions are inferior to those stipulated under the (white-collar) metalworking agreement and the scope for flexibility at company level is greater. In Italy, the major telecommunications companies moved from the metalworking agreement into a new ICT sector agreement in 2000, established to address a situation in which some companies had opted to apply the commerce sector agreement (regarded by employers concerned as more favourable). In addition, the 1999 metalworking agreement extended coverage to outsourced production units and services that have significant connections with metalworking activities. As a result, the outsourced logistics activities of *Italmetal* remain under the metalworking agreement (Pulignano, 2000). Even so, union respondents claimed that other employers were concluding company agreements rather than applying a sector agreement. And some sector boundaries remain unclear: with outsourcing, contractors can still apply a less favourable agreement than that which covers the original company.

In contrast, the ICT economy in Germany was said to be 'essentially an agreement free space. The big problem is not existing companies leaving the agreement but new companies not coming in' (union official). New ICT companies remain largely unorganized and, despite a demarcation agreement, the focus of competing aspirations from IG-Metall and Ver.di. 'Insourcing' of IT activities by large companies to newly established subsidiaries was perceived as less of a problem by union respondents, because such operations tend to stay within the scope of the agreement. IG-Metall has concluded supplementary agreements in such instances, which allow for greater flexibility of and prolonged working time. In other instances, new company agreements are being concluded, for example *Germetal's* agreement for technical staff at its R&D centre. In the UK, amongst established companies there is relative movement of employment into R&D and IT activities, where staff typically work in smaller units and are more difficult to organize. Even where they are, as at *Britmetal1*, new bargaining arrangements have been established outside the company's established area-based structures. As in Germany, the newly established part of the ICT sector remains very much an 'agreement-free' space.

Banking

The main challenges to existing sector collective bargaining arrangements across the three countries derive from three related sources: shifting 'back-office' operations into separate subsidiaries, the establishment of new direct banking subsidiaries and the growth of call centres (frequently employing new labour). The emergence of 'bancassurance' groups arising from recent mergers and acquisitions was only raised as a matter of concern for current collective bargaining arrangements in Italy.

In Belgium, the banks are adopting different approaches to new activities involving direct banking and call centres. Some were creating them from existing operations which were being retained within the mainstream business; in such cases employees remained under the coverage of the sector agreement. A second group were transferring employees into new subsidiaries; trade unions were pressing for these new subsidiaries to be included under the sector agreement but employers were resisting, arguing that they required further flexibilities. A third group were employing new people in the new operations, particularly call centres and some banks were placing these under the auxiliary sector agreement, referred to above. Trade unions were concerned that registration under the auxiliary agreement means inferior terms and conditions and greater scope for flexibility at company level. The 2002 sector negotiations became deadlocked over employer proposals to restrict the sector agreement to banking activities narrowly defined, with the consequence that larger numbers of staff employed in support services would be transferred to the auxiliary and other agreements with less favourable terms and conditions (EIRO, 2003c). In Italy, adjustments have been made to the sector agreement to accommodate direct banking and outsourcing. The (national and savings banks) sector agreement has special clauses for the flexibility required for seven-day, 24-hour working which are then fleshed out in company-level negotiations. On outsourcing, the 1999 sector agreement defined what activities could be outsourced, that they would remain covered by the banking agreement and made changes to job classifications for outsourced activities. Respondents further commented that the increasing fuzziness of the boundary between banking and insurance, as a result of recent mergers and acquisitions, was raising questions about the application of the respective agreements.

In contrast, the direct banks in Germany – which, as in the case of *Gerbank*, are mainly separate subsidiaries of the major private banks – are not members of the employers' association and not covered by the collective agreement. The direct banks have introduced a range of practices, especially working time arrangements and on flexibility, which would not be compatible with the private banks agreement. For their part, trade unions saw the direct banks, which usually employ new labour, as the biggest challenge to established sector arrangements. Placed outside the sector agreement, *Gerbank*'s call centres are not covered by a company agreement either. The unions' dilemma is whether to try and negotiate company agreements, on inferior terms and with greater flexibilities than the sector agreement, or to leave them in 'agreement-free' space. A second challenge for unions is outsourcing of back-office and IT operations to newly established subsidiaries. In the case of back-office operations, staff usually transfer across and the sector agreement is applied. In the case of IT operations, there is pressure to take these out of the sector agreement. A company-level agreement for part of *Gerbank*'s IT subsidiary was concluded in 2001. In the UK, IT staff in the main banks are increasingly covered by separate negotiating arrangements to those of banking staff. Restructuring of back-office operations was negotiated within the existing national company-level agreements. Subsequently, there has been a growing trend towards outsourcing such operations, with unions having some success in negotiating collective agreements with these new employers. As in Germany, call centres represent a considerable organising challenge to the unions.

The capacity of sector bargaining systems to adapt

Assessment of the ways in which existing sector-level structures are coping with the emergence of new business activities draws attention not so much to sector differences, but to marked variation in the capacity of national systems to adapt. In Germany, significant 'agreement-free' space has opened up within and on the boundaries of both metalworking and banking. Insofar as these new activities might become covered, the immediate prospect appears to be that of company-based bargaining arrangements. The establishment of new sector arrangements – or extension of the coverage of existing ones – was said to be unlikely in the foreseeable future. Industrial and business change appears to be the motor behind the growth of a significant 'disorganized' element to the collective bargaining system in Germany.

In Belgium and Italy, the consequences of similar change has not been the opening up of 'agreement-free' space, but two alternative developments. First, is the emergence of 'bargaining regime competition' as Belgian employers exploit the increased permeability of sector boundaries by applying other collective agreements more favourable from their perspective to new activities. Italy shows evidence of the same phenomenon. If left unchecked, the consequences of such competition might eventually undermine sector bargaining: as the provisions of the resulting 'polyglot' sector agreements have progressively less bearing on practice at company level, large employers may begin to question the relevance of remaining within a sector framework. Second, is adaptation of existing agreements to handle the particularities of new business activities and, in Italy, the growth of outsourcing. Also in Italy, new sector agreements have been concluded covering the emerging ICT sector. Overall, developments in Germany entail closer parallels to those in the UK than in the other two countries, which have displayed greater capacity for adaptation in their sector-based bargaining arrangements.

The cross-border dimension

As Chapter 6 noted, pressures for a 'Europeanization' of sector bargaining stem not so much from the development of a European labour market, of which there is little sign, but from the consequences of the further integration of the single European market. Increasingly collective bargaining systems are being set in competition with each other. The prospect of intensified regime competition, and resultant fears of a downward spiral of terms and conditions, has – as Chapter 4 described – prompted initiatives by European and national trade union organizations towards cross-border coordination of the agenda and outcomes of sector negotiations As UNI-Europa's initiative in finance signals, the company-level is also a potentially important focal point for such coordination. Hence, 'Europeanization' of collective bargaining also has implications for the balance between sector and company levels. This section confines itself to the sector-level evidence, presenting a 'bottom-up' perspective from the four countries and two sectors. Consideration of the company-level evidence awaits Chapter 8.

A tale of two sectors

Metalworking

The extent, intensity and nature of the use of cross-border comparisons in sector negotiations in Belgium, Germany and Italy, varied considerably. On the trade union side, the main metalworking unions in all four countries are involved in the EMF's bargaining coordination initiative (Schulten, 2001). On the employers' side, EMF's initiative has prompted WEM, the employers' organization at the European level, to step up its long-established system of information exchange. However, the actual impact of these developments on the negotiating practice of both trade unions and employers differed sharply across the countries.

In Belgium, according to both employers and trade unions, cross-border comparisons are regularly deployed by either side in sector negotiations.

Indeed, the practice was seen as nothing particularly new, dating back to government intervention in the 1980s aimed at tying the outcome of cross-sector negotiations to the movement of wage costs in Belgium's main European trading partners. The obligation for comparison laid down by the 1996 competitiveness law was said by union respondents to have prompted the launch of the 'Doorn' bargaining cooperation initiative, involving the union confederations in Belgium, Germany, Luxembourg and the Netherlands (see Chapter 4).

The Belgian metalworking unions have also been at the forefront of cross-border cooperation developments under the umbrella of the EMF's bargaining coordination initiative. Together with the NordRhein Westfalen district of IG-Metall and the Dutch metalworking unions, the two Belgian metalworking unions established a regional bargaining network in late 1997 (Gollbach and Schulten, 2000). Chapter 4 provides details. Union respondents said the network enables negotiators to be better informed when facing employers and to better understand developments in other countries. Both union and employer respondents cited an incident in the 1999 negotiations when some of the data on Germany underpinning the employers' comparative case was questioned by an observer from IG-Metall attending the session. The effect was said to be 'psychological' – both sides knew that the unions were negotiating in a cross-border context. The network's monitoring of bargaining outcomes indicated that the 2000 metalworking settlement in NordRhein Westfalen fell short of the EMF bargaining guideline. Some robust exchanges ensued which were said also to have underlined the difficulties in costing qualitative elements of settlements in such benchmarking exercises. (A similar general and specific assessment of the regional network was given by a union official involved in NordRhein Westfalen.) On the employer side, the Belgian employers' association has regular meetings and a lot of contact with their Dutch (but not their German) counterparts – 'it's a very open relationship' (employer respondent).

The deployment of cross-border comparisons in metalworking negotiations in Germany is of a rather different genre. Both employer and trade union respondents reported that general comparisons with other countries are used as 'propaganda' (union officer) in negotiations, but that neither side makes systematic use of cross-border comparisons. National reference points remain the more important for negotiations. Indeed, Germany was seen more as the object of comparisons by negotiators in other European countries, and especially its neighbours.

IG-Metall participates in the confederal 'Doorn' process, but more important from its perspective are the regional bargaining networks established with neighbouring countries/regions to each of its bargaining districts (Gollbach and Schulten, 2000), which Chapter 4 outlined. These were described as 'an information exchange initiative in essence' (union official) amongst which that between NordRhein Westfalen, Belgium and the Netherlands is the most advanced. More embryonic are the networks involving the Baden-Württemberg region and the Italian metalworking unions and that bringing together the Lower-Saxony region and the AEEU (now Amicus) in the UK. These cooperation networks were said to demonstrate to employers that the union was negotiating with a European perspective. This assessment reflected that made by an employers' association official, who saw the unions as exchanging information across borders but not coordinating bargaining as such. Given employers' systematic exchange of bargaining information through WEM, it was said that there was no need for a specific response to the regional bargaining networks.

In Italy, national reference points continue to predominate in sector negotiations: the use of cross-border references was said to be 'not frequent' (union official) and tends to be issue-specific. An example was the introduction of a 35-hour week, where bilateral contacts and exchanges of information had taken place with employers' organizations and trade unions, respectively, in France. Likewise in the UK, cross-border comparisons were reported not to be an important element in the preparation of major (company-level) claims in the sector. Cross-border comparisons are drawn, by both employers and unions, in negotiations in the major automotive manufacturers most usually on non-pay matters: a particular focus for cross-border comparison has been working time. Even in automotive, however, national reference points were said to remain the more important.

Banking

The use of cross-border comparisons in negotiations was, with the notable exception of banking in Italy, less marked than in metalworking. Respondents, however, drew attention to the potential consequences of the adoption by MNCs of common HR policies across European countries. In part, UNI-Europa finance section's bargaining coordination initiative is a response to this development. Its system for exchange of bargaining information is, however, only just being established (see Chapter 4). With the exception of banking in Italy, the same observation holds on the employers' side – regular meetings and informal contacts through the European Banking Federation notwithstanding.

In Belgium, beyond the evident impact of the 1996 law on competitiveness on the margin for sector salary increases, there appears to be little activity in terms of the use of cross-border comparisons in negotiations or the cross-border exchange of bargaining information. In Germany too, cross-border comparisons were reported not to be made 'as a rule' (employers' respondent) by either side. When they are, they 'tend to be used in a rhetorical way – for example over Saturday working' (union official). Like their metalworking counterparts, German employers' organizations and trade unions tend to be the recipients of requests from other European countries for information rather than seeking such information from others.

In Italy, a special tripartite agreement was signed in early 1998 motivated by the need under EMU to reduce the cost-base of banks towards the EU average (EIRO, 1998a). The same imperative led the employers' association to establish a systematic annual benchmarking exercise of compensation, labour costs, new skills and job classifications in other EU countries. It has also engaged in specific cross-border comparative projects with its counterparts in other countries. Trade unions accept the logic of the need for cross-border comparison, but question the indicators used and the conclusions drawn. In the UK, it was reported that there was little use of cross-border reference points in the major company-level negotiations; as in metalworking, national reference points remain predominant.

Europeanization at different speeds and levels

Consistent with Chapter 4, it is trade unions which are most active in developing a cross-border dimension to collective bargaining at sector level. Employers' organization activity tends to be more confined, focusing on information exchange and benchmarking of settlements. More active cooperation, as between the Belgian and Dutch metalworking employers, is in response to union initiatives.

Trade union cross-border bargaining cooperation initiatives have yet to have a widespread impact on the agenda and outcome of national negotiations in the two sectors. Even so, there is significant variation in the extent and intensity of cross-border activity between them. Whereas in banking cross-border cooperation remains largely an aspiration for which plans are being put in place, it has taken concrete shape amongst unions in metalworking and encompasses a series of cross-border structures. Differences between countries are also evident. 'Arm's-length' cross-border bargaining (Marginson and Sisson, 1998) appears to be developing involving Belgium, the Netherlands and the bordering region (NordRhein Westphalen) of Germany, in which the positions of both employers and trade unions in each country/region are increasingly coordinated even though there is no cross-border bargaining unit. In contrast, metalworking sector bargaining in Italy (and company-based bargaining in the UK) remains largely unaffected by any such cross-border dimension. 'Europeanization' of collective bargaining, it seems, is occurring at different speeds as between both countries and sectors.

Moreover, any 'Europeanization' of collective bargaining need not primarily be driven by sector-level developments. In banking, trade union respondents in Belgium emphasized the future tensions that might arise between the provisions of the sector agreements and the adoption of common HRM policies by large international groups such as Dutch-based ING (which owns BBL) and Fortis. In Germany too, both employer and trade union respondents underlined the way in which cross-border comparisons within the large private banks were increasingly impacting upon employment practice. As a result, both sides expected problems in maintaining the consistency across employers that a sector agreement requires.

Converging divergencies

The findings point to continuing differences between countries in the shifting balance between collective bargaining at sector and company levels, but also to similarities within sectors which transcend national borders. There is support for the proposition, outlined in Chapter 1, that trends towards greater differentiation within national systems and convergence between them are not incompatible but mutually reinforcing processes (Marginson and Sisson, 1998) resulting in what Katz and Darbishire (2000) describe as 'converging divergencies'. This dual process is particularly evident in finance, where the large banks are simultaneously developing human resource policies which reach across national borders and differentiating industrial relations arrangements and employment practice between different business activities within countries. At the same time, the persistence of country differences is consistent with Chapter 5's proposition that national systems continue to provide a coherent framework for handling the twin sets of pressures arising from decentralization and internationalization. Neither the country nor the sector effect appears to be dominant. The established presumption in comparative institutional analysis that country influences dominate those from the sector (Hollingsworth and Streeck, 1994: 273–9) would seem to need revisiting.

The top panel of Table 7.2 shows that differences between countries (and thereby similarities between the two sectors within a given country) are evident in the scope provided for company-level variation. Greater 'elasticity' was evident in the sector agreements in Belgium and Italy than in Germany. And the relationship of the company cases to the sector agreement was characterized as 'supplementary' in Germany and Italy, but as 'semi-autonomous' in Belgium. Country differences are further evidenced by the ways in which sector-based bargaining systems respond to the challenge of new business activities, leading to the creation of significant 'agreement-free' space in both sectors in Germany. This was evident in neither Belgium, where some employers are opting to register new activities under collective agreements deemed to be 'more favourable', nor Italy, where existing agreements have been modified and new ones established. Country differences are also evident in the greater degree to which Belgian and German trade unions in metalworking are bound in to cross-border cooperation arrangements as compared to their Italian and British counterparts.

Similarities within sectors across countries (and thereby differences within countries), shown in the lower panel of Table 7.2, are evident in the greater scope provided for company-level negotiations under sector agreements in metalworking, and the incidence of company-level bargaining – both authorized and unauthorized, as compared with banking. This reflects the strength and negotiating capacity of trade union and/or works council organizations at company level in metalworking. Yet, a further similarity was the greater salience of the external framework provided by the sector agreement to large companies in metalworking than in banking, where an internal, corporate framework loomed larger. And the large banks tended to favour more extensive reform of the sector agreement than their metalworking counterparts. Similarities are also evident in the bargaining agenda across countries in the two sectors: flexibility of working time, and in particular Saturday working, is a particular focus of sector negotiations in banking, whereas in metalworking there is a wider margin for company-level negotiations over working time flexibility. In both sectors too, the company-level bargaining agenda focused on questions of employment, adaptability and competitiveness; issues on which sector agreements have hitherto tended to be silent. In the banks a distinctive feature was the need to handle group-wide restructuring following either major mergers or internal business reorganization. A final sector similarity is apparent in

Table 7.2 Patterns of convergence and divergence across countries and sectors

	Differences between countries (similarity between sectors within countries)							
	Belgium		Germany		Italy		UK	
	Metalworking	Banking	Metalworking	Banking	Metalworking	Banking	Metalworking	Banking
De facto scope of company-level variation	♣	♣	♦	♦	◄	◄	n.a.	n.a.
Relationship of large companies to sector agreement	♣	♣	♦	♦	◄	◄	n.a.	n.a.
Agreement-free space in new business activities	♣	♣	♦	♦	◄	◄	□	□
Involvement in cross-border bargaining cooperation	♣ +	n.a.	♦ +	n.a.	◄ −	n.a.	□ −	n.a.

Cross-national similarity within sectors (differences between sectors within countries)

	Belgium		Germany		Italy		UK	
	Metalworking	*Banking*	*Metalworking*	*Banking*	*Metalworking*	*Banking*	*Metalworking*	*Banking*
Incidence of and scope for company negotiations in sector agreement	• +	∞ −	• +	∞ −	• +	∞ −	n.a.	n.a
Employer pressure for reform of sector agreement	• −	∞ +	• −	∞ +	• −	[∞ −]	n.a.	n.a
Recent sector-level bargaining agenda	•	∞	•	∞	•	∞	n.a.	n.a.
Use of cross-border reference points in negotiations	• +	∞ −	• +	∞ −	• +	∞ −	• +	∞ −

Key:
♣ ♦ ▲ □ denote country-specific effects in, respectively, Belgium, Germany, Italy and the UK.
• ∞ denote sector-specific effects in, respectively, metalworking and finance.
+, − denote, respectively, stronger and weaker effects.
n.a. denotes not applicable.

the extent to which the cross-border dimension is impinging on the negotiating process at sector level, something which at present is found only in metalworking.

Conclusions and implications

The consequences flowing from the further internationalization of markets that EMU heralds and the extensive restructuring that it has unleashed – alongside those stemming from rapid industrial change – are fuelling pressure for further decentralization. Although the industrial relations literature is replete with references to the decentralization of collective bargaining which has marked the past 20 years, beyond the fundamental distinction between 'organized' and 'disorganized' decentralization (Traxler, 1995), little attention has been paid to the different forms that greater scope for company-level variation within sector agreements is taking. This chapter has furnished detailed evidence of the variety of forms that decentralization is taking within agreements in two key sectors and three countries. The balance between sector and company levels is, according to this evidence, tipping further towards the company and is likely to continue to do so.

Findings from studies of other sectors suggest similar movement, more or less marked, elsewhere. Le Queux and Fajertag's (2001) survey of collective bargaining developments in chemicals across five EU countries suggests a shifting emphasis towards the company level similar to that found in metalworking. In the graphical sector, reflecting the continuing prevalence of large numbers of SMEs, the shift is less marked. Reminiscent of banking, however, company-level bargaining is becoming more extensive in the larger, international groups (Arrowsmith and Sisson, 1999; Leisink, 2002). In road haulage, although company bargaining remains rare, it is nonetheless emerging amongst the small but growing band of international logistics companies (Sisson and Marginson, 2000). Only under exceptional circumstances, such as those prevailing in the UK's engineering construction sector (Korczynski, 1997), is the balance shifting in the opposite direction.

Recent debate has tended to imply that decentralization is primarily a top-down process, steered and controlled by national-level actors. The bottom-up dynamic has been overlooked, reflecting a lack of attention to the role of management, which has replaced local trade union organization as the driving force behind company-level bargaining activity. The key role of MNCs in pushing out the boundaries of collective bargaining at company level and in reshaping the role of sector agreements is highlighted by our findings. Central to the continuing processes of 'authorized' decentralization within sector agreements, but also to the growth of 'unauthorized' bargaining at company level, is the reorientation of the bargaining agenda towards considerations of competitiveness, adaptability and employment. Unauthorized bargaining at company level is widespread amongst larger metalworking companies, such as our case companies, in all three countries. For the most part it addresses issues on which sector agreements are silent. It is becoming more extensive amongst the large banks, represented by our case companies, in Belgium and Germany; the Italian banking sector provides the exception that underlines the rule. Consideration of the bottom-up dynamic also underscores the contested nature of the competence of different levels, something which is most apparent in Italy's metalworking sector but which also arises in determining the level at which new bargaining issues are to be addressed.

MNCs in both sectors are using the opportunity that new business activities represent to take a step outside of the established sector arrangements. A sharp distinction is apparent between their approach to mainstream business activities, which continue to operate within the sector agreement, and to new business activities, which may be lodged outside of established arrangements, either under a more 'favourable' sector agreement – as in Belgium or Italy – or under company agreements or non-collectively-bargained arrangements – as in Germany. And it is the adoption of common cross-border policies and practices by MNCs, particularly in finance, which are introducing fresh tensions into sector agreements.

Wider questions about the conditions under which collective bargaining systems successfully adapt to new contingencies are raised by the findings on the ways in which existing sector-based bargaining structures are coping with the emergence of new business activities. In Germany, this has led to the emergence of significant 'agreement-free' space, a pattern more closely resembling developments in the UK, which no longer has a sector-based bargaining system, than in Belgium or Italy. Ferner and Hyman (1998: xxiv) discuss this capacity in terms of the 'flexible rigidity' of different national systems, as Chapter 6 outlined. In varying ways, existing arrangements in Belgium and Italy appear to possess a greater capacity for flexibility in continuing to provide the rigidity that the framework of a sector-level agreement entails than is the case in Germany. As Chapter 6 emphasized, the survival of sector-based, multi-employer bargaining depends not only on the legal framework, important though it is, but on employer and trade union preferences and policies.

Of the two sectors, the future of sector bargaining appears less assured in banking than in metalworking. In Germany, *Gerbank* seems to be loosening its ties with the sector agreement. In Belgium, the continuation of sector bargaining is being questioned by employers. Both sides acknowledged that considerable difficulties have arisen from the 1998 working time agreement, reflecting the disparity of the company-based arrangements that had developed since the previous agreement in 1982. Moreover, an employers' respondent stressed that the period of company-level bargaining over pay had not brought 'anarchy' – movements on pay had been tightly coordinated through the employers' association. The large Belgian banks are also casting an eye at their Dutch counterparts, which – as Chapter 6 described – have recently opted out of their sector agreement in favour of company-based arrangements. There are echoes here of earlier developments in UK metalworking, where the progressive withdrawal of large, international companies from the sector agreement preceded, and contributed to, its eventual demise (Brown and Walsh, 1991). In metalworking, large employers appear more committed to retaining sector bargaining. Even in Italy, where current arrangements are in a state of paralysis, the preference of *Italmetal* is for the reform of the sector agreement. Crucial to the difference between the sectors are trade union strength, noticeably greater in metalworking than banking, and industry concentration, higher in banking – thereby facilitating informal collusion between the key players – than in the more heterogeneous metalworking sector.

Even so, it would be rash to predict the demise of agreements in banking in either Belgium or Germany. As Chapter 6 underlined, their status, like that of sector agreements more generally in most of Western Europe, is altogether different from that of their (former) equivalents in the UK, being compulsory codes as well as binding contracts. A more likely outcome is a progressive erosion of the basic substantive function of sector agreements in specifying universal standards. Amongst large employers, decentralization is resulting in increasingly divergent arrangements across companies, rendering the notion of a universal sector standard increasingly diffuse. The wider consequence, as Hassel and Rehder (2001) contend, is a gradual inversion of the established relationship between the sector and company level, with sector agreements increasingly adjusting to company-level developments rather than mapping our directions for company-level negotiators to follow.

A cross-border dimension to sector collective bargaining is becoming apparent, but at different speeds as between sectors and countries. In metalworking, it is most evident between Belgium, the Netherlands and the bordering region of Germany; it has yet to develop in banking. The relative dynamics of cross-border developments at sector level and those at company level, to be considered in Chapter 8, will influence the balance between the two levels within national systems. The evidence of this chapter is of emerging tensions between the provisions of sector agreements and the adoption of common, cross-border human resource policies by large MNCs, particularly in banking. As yet, it is unclear how such tensions will be resolved. Nonetheless, a distinct possibility is that the cross-border dimension will tend to erode rather than bridge national, sector-based collective bargaining structures.

8
The Euro-Company: Focal Point for the Europeanization of Industrial Relations?

Singling out European-scale multinational companies for particular attention needs little justification in the light of previous chapters. MNCs have been key proponents of economic integration, championing the creation of the single European market and subsequent monetary union (Nollert, 2000). MNCs are also central protagonists driving forward the process of market integration. As Chapter 2 underlined, large companies have responded to EMU by seeking to extend their reach from particular national markets across the entire single market, and to reorganize production and market servicing on a continent-wide basis. In the process the number of companies within the EU which are multinational in scope has grown as has the geographical reach of established MNCs (Edwards, 1999). Chapter 2 went on to establish that the 'Euro-company' is a meaningful concept, distinct from the 'global' corporation and amounting to more than an umbrella term for a set of nationally differentiated MNCs. Legal accommodation to the scale and significance of these developments has come with the eventual adoption, in 2001, of the European Company Statute.

MNCs have also played a key role in the emerging multi-level industrial relations system. Chapters 6 and 7 emphasized MNCs' pacesetting role in the decentralization of collective bargaining within national systems, resulting in growing space for company-level negotiation. The effects are not only on the levels of governance, but also – as Chapter 3 discussed – on its scope, form and output. MNCs have exploited growing company-level negotiating space to expand the role of collective bargaining, using it to deal with a management agenda of competitiveness and adaptability. In so doing, the nature of the process and outcomes of bargaining have changed. MNCs have also provided major impetus towards the development of a cross-border, European, dimension to industrial relations, which is contributing to the changes in collective bargaining. Equally, MNCs are a central driving force behind both the convergence and divergence that is increasingly characteristic of the evolving multi-level system. For, in as much as they are bringing about a measure of cross-national convergence among their subsidiaries, they are adding to the diversity within national systems.

Any lingering doubts about the key role being played by MNCs in shaping a European-level framework of industrial relations are best allayed by recalling the high profile controversies which periodically surround the employment and industrial relations consequences of specific business decisions by these powerful non-state actors. In 1993, Hoover's decision to shift production of one product line from a plant in France, which was earmarked for closure as a result, to one in Scotland – on the back of a wide-ranging package of concessions in employment conditions and working practices negotiated with representatives of the Scottish workforce – became a totem for fears about the social dumping (see below) that might be unleashed by the creation of Europe's single market. In 1997, Renault's decision to close its plant at Vilvoorde in Belgium, and transfer the production involved to Spain, without fulfilling its national- and EU-level obligations to inform and consult the workforce, was widely seen as highlighting shortcomings in the EU's then recently adopted European Works Councils (EWCs) Directive. This gave early impetus to the process of review and, possibly, eventual revision of the Directive. In 2001, Marks and Spencer's decision to close all of its stores in France, as part of a more general withdrawal from its operations in Continental Europe, rapidly became the lightning conductor through which pressure for further EU-level measures to protect employees affected by large-scale restructuring was refracted. One result was to fracture remaining member state opposition to the draft directive on national employee information and consultation, which was adopted in early 2002.

Three particular sets of issues demand attention. The first is the extent to which an integrated European market opens up further scope for 'regime competition' – under which decisions on the location of investment and production are shaped by considerations of labour costs, labour standards and employment flexibility, but also the productivity, quality and adaptability of labour – between the EU's different national labour market systems. At worst, the fear has been of social dumping in which considerations of the lowest labour costs and standards and the greatest numerical flexibility become the driving forces behind investment location decisions. Although the actual scale of the problem has probably been exaggerated, the existence of the threat to do so has provided MNCs with a powerful lever to secure change.

A second set of issues involves the cross-border coordination of policy and practice by the management of MNCs that an integrated market is also stimulating. This is taking both explicit and implicit forms, the latter reflecting the 'isomorphism' pressures outlined in Chapter 3. In the first instance, some companies are developing common human resource policies, covering such matters as employee involvement and communication, financial participation and employee training and development. Typically, these conform to the principal of subsidiarity, leaving discretion to individual country operations and/or business units over their implementation. In the second and more widespread instance, benchmarking of working practices across national borders is resulting in growing use of mechanisms for the diffusion of best practice, reflecting 'mimetic' and 'normative' isomorphism processes on the one hand, and the deployment of comparisons in management's local negotiations with workforces in order to secure concessions, reflecting the 'coercive' process on the other. In addressing this and the next set of issues, findings from the company case studies introduced in Chapter 7 (see Appendix for summary details) are drawn on.

The third set involves EWCs. Recognition of the growing significance of the gap in employee rights to representation and participation at transnational level, which the first two developments in MNCs entailed, lay behind the Commission's commitment to introduce a measure providing for European-level information and consultation rights as a central plank of its proposals for a 'social dimension' to the single market. The commitment was delivered in 1994 with the adoption of the EWCs Directive. The Directive broke new ground, in that for the first time it prompted the establishment of transnational industrial relations structures within European-scale MNCs. Although only in their infancy, the question of whether EWCs will become a focal point for the Europeanization of industrial relations has already provoked sharp debate (e.g. Streeck, 1997). Research findings (Lecher *et al.*, 1999; 2001; Marginson *et al.*, 2004) point to the great variety of practice which characterizes EWCs, including some which are genuinely transnational in nature and others which have acquired de facto rights to formal consultation and even negotiation. Explaining what underlies such variation in practice is essential to our assessment of the potential of EWCs as a vehicle for the Europeanization of industrial relations.

Central to the argument of this chapter is the interaction between 'bottom-up' and 'top-down' developments. The emergence of a European dimension to industrial relations at company level has been driven by developments from 'below' – that is, within MNCs themselves – creating pressure for regulatory intervention from 'above' that is, by the EU – which in turn facilitates and shapes further developments from below, for example through EWCs. Thus, the process of EMU has increased the threat of 'social dumping' and scope for MNCs to benchmark the performance of operations in different countries against each other, generating pressure for supranational regulatory measures, amongst which the EWCs directive is the prime example, which – through the new transnational structures that it establishes – stimulates further developments from 'below', such as company-based European framework agreements (Carley, 2001).

Social dumping: the worst excesses avoided?

A major focus of concern for the Commission and some national governments, as well as for trade unions, has been the scope that an integrated European market potentially opens up for MNCs to engage in 'regime competition' resulting in social dumping, in which labour standards and wages and conditions are progressively undercut as countries, regions and existing sites of MNCs compete to secure existing production capacity and/or new investment (Moseley, 1990). At EU level, one important rationale underpinning the Community's 1989 Social Charter was to promote measures aimed at reducing the scope for social dumping between member states. These included the future directives on working time, part-time and temporary workers, posted workers and national-level employee information and consultation. Policy debate over social dumping has been periodically fuelled by high-profile instances of the phenomenon, such as Hoover's 1993 decision to transfer production from Scotland to France and Renault's 1997 decision to close its Vilvoorde plant in Belgium, referred to above. Renault's decision, which became the focus of European-wide protest action by trade unions, was reportedly influenced by the relatively high level of labour costs in Belgium as compared to Spain, even though the Vilvoorde plant had high productivity levels (EIRO, 1997a).

Amongst member states, sensitivity to the potential for social dumping has been particularly evident in Germany and France. In the former, there has been ongoing debate over whether high wages and extensive labour market regulation are deterring investment in Germany and therefore the future of 'Standort Deutschland' (Germany as a production location). Adding impetus to the Standort debate 'has been the sudden emergence of a large pool of cheap, but relatively well qualified labour on Germany's eastern borders' since 1989 (Ferner, 1997: 176). Indeed, German foreign direct investment into central and eastern Europe accelerated rapidly during the 1990s. In France, alarm over 'délocalization' (relocation to lower labour cost countries) was initially triggered by a 1993 parliamentary report which claimed that more than one million French jobs were at risk (Ferner, 1997) and fuelled by the Hoover controversy.

In the UK, by contrast, governments have made considerable virtue of the role of a relatively lightly regulated labour market in attracting the largest share of EU inward investment of any member state, feeding fears elsewhere about social dumping. Britain's success throughout the 1980s and 1990s was attributed by successive Conservative governments to successful policies to deregulate labour markets and constrain trade union organization and activity, and thereby restrain costs and promote (numerical) flexibility (Pain, 1997). The UK's commitment to competing for inward investment on this basis was underlined by its opt-out from the Maastricht Treaty's social policy protocol. Although this was subsequently reversed in 1997 by the incoming Labour government, the UK's commitment to a flexible labour market has been continued under the new administration – evidenced in its 2003 assessment of the economic conditions for joining the single currency (HM Treasury, 2003).

Yet the argument is not quite as straightforward as it seems. France, which has markedly higher labour costs, a more tightly regulated labour market and more extensive labour protection than the UK, attracted substantial flows of inward investment throughout the 1990s – on occasion exceeding those into the UK (Barrell and Pain, 1997). Moreover, the flexible nature of the UK's labour market which is held to be so attractive to inward investors is double-edged: it also facilitates easy exit. This 'perverse' impact (Ferner, 1997: 184) has become increasingly evident as the more internationalized MNCs rationalize and restructure their operations on a pan-European basis to benefit from the economies of scale that EMU promotes.

Overall, the evidence for European integration unleashing widespread social dumping appears somewhat limited: 'in some respects, the scale of the problem has been exaggerated' (Ferner, 1997: 165). In the few sectors where significantly lower labour costs are driving investment location decisions, activities are tending to be relocated outside of the

EU altogether. Whilst the accession countries of central eastern Europe have been the beneficiaries of some such relocation, particularly involving German-based companies, the main extra-EU destinations are the countries of Asia. Even here, market-seeking motives loom as large, if not larger, in investment decisions as (labour) cost factors. MNCs' location decisions are shaped by a range of factors, of which considerations of labour standards, costs and flexibility are only one element. Even on the labour dimension, companies are also concerned with quality, skills and productivity of labour: unit labour costs rather than labour costs per se are what matter. Yet, 'Whether or not "social dumping" is a serious reality, there is certainly evidence that many MNCs use the *threat* of relocation as a disciplining factor in collective bargaining' (Hyman, 2001: 288).

The evidence interrogated

A range of evidence confirms that the trajectory of MNCs' decisions on the location of new investments and site closures is far from being one-way traffic, under which activity moves away from locations which have higher labour costs and more restrictive labour regulation towards those with relatively lower labour costs and more flexible regulatory frameworks. Erickson and Kuruvilla (1994), analysing flows of foreign direct investment into EU member states from 1980–88, found no evidence that flows into relatively lower labour cost member states were higher than those into relatively higher labour cost states. Investigating the labour factors influencing flows of US foreign direct investment across a wider group of industrialized and developing countries, Cooke and Noble (1998) report that higher hourly wage costs in a country were positively related to the volume of inward investment, speculating that this reflects higher productivity, as were levels of education and skill. Low skills were negatively related with inward investment flows. Their findings on labour market regulation and labour protection show some features being negatively associated with foreign direct investment flows and others positively. Cooke and Noble conclude that investment location decisions are shaped by a complex of labour-related considerations with cross-cutting implications.

Within particular sectors indications also point to a complex geography of location decisions in which two-way flows into and out of particular countries are simultaneously evident. For example, since the early 1990s the UK automotive sector has seen significant investment in new car manufacturing facilities by Honda, Nissan and Toyota to supply the European market, and substantial investment by PSA at its UK facility to meet growing European demand for the company's models, as well as the closure over the same period of major assembly plants by Ford and General Motors as they seek to reduce capacity on a European-wide basis. At company level, Ford has committed major new investment to its engine manufacturing operation in the UK, whilst pulling out of volume car production and centralizing its R&D operation in Germany (and away from the UK).

Even in a country such as Portugal, which, because of its relatively lower labour costs, has been seen as a potential beneficiary of social dumping within the EU, a complex pattern emerges. The low cost base does seem to be important in attracting inward investment in traditional, labour-intensive sectors – such as clothing and footwear – but access to and presence in the local market appear the prime considerations behind inward investment in modern manufacturing sectors and commerce (Buckley and Castro, 2001). Likewise in the accession countries of central eastern Europe, whilst lower labour costs for given levels of productivity are a factor in attracting inward investment, as – if not more – important are considerations of market access and presence (Meardi, 2003).

Rather than evidencing widespread social dumping, such trends suggest a tendency amongst internationally integrated MNCs to segment and stratify activities according to the varying characteristics of different national labour market regimes within the EU in terms of wage costs and social charges, productivity, training and functional and numerical flexibility (Marginson, 2000b). This is consistent with official data showing convergent unit labour costs across EU member states but comprised of very different labour-cost and productivity configurations (Adnett, 1995; Eurostat, 2003). For example, Austria, the Benelux and Nordic countries all have relatively high levels of productivity, and relatively highly qualified and skilled workforces, offsetting higher labour costs, as compared to the UK, Spain and Portugal or Hungary and Poland, where the picture is reversed. Insofar as labour considerations are a factor shaping investment location decisions within the EU, the calculus encompasses productivity and quality as well as costs with, as suggested above, the relative emphasis between them differing according to the labour market regimes of individual countries. More widely, debate around social dumping has tended to neglect the extent to which market access and presence are a major motivation for foreign direct investment.

A credible threat?

Arguably more important than actual instances of social dumping has been the potential that regime shopping and the threat to relocate have offered MNCs in securing changes in industrial relations regulation at macro- and micro-levels. At national level, repeated recourse by MNCs to the threat to relocate has been a means of bringing pressure to bear for the introduction of measures to reduce the cost base and enhance the cost base. The shift in the bargaining agenda from a 'productivity' to a 'competition' orientation (Schulten, 1998: 209), emphasized in Chapters 5, 6 and 7, simultaneously reflects and legitimizes such pressure. Viewed in this light, the significance of the Standort debate in Germany and the controversy over délocalization in France is to have increased the pressure for reform within the respective industrial relations systems.

At micro-level, Mueller (1996) shows how, under a process of 'corporate investment bargaining', individual sites of MNCs are under continuous threat to improve performance with the risk otherwise of being starved of investment and ultimately run down and closed. Poor performance is punished by directing investment, and transferring production, to better performing sites in other countries. Conversely, strong performance is rewarded by new investment and augmented production mandates: Mueller and Purcell (1992) provide examples from car manufacture; Coller (1996) from food manufacturing. Crucially, the threat to relocate has to be credible. The initial decision of companies, such as Mercedes-Benz, to locate production facilities outside their home country provided management with a new and additional bargaining lever over its domestic workforce: threats to relocate overseas can no longer be seen as empty (Mueller, 1996). Similar reasoning in respect of its major domestic workforce in France was said by a manager at Peugeot to lie behind the company's renewed commitment to its UK plant (Sisson and Marginson, 2000). The significance of this 'politics of investment' for the implementation by MNCs of similar working practices across sites in different countries is explored below.

Two dimensions of cross-border management practice

As MNCs deepen their international management structures at European level, along the lines elaborated in Chapter 2, they increasingly have the capacity to develop transnational approaches to HRM and industrial relations, at European and also global level. The organization-specific employment systems that companies are developing, described in Chapters 6 and 7, can be extended across borders. The emergence of a pan-European approach is taking two main forms: explicit and implicit. Under the first, common policies are explicitly promulgated across different countries. Under the second, the pursuit of common policies is implicitly secured through a sequence of local decisions on implementation, underpinned by benchmarking processes, diffusion of best practice and deployment of 'coercive' comparisons of performance across countries and locations.

The explicit dimension: common policies

The adoption of explicit cross-border, common human resource and industrial relations policies has yet to become widespread, for non-managerial employees at least. Where they exist, such common policies tend to cover employee training and development, employee involvement and communication, equal opportunities and performance-related remuneration systems, including financial participation. Amongst our case companies, *Gerbank* has common worldwide policies on remuneration systems and training. These take the form of a 'global footprint' which lays down the main principles, but leaves the detailed implementation to the individual countries and businesses in the light of local regulation, customs and practice. These worldwide policies are recommended, but not binding, on individual countries and businesses – adding a further dimension to their 'softness' (in Chapter 3's terms). Much the same applies to *Italmetal*'s group-wide set of values and policies which covers aspects of industrial relations, such as recognition of the legitimate role and participation of trade unions, as well as HR matters. *Belmetal* is developing European-wide framework policies on remuneration systems, training and employee involvement and communication; policies on some other aspects, such as appraisal, are global in application.

A small but growing number of companies are elaborating such common policies through the negotiation of joint texts with their EWCs (see below). Notable amongst these is Groupe Danone, which has adopted European-level policies on training, equal opportunities, employee information and trade union rights (Carley, 2001). *Gerbank* has also concluded a European-level agreement with its EWC on employment security in the context of restructuring; likewise, the European headquarters of *Britmetal2* has concluded two European-level framework agreements on the handling of aspects of ongoing restructuring.

Fresh impetus to the promulgation of explicitly framed cross-border policies is coming from the mounting pressures on MNCs to demonstrate their 'corporate social responsibility'. A growing number of MNCs are adopting codes of conduct on a worldwide basis. Either drawn up unilaterally or, less frequently, negotiated with trade unions or works councils, many of these address employment and industrial relations issues, including child and forced labour, health and safety, freedom of association and the right to collective bargaining, minimum wages and anti-discrimination. A 1998 ILO study identified some 170 MNC codes which addressed such labour issues (EWCB, 2000). In mid-2002, some 25 MNCs operating in Europe were reported to have negotiated global agreements with international trade union organizations, or, in a few instances, EWCs, introducing codes of conduct covering labour matters. Reflecting developments in the EU's sector social dialogue, reported in Chapter 4, a feature of several of these agreements is the establishment of mechanisms to monitor application of the code (EWCB, 2002).

The implicit dimension: the two faces of benchmarking

Management's implicit pursuit of common, cross-border policies in internationally integrated MNCs occurs through processes of cross-border benchmarking. As Chapter 3 emphasized, these have two faces: one is the diffusion of those employment and work practices which are deemed to be examples of 'best' practice; the second is the deployment of coercive comparisons of performance between locations in negotiations over changes to employment and working practice. A growing number of MNCs have put in place management systems to diffuse best examples of working and employment practice across sites in different European countries (Coller, 1996; Edwards *et al.*, 1999). Such systems include the regular convening of meetings of production and personnel managers from sites in different countries, rotation of managerial staff from one site to another – both to champion the diffusion of particular initiatives and to learn about others – compilation of manuals of best practice and the assignment of a corporate management taskforce with a specific remit to identify and diffuse examples of best practice. The approach is frequently 'menu driven' in that local management are expected to choose from a range of best practices according to local production requirements and workforce circumstances. The emphasis is on implementing work practices tailored to business requirements on a site-by-site basis.

The process of diffusion of best practice is reinforced by the second face of cross-border benchmarking, which emanates from the systems of performance control utilized within major MNCs. Corporate and international business line management now have the capacity to compare the performance of workforces from sites across Europe, and beyond, across a range of productivity and labour-related indicators (Marginson *et al.*, 1995). Such coercive comparisons are being deployed by international management to place pressure on local management and thereby to lever concessions in working and employment practices from work-forces deemed to be performing poorly, under threat of loss of production mandates, disinvestment and ultimately run-down and closure. In locating production mandates and investment, corporate headquarters can thereby 'reward' strongly performing sites and 'punish' those that are performing poorly (Mueller and Purcell, 1992).

Findings from a survey of MNCs with operations in the UK (Marginson *et al.*, 1995) give an indication of the extensiveness of the practices involved. They also indicate variation according to international management structure and integration. Collection of data on indicators of labour performance was widespread, but not universal. Seventy per cent of the MNCs surveyed regularly collected data on at least one indicator of labour performance from sites in different countries, with 50 and 34 per cent, respectively, regularly monitoring labour cost and productivity data. The proportion was highest in the one-third of companies convening regular international meetings of personnel managers. Labour performance comparisons would appear to be very much on the agenda of such meetings; in almost three-quarters of relevant cases such data were utilized for comparisons between sites. In almost one-quarter of all cases, rising to nearly one-half where there were regular international meetings, these data were used in shaping investment and disinvestment decisions. The use of data for comparisons between sites and in (dis)investment decisions, was significantly more widespread in MNCs organized around international business streams which cut across countries, than in those which remained organized around national subsidiaries. The same held true comparing MNCs with internationally integrated operations with those where this was not so.

Although the corporate perspective on the benchmarking and diffusion processes is transnational, any negotiation over the implementation of working practices deemed 'best', and/or concessions in terms of more flexible and lower cost arrangements, remains at local or national level. The dynamics involved are well illustrated by changes in working time arrangements at General Motors' European operations. A 1997 'template' study involved an international unit which compared labour costs in the company's operations across Europe. The clear implication was that those sites wishing to maintain investment and employment would have to display a determination to make themselves the best in the group. It was only in 1998 that the effects became fully manifest, however. Hancké (2000: 45) describes developments at General Motors' operations in Belgium, Germany, Spain and the UK in that year:

> The competitive dynamic underlying the process explains this convergence. Management would start by singling out one plant as a pilot bargaining arena for changes in working time or work organisation. The agreement concluded in this 'most favourable' setting (for management) was then, in the next round, presented to every other plant in the company as a minimum standard. These other plants had no alternative but to follow suit, since they might otherwise find themselves in an unfavourable position in the next round of model planning.

Variation by sector and company

Differences are evident between sectors, and also between companies, in the extent to which such coercive comparisons are drawn and deployed by management in national and local company negotiations. The contrast between the automotive and banking sectors, drawing on Sisson and Marginson (2000) and our company cases, is illustrative. Amongst the major automotive manufacturers the use of such comparisons in company negotiations was widespread before the implementation of EMU. Increasingly it is reaching beyond Europe to companies' plants across the globe, as practice at *Belmetal*, *Britmetal2* and *Italmetal* confirmed. Nonetheless, the intensity of comparisons within the European operations remains greater. Such cross-country comparisons of costs and performance are increasingly evident, although not as intensive, in the components part of the sector. They are a routine feature, for example, of *Germetal*'s operations. Their deployment in negotiations with local workforces is aimed at securing changes in working practices and working time arrangements against future management commitments on investment and production for the plant concerned. In some instances, such as the General Motors example, the process involved can amount to a cross-border round of concession bargaining, resulting in a convergence of practice across countries. On the employee side, the use of cross-country comparisons by trade unions and works councils in company-level negotiations appears to be less well developed, a point developed in the next section. Management is the driving force behind this Europeanization of the agenda, process and outcomes of local and national bargaining.

In contrast, in banking management's use of such coercive comparisons in local and national company negotiations is effectively absent.

In *Belbank* and *Gerbank*, however, systematic comparisons of labour performance are beginning to be made in activities, such as back-office operations, which are being centralized and integrated across borders. Such developments aside, there is nothing like the level of homogenization of products of the automotive manufacturers or the integrated production arrangements that accompany them. For their part, employee representatives do not have the tradition of workplace organization that is found in the automotive sector, which provides the basis from which a coordinated cross-border response to management might be developed.

European Works Councils – providing the platform for 'Europeanization'?

The most significant institutional innovation in Euro-company industrial relations has been the establishment of EWCs. Their emergence represents a key instance of the interaction of top-down and bottom-up pressures. From above, proposals for employee rights to transnational information and consultation, which resulted in the EWCs Directive, were central to the European Commission's initiative for a social dimension (Hall, 1994). From below, a small number of French- and German-owned MNCs had already established voluntary European-level information and consultation arrangements prior to the publication of the draft Directive in 1991. Indeed, as Hall (1992) argues, the terms of the Directive were both prefigured and influenced by these prototype EWCs.

Originally adopted by 17 of the 18 EEA (European Economic Area) countries in September 1994, and subsequently extended to the UK in December 1997, the Directive requires 'Community-scale' companies to establish EWCs for the purposes of information and consultation on matters of a transnational nature affecting employees' interests. Under the Directive's provisions, the process of establishing an EWC is triggered by a request from representatives of employees in more than one country. 'Community-scale' companies are defined as those with 1,000 or more employees in the EEA and operations employing 150 or more in at least two EEA states; over 1,800 MNCs, including the EEA operations of companies headquartered in the US, Japan and other non-EEA countries, are estimated to be covered (ETUI, 2002). EU enlargement further extends the Directive's reach.

The framing of the Directive, which in its procedures for implementation provides scope for negotiated arrangements to take precedence over the statutory requirements which it specifies, has – consistent with the argument of Chapter 3 – been described as signalling a 'paradigm shift' (Müller and Platzer, 2003: 58) in EU social policy regulation. The novel nature of the EWC directive lies in 'its combination of three principles: regulation (procedural rules and an enforceable set of statutory minimum provisions), subsidiarity (adaptability to national and corporate conditions), and the primacy of negotiations (which give the parties at national level considerable leeway in shaping their institution)' (Müller and Platzer, 2003: 58). The primacy accorded to negotiated arrangements in implementing the Directive's requirements, has prompted European-level negotiations between management and employee representatives (frequently trade unions) on an unprecedented scale. By late 2002, an estimated 639 MNCs had negotiated agreements establishing a total of 739 EWCs (the difference being accounted for by two or more EWCs being established for the respective international divisions of the same MNC) (Waddington and Kerckhofs, 2003). Of these, no more than 40 were in existence at the time the Directive was adopted.

Yet the 'European' character of these new European-level industrial relations structures, and their potential effectiveness in advancing employee interests, has been forcefully questioned (Schulten, 1996; Streeck, 1997, 1998). Streeck (1997) argues that EWCs are 'neither European nor works councils'. In suggesting that they are not 'European', Streeck's contention is that 'one can expect European works councils to be heavily coloured by the national system of their company's country of origin' (1997: 331). This is because employee representatives of the MNC's home country workforce, by dint of their established relations with group management and their numerical dominance, are likely to play a decisive role in negotiations and thereby significantly influence the structure and role of the resulting EWC. 'In effect ... European works councils will be *international extensions of national systems of workplace representation*, instead of European institutions in a strict sense' (ibid., emphasis in original). In contending that they are not works councils, Streeck underlines that their formal consultation rights under the directive's statutory fall-back requirements are defined merely as 'dialogue' or an 'exchange of views'; there is no obligation to consult in the sense that management act only after employee representatives 'have had an opportunity to present a considered opinion' (Streeck, 1997: 329) and less still co-determination on any matters.

Engaging with Streeck's twin propositions, this section establishes that EWCs can – but not that they necessarily will – develop as European entities and that they are not necessarily doomed to being shadows of the real thing (i.e. national works councils with strong consultation rights). The considerable variety in the provisions of the agreements negotiated between management and employee representatives and in the practice and impact of EWCs is underlined. Cross-cutting differences are evident by country of origin of MNC, sector, and company structure and organization. The discussion proceeds by reviewing the diffusion of EWCs, the provisions of EWC agreements and the practice of EWCs, before considering the potential for EWCs to prompt European-level bargaining.

Diffusion of EWCs

According to the country of origin of the MNC concerned, EWCs are concentrated amongst seven countries: companies based in France, Germany, the UK and the US account for almost 60 per cent, with multinationals based in the Netherlands, Sweden and Switzerland accounting for a further 20 per cent (calculated from Waddington and Kerckhofs, 2003: 325–6). There are differences in the 'strike rate' of agreements concluded to companies covered by MNC country of origin, suggesting some influence of national systems on the diffusion of EWCs. Amongst the large European economies, for example, Germany has a relatively low strike rate at 25 per cent, whereas at 40 per cent the UK's is relatively high (Waddington and Kerckhofs, 2003: 325). The precedence which the Directive accords to agreements negotiated between the parties to establish EWCs leaves scope for the conclusion of arrangements which extend beyond the EEA in their geographical coverage. In a sizeable minority, EWCs provide for representation from operations in European countries outside the EEA, and in a handful arrangements are world-wide. One in five agreements extend coverage to Switzerland and – some five years prior to EU enlargement – a similar proportion to one or more of the countries of central Europe (Carley and Marginson, 2000). Considerations of companies' production and management organization within Europe, rather than minimal compliance or the political boundaries of the EEA, seem to be driving the way in which 'Europe' is operationalized in EWC agreements.

As between sectors, manufacturing dominates the picture, accounting for almost 80 per cent of agreements, construction and the utilities account for 7–8 per cent and services for just under 15 per cent. There are considerable differences in the sectoral 'strike rate' of agreements concluded compared to the number of MNCs covered by the directive. Important influences are the extent to which production is internationally organized and integrated and the strength of trade union organization. Overall, the 'strike rate' of agreements in the more internationalized manufacturing sectors are double that in the service sectors, where competition tends to be more nationally bounded and trade union organization less extensive (Carley and Marginson, 2000). The first factor also suggests why, within manufacturing, strike rates in the oil and chemicals sectors are markedly higher than those in paper and printing and textiles, clothing and footwear; and both factors help explain why the strike rate in financial services is considerably higher than in any other service sector. Differences in the penetration of EWCs according to type of company reflect the operation of three influences (Waddington and Kerckhofs, 2003: 326). Penetration rises with: company size (in employment terms); spread of the workforce across two or more countries (as compared with concentration in a single country); and the extent of internationalization (the number of countries in which an MNC has operations).

EWC agreements

Four influences on the contents of EWC agreements are apparent (Gilman and Marginson, 2002). First are the terms of the EWC directive itself, or a 'statutory model effect'. For example, as compared with so-called 'Article 13' agreements concluded in the period before the Directive came into force in September 1996, later 'Article 6' agreements are more likely to contain provision for the employee side to have access to independent experts and to convene additional EWC meetings should extraordinary circumstances arise. Both these are matters directly covered in the Directive. Second is a 'country effect' under which industrial relations arrangements in the European country in which an MNC is headquartered, and those for employee information and consultation in particular, influence the provision of EWC agreements. There is a tendency – but not a rule (Marginson, 2000a) – for EWCs to reflect nationally-based structures for employee consultation: that, for example, following the French model, EWCs in French-based MNCs are constituted as joint management–employee structures whereas, in accordance with the German model, their counterparts in German-based MNCs are employee-only structures. The influence of different systems of corporate governance is also evident in the stipulation of confidentiality clauses, which are significantly more widespread amongst EWCs in UK-based MNCs than amongst their counterparts in French-, German- or Nordic-based companies.

Third is a 'sector effect', which cuts across countries. This arises from the similarities in production methods, employment practice and industrial relations traditions within sectors, but also from the influence of the trade union EIFs. These have played an important role in initiating and coordinating negotiations within their respective sectors (Rivest, 1996). Such an effect is evident, for example, in the basic structure of EWCs where, controlling for country, joint structures are significantly more evident in chemicals and food and drink as compared with metalworking, reflecting different sectoral industrial relations traditions. There are also sector differences over whether agreements explicitly provide for trade union officials to participate in the EWC. Such participation is more common in EWCs in chemicals and food and drink than metalworking. Following Rivest (1996), this reflects the differing emphasis placed on such provision by the respective EIFs. Fourth, a 'learning effect' is evident, under which innovations in earlier agreements which come to be regarded by the parties as good practice become generalized in later agreements. Like the 'sector effect' the 'learning effect' cuts across countries. It is evidenced by the growing incidence of clauses in agreements dealing with training for employee representatives – a matter on which the Directive is silent.

Overall, the evidence on the provisions of EWC agreements shows that national systems of workplace representation and consultation do have an influence, as also do systems of corporate governance. But it also points to the salience of sector influences and learning effects which are cross-country in nature: cross-border processes and European-level actors – trade unions and MNCs – are also influential in shaping the provisions of agreements.

The contention that EWCs are not works councils would appear to be on firmer ground. The overwhelming majority of agreements define consultation in terms of 'dialogue' or an 'exchange of views'; only one in ten agreements make provision for a more formal consultation process, including the right for the employee side to give considered comments or opinions or to make recommendations, and just 3 per cent of agreements anticipate a negotiating role for the EWC (Carley and Marginson, 2000). Moreover, the provisions of some EWC agreements fall short of the requirements incorporated in the statutory fallback model, particularly on the rights of employee representatives to an additional EWC meeting in the event of exceptional business decisions affecting employees' interests and to be assisted by experts of their own choosing (Marginson *et al.*, 1998). Such shortcomings are mostly evident amongst 'Article 13' agreements. 'Article 6' agreements, negotiated under the Directive's procedures, almost all conform with the minimum requirements on these and other matters laid down in the statutory fall-back model (Carley and Marginson, 2000).

The actual practice of EWCs cannot, however, be read-off from the provisions of agreements, still less from those of the Directive:

> the Directive's lack of rigorous regulatory specification does not mean that the EWC as a company-level forum for 'social dialogue' and an instrument of participation is necessarily weak. Rather its effectiveness is achieved [or not] by practical operation. (Müller and Platzer, 2003: 68)

At best, EWC agreements are likely to provide only an approximate guide to the practice evolved by the parties. Practice may differ from, or have moved beyond, the provisions laid down in agreements. The formal provisions of agreements serve to facilitate or constrain the development of EWCs in particular directions. Accordingly, Marginson *et al.* (1998) drew a distinction between agreements whose provisions seem likely to constrain the EWC to a formal or 'symbolic' role – in which there is a ritual annual meeting but little or no contact between employee representatives in-between, and none with management – and those whose provisions are likely to promote an EWC with an 'active' role in which there is contact and networking amongst the employee representatives and liaison with management, the provision of information and dialogue are ongoing.

EWC practice

Evidence on EWCs' practice suggests that they are not in general bound by the tradition of employee information and consultation in the country in which the respective MNC is headquartered. Neither are all EWCs confined to information provision: 'their internal structure, cohesiveness and capacity for information, consultation and negotiation all vary considerably' (Müller and Platzer, 2003: 60). There is a considerable variety of practice, in which some EWCs acquire de facto rights beyond their limited formal entitlement.

Drawing on a study of eight EWCs in multinationals based in four European countries, Lecher and Rüb (1999) identify three trajectories of development. Under the first two, the operation of EWCs results in bodies which, in contrasting ways, are indeed no more than extensions of national systems. But under the third, the functioning of the EWC is creating a genuinely transnational form of interest representation. The first path is where the EWC is essentially the meeting point of different national representatives: each national delegation regards the EWC as an extension of its national system and attempts to use the EWC to promote issues which accord with national priorities. Such EWCs develop a largely symbolic existence confined to an annual meeting. Following Levinson's (1972) classic analysis of the potential for transnational collective bargaining, these are 'polycentric' in orientation. Second are those EWCs in which representatives of the home country dominate its functioning, providing the secretariat and leading officers. Nonetheless, the EWC assumes an active rather than symbolic role, characterized by communication between employee representatives in between meetings and ongoing contact with group management. In Levinson's terms, this represents an 'ethnocentric' approach. Third are those EWCs which are developing a new, European, identity distinct from that of the structures of representation in the home country. These correspond to Levinson's 'geocentric' orientation. Continuing communication and activity on the employee side is not necessarily coordinated by home country representatives, who do not have a monopoly of leading positions on the EWC. Such EWCs are more than the sum of the national delegations, developing a European agenda which is not nationally driven, and beginning to regulate some matters at European level.

Lecher and Rüb (1999) find evidence of all three types of EWC. Crucially, even though many of the EWCs in question had only been in operation for two to three years, some were already evolving a transnational or 'European' mode of operation where the network of contacts and control of resources is not nationally-centred. More recently, surveying 165 European-based MNCs with EWCs Vitols (2003) finds little evidence of a 'home country' effect on managers' assessment of EWC effectiveness and impact. EWCs, according to Vitols, can be as effective in countries, such as the UK and Italy, with weaker traditions of enterprise-based partnership, as in those with stronger ones, such as Germany and the Nordic countries. In general, EWCs seem not to be primarily an extension of national systems.

The considerable variety of EWC practice is underlined in further work by Lecher and his colleagues (Lecher *et al.*, 2001). Their comparative, cross-country and cross-sectoral, analysis of EWCs' role and functioning in 23 MNCs is structured according to four fields of interaction between the actors involved: the (employee-side) EWC and central management; amongst the EWC employee representatives; the (employee-side) EWC and national and local structures of employee representation; and the (employee-side) EWC and trade unions. Analysing the interplay between the four different fields of interaction under this framework yields four empirically distinctive types of EWC, differentiated according to their capacity to act: the 'symbolic', 'service', 'project-oriented' and 'participatory' EWCs. The 'symbolic' EWC, in which there is a low level of information provision and no formal consultation, resembles that suggested by Marginson *et al.* (1998) as outlined above. The 'service' EWC engages with the (better quality) information it receives from management and exchanges information between employee representatives, with both kinds of information being utilized by representatives locally. There is ongoing contact between meetings on the employee-side and liaison with management. The 'project-oriented' EWC differs from the 'service' EWC in the degree of organization and capacity for cooperative action on the employee side. Projects undertaken by the employee side might be a systematic exchange of information across countries on a particular matter or framing ground rules on how to respond to management decisions, for instance restructuring which involves job loss. In a 'participatory' EWC, dialogue goes beyond the provision of information by management and an exchange of views to embrace some kind of formalized consultation procedure and even negotiation over particular matters. The employee side has the organized capacity to deliver coherent positions to management on issues arising, and has close relations with and is effectively resourced by trade unions.

Lecher *et al.* (2001) firmly establish that some EWCs are more than mere shadows of the real thing. The most advanced are acquiring de facto rights to the more formalized consultation found under some national works council provisions, and thereby exercising influence beyond the relatively limited formal rights envisaged under the directive. Equally, the fact that around one-half of Lecher *et al.*'s cases fall under the 'symbolic' type indicates that the grounds for pessimism articulated by Streeck and others have real substance. Nonetheless, the proposition that EWCs are doomed to be ineffective as structures of employee interest representation turns out to be a contingent and not a general one.

Two further questions arise: given the as yet relatively short life of many of these European-level structures, are more EWCs likely to develop into active and even 'participatory' bodies? Second, what are the conditions that facilitate the emergence of an active rather than a symbolic

EWC? On the first, an initially pessimistic conclusion is suggested by Hancké's (2000) study of the role of EWCs in restructuring in car manufacture. The significance of the study is that the industry can be considered a critical case: one where EWCs are likely to have the most impact, because of the strength of union and works council organization at national and local levels and given the presence of pre-existing international trade union networks. Yet reviewing experience across 11 car manufacturing EWCs, Hancké concludes that it is management which was better able to utilize the EWC – to secure legitimacy for its restructuring decisions at European level and thereby help to diffuse national and local opposition from affected sites. Employee and union representatives largely utilized the EWC to pursue local interests, and in the face of a regime of internal competition between sites, experienced acute difficulty in forging common positions. This rather bleak assessment needs, however, to be tempered in the light of subsequent developments. These have seen workforce representatives successfully press central management into the conclusion of European-level framework agreements on the implementation of restructuring programmes with EWCs at Ford and General Motors (Carley, 2001). These agreements are amongst the most advanced instances of EWC practice, coming close in the substantive matters that they address – employment terms and conditions and employment rights – to those traditionally concluded in national systems.

Further understanding of the factors shaping the future development of EWCs lies in the answer to the second question. Lecher *et al.* (1999, 2001) take an 'actor-centred' approach which underlines the importance of such factors as organizing capacity and effective networking between the employee representatives, strong links between EWC employee representatives and those at national and local levels, close relations with trade unions which in turn provide resources and expert assistance and cooperative, and high trust, relations with management. Yet also important in shaping or constraining EWCs' capacity to act are a range of structural preconditions, including the degree of internationalization of the business operations of the MNC concerned.

Examining EWCs in eight UK- and US-based MNCs, a Warwick-based team (Hall *et al.*, 2003; Marginson *et al.*, 2004) find that the organization and networking activity of the employee side and, in turn, the capacity of the employee side to influence the outcome of management decisions on transnational business matters, are conditioned by the nature of companies' business operations and the degree to which they are internationalized. Three considerations are important. First, the extent to which business operations are spread across several countries or concentrated in one, and therefore whether the EWC is numerically dominated by representatives from a single country. Second is the business portfolio of the company, and whether this extends across a range of business activities or is focused on a single business. Where there are multiple business activities, which may be differentially spread across countries, similarities of interest amongst employee representatives are more difficult to establish. Where there is a single business focus, such similarities of interest are more readily established amongst representatives. This second consideration is intensified or attenuated by the third, which is integration of production and other activities across borders. With integrated production across national borders, employee interests are not only similar but become directly interdependent. Accordingly, employee-side organization and networking activity was found to be strongest, and the impact of the EWC on management decision making greatest, in single business companies whose operations are spread across countries and where production and other activities are integrated across European borders. It was least, and no EWC impact on management decision making was evident, in multi-business companies whose operations tended to be concentrated in one country and/or where there was little cross-border integration of production.

EWC practice in the eight MNCs was further shaped by a range of other factors, some structural and some behavioural. Management structure and management policy are both important. How far EWCs are 'active' rather than 'symbolic' was facilitated or constrained by whether there was a European-level management structure which actually corresponded to the EWC. Where there was 'fit' between the management structure and the EWC at European level, the EWC was more likely to be active and to have an impact on management decisions, than where there was not. And EWCs were more likely to exercise influence where management's approach to the EWC was proactive, seeing it as a mechanism that could be harnessed for management purposes – such as improving employee understanding of the rationale for business decisions and hence the legitimacy of management actions – than where management's approach was minimalist, primarily concerned to comply with its legal obligations and strictly circumscribing the activity of the EWC. The nature of pre-existing structures of employee representation was also important in facilitating the development of employee-side organization and activity; in particular, the existence of representative structures at national group level in the main countries of operation and/or a pre-existing international network amongst representatives on which the EWC can build. It was in the single case, one of the large automotive manufacturers, in which all these preconditions were present that the employee side exercised the strongest influence amongst the eight cases, embracing de facto rights to more formalized consultation and the negotiation of European-level agreements with central management on the handling of restructuring (Marginson *et al.*, 2004).

Both sector and, seemingly, variety of capitalism (Hall and Soskice, 2001) – rather than country-specific – differences in EWC practice are apparent. The structural features of companies to which the Warwick research draws attention are more prevalent amongst MNCs in some sectors than others, as the comparison between automotive and finance below underlines. In general, the combination of internationally integrated operations and well organized trade unions and works councils within companies which underpins the more advanced forms of EWC practice is more widespread in key manufacturing sectors such as metalworking and chemicals than in the service sectors. Lecher *et al.* (2001) report few differences in EWC practice according to the country of origin of the MNC concerned. Surveying employee representatives on EWCs across five countries, however, Waddington (2003) finds differences consistent with the contrasting types of corporate governance arrangements found in Hall and Soskice's two main forms of capitalism, introduced in Chapter 2. Employee representatives in MNCs based in the 'liberal market' economies of the UK and US, irrespective of which country they are working in, report that the EWC agenda is narrower, the quality and timeliness of the information provided by management is poorer, the occurrence of consultation least widespread and its extent more limited as compared to their counterparts in MNCs based in the 'coordinated market' economies of continental Europe.

Three conclusions emerge from this review. First, the 'capacity to act' of EWCs, and the influence they wield, varies considerably, from engaging in a symbolic exercise largely devoid of any outcome of consequence to bodies which wield a measure of influence over management decision making to those which exercise de facto rights of consultation and even negotiation beyond that envisaged in the Directive. Second, this substantial variation is shaped more by the international nature of the company concerned, and the sector in which it operates, than by features of the particular country in which a given company is headquartered. Third, to date only a minority of EWCs have evolved as effective means of employee interest representation at European level. Yet insofar as international integration of operations is progressively spreading across sectors, and tending to deepen further within given sectors, a crucial element of the preconditions for the development of a larger number of EWCs which possess this capacity is becoming more widely diffused.

Opening the door to European-level collective bargaining?

Are EWCs likely to provide a focal point for the further Europeanization of industrial relations at company level? And, are they opening the door to European-level collective bargaining? The potential of EWCs as a focal point for employee action at transnational level has already been glimpsed in the European-level mobilization of workforces from different countries in protest action following Renault's 1997 announcement to close its plant at Vilvoorde in Belgium (EIRO, 1997a) and again following General Motors' European-wide restructuring plans announced in 2000 (EWCB, 2001). In 2002 Fiat's EWC organized a day of protest action across the company's European sites in the face of the group's restructuring plans (EWCB, 2003). Restructuring plans at other companies, including ABB Alstom, Goodyear and Levi-Strauss, have been the focus of European-level demonstrations and lobbies and coordinated union activity across borders. Conversely, the potential of EWCs as a mechanism through which management can secure enhanced legitimacy for its cross-border restructuring decisions, and better facilitate their implementation, has also been evidenced in the automotive sector (Hancké, 2000). Elsewhere, amongst the large Dutch banks the potential of EWCs to facilitate the promotion of common, European-wide human resource policies has been recognized by management (Sisson and Marginson, 2000).

In the lead-up to the Directive's adoption, employers voiced widespread concern that EWCs would provide a stepping stone towards European-level collective bargaining over substantive industrial relations matters. Conversely, on the trade union side, there were aspirations that EWCs would provide just such a platform. In general, such fears and aspirations remain far from being fulfilled. If the EWCs Directive has promoted substantial negotiating activity towards the establishment of European Works Councils, the remit of most EWCs nevertheless remains confined to employee information and consultation. Yet EWCs are prompting forms of 'virtual collective bargaining' at Euro-company level, embracing two kinds of process (Marginson and Sisson, 1998). First, the conclusion of European-level framework agreements or joint texts. Second, 'arm's-length bargaining' in which management and employee or union representatives do not negotiate face-to-face at European level, but in which bargaining agenda (and outcomes) within the different national operations of an MNC are increasingly coordinated across countries.

On the first process, a small number of EWCs have agreed joint texts; Carley (2002a) identifies 26 such texts concluded by 12 EWCs. Analysing 14 of these texts, Carley (2001) notes considerable variation in the nature of the regulation provided, echoing Chapter 4's assessment of the output from the sector social dialogue. In some instances, the texts spell out general frameworks for company policy – as at Suez-Lyonnaise des Eaux and Vivendi – with no indication as to how their implementation will be effected or monitored. In others, they commit the signatories to specific actions – such as the establishment of a health and safety observatory at ENI. A further group take the form of framework agreements for lower-level action, with a crucial distinction between those that are permissive, inciting follow-up at lower levels – such as Danone's 1996 agreement on training and *Gerbank*'s joint text on employment security in the context of restructuring – and those that are obligatory on the parties at lower levels. Of the latter, the agreements coming closest to traditional 'hard' collective agreements are those concluded during 2000 by the EWCs at Ford Europe and GM Europe dealing with the status, rights and terms and conditions of employees being transferred into the Visteon spin-off and to a new power train joint venture with FIAT, respectively. The subsequent 2001 agreement at GM Europe on handling its European-wide restructuring also falls into this category.

'Soft' issues such as training, equal opportunities and employment policy, which might not necessarily be addressed in national and local collective agreements, are prominent amongst the subject matter addressed by several of these jointly agreed texts. Yet, as indicated above, 'hard' issues which are central to national and local negotiations are also in evidence. Context is important too, with half the texts analysed addressing issues arising as a result of company restructuring (Carley, 2001). The innovations in collective bargaining prompted by management's need to handle restructuring would seem not to be confined to the within-country PECs analysed in Chapter 6, but extend to new pan-European forms of agreement.

On the second process, the cross-border dimension to management's approach to local negotiations has been addressed earlier, evidenced in the use of cross-border comparisons of performance and pursuit of similar concessions in working practice in local negotiations across sites in different countries. On the employee side, EWCs represent a potentially vital resource for organizing cross-border exchanges of information on bargaining matters and, in the medium term, coordination of bargaining agenda with the aim of securing similar bargaining outcomes. As yet, however, such cross-border bargaining cooperation seems confined to relatively few instances, with a distinctly uneven pattern across sectors. A comparison of automotive, where such activity is most prominent, with finance – drawing further on Sisson and Marginson (2000) and our company cases – is again instructive.

EWCs are almost universal amongst the large automotive manufacturers and originated relatively early; coverage is less comprehensive amongst the multinational automotive suppliers. In banking, EWC coverage amongst the large financial groups is more patchy – as yet, *Italbank* has no EWC, for example – and the EWCs that have been established are of more recent origin. Concerning practice in the two sectors, Sisson and Marginson (2000: 92) report that instances of 'active and effective EWC arrangements appear to be largely confined to the automotive [manufacturing] sector'. In some manufacturers employee representatives were utilizing EWCs for a systematic exchange of information on matters related to company-level negotiations – with working time arrangements a particular focus. These EWCs were frequently preceded by trade-union-sponsored contacts between local representatives, who themselves have considerable company-level negotiating experience. Amongst the case companies, employee representatives at *Britmetal2* were actively engaged in the systematic exchange of information relevant to local and national negotiations, and in attempting to forge common positions. Their counterparts at *Germetal* had undertaken a comprehensive survey of working time arrangements across the group's European operations to provide contextual data for local negotiations. At *Belmetal*, information exchange on terms and major conditions between the unions at the large Belgian and French sites is of long standing, although it had not embraced other countries. Contact between representatives at *Italmetal* was said to be useful for improving understanding across countries, but was not oriented towards bargaining matters. For their part, management at *Britmetal2* and *Belmetal* commented on the usefulness of the EWC in enabling it to present the wider context in which local negotiations occur. At *Germetal*, the EWC was said to provide a valuable interlocutor at European level from which the employee response at country level to upcoming decisions could be gauged.

In contrast, EWCs in banking represented the first opportunity that employee representatives have had to meet each other. Coming from a less entrenched tradition of local, company-level negotiations these representatives were not engaging in any systematic exchange of bargaining information. At *Belbank* and *Britbank1* both sides observed that to date relatively few genuinely transnational issues had arisen, although in the future, as some back-office activities become cross-border, the picture might change. The same observations apply to *Gerbank*, although here – as already noted – the EWC has agreed a European-level framework for handling restructuring in ways consistent with employment security.

EWCs are incrementally opening the door to forms of European collective bargaining. At the European level, in promoting common HR policies which reach across borders an increasing number of MNCs might see advantages deriving from agreeing a framework of principles or guidelines with workforce representatives through the EWC; alternatively, in implementing cross-border restructuring programmes in the face of a well-organized workforce further MNCs might follow Ford and GM Europe in concluding agreements which map out a European framework for handling the consequences. Across Europe, management's continued use of cross-border comparisons in local negotiations in the growing number of MNCs which have internationally integrated operations can only serve, in the medium term, to encourage employee representatives to counter with comparisons of their own. EWCs provide a platform from which to organize this.

Conclusions and implications

European-scale MNCs are playing a key role in the development of industrial relations at European level. They have been integral in driving forward the regime competition which the single market and then monetary union have stimulated, and the social dumping that it threatens to unleash. The threat of social dumping has proved potent, even if the actual incidence has been modest. In turn, this has been a crucial ingredient in the pressure for 'spillover' in the shape of an accompanying social dimension to market integration, realized in measures to reduce the scope for damaging competition in labour standards between member states and new information and consultation rights for employee representatives aimed at enhancing employee voice over restructuring decisions. At the same time, the implications of managing business operations which are increasingly pan-European in scope and organization has prompted a growing number of MNCs to develop a cross-border, European dimension to their own company-specific industrial relations practice. This is taking either an explicit, 'formal' or an implicit, 'informal' form – based on benchmarking, diffusion of best practice and coercive comparisons. The effect has been to articulate legislative initiative from 'above' with emerging transnational practice from 'below'. As a result, some EWCs are becoming a focal point for two processes of 'virtual' collective bargaining (Marginson and Sisson, 1998), involving the conclusion of European-level framework agreements and/or 'arm's-length' bargaining in which local company negotiations are coordinated across borders.

Taken together with the prominence of MNCs in the decentralization from sector to company level occurring within national industrial relations systems (see Chapters 6 and 7), the emergence of a Euro-company level of industrial relations confirms the central contribution of these powerful non-state actors in developing the multi-level character of governance arrangements in industrial relations. Insofar as the Euro-company level of industrial relations has taken a formal shape, it has also contributed to the changes in the nature and scope of regulation introduced in Chapter 3. The nature of the regulation involved reflects the wider shift in emphasis from 'hard' to 'soft' forms evident at other European levels, and also at higher levels within national systems. The information and consultation rights accorded to EWC employee representatives are 'softer' than those found in some – but not all – national systems, leading some to presume that EWCs would be rather ineffective. This chapter has shown, however, that an absence of hard rights does not necessarily translate into a lack of employee influence, a conclusion which echoes that of Chapter 4's assessment of the social dialogue. In terms of company-specific regulation, common, cross-border, management policies tend to be framework in form, leaving the details of implementation to the local businesses; some are advisory rather than mandatory in status. Joint texts concluded with EWCs vary in the degree of 'softness' from statements of principle which national and local negotiators may or may not take into account to those which establish a mandatory European-level framework. In their scope, the emphasis on handling restructuring in the joint texts parallels the extension of the company-level bargaining agenda at lower levels to questions of employment, competitiveness and adaptability.

In addition to, and more widespread than, these formal developments are the informal processes through which a Euro-company dimension to industrial relations is emerging. The chapter has highlighted the role of management's cross-border benchmarking of practices and performance in underpinning a dual process. On the one hand, mimetic and normative pressures are mobilized to drive the diffusion of 'best' working practices across countries and locations. On the other, coercive pressures underpin the deployment of cross-country, cross-site comparisons in local negotiations aimed at securing cost and flexibility concessions from the workforces involved. In a context which is structured by the scope for regime shopping which market integration fosters, it is management which is propelling forward these informal processes. Trade union and employee representatives, often preoccupied with local concerns rather than building wider solidarity across a company's operations, have – with some exceptions – yet to respond with their own cross-border benchmarking. The infrastructural potential that EWCs offer trade union and employee representatives for coordinating local bargaining remains to a large extent unfulfilled.

The emergence of the Euro-company level is not only further elaborating a multi-level system of industrial relations at both the EU and company levels; it also has implications for established sector-level arrangements within national systems – as Chapter 7 contended. Company-level negotiators nationally and locally can find themselves operating within twin sets of parameters, one emanating from the national sector agreement the other from company-specific policies and practices. The tensions arising are likely to be ameliorated to the extent that sector agreements tend towards establishing a framework – leaving space for company-specific variation – rather than specifying detailed standard provisions. At the least, the developments surveyed in this chapter are likely to further increase the pressure for reform of national, sector agreements. Alternatively, resolving such tensions might prompt some leading MNCs to abandon sector agreements altogether, as in the case of the large Dutch finance groups considered in Chapter 7. Either way, company-based 'Europeanization' looks set to reinforce pressure for decentralization from the sector level.

There is considerable variation by sector and company structure in management's cross-border industrial relations practice and in the operation and impact of EWCs. This chapter's cross-sector comparison highlighted the marked differences evident between the automotive and banking sectors, and explained them in terms of structural and agency factors. Likewise differences between companies, in terms of the internationalization of their business operations across the EU, their management structures and the cross-border integration of market servicing, but also in management policy and employee and trade union organization, have been shown to underpin substantial variation in EWC effectiveness. The convergence occurring across countries between the operations of the same MNC, and amongst some MNCs within the same sector, simultaneously represents increased differentiation within countries. Differences are also evident between different types of company, leading to increased differentiation within sectors as well as within countries.

This chapter confirms the necessity of combining 'bottom-up' and 'top-down' analysis in analysing the repercussions of European integration for industrial relations, which is one of the book's key themes. The established view in political science is that 'formal integration' precedes 'informal integration' (Wallace, 1990) in which 'Decisions made by governments create the space for cross-border activity to occur' (Rosamond, 2000: 79). As Chapter 1 observed, formal (market) integration would cause a steady increase in transnational activities, especially those of MNCs, leading to 'declining domestic governability', i.e. a mismatch between an essentially regional or global economy and nationally based institutions, resulting in pressure for supranational arrangements. Yet a much more iterative process seems to be at work, in which top-down and bottom-up pressures interact. 'Formal' integration has encouraged developments from 'below' – within MNCs – which creates pressures for regulatory intervention from 'above' – the EU – which in turn then facilitates and shapes further developments from 'below'.

9
Wage Developments in a Multi-Level System: A Case of 'Convergence Without Coordination'?

Our focus in this chapter and the next shifts to the impact of European integration on the outcomes of industrial relations. Singling out wages for special attention needs little justification. The levels of wages, and the wages structures they are embedded in, lie at the heart of the employment relationship and the negotiations that surround its governance. Following Brown and Walsh (1994: 437), being quantifiable, and thus generalizable across all manner of jobs and employees, wages are the common focus and language of policy makers and negotiators alike, albeit their interests may differ. For policy makers, as Chapters 4 and 5 have shown, wages are a key element in the macroeconomic policy mix, with links to employment, social security and taxation; changes in the levels of wages are fundamentally important in maintaining price stability. The wage structure shapes the distribution of employment between skills, employers and regions. For negotiators, the interests of their constituents are paramount. For workers, the level of wages is both the means to livelihood and a measure of self-esteem, explaining the focus on both real wages and relative wage levels or differentials. For employers, the levels of wages (both absolute and relative) are not only a key component of costs, but also instruments of motivation, performance and productivity.

In speculating about the impact of European integration on labour markets and industrial relations, much attention has focused on wages (along with employment) reflecting the contradictory implications of the contrasting scenarios mapped out in Chapter 1. One possibility, consistent with 'Europeanization' as the dominant tendency, is that integration will lead to greater homogeneity of wage levels and/or rates of increase insofar as it encourages, through processes of institutional and/or competitive isomorphism, negotiators to increasingly coalesce around similar outcomes across countries. By contrast, 'Americanization' as the prevailing tendency suggests the opposite. Widespread decentralization of bargaining arrangements, involving the fracturing of multi-employer structures, coupled with ineffective coordination, will lead to greater variation within as well as between countries. The third possibility, associated with the tendency towards re-nationalization, is relative homogeneity within countries, but persistent diversity between them. For, if social pacts are to be viewed as a form of 'regime competition' (Schulten, 2002), they raise the prospect of some countries favouring exceptionally low wage settlements in the hope of maximizing inward investment opportunities.

In practice, as Chapter 1 contended and subsequent chapters have demonstrated, these tendencies are not mutually exclusive: European integration is resulting in both convergence and divergence in the processes and outcomes of industrial relations. Convergence might be evident amongst groups of countries, whilst continued heterogeneity continues to characterize the EU-15. Or greater convergence across national boundaries might be apparent in some sectors, such as metalworking, where there is greater exposure to international competition and cross-border trade union coordination is more advanced, than in others where such is not the case. In other sectors, there might be little or no impact, given that the competitive pressures that EMU is encouraging are uneven in their effects and that trade union coordination hardly features in many service sectors. The result would be greater diversity between sectors within national systems.

Patterns of convergence and divergence are likely to vary according to the different dimensions of wages and labour costs. Differences in levels of wages and labour costs as between member states may persist, at the same time that convergence is apparent in the rates of change of these variables reflecting the effects of similar changes in economic conditions, an emphasis by employers in maintaining the relative competitiveness of operations in different countries and/or a focus on wage settlements rather than wage levels by trade unions in attempting to coordinate outcomes across countries. Differences in levels of wages and labour costs may also be sustained alongside convergence in unit labour costs across countries, reflecting differing productivity outcomes. A further dimension, which is beyond the scope of this chapter, is wage dispersion where Schulten (2002: Fig. 3 and 179) reports that the long decline in wage inequality from 1950 up until 1975 'came to a standstill in the 1980s, and in some [European] countries has since been reversed'.

To establish the patterns of divergence and convergence emerging from the interaction of the three tendencies, this chapter analyses the available data on the levels and rates of change of three key dimensions of wages:

- earnings;
- labour costs (which take into account direct and indirect labour costs, such as social security) and;
- unit labour costs or, in the absence of such data, productivity which together with labour costs constitute the relevant components.

The term 'available data' is used advisedly: any empirical study of wages is an exercise in the art of the possible. Ideally, the present task requires cross-national time series data on the three key variables at the three main levels of activity: national, sector and company. For the first, comprehensive cross-national data are available for two of the three main indicators, but not levels of unit labour costs (ULCs), and even then not necessarily as time series; for the second, they are patchy with those for the public services especially being in short supply; and for the third, they are virtually non-existent.

Aggregate wages

Wage levels – cross-national disparities persist?

The EU-15 embraces countries with not only diverse industrial relations systems, but also some substantial differences in the levels of wages. Just how substantial is indicated by Figure 9.1, which charts monthly earnings of full-time employees in industry and services across these countries for 2000. The data shown are in Euros and in purchasing power parity (PPP), which adjusts the initial Euro amounts for differences in the cost of living as between countries. Average monthly earnings ranged between 3,350 Euros in Denmark and 950 in Portugal. The EU average of 2,390 Euros was exceeded by 10 per cent or more in Denmark, Germany, Luxembourg, Sweden and the UK. Monthly earnings were more than 10 per cent below the EU average in Italy, Greece, Spain and Portugal. Adjusting for purchasing power, the range narrows (2,760 in PPP in Denmark to 1,300 in Portugal around the same EU average of 2,390) but the ranking remains broadly the same. Although there are considerable variations in monthly working hours across the EU, inter-country variations in hourly earnings are broadly similar to those in monthly earnings (European Commission, 2003a: 94). Denmark, Finland, France, Germany and the Netherlands have higher relative hourly than monthly earnings, reflecting comparatively shorter working hours, whilst the opposite is the case for Ireland and the UK.

If earnings data are those of immediate concern to workers and their trade unions, it is those on labour costs – covering both direct, wage and salary, costs and indirect costs, such as social security – which are of more immediate relevance to employers. Table 9.1 reports figures on hourly labour costs per employee for industry and services. Since the proportion of labour costs accounted for by direct costs differs between countries (see the fourth column of the table) countries rank slightly differently from Figure 9.1. Nonetheless, Table 9.1 shows a similar picture in terms of the range between countries. In 1999, which is the most recent year for which comprehensive cross-country data are available, labour costs in the highest three countries – Austria (27.2 ECU per hour), Denmark (27.0) and Germany (26.8) – were almost four times those in Portugal (7.0 ECU per hour) – the lowest country – and 1.8 times those found in Spain (15.3). The gap between highest and lowest had actually widened since 1992, when the difference between Belgium and Germany (21.5 and 21.3 ECU per hour) and Portugal was a factor

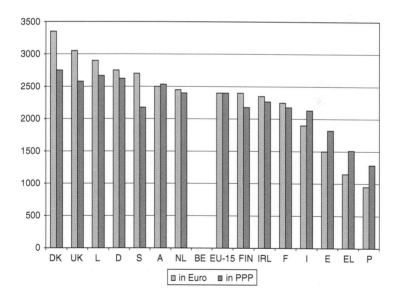

Figure 9.1 Monthly gross earnings in industry and services, 2000

Source: European Commission, *Employment in Europe*, 2003, Chart 67.

Table 9.1   Hourly labour costs in industry and services (ECU)

	1992	1996	1999	% direct costs (1996)
Belgium	21.5	25.0	26.2	68
Denmark	19.9	24.1	27.0	90
Germany	21.3	25.9	26.8	75
Greece	6.9	9.5	11.8	76
Spain	15.2	14.4	15.3	74
France	19.3	22.3	23.8	67
Ireland	13.1	14.0	16.2	84
Italy	19.1	19.2*	18.8	65*
Luxembourg	18.6	21.4	22.7	84
Netherlands	18.0	20.4	21.7	76
Austria	—	25.9	27.2	71
Portugal	6.3	6.9	7.0	76
Finland	—	19.4	20.8	75
Sweden	—	23.9*	25.8	68*
UK	12.8	13.5	19.3	87
EU-15	**	19.4	21.5	74
COV	**	0.32	0.29	
COV [EU-12]	0.33	0.27	0.25	
EUR-11	**	21.2	22.1	71
COV	**	0.30	0.29	

Notes: EUR-11 is the eleven founding member states of the Euro zone.
* 1997 figures for Italy, Sweden.
** no equivalent figures available for 1992, as pre-dates accession of Austria, Finland, Sweden.
Source: *European Social Statistics: Labour Costs, Series 1988–99*, Eurostat (2001).

of 3.4. Yet, over the same period the overall dispersion of hourly labour costs amongst EU member states narrowed: the coefficient of variation for the 12 member states (as at 1992) declining from 0.33 in 1992 to 0.25 in 1999. The equivalent statistic for the EU-15 shows a similar trend between 1996 and 1999. In further integrating markets and establishing common economic policy parameters, EMU seems to have prompted some convergence of labour costs. However, the prospect of the single currency and a common monetary policy within the Euro zone was not reflected in a stronger trend amongst the original 11 member countries: the relevant coefficient of variation barely changed between 1996 and 1999.

The variation in the composition of labour costs into direct and indirect components across countries is marked, reflecting the different traditions for funding pension and social security systems discussed in Chapter 2. Table 9.1 indicates, for example, that in 1996 indirect costs comprised 10 per cent of hourly labour costs in Denmark and 13 per cent in the UK, but 33 per cent in France and 35 per cent in Italy. Put simply, Italy and France depend on employers' contributions to finance social protection whereas Denmark and the UK rely on income tax. Data for 1992 and 1999 were little different from the 1996 figures reported, confirming the enduring nature of such differences. More recently, levels of indirect labour costs have become a focus of welfare and fiscal reform proposals in several countries suggesting that the picture may begin to change.

Comparable cross-country data on levels of unit labour costs are not available, due to differences in definitions and concepts. Instead Figure 9.2 shows, for 2000, the productivity and labour costs components which go to comprise unit labour costs for each member state as a percentage of the EU average for both variables. Two main patterns are apparent. First, there are markedly different configurations of productivity and labour costs within the EU. Most striking is the position of Spain, Greece and Portugal as relatively low productivity (25 per cent

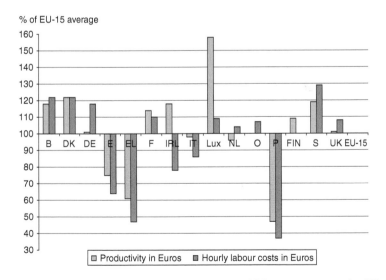

Figure 9.2   Relative levels of labour productivity and labour costs across the EU

Sources: compiled from CEC (2003) *Employment Trends 2003,* p. 97 (Chart 70) and Eurostat (2003) 'Labour Costs Survey 2000', *Statistics in Focus, Population and Social Conditions,* Theme 3–7/2003.

and more below the EU average) and low labour cost economies (35 per cent and more below the average). At the other end of the spectrum, setting aside Luxembourg, productivity differences are less marked, with levels in the highest four countries being no more than 20 per cent above the average, although labour costs in Sweden are almost 30 per cent higher than the average. Second, there are differences in the relative levels of productivity and labour costs for some countries. Relative levels of productivity are noticeably more favourable than relative labour cost levels for Ireland, Italy, Luxembourg and also Spain, Greece and to a lesser extent Portugal. The converse is the case for Germany and to a lesser extent Sweden. Overall, insofar as pressures from EMU might be leading to convergence of unit labour costs across countries, the figure indicates that this will be around differing configurations of productivity and labour costs. EU enlargement to central eastern Europe will reinforce this diverse pattern.

Wage increases – a 'European going rate'

In surveying the cross-national data on rates of changes in earnings and labour costs, the most striking impression is of what countries have in common. Notwithstanding continuing differences in wage levels between countries, there has been convergence in the rate of increase of nominal wages compared to the picture prevailing in the 1970s and 1980s (Fajertag, 2000). For economy of presentation, Table 9.2 provides average annual periodised changes in prices and nominal and real earnings from 1985, the year in which the Commission launched the single market project, up to 2002, for the EU as a whole and for selected countries: the largest five EU economies (France, Germany, Italy, Spain and the UK), Sweden (as the largest economy in the Nordic area and part of the 1995 'northern' enlargement of the EU) and two of the smaller and comparatively less industrially-developed countries, Ireland and Portugal (and part of the 1986 'southern' enlargement of the EU). The patterns and trends highlighted below carry over to the remaining seven member states not reported in the table.

A first common feature apparent from Table 9.2 is that throughout the period nominal earnings increases have tended to track inflation, rising in 1990–94 as compared with 1985–89 and declining again thereafter. Second, nominal wage growth throughout the period has been sufficient to more than offset price inflation. Third, average annual increases in real earnings have rarely exceeded 2.5 per cent and (with some exceptions) recorded a marked slowdown in the second half of the 1990s, continuing into the most recent period. These three features

Table 9.2 Prices and earnings, annual average percentage change

	1985–90	1990–94	1994–99	1999–2002*
Germany				
Consumer prices	1.4	4.0	1.3	1.6
Average earnings	3.5	6.0	2.1	1.8
Average real earnings	2.1	1.9	0.8	0.1
Spain				
Consumer prices	6.5	5.3	2.9	3.3
Average earnings	7.9	7.3	3.0	3.9
Average real earnings	1.4	2.0	0.1	0.6
France				
Consumer prices	3.1	2.3	1.2	1.8
Average earnings	4.0	3.3	2.4	2.6
Average real earnings	0.9	1.0	1.1	0.9
Italy				
Consumer prices	5.7	5.0	2.9	2.5
Average earnings	8.5	5.5	2.9	2.8
Average real earnings	2.7	0.5	-0.1	0.1
Sweden				
Consumer prices	6.2	4.6	0.8	1.8
Average earnings	9.2	5.0	3.5	5.3
Average real earnings	2.8	0.4	2.7	3.4
UK				
Consumer prices	5.9	3.4	2.8	1.1
Average earnings	8.4	5.5	4.2	4.7
Average real earnings	2.4	2.1	1.4	3.9
Ireland				
Consumer prices	3.3	2.5	2.0	4.7
Average earnings	5.6	5.0	4.5	8.2
Average real earnings	2.2	2.5	2.5	3.7
Portugal				
Consumer prices	11.3	7.9	2.8	3.6
Average earnings	16.7	11.3	4.9	5.6
Average real earnings	4.8	3.2	2.0	2.0
EU-15				
Consumer prices	4.4	4.1	2.1	2.1
Average earnings	6.4	5.5	3.0	3.3
Average real earnings	1.9	1.4	0.8	1.2

Note: * definitions of prices and earnings variations changed for 1999–2002.
Sources: *Employment in Europe 2000* (CEC, 2000), pp. 101–3 for 1975–99; *Employment in Europe 2003* (CEC, 2003a), pp. 202–6 for 1999–2002.

appear to hold true regardless of the structure of collective bargaining and levels of unionization; or of employment performance (Fajertag, 2000). Fourth, the table confirms the downwards 'stickiness' of nominal earnings: there are no instances of a decline in nominal wages sustained over a five-year period. Moreover, instances of real wage cuts are rare, occurring only (marginally) in Italy in 1994–99 (and, although not shown, more substantially in Greece in 1985–89 and 1990–94). Negotiators do not appear prepared to contemplate real wage reductions in order to secure competitive advantage.

Two variations on these common themes are apparent. First, there is evidence of 'catch-up': average real earnings increases in Portugal comfortably exceeded those in the main EU economies in 1985–89 and 1990–94 and were at the top end of the 1994–99 range, whilst in Ireland increases since 1990 were also at the top end of the range. Second, the most recent period shows evidence of a bifurcation between the major economies of the Euro zone – France, Germany, Italy and Spain – on the one hand – where real earnings growth has been less than 1 per cent p.a. – and Sweden and the UK (together with Ireland), on the other – where real wage growth has averaged 3–4 per cent p.a..

Table 9.3 gives coefficients of variation of price inflation and nominal earnings increases for the main sub-periods since 1985 for the EU-15, the original 11 members of the Euro zone and the smaller group of countries frequently regarded as having constituted the earlier, de facto

Table 9.3 Coefficients of variation of average annual increases in prices and earnings

	1985–89	1990–94	1994–99 (A)	1994–99 (B)	1999–2002
EU-15					
Consumer prices	0.85	0.74	0.61	0.37	0.37
Average earnings	0.60	0.46	0.51	0.56	0.40
Euro zone					
Consumer prices	0.78	0.44	0.39	0.40	0.34
Average earnings	0.63	0.41	0.35	0.54	0.47
BeNeLux+D					
Consumer prices	0.37	0.17	0.25	0.23	0.36
Average earnings	0.41	0.18	0.05	0.25	0.37

Note: (A) signifies 1994–99 calculated using price and earnings definitions consistent with earlier periods; (B) signifies 1994–99 calculated using definitions consistent with 1999–2002.
Source: Own calculations from Table 9.2.

'D-mark' zone i.e. Germany and Benelux – which were also the focus of the pioneering 'Doorn' cross-border trade union bargaining coordination initiative. It provides evidence of a convergence of inflation rates and nominal earnings growth. Amongst the EU-15 there is a clear convergent trend in rates of inflation over the period. A similar, although less pronounced convergent trend is evident for the rate of growth in nominal earnings. Equivalent statistics for the Euro-zone countries show a sharp convergence in inflation rates and nominal earnings growth in the early 1990s, with a more modest trend in the same direction in later periods. For the countries of the 'D-mark' zone, a sharp convergence in both indicators is also evident in the early 1990s and continues for earnings (but not prices) through to 1999. The convergence apparent in growth rates of nominal earnings largely predates the 1998 Doorn initiative. The effect of Euro-zone membership and the removal of direct or proxy discipline exercised by the Bundesbank seems, however, to have prompted greater dispersion amongst Germany and the Benelux countries since 1999.

Overall, following Hassel (2002b: 165), it seems not unfair to talk in terms of a new 'European going rate' for wage increases: an assessment which is confirmed by Figure 9.3, which shows annual changes in hourly labour costs from 1996 to 2002 broadly tracking each other across six of the eight countries (Ireland and Italy being the exceptions).

Table 9.4 presents cross-national data on rates of change of productivity (GDP per person employed), average real labour costs (which reflect changes in average real earnings) and real unit labour costs (ULCs) for the same eight countries as Table 9.2. It also reveals common cross-country patterns, albeit with some country-specific variations around these. First, productivity growth has tended to outstrip growth in real labour costs (and therefore real earnings), which is in sharp contrast with the pattern of the 1960s and early 1970s (Schulten, 2002: 178–9) when real wage increases matched and even exceeded productivity gains. Only in Sweden and the UK in 1985–90 and Portugal in 1994–99 have increases in real labour costs run ahead of productivity growth. Ireland stands out as securing high rates of productivity and of average earnings growth during the 1990s, which combined to generate a substantial reduction in real ULCs in 1994–99. Data on real labour costs changes are not available for the period 1999–2002, but the changes in real earnings reported in Table 9.2 for this period suggest that increases in real labour costs might have exceeded productivity growth in several countries. This is confirmed by Commission analysis of the pattern of nominal wage increases against the sum of inflation

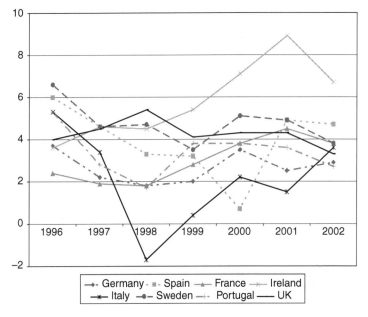

Figure 9.3   Annual percentage change in total hourly labour costs (nominal) for selected EU countries, 1996–2002

Source: Eurostat (2003) *Labour Cost Index.*

and labour productivity for 2000–02 as compared with the late 1990s (European Commission, 2003a: Table 33). Second, and largely as a result of productivity increases running ahead of those in real labour costs, the general tendency up until 1999 is of a sustained reduction in real ULCs. Third, up until 1999 there was some modest convergence in the rate of change of real ULCs over time: the coefficient of variation for the EU-15 declining from 1.36 in 1985–89 to 1.32 in 1990–94 to 1.16 in 1994–99. Figures for the three years 1999–2002 show a sharp widening, however, due to large reductions in productivity in some but not all countries as a result of recession.

A significant consequence of the first two trends has been the trend decline in labour's share of GDP (i.e. the proportion of national income accounted for by wages) evident across the EU since the 1970s. Schulten (2002: Table 1) reports that after rising to an average of 75.3 per cent during the period 1971–80, the share of wages in GDP for the EU as a whole declined to 73.0 and then 69.7 per cent in the following two decades capturing a common cross-national development.

Table 9.4 Productivity and costs, annual average percentage change

	1985–90	1990–94	1994–99	1999–2002
Germany				
GDP/number employed	1.9	2.4	1.7	0.7
Average real labour costs	1.0	2.1	1.0	—
Real unit labour costs	−0.8	−0.3	−0.7	0.2
Spain				
GDP/number employed	1.2	2.0	0.7	0.6
Average real labour costs	0.5	0.6	1.7	—
Real unit labour costs	−0.7	−0.4	−0.9	−0.7
France				
GDP/number employed	2.2	1.3	1.3	0.6
Average real labour costs	0.6	1.1	1.2	—
Real unit labour costs	−1.6	−0.5	−0.4	0.5
Italy				
GDP/number employed	2.0	1.5	1.4	0.3
Average real labour costs	1.3	0.6	−0.5	—
Real unit labour costs	−0.8	−1.2	−1.7	0.1
Sweden				
GDP/number employed	1.2	2.9	1.9	0.9
Average real labour costs	2.0	1.5	1.8	—
Real unit labour costs	0.8	−1.3	−0.1	2.7
UK				
GDP/number employed	1.5	2.5	1.2	1.5
Average real labour costs	2.4	1.7	1.2	—
Real unit labour costs	0.9	−0.8	−0.1	0.6
Ireland				
GDP/number employed	3.5	2.2	3.9	4.3
Average real labour costs	2.3	2.1	0.9	—
Real unit labour costs	−1.1	−0.1	−3.1	−1.0
Portugal				
GDP/number employed	4.4	2.0	1.8	0.8
Average real labour costs	2.9	2.4	1.2	—
Real unit labour costs	−1.4	0.4	−0.6	0.6
EU-15				
GDP/number employed	1.7	1.9	1.3	0.9
Average real labour costs	1.4	0.8	0.8	—
Real unit labour costs	−0.8	−0.7	−0.7	0.2

Sources: *Employment in Europe 2000* (CEC, 2000), pp. 101–3 for 1975–99; *Employment in Europe 2003* (CEC, 2003a), pp. 202–6 for 1999–2002.

From productivity- to competition-based bargaining

Convergence in the rate of increase of average earnings and in levels of labour costs look like convincing evidence of a tendency towards 'Europeanization'. Yet, as Hancké (2002: 134) suggests, there is a 'remarkable and surprising puzzle' to be resolved. Although the outcomes of wage-setting would be consistent with 'regime collaboration' (Dølvik, 2000) in the negotiation of social pacts and strong forms of cross-border wage coordination at sector level, it is difficult to argue that they are actually the result of any such formal arrangements for cross-border coordination. The ECB's regime, along with the Cologne process establishing a macroeconomic dialogue, did not commence until 1999. Trade union cross-border coordination is also in its infancy, as Chapter 4 has confirmed. The ETUC's third annual assessment of bargaining outcomes across countries in respect of the 'inflation plus increase in productivity' bargaining guideline is candid. Although 2001 was an exceptional year, in that the sharp downturn in labour productivity brought on by recession in many countries, meant average wage settlements above the guideline, '2002 should mark a return to the 2000 situation' with wage rises at a little over inflation being below the guideline (Mermet and Clarke, 2002: 4)

At first sight, attributing the convergence to greater formal coordination within countries looks more promising. As Chapter 5 showed, governments have been directly involved in seeking to influence the course of wage developments and moderation has been a key element of national social pacts. In most cases, however, these initiatives involve what Hassel (2002b) has described as 'soft' incomes policies, in which strict limits have been eschewed in favour of broad guidelines. Further, as Traxler *et al.* (2001) demonstrate, there are considerable differences from country to country in the capacity of national-level negotiators to call on the kind of horizontal and vertical coordination necessary to deliver wage outcomes in line with such guidelines. To secure the degree of convergence observed through formal coordination would have required France and the UK, for example, to have developed arrangements akin to those associated with the Rhineland and Nordic countries – something that clearly has not happened. Perhaps even more telling is Traxler *et al.*'s (2001) finding that the systematic relationship between horizontal and vertical coordination of bargaining, on the one hand, and economic performance on the other, seemed to break down in the 1990s:

> After a time of significant fluctuations and divergence across countries, labour costs – as well as inflation – have converged more and

more in relation to declining growth rates since the mid-1990s. It is especially the convergence of labour-cost growth that calls into question the economic importance of labour relations in general and bargaining in particular. Due to declining variation in labour-cost growth across countries, variations in labour relations seem to have lost their economic relevance. (p. 253)

In the transition from a productivity- to a competition-oriented wage policy (Schulten, 1998; 2002), it is the informal processes of institutional and competitive isomorphism elaborated in Chapter 3 which have been the most influential. The context of this shift in wage policy is the fundamental change in macroeconomic policy regimes. As Hassel (2002b) contends, in the light of the failure of Keynesian policies to deal with the external shocks of the 1970s, the accumulating burden of public debt and the relative success of the German *Bundesbank*'s non-accommodating monetary policy, most west European governments adopted non-accommodating monetary regimes and strict control of public expenditure. A second consideration, as Chapter 6 emphasized, has been the rise of company bargaining. Negotiators have taken and been given greater scope to negotiate arrangements that take into account the particular competitive position of individual companies. Related to these considerations has been the weakened bargaining power of unions in a period of persistently high unemployment and, in several countries, declining levels of union density.

In effect, as Hancké (2002) contends, there has been a process of 'convergence without coordination'. Regardless of the structure of collective bargaining or the formal processes of co-ordination, negotiators have reacted to the introduction of non-accommodating monetary policy across the EU by adjusting their point of resistance to the prevailing level of inflation in order to maintain living standards. Convergence in policy, in the guise of the stance of the monetary authorities, has – by eliciting a similar response from wage negotiators in different countries – combined with convergence in rates of inflation to produce convergent average wage settlements. Such similarity of behavioural response reflects the influence of 'mimetic' and 'normative' isomorphism processes amongst negotiators, who are motivated to achieve the pattern of settlements elsewhere. The more this happens, the more normative such behaviour becomes, as Chapter 3 underlined. Moreover, 'bargaining governability' becomes less of an issue, helping to explain why the relationship between bargaining arrangements and economic performance is seemingly breaking down.

An important piece of the puzzle is nonetheless missing. Not surprisingly, trade unions have pushed to achieve settlements which at least match the level of inflation. Maintaining standards of living along with securing a share of productivity gains and economic growth are primary considerations for trade union negotiators across the EU (Mermet, 2001: Table 4), matching inflation constituting the 'determinant' factor in the wage bargaining for trade unions in most countries. Less obvious is why employers have not behaved as neo-liberal economic orthodoxy would have them do: why they have not insisted on freezing, if not reducing, wages until the market 'cleared'. It is debatable whether Hancké (2002) has got the emphasis right in suggesting that the major consideration has been a shortage of labour. Some companies may have experienced shortages of key groups, but overall those in the internationally exposed sectors especially have been shedding labour – as the evidence of changes in employment (see next section) confirms. Crucially, the process of wage setting has effectively become detached from that of determining costs. The quantitative data are at one with the case study evidence in confirming that in most cases employers have been meeting employees' expectations in terms of maintaining living standards by agreeing to inflation-equaling wage rises (Arrowsmith and Sisson, 1999). In return, however, they have been demanding acceptance of major changes in work organization, including reductions in employment, reflected in rising productivity and the sustained reduction in unit labour costs. The trade-off can be likened to an 'implicit contract': it is not formally agreed, but is a shared informal understanding which has become more or less generalized (Arrowsmith and Sisson, 2001).

Contrary to neo-liberal economic prescriptions, the wages of so-called 'insiders' are being maintained at the expense of the employment potentially available to 'outsiders' in the labour market. The failure of the market to clear arises because labour is not merely a factor of production to be bought or sold like any other. 'The act of hiring an employee is not sufficient to ensure that the job in question gets done in an acceptable way . . . The employee has to be motivated – by encouragement, threats, loyalty, discipline, money, competition, pride, promotion, or whatever is deemed effective to work with the required pace and care' (Brown and Walsh, 1994: 440). Wages, in other words, are important for reasons other than direct cost. The dividends of meeting employee expectations over wages by offering so-called 'efficiency wages' above the market-clearing rate lie in maintaining or improving performance, a reduction in turnover and a better pool of labour from which to select. Maintaining real wage levels in circumstances where management has simultaneously to minimize costs *and* elicit cooperation and performance from the remaining workforce may be irrational from a neo-liberal economic perspective, but is wholly rational from an industrial relations one.

The sector dimension – a case of 'converging divergencies'?

To establish the impact of European integration on wage and labour cost outcomes, it is not sufficient to focus exclusively on aggregate level data. A disaggregated analysis, which investigates developments at sector level, is also needed. The reason is that the competitive pressures that integration is encouraging are extremely uneven in their effects. Salient factors which differ from sector to sector include exposure to international competition and reliance on 'high road' quality as opposed to 'low road' cost-minimization strategies. Although, given data limitations, a company-level analysis cannot be pursued here, divergences within sectors might also be expected, reflecting the specific position of individual companies. As Scharpf (2000a: 225–6) observes in explaining why the switch to the ECB regime has not resulted in the above average wage increases in Germany expected by some commentators (e.g. Soskice and Iversen, 1998):

> International competitiveness is no longer merely a balance of payments problem constituted by differences among national averages of cost and productivity increases. Instead, it is a problem of individual products and producers. Within the monetary union, each national branch is in competition with unions organising the same branch in other countries.

In the light of the previous discussion, there are three possible outcomes to be considered. First, there are substantial differences in the rate of increase in wages, with internationally competitive sectors falling behind more sheltered ones. Second, there are again substantial differences, but increases in internationally-exposed manufacturing are higher than those in the service sectors because of the greater scope for productivity trade-offs. Third, wages rise in line with, or a little above, inflation in internationally competitive and sheltered sectors alike, with the former under pressure to make substantial increases in productivity and/or reductions in costs to cover such rises. Intermediate outcomes between either the first or second and the third are also possible.

Inter-sector levels of labour costs and productivity

In the absence of comprehensive cross-country, cross-sector data on wages, Table 9.5 presents hourly labour costs per employee for manufacturing, construction and three main service sectors for the eight countries selected in the previous section: the data are the sectoral equivalents of the aggregate levels reported in Table 9.1. Similar data are not available for public services. For the three service sectors, given the absence of equivalent figures for 1999, the final two columns give information for the whole of the private services sector for 1996 and 1999. Two features are immediately apparent. First, average hourly labour costs are lowest in hotels and restaurants and highest in financial services, and those in manufacturing are above those in construction and distribution but below those in finance. Second, there is variation in the size of inter-sector differentials, and in the ranking of sectors, across countries. For example, the gap between labour costs in manufacturing and construction is relatively large in Germany but relatively small in Italy and the UK. In Ireland, labour costs in construction are higher than those in manufacturing, whereas in the other seven countries they are lower. The coefficients of variation (which, because of missing data, exclude Austria) enable two kinds of comparison. First, looking across the seven sectors for 1996, there are few marked differences: the cross-country dispersion of labour costs within a sector does not appear to be smaller in more internationally exposed sectors, such as manufacturing, and larger in those, such as the service sectors, which are less exposed. Second, comparing 1999 with 1996 for manufacturing, construction and private services, the coefficients of variation in all three cases evidence some modest convergence of levels of labour costs – consistent with the aggregate analysis of Table 9.1.

Sectoral differences in hourly labour costs, and therefore hourly wages, are reflected in differences in labour productivity – 'the spread of wages across sectors roughly matches that of relative productivity' (European Commission, 2003a: 95). Whilst differences in productivity between sectors are larger than those between wage costs in the Nordic countries, there is a close fit in the four large economies and Spain. The Commission's multi-variate analysis of inter-sector wage differentials confirms the link: across the EU-15, more than 80 per cent of inter-sector variation in wage levels is accounted for by differences in labour productivity and price level (European Commission, 2003a: 99).

Rates of change of labour costs

Time series data for annual increases in hourly labour costs are available for most EU countries for the period 1996–2001. Again, equivalent data

Table 9.5 Hourly labour costs by sector in selected EU countries (ECU)

	Manufacturing		Construction		Wholesale & retail distribution	Hotels & restaurants	Financial services	Services (private sector)	
	1996	1999	1996	1999	1996	1996	1996	1996	1999
Germany	27.4	28.4	21.3	21.8	21.3	15.5	32.8	23.5	25.4
Spain	15.0	16.2	12.3	13.4	11.5	9.8	25.5	14.0	14.8
France	22.4	23.7	19.6	20.5	19.5	16.5	33.0	22.2	23.4
Ireland	13.4	15.6	14.6	18.6	11.6	8.4	21.5	14.3	18.2
Italy	17.8	17.9	17.2	17.3	16.1	13.7	36.6	21.2	21.2
Portugal	6.0	6.2	5.3	5.8	6.9	4.7	16.9	8.2	8.3
Sweden	24.1	25.6	21.9	23.5	22.7	16.9	30.1	23.9	26.3
UK	13.8	19.2	13.5	19.7	11.4	8.0	21.0	13.1	19.2
EU-15	20.3	—	17.9	—	16.2	11.7	29.2	18.2	—
COV (EU-14*)	0.34	0.32	0.33	0.31	0.34	0.32	0.26	0.31	0.29

Note: * excluding Austria due to missing data.
Sources: Eurostat (2001) European Social Statistics: Labour Costs, series 1988–99; Eurostat (2001) 'EU Labour Costs 1999', Statistics in Focus, Population and Social Conditions, Theme 3–3/2001. Coefficients of variation are own calculations.

are not available for public services. Two main patterns are evident from Figure 9.4, which shows annual increases for manufacturing, construction and two sub-divisions of private services – wholesale and retail distribution and hotels and restaurants, and financial services and real estate – for five of the eight countries (complete data being unavailable for France and Ireland and not shown for Portugal) focused on above and for the EU-15. First, there is some indication that labour cost increases in the more internationally exposed manufacturing sector have been below those in the less exposed service sectors. This is most clearly the case for financial services, where average increases across the EU-15 were higher than in manufacturing in each year after 1996, except in 2000 when they were the same. Second, the rate of increase in labour costs in all sectors was normally above the rate of inflation confirming the aggregate picture of Table 9.2. The main exception was Italy, where for four consecutive years, 1998 to 2001, increases in labour costs in all or three of the four sectors were below the rate of inflation. Given this second observation, the above-inflation margin involved was generally larger in financial services than it was in manufacturing.

Two further findings from analysing the data are not apparent from Figure 9.4. Average annual increases in the 11 original Euro-zone countries were below those of the EU-15 in all sectors throughout the period. This suggests that the pressures placed on wage negotiators to deliver settlements consistent with the convergence criteria for Euro-zone membership in the run-up to the launch of the single currency, and subsequently to accommodate to the ECB's restrictive monetary policy, have had an additional effect beyond those arising from the intensified competition across the single market which further integration brings. Also striking is that over the period annual increases in labour costs were the product of influences which were both cross-sector within countries and cross-country within sectors. An analysis of variance across the 12 countries (Austria, France and Greece being the exceptions) and three sectors (manufacturing, construction and finance) for which the data series were complete revealed that both country and sector constituted significant (at the 99 per cent confidence level) sources of variation. This is persuasive evidence, albeit indirect, of converging divergences in wage settlements.

In order to bring the public services into the picture, Table 9.6 summarizes information on collectively agreed wage settlements for three sectors, metalworking, banking and public services – across seven of the eight countries (data for France being unavailable) compiled by the European Industrial Relations Observatory (e.g. EIRO, 2002b).

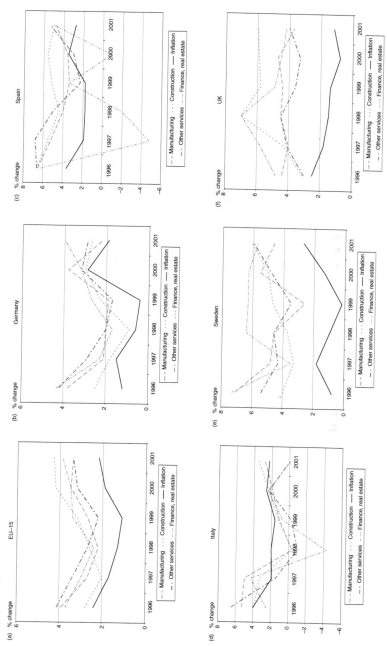

Figure 9.4 Annual changes in sectoral hourly labour costs for selected EU countries, 1996–2001

Source: Eurostat (2003) *Labour Cost Index.*

Table 9.6 Collectively agreed wage settlements: average annual percentage change in metalworking, banking and public services

	1991–94			1995–98			1999–2001		
	Metal working	Banking	Public services	Metal working	Banking	Public services	Metal working	Banking	Public services
Spain	6.0	5.2	5.0	3.4	3.2	2.6	3.4	2.3	2.0
Germany	4.4	4.1	3.9	2.8	1.9	1.8	3.1	3.0	2.4
Ireland	2.7	3.2	3.2	2.4	2.4	2.6	5.2	5.2	6.2
Italy	5.7	3.9	2.6	3.8	2.1	3.7	1.8	1.1	2.3
Portugal	7.5*	5.4*	4.0*	4.4	3.6	3.7	3.5	3.5	3.2
Sweden	–	–	–	3.2	2.9	3.3	2.4	3.2	3.1
UK	4.9	4.0	–	3.1	3.2	2.6	3.0	2.9	3.2

Note: *Average of 1992–94 for Portugal.
Source: EIRO, Pay Developments – annual update 2001 and previous years.

Collectively agreed settlements are not the same as wage increases and there are important caveats concerning differences in definitions and sources across countries: nonetheless, the data suffice for present purposes.

There are indications of a squeeze on settlements in public services as compared to metalworking – but less so when compared with banking – up until 1998. The pressures on wage settlements generated by preparations for EMU would appear to have been most sharply felt in public services. After 1999, there are signs of 'catch-up' by the public services in some countries, both outside and within the Euro zone. Second, metalworking settlements tend, if anything, to be slightly ahead of those in banking. The greater international exposure of metalworking appears not to have resulted in lower settlements; rather, metalworking's enhanced scope for productivity trade-offs seems to have offset such pressure.

Productivity considerations

Although wages rose a little above inflation, and there is some evidence of a higher rate of increase in sheltered than internationally exposed sectors, the possibility that there were differential increases in productivity remains. Table 9.7 confirms considerable differences between the main industry (manufacturing, mining and utilities), construction and (private) service sectors of the economy in productivity – and also employment share – trends amongst the EU's five main economies. In particular, comparing industry with services there is evidence of both similarity *between* and greater diversity *within* countries. In industry, the cross-country pattern is of a trend increase in productivity and a trend decline in employment share. Although declining employment share does not necessarily translate into declining employment levels, the implication is that reductions in employment in order to secure cost savings have contributed to rising productivity. In services, by contrast, productivity improvements are markedly below those in industry. And employment share shows a general trend increase – reflecting growing demand for services. For construction, the increase in productivity has tended to be lower than in industry, and there is no overall discernible trend in employment share.

In sum, to answer the conundrum posed at the beginning of this section, negotiators in internationally competitive and sheltered sectors alike seem to have been able to achieve increases in wages a little above inflation. The price of doing so in the internationally exposed industrial sectors, such as manufacturing, has been sustained increases in productivity attained in part by reductions in employment in order to cut costs.

Table 9.7 Sectoral dynamics of productivity and employment share (compounded annual growth rates in %)

	Germany		Spain		France		Italy		UK	
	Productivity	Employment share	Productivity	Employment share	Productivity	Employment share	Productivity	Employment share	Productivity	Employment share
					Industry					
1980–90	1.6	−0.7	2.8	−1.5	3.1	−1.8	2.9	−1.8	na	na
1991–99	3.0	−3.3	1.4	−0.4	3.5	−2.0	2.3	−0.7	3.0	−1.8
					Construction					
1980–90	0.9	−1.6	2.0	0.6	2.4	−1.7	2.2	−1.8	na	na
1991–99	−0.1	0.3	0.3	−0.1	−1.4	−2.4	0.1	−0.7	2.5	−2.3
					Services					
1980–90	1.6	1.0	0.6	1.7	1.6	1.4	0.1	2.2	na	na
1991–99	1.1	1.6	1.0	0.6	0.4	1.0	1.0	0.8	2.0	0.8

Source: European Commission (2001b: 60).

Conclusions

There continue to be significant differences between countries in the level of wages and labour costs per employee. European integration has nonetheless prompted some convergence in levels and, more noticeably, in the rates of change of earnings and labour costs. There is little evidence to suggest, however, that convergence in rates of increase across countries is the result of any formal coordination through either EU-level intergovernmental arrangements or trade union cross-border bargaining initiatives. Rather it seems to be a case of 'convergence without coordination' (Hancké, 2002: 134), encouraged by the adoption of non-accommodating monetary policies. Trade union negotiators, it seems, have adjusted their sights in the light of the new macroeconomic policy framework to achieve something above the level of inflation but less than the productivity margin. In return, employers have insisted on reductions in employment. This pattern of settlement emerges regardless of bargaining structure, being as apparent under single-employer bargaining in the UK as it is under differing multi-employer bargaining arrangements elsewhere.

The quantitative data analysed above are consistent with the case study evidence (Arrowsmith and Sisson, 2001; Sisson and Artiles, 2000) in suggesting that there is a need to focus on (unit) labour costs to understand developments on the ground. Employers' efforts to respond to intensifying competitive pressures have not primarily been directed at wages. In particular, reductions in wages – both nominal and real – have been rare. Rather costs have been the main focus and there has been action on two main fronts: a reduction in employment and the introduction of more efficient forms of work organization, including working time initiatives such as increased shift working, part-time working or more variable hours to be considered in Chapter 10. Employers continue to meet worker aspirations in terms of the maintenance of living standards. In return, the employer is given some de facto flexibility to make the adjustments necessary to allow unit labour costs to be progressively reduced, thereby enabling profit margins to be sustained.

The sector analysis offers further support for this conclusion. It also throws light on the relative balance between the tendencies towards Europeanization, Americanization and re-nationalization, introduced at the outset of this study. Rates of increase of labour costs and collectively agreed wages do exhibit sector-specific patterns, but in the private sector the differences between sectors have not been large. The picture is markedly different for productivity and employment. In the exposed manufacturing sector, negotiators have had to dig deep in terms of productivity improvements, including cost-saving reductions in employment, to maintain and marginally improve real wages. In the service sector, by contrast, wage increases a little above inflation have involved nothing like such levels of adjustment: there has been a growth rather than a reduction in employment. Overall, there is cross-national convergence in the rate of increase in wages and cross-sector diversity in the trends in productivity and unit costs. A tendency towards Europeanization is confirmed in the convergence across countries apparent in wages and labour costs, more marked for rates of increase than for levels. The evidence for a process of Americanization is altogether less persuasive: greater within-country diversity between sectors has not gone hand-in-hand with greater sector-level divergence across countries. Our findings are also consistent with a tendency towards re-nationalization – most clearly that which underlines that sector changes in labour costs continue to be the subject of significant country influences. That they also exhibit significant sector influences confirms that wage setting entails a complex pattern of 'converging divergences'.

10
Working Time Patterns: Confirming the Significance of the Sector

Along with wages, working time is a defining feature of the employment relationship and needs little justification for special attention – 'Time is at the heart of industrial relations' suggests the European Commission (2000: 66). As previous chapters have pointed out, the two main dimensions of working time – duration and flexibility – have been significant factors in the development of the EU's multi-level system of industrial relations. They have been one of the main vehicles of bargaining decentralization within national systems (Traxler *et al.*, 2001: 128–9) – notable examples include the 1984 settlement reducing the working week below 40 hours in German metalworking and the French Aubry legislation of 1998 and 1999 implementing the 35-hour week. They have also constituted a major focus for Community-level activity. Substantively, the duration of working time figures prominently in the 1993 EU Working Time Directive under its provisions for a 48-hour average weekly maximum and four weeks paid holiday entitlement. The flexibility of working time is seen as making a major contribution to the modernization of work organization, being vital to each of the main objectives of the EU's employment strategy, i.e. full employment; quality of work (better jobs) and productivity or competitiveness; and cohesion and an inclusive labour market providing for greater access (European Commission, 2003b). Procedurally, too, working time has been significant. The 1993 Working Time Directive pioneered derogations for collectively agreed arrangements between the parties and three of the four agreements reached under the Maastricht social policy process deal with issues of working time flexibility: parental leave, part-time and fixed-term contracts. At the sector level, the EMF's 'Working time charter' outlined in

Chapter 4 signals the centrality of working time to trade unions' cross-border bargaining coordination efforts.

It is one thing to suggest that working time is integral to the development of a multi-level system; it is another to show a demonstrable impact of European integration on working time. For a start, there is the problem of measurement. The duration of working time and flexibility practices such as part-time, temporary and shift working can be charted. Much more difficult to establish is the variability of working time, where the differing interpretation possible of such practices as 'personal time accounts' or 'overtime corridors' or 'flexible rostering' or 'annualization' is a major problem (Bosch, 2001: 106). Moreover, unlike wages, the nature of working time means that a similar regularity of changes, in the form of annual or multi-annual adjustments, cannot be expected.

Complicating matters is that the pressures for change are often contradictory. In the case of duration, the long-standing trade union objective of reducing working hours is increasingly meeting employer demands for extended hours of operation. In the case of flexibility, supply-side and demand-side considerations are interacting in the context of the global trends concerning the 'tertiarization' of economic activity and changing demography considered in Chapter 1 (Sarfati, 2001; Dølvik, 2001a). Thus, as the balance of employment has shifted from manufacturing to services, demands for more 'family-friendly' arrangements have grown, reflecting the increasing proportion of women in the labour force, allied to the expansion of dual-income and single-parent families, and, in some countries, the privatization of care arrangements.

There are strong grounds for being cautious in expecting significant changes in working time arrangements, let alone convergent trends (Arrowsmith and Sisson, 2001). If anything, working time patterns are even more 'path-dependent' than wages, the household rather than the individual worker being the critical unit. Bosch (2001: 72) offers a useful catalogue of the deeply rooted institutional arrangements where differences have been shown to be particularly important in accounting for continued cross-national variations: the regulatory framework; wage levels and income distribution, which affect the 'affordability' of working time; tax and social security arrangements, which provide incentives/disincentives for workers and employers respectively; childcare arrangements, which affect the ability of women to work full-time as opposed to part-time; and education and training policy, which influences the quality as well as the quantity of employment.

Even so, it might be expected that competitive pressures would impact on working time in different ways from sector to sector. Most

Fluctuations

		Longer-term (Seasonal/Periodic)	Shorter-term (Weekly/Daily)	None
Predictability	High	A	C	E
	Low	B	D	F

Figure 10.1 Working time patterns

sectors have been under pressure to extend operating hours: in manufacturing, increasing capital intensity means pressure to amortize investments more effectively in order to reduce marginal costs; in services, the main driver is the demand from customers for greater availability. As Figure 10.1 portrays, however, there can be significant fluctuations in demand of a short-term or longer-term nature and in operational predictability, which differ between sectors and sub-sectors (Bloch-London *et al.*, n.d.). Thus fluctuations may be within the cycle of the extended working day, as in banking or restaurants (cells C/D), or the 7-day cycle of the week of hotels (also cells C/D), for example, or the seasonal or 52-week cycle as is the case in agriculture, parts of food processing and also hotels and catering (cells A/B). In some sectors, there may be no regular fluctuations, as in private security or emergency maintenance services (cells E/F). Operational predictability can range from the very low to the very high. In chemicals, for example, there can be considerable fluctuations in demand over the year, but these are relatively easy to predict (cell A). In much of metalworking, by contrast, changes in production processes such as 'just-in-time', combined with the fluctuating volume and design stipulations of customers, mean that predictability is much less (cell B). In retail, operating hours in large superstores can involve round the clock working seven days a week with considerable fluctuation in demand depending on the time of day and week, but predictability is relatively high (cell C). In hotels and restaurants, demand can also fluctuate considerably, but it is more difficult to predict (cell D). In private security the predictability of operating hours is high (cell E), whereas in emergency maintenance services predictability is markedly lower (cell F).

A different mix of working time patterns can be expected in the light of these complexities. Predictable fluctuations might be met by a combination of annual hours, part-time and temporary working and different forms of shift working. Unpredictable fluctuations might involve longer hours – either voluntary or contractual overtime, along with greater variability in starting and finishing times and/or the days worked.

In the circumstances, this chapter has a modest aim. This is to establish whether, in the light of the expectations suggested by Figure 10.1 but also in the face of the enduring institutional and other differences between countries underlined by Bosch (2001), there are cross-national differences by sector that are consistent with the 'converging-divergences' proposition which has found support in the findings of Chapters 6, 7, 8 and 9. The chapter can test for the connections between European integration and working time developments, in other words, even if it cannot prove that European integration is the main cause.

As in the case of Chapter 9's consideration of wages, the task ideally requires cross-national data on the key dimensions at the three main levels of activity: national, sector and company. Such data are only available for some of the main indicators at the first two levels, however. At company level, where Chapter 7 has shown the flexibility of working time to be central to recent developments in collective bargaining (see also Arrowsmith *et al.*, 2001), systematic cross-country data are again virtually non-existent.

The duration of working time

Although there are aggregate dimensions, such as seasonal or annual hours, the duration of working time is usually associated with the working week. Two measures deserve attention: collectively agreed working time, which focuses on basic hours and provides some indication of the success or otherwise of trade union pressure to regulate working time; and usual working hours, which better reflect demand pressures from employers. The difference between the two is accounted for by overtime, which can be contractual or voluntary, paid or unpaid.

Collectively agreed working time

Although collective agreements may deal with aspects of part-time working, when addressing hours of work, most restrict themselves to full-time working, which is generally taken to mean more than 30 hours a week. Table 10.1 gives details of collectively agreed hours in two main sectors – metalworking and banking – as well as the cross-sector average. The key point to note is that there are not only differences between countries, but also sectors. Indeed, in only four countries were hours the same across the two sectors: Austria, Denmark, France and Ireland. In

Table 10.1 Collectively agreed normal working hours, 2001

	All sectors	Metalworking	Banking
Belgium	39.0	38.0	35.0
Denmark	37.0	37.0	37.0
Germany	37.7	35.0	39.0
Greece	40.0	40.0	38.3
Spain	38.6	38.6	38.4
France	35.0	35.0	35.0
Ireland	39.0	39.0	39.0
Italy	38.0	40.0	37.5
Luxembourg	39.0	37.5	40.0
Netherlands	37.0	38.0	36.0
Austria	38.5	38.5	38.5
Portugal	38.7*	40.0	35.0
Finland	39.3	39.9	39.6
Sweden	38.8	40.0	38.5
UK	37.5	37.5	35.1
EU average	*38.2*	*38.2*	*37.5*

*1999 figure.
Source: EIRO (2002c), where detailed sources and calculation method will be found accompanying Figures 1, 2 and 3.

the other 11, there was a difference, the advantage being with metal-working in two, Germany and Luxembourg, and with banking in the remainder. Moreover, the differences between sectors were sizeable in several countries. In Italy, the difference was 2.5 hours, in Belgium three, in Germany four and in Portugal five.

Self-evidently, the differences cannot be explained in terms of the operating requirements of the two sectors. If they could, the direction of difference would be the same across all 15 countries. The differences are also long-standing, despite more or less continuous pressure for reductions from trade unions. It is not so much a question of it being 'difficult for [trade unions] to argue for working time reductions – in competition with wages' in times of low rates of growth in GDP and labour productivity (Lehndorff, 1998: 613). Rather low inflation may mean workers are more rather than less indifferent to accepting reduced working time as compensation for increased productivity. Crucially, employers oppose conceding working time reductions in exchange for wages, because these are so difficult to reverse (Arrowsmith, 2002). The differences identified reflect two main considerations: the bargaining power and priorities of trade unions, with the position of IG-Metall in respect of both these considerations helping to explain the comparatively shorter hours in metalworking in Germany; and the association of banking with staff status conditions, which accounts for this sector's comparatively shorter hours across a larger number of countries.

Usual working hours

Usual working hours include paid and unpaid overtime. The overall picture is reasonably well established and confirms the enduring significance of country. On the basis of the distribution of employment by groups of hours, three main patterns may be identified (European Commission, 2000: 69):

- A 'highly regulated' model such as Luxembourg where the bulk of the labour force works full-time with hours concentrated around a single peak or two, or at most three peaks.
- An 'unregulated' model such as the UK, where there is a fairly even spread across the distribution for women, in particular, but an upturn in the distribution at long hours of work for men.
- A 'progressive' model such as the Netherlands, where there is a wide spread of hours worked up to 40 hours, especially by women, reflecting extensive part-time working, but with very few workers, men or women, working longer.

Although a comparison between 1990 and 2000 (Eurostat, 1991, 2001) confirms the enduring nature of many of these features, there has been some change in composition. As Lehndorff (1998: 602–5) reminds us, the aggregate reduction in working hours is a statistical 'illusion', being less a product of collective bargaining and more a question of changes in the composition of the labour force (i.e. between men and women, full-time and part-time) and its distribution across sectors. Indeed, the European Commission (2000: 67) emphasizes that, whereas there was a reduction of 0.36 in the average usual hours per week between 1994 and 1998, when account is taken of sectoral and compositional changes, there was an increase of 0.15 in individual working hours per week.

Table 10.2, which gives average usual weekly hours for men and women working full-time, shows the strength of the country effect, reflecting the continued salience of the factors – outlined earlier – identified by Bosch (2001). Take the spread of male hours across the sectors. In some countries the spread is minimal – Belgium is the most homogeneous (1.0 hours), followed by Sweden (1.4 hours) and the Netherlands (1.7 hours). In others, however, the spread is quite substantial, the widest gaps being found in Portugal (7.1 hours) and Greece (6.5 hours). As compared with other countries, the UK is an outlier in the length of usual weekly hours worked by men. These long hours are not just a manufacturing phenomenon, as is sometimes suggested: Table 10.2 shows that the UK had the longest usual hours in five of the six sectors, the exception being hotels and restaurants where it was exceeded only by Greece. Women working full-time in the UK are closer to the EU average than their male counterparts across all sectors. Given that Table 10.1 indicates that collectively agreed hours in the UK are not out of line with those in other countries, the implication is that overtime working – both paid and unpaid – is significantly higher in the UK, for men in particular, than it is elsewhere amongst the EU-15. Such data are not currently available on a comparative basis: as the ETUI (2003: 41) observe, 'measurement of the amount of overtime worked would further complete the picture'.

Important though country is, sector differences are also apparent. As Table 10.2 shows, the hierarchy of sectors is similar between countries. Overall, the longest hours for men are to be found in hotels and restaurants and transport and communications (44.4 and 42.5 hours respectively). Indeed, these two sectors have the longest weekly hours in all but two of the countries, the exceptions being Belgium and Sweden. Hours in finance are the lowest in six countries. The pattern is only slightly different for women. Hotels and restaurants has the longest hours in ten of the 15 countries, although transport and communications is less marked in terms of long hours. Hours are lowest in finance in eight countries.

As in the case of collectively agreed working time, therefore, the country effect is pronounced. There are nonetheless some marked differences between sectors in the majority of countries. Moreover, the pattern of differences between sectors bears a degree of similarity from country to country.

The flexibility of working time

Recent initiatives to increase the flexibility of working time have focused around four main developments: part-time working, temporary work and non-standard and variable hours arrangements. Each of these is considered in turn, together with the extent to which employees have discretion over their working time arrangements. Overtime, which the preceding section included as an integral component of the duration of working time, could equally have been treated as a means of working time flexibility. For overtime working is increasingly being 'engulfed in a more sophisticated set of methods [of working time flexibility] from

Table 10.2 Average weekly hours of full-time employees by economic activity, 2000

	Men						Women					
	Manufacturing	Construction	Wholesale & retail distribution	Hotels & restaurants	Finance	Transport & communications	Manufacturing	Construction	Wholesale & retail distribution	Hotels & restaurants	Finance	Transport & communications
Belgium	39.3	40.1	40.0	39.6	40.3	40.2	39.9	39.0	38.4	39.9	38.2	38.8
Denmark	39.2	38.8	40.5	40.6	40.9	41.6	37.7	37.4	37.6	39.1	38.2	38.3
Germany	39.3	40.4	41.2	45.1	41.3	42.5	38.7	39.8	39.4	43.3	39.1	39.6
Greece	42.1	42.7	43.3	47.0	40.5	45.2	41.2	–	42.6	44.6	39.9	41.1
Spain	41.0	41.0	42.2	44.7	40.9	42.3	40.4	40.1	41.1	42.4	40.2	39.6
France	38.7	39.5	40.1	43.3	40.9	40.0	38.1	39.0	38.3	40.6	38.3	37.8
Ireland	40.8	41.9	41.5	43.1	41.1	41.8	39.2	40.4	39.1	39.9	39.3	39.3
Italy	40.6	40.7	42.1	44.0	39.6	40.2	39.6	39.7	40.5	40.6	38.3	37.5
Luxembourg	40.4	40.4	41.0	45.2	41.7	41.0	38.8	39.1	39.2	41.9	39.2	39.6
Netherlands	39.0	39.5	39.6	39.4	38.7	40.7	39.1	39.2	38.5	39.2	37.6	39.3
Austria	39.5	38.8	40.0	42.6	40.0	41.1	40.3	39.2	39.4	40.8	38.9	40.0
Portugal	41.0	41.7	42.2	45.4	38.3	42.7	39.2	39.4	41.1	44.2	37.6	38.8
Finland	39.8	40.7	40.6	39.3	43.1	41.4	39.3	38.6	37.9	38.6	38.4	38.0
Sweden	39.7	40.1	41.1	40.2	40.5	40.0	39.3	39.8	39.5	39.6	39.0	39.6
UK	44.6	45.8	45.5	46.1	43.8	47.1	40.5	39.7	40.2	41.0	39.5	41.4
EU-15	40.5	41.2	42.0	44.4	41.2	42.5	39.3	39.6	39.7	41.7	39.0	39.3

Source: Eurostat (2001) Labour Force Survey 2000, Table 47.

working time variation around an average to annualisation, personal time accounts, part-time work and additional hours etc' (Freyssinet and Michon, 2003: 19).

Part-time working

Part-time working has come to be seen as one of the main forms of flexibility. It is very much a gendered phenomenon. The absolute number of men working part-time is not insignificant, but the proportion is – the 5.7 million who worked part-time in 2000, amounted to only 6.3 per cent of the total number of men in employment. In manufacturing, only in Denmark and the Netherlands did the proportion exceed 5 per cent with just the Netherlands reaching double figures. Even in services, in only five countries did the proportion reach double figures (Denmark, Finland, Sweden, the Netherlands and the UK). By contrast, the 22.6 million women working part-time in 2000 accounted for 35 per cent of female employment.

Throughout the 1990s, part-time working increased in both absolute and proportionate terms in the case of men and women. The increase has not been across the board, however. In manufacturing there has been little or no change in most countries. In services, there appears to be a strong country effect. Some countries that started with a low proportion have seen growth, most notably Italy, where there has been a doubling in the proportion of part-time working among women from just over 9 to 18 per cent. By contrast, Greece shows little change. The Netherlands had a high proportion of part-time workers at the start of the 1990s and this has continued to grow. Denmark, Sweden and the UK, on the other hand, which also started with relatively high proportions, have shown little increase or even a decline since 1990.

Focusing on women, Table 10.3 shows the proportion in part-time employment by country and sector in 2000. Both country and sector influences are evident. In the first instance, there is a group of eight countries (Belgium, Denmark, Finland, France, Germany, Ireland, Sweden and the UK) sharing similarly high levels – in wholesale and retail distribution and hotels and restaurants – amongst the service sectors. In each case the proportion exceeds 30 per cent. By contrast, in Greece, Italy, Portugal and Spain part-time working was proportionately relatively low in both services and manufacturing. Extreme is Greece, where the proportion is one-fifth or less of the EU average in each of the six sectors. The Netherlands stands out for the opposite reason. More than 50 per cent of women in employment in manufacturing and more than 70 per cent in wholesale and retail distribution and hotels

Table 10.3   Female employees working part-time by economic activity, 2000

	Manufacturing (%)	Construction (%)	Wholesale & retail distribution (%)	Hotels & restaurants (%)	Finance (%)	Transport & Communications (%)
Belgium	18.1	18.1	34.3	33.8	28.0	20.6
Denmark	18.6	18.6	45.7	50.0	20.4	26.4
Germany	29.8	29.8	46.1	37.5	28.2	33.6
Greece	4.7	4.7	5.9	7.3	*	*
Spain	8.5	8.5	13.8	20.7	8.5	13.4
France	15.1	15.1	32.6	38.7	20.6	27.2
Ireland	13.8	13.8	41.2	48.4	17.9	20.0
Italy	12.8	12.8	19.2	24.7	14.8	12.9
Luxembourg	*	33.3	27.2	25.0	12.5	*
Netherlands	54.4	54.4	70.6	79.0	48.3	62.7
Austria	24.7	24.7	42.5	26.4	31.8	31.0
Portugal	5.7	5.7	9.5	6.5	*	*
Finland	6.9	6.9	33.6	32.1	20.6	16.3
Sweden	21.2	21.2	41.7	40.3	20.8	27.8
UK	24.2	24.2	59.4	63.1	26.6	31.4
EU-15	20.2	20.2	39.3	38.4	23.7	27.7

* Insufficient numbers for reliable calculation.
Source: Eurostat (2001) *Labour Force Survey 2000*, Tables 17 and 36. Own calculations.

and restaurants were part-time. No other country exceeded 50 per cent in manufacturing and only in the UK were more than half of women employees working part-time in the two service sectors.

Turning to sector, part-time working is much more prevalent in services than it is in manufacturing, reflecting relatively predictable daily and weekly fluctuations in demand in service sectors such as wholesale and retail distribution. The proportion in this sector, and also in hotels and restaurants, is around twice that in manufacturing. Part-time working in finance is much less pronounced in every country, however, with the proportion being less than half that in the other service sectors in many cases. The changes taking place in the sector discussed in Chapter 7, such as the expansion in call centres, might have been expected to lead to significant part-time working. One explanation might be that moves to extended operating hours have been relatively modest as compared with other service sectors, and employer demand for part-time working correspondingly less. Overall, the pattern is generally consistent with the opening discussion about the significance of operating hours and operating predictability, as portrayed in Figure 10.1, in underpinning sector differences.

Temporary working

Temporary working enables employers to vary the total hours worked by changing the numbers employed on contracts of limited or predetermined duration. It can take the form of engaging employees on fixed-term contracts either directly or indirectly from agencies. It is generally regarded as an important means by which employers can respond to market pressures through numerical flexibility, reducing or increasing total hours worked through rapid and low cost changes in employee numbers (Casey *et al.*, 1997). Overall, some 17.7 million workers were in temporary employment in 2000, representing 11.2 per cent of total employment. The gender differences evident in the incidence of part-time working are barely discernible in temporary work, with just under 13 per cent of women in employment being temporary and some 10 per cent of men (Eurostat, 2001: Table 36).

The country effect is especially noticeable. Austria, Belgium, Italy, Luxembourg and the UK have a relatively low incidence of temporary working, with levels below 10 per cent of the workforce. By contrast, Spain stands out as having a comparatively high level – no fewer than 24 per cent of men and 29 per cent of women were in temporary employment in 2000. The legacy of stringent job protection legislation is that almost all new employees start on such contracts. Portugal, Finland and Sweden also have relatively high levels of temporary working, accounting for at least 15 per cent of the workforce in each case. The main sector differences are in construction, where there is a comparatively high incidence of temporary working amongst the predominantly male workforce and finance, where the proportion of temporary working is – like part-time working – noticeably lower than in other service sectors.

Non-standard hours

Longer operating hours raise the prospect of round the clock working (Kauppinen, 2001). One of the main ways in which employers can increase the coverage of working time beyond the working day is through shift working. Strictly speaking, shift working means two or more periods of working within the same 24 hours by different employees usually organized in crews or teams. It may involve split shifts as in the case of hotels and restaurants. More generally, shift working involves individuals working at different times of the day and/or week. Employees can be asked to work on a Saturday or a Sunday, which have traditionally been seen as days of rest, or in the evening or at night.

Data from the third survey of working conditions carried out by the European Foundation for the Improvement of Living and Working

Conditions (2001) make it possible to gauge the extent of such practices in 2000. The results, which combine men and women, appear in the top panels of Tables 10.4 and 10.5, which report the incidence of various practices by country and sector respectively. In the case of Table 10.5, the eight countries selected for economy of presentation are the same as those in Chapter 9's consideration of wages. The averages and the coefficients of variation, however, are for the EU-15.

The first point to note is that, despite impressions to the contrary, most of these practices continue to be the exception rather than the rule. Shift working strictly defined remains a practice involving only around one-fifth of the labour force. A similar proportion of employees works at night. One in four employees works on Sunday. Around one in three, however, report that they sometimes work more than ten hours a day and as many as one in two that they sometimes work in the evening or on Saturday.

The second point involves country and sector influences: both, it seems, are important. As the coefficients of variation in the final column of the top panel of each table indicate, however, the variation tends to be greater in the case of the sector, suggesting that this influence is the stronger. Shift working, for example, was six times more likely in mining and manufacturing, hotels and restaurants and transport and communications than it was in finance or in construction. Similarly, very few employees worked nights in wholesale and retail or construction, but more than one third did so in transport and communications and almost one half in hotels and restaurants. Overall, the extent of non-standard working was especially high in hotels and restaurants, which recorded the highest figures for long hours, evening, night, Saturday and Sunday working. The sector composition of the labour force also has a bearing on the differences between the countries. Of the eight countries, Italy, Portugal and Spain show a comparatively high incidence of non-standard working. These are countries in which hotels and restaurants and wholesale and retail – sectors where the incidence of non-standard practices is also comparatively high – employ a disproportionate share of the labour force (Eurostat, 1999: 91).

Variable hours

The arrangements considered so far have for the most part involved essentially fixed hours worked on a weekly basis. Our attention now turns to arrangements under which hours worked are variable. Here the European Foundation's survey (2001) contains information on four dimensions of working time flexibility, which capture some of the basic

Table 10.4 Incidence of flexible working by economic activity, 2000 (all employees)

	Manufacturing & mining	Construction	Wholesale & retail distribution	Hotels & restaurants	Finance	Transport & Communications	All sectors: EU-15	Coefficient of variation
Non-standard working patterns								
% working shifts	30	5	13	30	5	30	19	0.60
% working ten hours+ a day	28	40	32	43	30	44	33	0.19
% working in the evening	44	35	45	75	35	55	46	0.26
% working at night	22	7	6	46	10	37	19	0.60
% working Saturday	42	45	70	81	33	65	52	0.32
% working Sunday	17	12	22	65	11	41	27	0.57
Variable hours								
% with fixed starting/finishing times	74	61	65	52	58	54	64	0.23
% working same no of hours each day	70	57	59	50	62	49	58	0.17
% working same no of days each week	80	73	77	70	80	61	74	0.10
% experiencing changes in scheduled working times	22	23	22	31	21	33	24	0.39
Employee discretion								
% reporting they can influence working hours	36	44	50	42	57	41	44	0.22
% reporting they can take their break when they wish	57	64	64	46	76	59	61	0.17
% reporting freedom to decide holiday dates/days off	56	55	61	50	68	50	56	0.13

Source: Unpublished tables from *Third European Survey on Working Conditions* (2000), kindly supplied by European Foundation for the Improvement of Living and Working Conditions. Own calculations.

Table 10.5 Incidence of flexible working by country, 2000 (all employees)

	Germany	Spain	France	Ireland	Italy	Portugal	Sweden	UK	EU-15	Coefficient of variation
Non-standard working patterns										
% working shifts	19	22	19	17	21	8	17	23	19	0.27
% working ten hours+ a day	30	26	31	39	33	25	47	37	33	0.21
% working in the evening	39	34	45	51	45	34	55	47	46	0.21
% working at night	18	19	18	20	15	15	18	22	19	0.16
% working Saturday	48	51	52	55	63	47	41	54	52	0.15
% working Sunday	22	22	27	31	22	18	38	32	27	0.24
Variable hours										
% with fixed starting/finishing times	67	69	67	65	61	66	62	61	64	0.08
% working same no of hours each day	56	66	58	67	62	70	48	56	58	0.15
% working same no of days each week	73	80	77	80	73	82	69	73	74	0.07
% experiencing changes in scheduled working times	36	15	20	19	18	6	46	24	24	0.45
Employee discretion										
% reporting they can influence working hours	40	30	44	46	42	42	56	52	44	0.15
% reporting they can take their break when they wish	48	56	69	60	74	73	62	61	61	0.11
% reporting freedom to decide holiday dates/days off	50	44	50	60	62	46	52	68	56	0.17

Source: Unpublished tables from *Third European Survey on Working Conditions* (2000), kindly supplied by European Foundation for the Improvement of Living and Working Conditions. Own calculations.

parameters. These are: fixed starting/finishing times; the regularity of the hours worked each day; the regularity of the days worked each week; and the extent of changes in working time schedules. The middle panels of Tables 10.4 and 10.5 show the findings by sector and country, respectively. Overall, two out of five employees reported that they did not work the same number of hours each day, with one in four saying that they did not work the same number of days each week. Around one-third have variable starting/finishing times and one-quarter experienced changes in their working schedules.

The variation between sectors is not as pronounced as that for non-standard forms of working; the magnitude of the coefficients of variation in the final column of the middle panel of Table 10.4 being generally smaller than those in the top panel. Even so, some sectors stand out. In the case of variable starting/finishing times, hotels and restaurants and transport and communications are prominent, such arrangements accounting for almost one-half of employees in either case. The same two sectors are also distinctive for having the lowest proportion of employees reporting that they worked the same number of hours each day – a degree of irregularity which is consistent with the further finding that employees in these two sectors also are the most likely to experience changes in scheduled working times. Sector variation is not consistently more marked than country; comparing the coefficients of variation in the middle panels of Tables 10.4 and 10.5 the magnitude of the sector statistic for fixed starting and finishing times is rather greater than that for country, with no great difference for two of the other practices, and the magnitude of the country statistic is greater for changes in scheduled working times. On this last aspect there is a substantial difference between Sweden and Germany on the one hand, where over one-third of employees experience such changes, and Portugal and Spain on the other, where fewer than one in six employees are affected.

Employee discretion

The European Foundation's survey (2001) also offers information on three dimensions of what might be determined 'employee discretion'. There is a general question about being able to influence working hours and specific ones about the ability to take breaks when desired and the freedom to decide when to take holidays or days off. In practice, answers probably capture the influence of formal flexi-time schemes but also that of informal arrangements. The findings, by sector and country, will be found in the bottom panel of Tables 10.4 and 10.5, respectively.

Employee discretion over working time, whilst widespread, is far from universal: fewer than one-half of employees (44 per cent) say they can influence working hours. On specific matters, the proportions are somewhat higher: 56 per cent report that they take their break when they want and 61 per cent that they are free to decide when to take their holidays or days off.

Comparing the coefficients of variation in the bottom panel of Table 10.4 with those in the top and middle panels, the variation between sectors is not as pronounced as in the case of the non-standard forms of working and is broadly similar to that for variable hours. Comparison of the coefficients of variation in the bottom panel of Table 10.4 with those in the same panel of Table 10.5 indicates that the sector effect is neither greater nor less than that of country. The sector patterns are generally consistent with the considerations of operating hours discussed earlier. Where work is highly integrated and/or process driven, as in mining and manufacturing, employees have relatively low levels of influence over their working hours. The same applies where work is customer driven, as in hotels and restaurants. In finance, where such considerations are less stringent, employees enjoy a comparatively high level of influence over working hours.

Why the sector makes a difference

While there continues to be a strong country effect, reflecting the enduring influence of the institutional and other factors identified by Bosch (2001), the sector appears to be as important in shaping patterns of flexible working time. Part-time working is especially prominent in service sectors. Shift working is more likely in manufacturing. Irregular patterns of working are a distinctive feature of transport and communications, and hotels and restaurants. Employee discretion is greatest in finance.

Crucially, the sector defines operational requirements and therefore, as Figure 10.1 suggested, the available options for change. At the most basic level, there are 'technical' factors, such as the nature of the product (for example, the balance between quality and quantity or between standardization and heterogeneity), patterns of demand, technology and, therefore, skill and training requirements. Take, for example, two sectors with extended operating hours. In retail the peaks and troughs of demand over an increasingly lengthy cycle of seven days a week are massive but predictable, which encourages the development of a plethora of part-time as opposed to full-time shift patterns. In a continuous process industry such as chemicals, peaks and troughs in demand occur over a longer period but are still relatively predictable. There are full-time shifts organized on a round the clock basis, along with annualized hours arrangements. It is also clear that the diversity *between* service sectors is as important as the manufacturing-service distinction. Prominent are sectors such as hotels and restaurants and transport and communications, where long hours are being combined with the various forms of flexible working, reflecting the greater fluctuations in demand and operational predictability discussed in the opening of this chapter. By contrast, finance does not show anything like the same incidence of flexible working time arrangements.

Also important is the sectoral segmentation of the labour market, which is linked to national arrangements for social/welfare provision, childcare, tax and social security, pensions, plus the nature and extent of employment regulation. Skilled metalworking workers, for example, are overwhelmingly male looking for full-time employment; part-time work is less likely to be attractive. In contrast, in much of the service sector a large proportion of the workforce – those with other household, care or educational responsibilities – might be willing only to work on a part-time basis. Once established, such patterns themselves become crucial in circumscribing the options for change. The path dependency which is so frequently underlined in cross-country analysis, can be an equally powerful influence on sectoral patterns.

Conclusions

Considering European integration, it is important to distinguish between the causes and effects of the working time patterns discussed here. European integration has encouraged pressure to create a level playing field underpinned by legislation and collective agreement; through market integration it has intensified the competitive pressures coming from employers for greater flexibility; it has helped to keep working time in the forefront of debate, leading to change at every level. Less obvious, but perhaps more important in the long run, is its promotion of higher employment rates in the service sector through the European Employment Strategy and the targets adopted at the Lisbon Summit. Even so, it is necessary to go beyond European integration to fully account for the incidence of many of the practices surveyed. Especially important has been the 'tertiarization' of economic activity associated with the rise of the service sector. Indeed, once the changing structure of employment between manufacturing and services is factored in, innovations in working time arrangements have not been as extensive as many commentators have suggested. For, unlike productivity discussed in Chapter 9, many of the aggregate developments reflect not so much changes within sectors, but the changing balance between them.

Although some of the causes of working time developments are relatively independent of European integration, their effects are a very different matter. Working time is a major consideration not only in the development of the EU's multi-level industrial relations system, but also in the tendency to 'convergent divergences' that European integration is promoting. For, as in the case of Chapter 9's consideration of wages, the sector emerges as a crucial variable. True, some working time patterns, such as usual weekly hours or temporary working, continue to mainly reflect different national frameworks and legacies. Yet the nature and extent of the fluctuation and predictability of operating hours, which are sector phenomena, are also integral in accounting for the incidence of specific flexibility practices.

Working time patterns not only underline the diversity within national systems and the similarities between them, but developments are also encouraging cross-national convergence. This is because management and trade unions and works councils at the company level, which data limitations have obliged us to exclude in this chapter, are contrasting and comparing practices in other countries, as demonstrated in Chapter 8. Bearing in mind that with working time it is easier to make comparisons but more difficult to justify differences than with wages, working time is likely to become a central focus of cross-national attention for both management and employee representatives. Examples of this happening already, reported in Chapter 8, include the extension of 'working time corridors' throughout General Motors' operations in Europe and systematic exchange of information on working time arrangements between local and national employee representatives being undertaken by the employee side of the EWC at *Germetal*. The greater domestic focus of much business activity, coupled with relatively weak trade union organization, means that there has not yet been the same resort to international comparisons in the service sector. That similarities in working time duration and arrangements across countries are likely to progress faster in internationally exposed sectors such as manufacturing than in the more sheltered service sectors underscores the multi-speed nature of Europeanization.

11
'One Europe' *and* 'Several Europes'?
A Review of the Findings

Contrary to the hopes of some, European integration has not brought about an industrial relations system that is comparable to national ones. Equally, however, it has not yet brought about the worst nightmare of many – the collapse of multi-employer bargaining and the fragmentation of existing national systems. Indeed, on the surface there has apparently been little change in the formal institutions of national systems. Instead, a complex multi-level system is emerging. Like the EU polity's multi-level governance system, it reflects a history of informal and gradual development as well as deliberate institution building. National industrial relations systems have always been multi-level in some degree, with national, sector, company and workplace levels interacting with one another. Making the difference is the international dimension that European integration brings. Cross-national (horizontal) influences mix with national (vertical) ones and involve the sector and Euro-company levels as well as the Community level. Moreover, it is not only the formal processes of legal enactment, collective bargaining and coordination that are important. Coping with common constraints is encouraging the informal processes of isomorphism ('competitive', 'coercive', 'mimetic' and 'normative'). In Teague's (2001: 23) phrase, 'Europe is learning from Europe'. Paradoxically, the result is a mix of 'Europeanization', 're-nationalization' and 'Americanization'. National-level social pacts are instances of both 'Europeanization' and 're-nationalization'; the development of organization-specific arrangements by large employers represents 'Americanization' from the position of national sector agreements, but 'Europeanization' from the perspective of the Euro-company.

A multi-level system is not just a descriptive metaphor, however. It is the system's evolving patterns of regulation, policy networks and opportunities for mutual learning that are simultaneously prompting *both* greater convergence *and* diversity. The convergence is apparent along the policy, process and output dimensions distinguished by Hay (2000), taking the form of a number of common changes at national, sector and company levels in the levels of governance, but also its scope, form and output. Divergence nonetheless persists between countries, underlined by the variants of the European social model which coexist within the EU. Growth in diversity is within national systems and reflects the different speed of 'Europeanization' *between* sectors and companies. In bringing about a measure of convergence *within* companies and sectors *between* national systems, the multi-level system is also promoting greater diversity *between* companies and sectors *within* national systems. The result is considerable instability, which EU enlargement is likely to exacerbate. This chapter expands on these findings, with Chapter 12 developing their wider implications both for policy and practice and for industrial relations theorizing.

The genesis of Europe's multi-level system

European integration has prompted a multi-level governance framework in introducing three supranational levels – the Community, EU sector and Euro-company – and in extending the range of reference groups with which comparisons are made. Less obviously, it is also encouraging resort to 'subsidiarity' within national systems, leading to further decentralization *and* new forms of centralization.

The significance of the EU's multi-level system of governance

The emergence of a multi-level system of industrial relations is inextricably linked to the multi-level system of governance that the EU has produced. Explaining the lack of a strong state protagonist (Traxler, 1996) with the authority to sponsor the construction of supranational collective bargaining arrangements, is the reluctance of national states to cede sovereignty to the EU and the immensely practical problems of resolving the collective action problem. The preference has been for negative integration and 'soft' forms of coordination rather than 'hard' regulation. Even so, there has been considerable 'spillover' from economic integration. The Community has become an important level, with an industrial relations framework that can lay claim to principles, procedures and substantive outcomes. Since the Maastricht social policy agreement of 1991, a social policy process has become embedded, prioritizing social dialogue and collective agreement as an effective means of handling change, and hence the role of the European-level social partners. The industrial relations *acquis communautaire* has been substantially augmented, embracing minimum standards on information and consultation as well as the freedom of movement and the exchange of qualifications, equality, health and safety and working time. A long-term employment strategy involves targets, benchmarking of progress and peer group review, along with a forum for ongoing dialogue about the links between prices, wages, employment and economic performance. Underpinning these developments, and a key factor in their emergence, is the development of a well-organized policy community involving representatives of the Commission, national governments and social partners.

These developments entail certain features which temper their impact, however. The directives which form a core part of the industrial relations *acquis communautaire* have for the most part established a minimum floor by addressing the extremes of the range of prevailing (non-) regulation across member states. Those on working time and national information and consultation are examples, the principal impact bearing on two of the pre-enlargement member states – Ireland and the UK. Further, the softer regulatory form which directives have increasingly taken, introducing a double-form of subsidiarity opening up possibilities of variation to national governments in transposing them and also to the social partners via negotiation (Hall, 1994), has had the effect of softening the minimum standard applied.

The EU sector and Euro-company levels have also become sources of 'Europeanizing' initiatives, albeit here there is enormous variation. At EU sector level, there is an active social dialogue in some sectors and agreement-making in a few. The ETUC and its industry federations have also begun to put in place cross-border coordinating procedures and common 'rules' to influence national bargaining agendas. At Euro-company level, the EWC Directive has been the catalyst for transnational agreements in some 650 MNCs establishing EU-wide information and consultation arrangements. Ford and General Motors have set important precedents in using their EWCs to negotiate European-wide framework agreements to implement restructuring, involving representatives of European and national trade unions as well as their own employees. 'Mimetic' and 'normative' forms of isomorphism are also encouraging greater harmonization within MNCs regardless of the presence of trade unions. Coupled with the adoption of European-wide management structures in many Euro-companies, the effect is to promote the use of cross-national 'coercive' comparisons by managers and, as yet less commonly, employee representatives.

Weaknesses are also apparent at these levels. The sector-level social dialogue remains underdeveloped in most sectors as compared to its cross-sector counterpart, with little by the way of regulatory output likely to impact at national and local levels. It has yet to be established in some key manufacturing sectors. Coordination of sector bargaining agenda and outcomes across borders by trade unions presently appears more of an aspiration than a reality. There is neither a strong state protagonist nor strong non-state actors promoting the development of industrial relations at EU sector-level. As a result, the EU sector-level represents the weak link in the emerging multi-level system. At Euro-company level, the enormous variation which is apparent embraces a substantial minority of European-level industrial relations structures which are no more than 'symbolic' in nature, in the form of sizeable numbers of EWCs which are inactive beyond the ritual of an annual meeting.

Centralization and decentralization within national systems

Also important in the emergence of multi-level governance have been developments within national systems. Most west European countries are characterized by an inclusive structure of multi-employer bargaining at national and/or sector level. Increasingly, however, there has been a widespread trend towards more decentralized arrangements, reflecting employer demands for greater scope to negotiate working practices appropriate to local circumstances. EMU has reinforced this long-running development by unleashing pressures for extensive restructuring and rationalization. One result is the spread of 'pacts for employment and competitiveness' (PECs), in which management and employee representatives trade off employment guarantees against reductions in costs, working time flexibility and improvements in adaptability.

Although sector agreements are now tending to respond to developments in company negotiations rather than vice versa, they nonetheless continue to be a key level. In most cases, decentralization has followed Traxler's (1995) 'organized' trajectory involving 'opening', 'hardship' and 'opt-out' clauses in sector agreements, along with a shift from detailed to framework provisions and uniform to minimum standards. Only in the UK, reflecting the very different form and status of multi-employer agreements, has decentralization been 'disorganized', with sector agreements disintegrating and being displaced by company bargaining or unilateral management regulation. Nonetheless 'organized' decentralization entails some developments which may eventually corrode the relevance and purchase of sector-level agreements under a process of 'evolutionary decay' (Traxler *et al.*, 2001: 206). The 'hardship' and 'opt-out' clauses which result from the shift from productivity- to competition-oriented bargaining (Schulten, 1998) qualify universal standards and undermine the traditional basis of worker (and employer) solidarity on which sector regulation has rested. Simultaneously the increasingly framework character of sector agreements tends to empty them of substantive content, threatening a retreat towards hollow shells specifying procedural rules.

Integral to organized decentralization in many countries has been a strengthening of the national level or the addition of a national level where one did not previously exist, thereby contributing to the development of the multi-level system. Under pressure to contain inflation and reduce public sector deficits in line with EMU convergence criteria, many governments – France, Germany and the UK excepted – have sought agreements with the social partners on wage moderation, greater labour market flexibility and reform of social protection systems. In some cases, such as Italy and Spain, national agreements have also sought to formalize the respective competence of the different bargaining levels. Even where there has been no formal agreement, as in Germany, there has been extensive macro-level social dialogue. The coming of EMU has given added legitimacy to social dialogue and an inclusive structure of multi-employer collective bargaining as the vehicles for handling economic and social change.

The effects of Europe's multi-level system

The EU's emerging multi-level system is simultaneously prompting *both* convergent and divergent developments, with the processes and the outcomes of industrial relations being affected. In Hay's (2000) terms introduced in Chapter 1, European integration (input convergence) is resulting in elements of process and output convergence. Yet the pace at which developments are taking place varies considerably *between* and *within* sectors as well as *between* and *within* countries, making it appropriate to refer to a process of multi-speed 'Europeanization'. The result is considerable complexity, uncertainty and instability.

Changing patterns of regulation

Turning first to processes, there are both striking parallels in the developing patterns of regulation across national systems and similarities with developments at EU level. Most evident is that collective bargaining is assuming a wider range of functions, with the supremacy accorded to social dialogue and collective agreement by the Maastricht social policy process being refracted within national systems. Following the Supiot report (1999: 140–7), collective bargaining is no longer seen solely as a means of improving on the legal status of employees. It has also acquired *a flexibility* and a *management* function. At national level, social pacts can cover employment policy and social protection arrangements as well as issues more traditionally associated with the employment relationship. At company level, PECs can include fundamental changes in work organization and working time arrangements, the handling of substantial job reductions and guarantees of employment security. Significantly too, such 'pacts' typically do not just involve a one-off 'agreement'. Many make explicit provision for ongoing joint implementation and development.

As collective bargaining assumes a wider range of functions, common changes are also taking place in other dimensions. Most attention has focused on the levels and the greater decentralization of bargaining structures. Yet, as confirmed above, there is centralization as well as decentralization. Developments are best understood as acceptance of the subsidiarity principle that matters should be handled at the appropriate, rather than one single, level. An increase in the subjects of collective bargaining and its greater devolution is also affecting the form. Rather than resembling Walton and McKersie's (1965) *distributive bargaining*, in which there are winners and losers in a 'zero-sum' game, recent developments are better comprehended in terms of their *integrative bargaining*, involving a 'variable-sum' game in which the parties seek to integrate their objectives to some degree. There is a strong element of problem solving about the process of negotiating social pacts and PECs. Also noticeable is the key role played by management. Under distributive bargaining, it has tended to be trade unions that take the initiative in formulating demands, while management is largely reactive. In the case of PECs, the opposite tends to be the case, with management initiating negotiations around its own agenda which often includes matters previously regarded as falling within its prerogative, such as changes in work organization.

A further effect is a shift in emphasis in output from 'hard' to 'soft' regulation. More issues are being decided by collective bargaining, involving a tendency to divest laws of substantive rules, which tend to be 'hard' in form', in favour of rules on negotiation, which tend to be 'soft'. In addition, 'proceduralization' has been affecting collective bargaining as well. Typically, the higher the level at which an agreement is reached, the more likely it is to take the form of a framework agreement or *accord cadre*, wherein much of the regulation is of the 'soft' or *incomplete* variety. A key rationale of much higher-level activity – indeed, it is the very essence of 'organized decentralization' – is to lay the way for more detailed negotiations at lower levels that can embrace 'hard' regulation tailor-made to the specific circumstances of individual units. Most social pacts between national social partners take the form of framework agreements, as increasingly do many sector agreements. A further consequence is that collective bargaining begins to look more like ongoing dialogue than a process of agreement making.

Underlying these developments is the increasing complexity of the collective action problem and the need for legitimacy in its resolution. The nature of the employment, competitiveness and adaptability agenda makes it more difficult to pin down the outcome in the form of 'hard' regulation. Legitimacy enters the equation because intensifying competition makes it essential both to minimize costs *and* to promote the cooperation and commitment of the workforce necessary for the adaptability required to underpin continuous improvement. In these circumstances decentralization makes it possible for the principals to set a sense of direction and yet to avoid failures to agree over the details that can so easily bedevil negotiations on the horizontal dimension. At the same time, by devolving responsibilities to representatives at lower levels, it helps to relieve the collective action problem on the vertical dimension: enabling representatives to tailor solutions to their immediate situation within parameters jointly agreed at a higher level considerably enhances the legitimacy of the outcome.

Changing patterns of outcome

Wages

Although there continue to be significant differences in their levels, European integration has helped to bring about a convergence in the rate of change in wages and labour costs. It has also prompted convergence in levels of unit labour costs. The adoption of non-accommodating monetary policies has encouraged the shift from productivity- to competition-oriented bargaining. The quantitative data are consistent with case study evidence (Arrowsmith and Sisson, 1999; 2001) in confirming that, for the most part, employers have been prepared to meet employees' expectations in terms of standard of living by agreeing to trade union demands for inflation-matching wage rises. In return, however, they have demanded acceptance of major changes in work organization entailing reductions in employment, helping to explain falling unit labour costs. Cross-national convergence in the rate of increase in wages has been accompanied by cross-sector diversity in productivity trends. In the exposed manufacturing sectors, negotiators have had to dig deep in terms of reductions in employment to maintain real wages. In the service sector, by contrast, wage increases in line with inflation have involved nothing like such levels of adjustment and there has been a growth rather than a reduction in employment.

Principally accounting for these developments are the informal processes of isomorphism that Europe's multi-level system is encouraging rather than any formal macro- or sector-level coordination mechanisms. Regardless of the structure of collective bargaining, negotiators have responded to the introduction of non-accommodating monetary policy by adjusting their resistance points to the level of inflation in order to maintain living standards. The more salient the process of 'unintended pattern bargaining' has become, with the prime motivation being to achieve the level of settlements elsewhere, the more such behaviour has assumed 'normative' status.

Working time

Compared to wages, the effects of the emerging multi-level system on working time have so far been more limited. European integration has intensified the pressures for greater flexibility – both in terms of the duration and predictability of operating hours. It has also helped to keep working time in the forefront of debate, leading to legal and collective bargaining change. Pressure to negotiate more flexible working time has provided important impetus towards organized decentralization, thereby developing the multi-level character of national systems. Sector variations in working time arrangements are marked, reflecting differing requirements in terms of operating hours and operating predictability. Path dependency is especially strong in the case of working time, reflecting sector specific forms of segmentation as well as wider societal considerations, such as the legal framework and tax, social security and childcare arrangements. The length of the working week, which continues to differ between countries, is the clearest example. Furthermore, it is the growth of the service sector that has been primarily responsible for many developments, in particular the growth of part-time and variable hours working.

Multi-speed 'Europeanization'

Multi-speed Europeanization is arising from the varying pace at which the developments described above are taking place *between* and *within* sectors as well as *between* and *within* countries. Differences *between* sectors are inextricably bound up with both industrial structure and industrial relations institutions. A comparison of the automotive and finance sectors, which feature in Chapters 7 and 8, illustrates the point. Automobile manufacture is exceptional in the degree of homogenization of activities and the accompanying integration of operations for their delivery, being dominated by a small number of large MNCs with increasingly integrated European and in some cases world-wide production operations. An internal market for capital has long been a feature and the use of 'coercive comparisons' integral to its operation. Financial services are also increasingly dominated by large MNCs. Yet most of these organizations are involved in an increasingly diverse range of activities embracing both banking (retail, corporate and investment) and insurance. Most importantly, retail banking, where most unionized employees are to be found, has so far remained largely a domestic affair. In automotive, union organization at company level is robust and company-level negotiation is well developed. The result of the influence of both industrial structure and industrial relations institutions is that cross-national comparisons at company level are already an important consideration. In finance, union organization at company level is less assertive and company-level negotiations less well developed. The result, as Chapters 7 and 8 found, is that cross-border comparisons hardly feature – except in the case of specialist groups. Differences *within* sectors relate to companies' specific circumstances, including ownership, market, geographical spread, the nature and extent of international integration and management structure. Also relevant is the extent and strength of trade union organization, and the capacity of employee representatives to mount their own 'coercive comparisons' across borders.

Differences *within* countries reflect those between and within sectors described above. Under EMU, these are becoming more pronounced according to the varying degree of exposure to competition of different sectors and companies within them to international competition. As between sectors, points of convergence are emerging more rapidly in more internationally exposed sectors such as automotive than in less exposed activities such as retail banking. Conversely, processes, practice and outcomes in sectors such as automotive are becoming relatively less nationally bound, thereby augmenting the internal diversity within any given country. The tendency for pressures deriving from exposure to international competition to impact more on larger international companies than small and medium-sized ones is also opening up significant differences in industrial relations policy and practice within sectors.

Differences *between* countries reflect three factors. One is the historical particularity of individual nation states. In most countries associated with the 'Latin', 'Rhineland' and 'Nordic' models, the industrial relations *acquis communautaire* has had relatively little effect. In the two countries characterized by 'voluntarism', Ireland and the UK, however, it has had a substantial effect, with much 'soft' regulation establishing minimum standards being tantamount to 'hard' regulation. The second and third are closely related: the extent to which the economies of sub-groups of countries are already more integrated with each other than they are with those of the wider EU; and the similarity or otherwise of industrial relations structures and traditions, as outlined in Chapter 2's account of the main variants of the European industrial relations model. These shape the immediate potential for coordination initiatives. Thus, cooperation amongst both employers' organizations and trade unions in the Nordic countries reflects both the comparative depth of the economic integration that already exists between these countries and important similarities in industrial relations institutions and traditions. A similar argument applies, perhaps less forcefully, to the countries previously part of the unofficial 'Deutsche-Mark zone' – Austria, Belgium, Germany and the Netherlands – which have been the focus of pioneering trade union initiatives in bargaining coordination. More generally, the 'dual convergence' thesis (Hall and Soskice, 2001) would suggest that cross-border coordination is more likely either amongst countries with coordinated market, or even amongst those with liberal market, economic regimes – than between countries with contrasting regimes – reflecting the fundamental distinction between those countries with multi-employer bargaining and legal frameworks which support collective bargaining and those with single-employer bargaining and less supportive frameworks (Traxler, 2003). A central implication is that 'Europeanization' may flow from arrangements that embrace varying geographical configurations of European countries, thereby intensifying the tendency toward multi-speed Europeanization.

Complexity, uncertainty and instability

In contributing to handling European integration, the EU's emerging multi-level industrial relations system has demonstrated several advantages attributed to multi-level governance systems in the political domain, namely adaptability, openness to experimentation and innovation, and the facilitation of commitments (Hooghe and Marks, 2002). It is also confirming major weaknesses of such systems, however. These entail the transaction costs involved in coordinating multiple jurisdictions, costs compounded by the fact that the system has not been 'decided', let alone 'designed', as is typically the case in the political domain. Rather its evolution reflects a mix of intentional and unintentional developments, as major players exploit opportunities to promote their particular interests. The weakness of the EU sector level, already noted, is one result.

Tensions abound, with complexity, uncertainty and instability set to be the defining characteristics of industrial relations in Europe for the foreseeable future. Unresolved is the balance of responsibilities between the different levels, which 'subsidiarity' deals with only superficially. At issue is the balance between Community, EU sector and Euro-company levels as well as that between the EU and member states. Within countries there is the balance between national and sector, and sector and company, arrangements. Employers' representatives in particular complain about the costs and time involved in so many levels, with practitioners in the larger workplaces potentially having to cope with regulation from no fewer than six levels – Community, EU sector and Euro-company; national, sector and national company. Moreover, instead of being complementary, the different levels can be competitive, with arguments about their appropriateness being a major issue in failures to progress substantive issues.

Accompanying what might be described as *levels overload* are *issue overload* and *methods overload*. Arguably, practitioners are being asked to cope with too many issues and too many methods at the same time. The result is an increasingly complex *linkage problem*. 'Linkage strength' (promoting agreement by widening the scope of negotiations) is giving way to 'linkage stress' (the danger of failure in one area putting everything else at risk). There are also difficulties in *articulating* relationships between the different levels – for example, specifying 'framework agreements' that do not merely shift the problem from one level to another; balancing 'top-down' with 'bottom-up' initiatives; combining different methods; balancing/combining different issues, levels *and* methods.

The more issues, levels and methods, the more complex becomes the *collective action problem*. In addition to problems of employers and trade union representatives reaching agreement on the horizontal dimension, *second-order* coordination problems are also mounting on the vertical dimension. Employers' organizations and trade unions are finding it increasingly difficult to get internal consensus among their members; where the parties are involved in bargaining coalitions, as in the case of social pacts, the problems are doubly difficult. The representativeness of established employers' and trade union organizations is also being called into question, leading to calls for involvement of other groups. There are also problems of *monitoring and control* – it is difficult to be informed about, let alone control, developments at company and workplace levels – with consequent implications for enforcement.

Complicating matters further are the coordination processes at work. Most apparent is the sharp asymmetry between trade unions and employers at European levels. Trade union initiatives aimed at cross-border coordination of bargaining are focusing on the sector level, whereas the potential offered by EWCs for similar coordination at company level appears to remain largely unfulfilled. Amongst employers, the sector-level negotiating organizations are strongly opposed to cross-border coordination. The management of MNCs, by contrast, is increasingly coordinating local bargaining over working practices and working time arrangements across countries. In so doing, the role of headquarters management in enforcing coercive comparisons is becoming increasingly transparent, potentially exposing it to future demands from employee representatives for European-level negotiations.

The greater diversity within countries arising from the differing intensity of competitive pressures for change at sector and company levels is also generating problems. It is exacerbating long-standing differences between large and small employers, making it more difficult for employers' organizations to achieve consensus over the agenda and outcomes of sector negotiations. Indeed, the weakness of employers' organizations poses at least as big a threat to the future of the European social model's inclusive structure of multi-employer bargaining as that of trade unions. Simultaneously, greater diversity within countries is intensifying the long-standing differences between 'sheltered' and 'unsheltered' sectors, complicating the realization of national social pacts. The emergence of new sectors and business activities is creating further difficulties: concluding new agreements presumes sufficient levels of organization, representation and commitment on both sides, whilst incorporating these into existing agreements has significant implications in terms of their scope and form.

Fundamental is the tension at the heart of collective bargaining itself. It is captured in policy makers' emphasis on the need for flexibility *and* security. In practice, the changing roles of collective bargaining discussed above mean a shift of emphasis from workers' substantive rights to the management agenda of change and competitiveness, less distributive and more integrative bargaining, decentralization of much of the substance of collective bargaining to the company/workplace, and a tendency for 'soft' regulation to replace 'hard'. The more the emphasis shifts from common standards to flexible frameworks and from agreement-making to social dialogue, however, the more important becomes the issue of trust. Yet trust does not exist in a vacuum. Following Wedderburn (1997: 11), the effectiveness of processes such as integrative bargaining and social dialogue depend upon a 'fundament' of 'hard' regulation, be it constitutional principle, legislative provision, 'tough judges' or collective agreements. It is this fundament of hard regulation that gives employee representatives the sense of security that is necessary to engage in these processes as well as legitimizing them in the eyes of managers.

The trajectory of the EU's social dimension and the European industrial relations model, identified in Chapter 2, will depend upon how these tensions are managed. Indeed, EU enlargement looks set to augment the complexity, uncertainty and instability which characterize the pre-existing situation and thereby exacerbate the tensions arising. Major revisions in macroeconomic policy in the direction of 'Euro-Keynesianism' would considerably ease the social dimension's further development (Schulten, 2002). The same is true of greater Community-level coordination of the various strands of economic, employment and social policy. Yet top-down developments such as these can only deal with some of the issues and only in general terms – even their impact in the areas they cover will not be automatic, but will depend upon how they are implemented at national, sector and company levels. The linkages and integrating mechanisms of the increasingly complex multi-level industrial relations system will be central (Molina and Rhodes, 2002). Here the weakness of the EU sector level, noted above, poses a considerable challenge, as does the absence of strong sector-level institutions at national level in the Anglo-Saxon and most central European accession countries.

The impact of enlargement: more of the same or an unravelling of the balance?

By embracing countries where 1998 gross wages and salaries and GDP per capita were on average 15 per cent of the average levels prevailing across the EU-15 (European Commission, 2000; Kittel, 2002), EU enlargement into central eastern Europe (CEE) places the European social model under unprecedented strain. Of the CEE accession countries, only Slovenia reached levels of wages and salaries comparable with those of Greece and Portugal – the lowest two amongst the EU-15. The increase in wage inequality that enlargement to the east signals is indicated by the change in the coefficient of variation of gross wages and salaries entailed. Standing at 0.32 amongst the EU-15 in 1998, Kittel (2002) calculates that it would have more than doubled to 0.73 with the inclusion of ten CEE countries (the eight accession states plus Bulgaria and Romania). Even allowing for differences in purchasing power, differences in living standards remain large, with the CEE average reaching only 32 per cent of that in the EU-15 and the coefficient of variation still doubling when including the ten CEE countries (Kittel, 2002). Unemployment rates, which averaged 8 per cent across the EU-15 in 2000, were on average half as much again amongst the ten CEE countries at 12 per cent (European Commission, 2001b). The kind of regional disparities and tensions that Germany has discovered east and west, and Italy has long experienced south and north, look set to become a pronounced feature of the EU.

One fear is that inequality of living standards and disparities in unemployment will lead to substantial labour migration, threatening to undermine wages and conditions elsewhere in the EU. According to Kittel (2002), the total of foreign residents migrating from the CEE countries in 1998 was small, at 850,000 (or 0.2 per cent of the enlarged EU's population). Once labour mobility becomes unrestricted, five years after accession, considerable change is anticipated in the volume of migration. Estimates suggest that some 11 per cent of the citizens of CEE countries (or 2.3 per cent of the enlarged EU's population) are likely to migrate to the EU-15. The impact is expected to be most sharp in neighbouring Austria and Germany, which are the current destination of four out of every five CEE migrants, and in labour markets for manual occupations. Mitigating the effects will be the tendency for migrants to move to the more prosperous regions, increasingly characterized by labour shortages for such occupations.

A second fear is that of widespread social dumping as capital takes advantage of markedly lower labour costs in the CEE countries to relocate production. The available evidence, however, suggests that this is likely to be rather limited in extent. For a start, the substantial differences in gross wages and salaries, which translate into similar differences in labour costs, between the CEE accession countries and the EU-15 are in large part offset by lower levels of productivity. As a result differences in unit labour costs 'are marginal compared with the wage gap . . . reduced to a few percentage points' (European Commission, 2000: 64). In these circumstances, it is only low-wage, low productivity sectors in the current EU-15 which might be exposed to the full force of significant eastwards relocation of capacity. This is confirmed by Boeri and Brücker's (2001) authoritative study, which in most sectors found little evidence of ongoing cost-driven relocation processes and confirmed market access as the main motivation for inward investment into the CEE countries. Even so, the combination of lower labour costs, relatively high levels of workforce qualification and more lightly regulated labour markets than many of those in the EU-15, is likely to make the CEE countries an attractive location for investment in industries where labour costs are proportionately relatively high, production integrated across borders and market presence is defined in terms of 'Europe' rather than individual countries. In so doing, enlargement will increase the scope for the exercise of coercive comparisons by the management of integrated MNCs, as discussed in Chapter 8.

The most striking implication of enlargement for industrial relations regulation is that the EU's collective action problem will deepen and its character change. At its baldest, the accession of ten new countries increases the number of member states by two-thirds. The difficulties of reaching agreement have been substantial enough with the present 15. They will become even greater when the EU expands to embrace 25 countries. Insofar as the inclusion of more players – governmental, employer and trade union, company management and employee representatives – at each level results in the complexity and associated uncertainty and instability considered in the previous section being further augmented, enlargement might be seen as holding out the prospect of more of the same by compounding the degree of the collective action problem. It might nonetheless be argued that industrial relations' emerging multi-level system of governance can and should be adapted to the challenges involved. Its multi-level nature allows for issues to be addressed at the level most appropriate – the 'subsidiarity' principle; it has the capacity to establish overall parameters whilst leaving implementation to be decided at devolved levels – thereby taking account of the increased heterogeneity that enlargement brings; it has the potential to connect 'bottom-up' developments with 'top-down' initiatives; and it is permissive of Europeanization at different speeds as between countries – likely to loom larger following enlargement.

Yet enlargement will also change the character of the EU's emerging multi-level system. Crucially, it shifts the balance between countries with inclusive structures of multi-employer bargaining – in which the sector-level is a cornerstone – and those where single-employer bargaining prevails, and the sector-level is marginal or non-existent. Amongst the EU-15 the UK's single-employer collective bargaining arrangements are the exception. Amongst the eight CEE accession countries, multi-employer bargaining arrangements have become well entrenched only in Slovenia – where the cross-sector level is the most important for wage bargaining – and Slovakia, where sector-level wage agreements are the norm (Carley, 2002b). In the other six countries, insofar as wages are determined through collective bargaining, single-employer bargaining prevails. Only in Hungary is sector bargaining relevant in some industries. The prevailing pattern of single-employer bargaining in these six countries is reflected in levels of collective bargaining coverage, which are at or below the 35 per cent level prevailing in the UK, and a lack of representative employers' organizations at sector level. In Slovenia and Slovakia, by contrast, coverage levels are higher – almost universal in the former and 48 per cent in the latter – and strong sectoral and (in Slovenia) cross-sectoral employers' organisations have developed. Levels of union density in these two countries are also – at just over 40 per cent – noticeably higher than in the other CEE countries (Carley, 2002b).

A combination of reasons appears to account for the weakness of sector-level industrial relations institutions in most CEE countries (Carley, 2002b; Kohl *et al.*, 2000). These include weak institutional capacity, including meagre financial and human resources as well as problems of representativeness, of the social partners at the sectoral level. This prevents them from fully engaging in bipartite social dialogue, let alone conducting effective collective bargaining. In addition, state authorities have not taken the legal and administrative measures required to support the development of sector bargaining, or promoted supportive institutional conditions. The result is the absence of a stable institutional framework within which sector bargaining can take place, including sound machinery for settling labour disputes arising out of the negotiation process. Compounding these difficulties has been the rapidly changing economic environment, which has entailed major upheavals in sectors and the companies within them further mitigating against the establishment of a stable sector framework.

The absence of generalized structures of multi-employer bargaining and the weakness of the sector level in the majority of CEE countries carries profound implications. The European model of industrial relations can no longer unequivocally be presented as one characterized by strong interest associations, regulating the labour market through inclusive agreements concluded at sector and/or cross-sector levels in which decentralization towards the company level has been 'organized' within frameworks elaborated at these higher levels. Conversely, the UK case of 'disorganized' decentralization in which company-level bargaining displaces sector agreements, and collective regulation of the labour market is partial in its coverage, no longer remains an exception. The weakness of the sector level in a significant group of member states in the enlarged EU – described by Kohl *et al.* (2000: 15) as the ' "hole in the middle" . . . between the company and national level' – combined with the underdeveloped nature of the EU sector level threatens to deprive the multi-level system of a key linkage and therefore integrating mechanism. The possibilities for resolving the collective action problem through invoking the twin principles of subsidiarity and devolution become more constrained. The resulting spectre is of EU enlargement unravelling the balance between the cross-sector, sector and company levels that has evolved under the multi-level framework which EU integration has driven forward. As Meardi (2002) has argued, the CEE accession countries could conceivably turn out to be the 'Trojan Horse' for the 'Americanization' of industrial relations across the wider EU.

12
Implications

Policy and practice – promoting 'regime collaboration'

Chapter 11's elaboration of the complexity, uncertainty and instability surrounding Europe's multi-level system of industrial relations will no doubt invite some to conclude that it is, in the language of Scharpf's (1988) 'joint decision trap', 'sub-optimal'. Centralized or decentralized arrangements, they might contend, are surely preferable. Yet, however compelling the reasoning may be, neither centralization nor decentralization represent a realistic, or indeed desirable, way forward. This is all the more true given that industrial relations governance concerns much more than wage determination, with issues such as restructuring now prominent on the agenda.

In the case of centralization, it seems inconceivable that, with 'subsidiarity' enshrined in the Treaty, member states will cede competence in the key areas necessary to achieve a vertically integrated system, i.e. wage determination, the right of association, the right to strike and the right to lock-out. Moreover, such a model cuts against the grain of the greater devolution taking place within national systems and cannot cope with the increasing diversity that is resulting. Decentralization, whilst perhaps less implausible, is no more desirable. It would mean unscrambling most of the 15 member states' national industrial relations systems. It would also put the clock back on some thirty years of EU developments, culminating in the social chapter's inclusion in the 1997 Amsterdam Treaty. Although there is a powerful logic behind transferring issues for implementation to lower levels, there remains a fundamentally important role for an inclusive structure of multi-employer bargaining in setting the main directions and parameters as well as establishing minimum standards. Moreover, the ambitious aims of the Lisbon Summit, i.e. 'to become the most competitive and dynamic knowledge economy in the world, capable of durable economic growth, of higher employment levels and jobs of a better quality and of improved social cohesion' (EIRO, 2000) are, following Weiss (1998), extremely unlikely to be achieved through the cathartic 'institutional cleansing' that decentralization would involve. Rather, it will depend on the ability to adapt existing institutions and patterns of state intervention. The experience of handling the introduction of EMU suggests that there is much to gain from doing this on the basis of 'regime collaboration' rather than 'regime competition' (Treu, 2001: 8).

In principle, there are two strategies for dealing with the 'coordination dilemma' of multi-level governance systems (Hooghe and Marks, 2002). The first is to limit the number of decision levels and the number of jurisdictions at each level. The second is to limit interdependence among jurisdictions by carving out functionally discrete areas for them to deal with. Four main suggestions can be made with these parameters in mind.

First, there needs to be a better differentiation of the roles and responsibilities of the EU Community and EU sector levels. Effectively, these levels are in competition with one another, dissipating energies and acting as a drag on further developments. At the Community level there are limits to the legal enactment and collective agreements required to provide the 'fundament' of 'hard' rights (Wedderburn, 1997: 11) which establish a minimum floor of substantive and industrial citizenship rights. Whilst gaps remain, key roles for the future are the setting and monitoring of a wider range of procedural and substantive standards – which can be dynamically adjusted – via the 'open method of coordination' (OMC) as suggested by the European Commission's High Level Group (European Commission, 2002b). The focus for collective agreement should be shifted to the EU sector level, recognizing the force of the book's 'multi-speed Europeanization' argument. Many issues are sector-specific, including those relating to work organization, working time arrangements and forms of employment contract, changes in which are integral to pursuing the Lisbon Summit aims. Coupling productivity growth with employment growth crucially depends upon not only competition policy, but on adapting deeply-entrenched institutional arrangements. The provisions of EU sector agreements should be implemented through national collective bargaining procedures with legislation – or a transnational form of extension arrangement – as a fall-back only in the absence of comprehensive coverage of such.

This would have the added benefit of underscoring multi-employer bargaining within national systems.

The opportunity of such a shift in emphasis should be taken to re-visit the Maastricht social policy process. If collective agreement is to be restricted to the negotiation of minimum or equivalent standards, as is presently the case under Article 137, there is not much incentive for employers to engage, especially since a floor of both procedural and substantive rights is now in place. Provisions need to be built in to enable trade-offs to be made, as occurs in sector or company negotiations within national systems.

Second, there is also scope for a better articulation between sector and company arrangements – at both national and EU levels. Arguably, at the national level, it no longer makes sense to think in terms of 'standard' agreements covering the operations of large MNCs' subsidiaries at one end of the spectrum and SMEs at the other – allowing 'opt-outs' from supposedly 'standard' sector agreements devalues the coinage. It is better to think in terms of two-tier arrangements, under which the role of the sector agreement is seen as threefold: establishing an effective minimum floor of standards, providing frameworks which specify the main parameters and setting directions. There is also growing experience of changes of emphasis that can build in flexibility – for example, providing for annual as opposed to weekly hours. Management and employee representatives in the large companies could be encouraged to negotiate on subjects not normally dealt with in sector negotiations, with the results generalized to SMEs through subsequent multi-employer negotiations. Moreover, in most countries there is also scope for trade union involvement in negotiating company agreements to ensure better consistency between the outcomes of the two levels. This could take the form of direct involvement by officials, as already happens in some larger companies, or approval of agreements negotiated by local representatives.

Some of these arguments also apply at the EU level. MNCs are in a unique position to exercise a pattern-making role. They are at the forefront of developments in employment practice, with the networks and resources to develop and learn from innovations across countries. They have a major presence in most EU member states and, through their supply chains, an organizational as well as economic relationship with other companies, including SMEs. The principles established in agreements reached in the larger Euro-companies, for example those dealing with restructuring, might in turn form the basis of EU sector-level framework agreements covering the full range of employers.

Our third point concerns methods. As Chapter 3 emphasized, the distinction between 'hard' and 'soft' regulation is not watertight – it is useful to think in terms of a continuum running from 'soft' to 'hard'. The degree of 'softness' of different forms of regulation varies and, as in the cases of framework directives and agreements, regulation can combine both 'soft' and 'hard' dimensions. Concerning agreements, joint texts adopted by the social partners at sector or company levels may simply elaborate a set of principles, which have no further consequences for constituent organizations at national and local levels. Or they may have the express intention of 'inciting' negotiations on the matter in questions at other levels within the sector and/or company and also establishing mechanisms to monitor implementation at these other levels. The contrast is even greater with a framework agreement establishing a set of principles or minimum standards that is binding on the parties at other levels (the 'hard' dimension), but within which employers and trade unions at national and local levels within the sector or company have scope to fashion their own solutions (the 'soft' dimension).

The aim of higher-level activity, be it in the form of legislation, 'hard' collective agreements or 'soft' frameworks, should be to incite negotiations and establish mechanisms to monitor the implementation of their outcome. Similar arguments for what might be termed 'positive subsidiarity' can be made about the form of the OMC-type mechanisms on which soft regulation is coming to rely for implementation. The nature and quantifiability of the benchmarks utilized in peer group review processes can vary considerably in terms of the transparency required and hence their potential to be the focus of 'moral suasion'.

Our fourth point cannot be avoided in the light of earlier analysis. A multi-level system is no less in need of a 'fundament' of rights, as Wedderburn (1997: 11) puts it, than a vertically integrated one. The key to striking a balance is the level and the form. The logic of the model would suggest a combination of Community- and national-level activity. The EU constitutional convention's proposal that the Charter of Fundamental Rights proclaimed at the Nice Summit on 7 December 2000 be incorporated into the draft EU constitution (EIRO, 2003h) offers a promising opportunity for advancing towards the entrenchment of such a 'fundament' of rights. Confirmation of the Charter's constitutional status by the Intergovernmental Conference commencing in late 2003 would provide the legal basis for national-level activity in the form of 'hard' regulation and judicial review by the European Court of Justice. It could also be the platform for 'soft' regulation at the

EU levels in the form of targets, core standards and guidelines involving peer group review. And it could provide the basis for further EU-level hard regulation where transnational issues are involved – collective bargaining and collective action are obvious candidates. Combining OMC-type arrangements with the harder edge of framework directives and/or collective agreements intended to be legally enforceable within national systems is a further way of tackling the trust problem that the existence of a 'fundament' of 'hard' rights helps overcome.

A 'hard' edge is also needed to ensure that MNCs exercise their pattern-making role in socially-enlightened directions, especially as many of the SMEs with which they have a close relationship are often de facto beyond the scope of collective bargaining. The recommendations of the European Commission's High Level Group Report on industrial restructuring (European Commission, 1998b), resurrected in the European Commission's Green Paper on corporate social responsibility (European Commission, 2001a), suggest a way forward. These included proposals for large companies to produce annual social audits, a so-called 'management of change' report, which would involve employee representatives and go beyond the bland public relations exercises that many companies presently engage in. Rather than being voluntary, as the High Level Group's final report recommended, such audits should be compulsory – as its interim report advocated. There is also a role here for EWCs, both in the ongoing development of such codes and the monitoring of their diffusion down to SMEs through supply chains. The revision of the EWCs Directive and the employee participation arrangements under the ECS would be an opportunity to provide for such a role along with the resourcing of employee representatives that would be required.

Failing consensus in these areas does not necessarily mean the end of matters. There is a great deal that trade unions can do to move things in the directions indicated. In some areas, trade unions are already active: for example, the promotion of information exchange through databases, establishing targets and benchmarking progress towards these, including through bargaining coordination at EU sector level. The scale of the task is nonetheless daunting. Will national trade unions, under the umbrella of their European sector federations, be able to achieve what national governments are doing in terms of open coordination, thereby forcing employers to respond? A further challenge remains, which is to achieve a better articulation of sector and company levels. There is a widespread reluctance to accept the force of the argument for change. Company bargaining, it is contended, will only serve to undermine sector agreements. Attempting to force large and small companies into 'one-size-fits-all' agreements, however, is likely to be counter-productive, compounding the difficulties employers' organizations face in holding these two groups together. Equally, an exclusive focus on the sector will do little to counter the force of management's use of coercive comparisons in internationally integrated MNCs. Sector-based coordination of EWCs needs to be fostered. More widely, there is a need to develop trade union organization at both national-company and Euro-company levels with a view to generalizing achievements attained through company bargaining into sector agreements.

It would also be possible for like-minded governments to pursue some of these objectives. For example, some countries already have provision for compulsory audits, which could be refashioned. Conceivably, there could even be 'differentiated framework directives' combined with the OMC, as Scharpf (2002: 663) has proposed in connection with social protection. 'Instead of striving for uniformity, European social law should allow different types of welfare states to maintain and develop their specific institutions in response to different understandings of social solidarity'. Member states would retain considerable discretion in shaping the substantive and procedural content of framework directives to suit specific local conditions and preferences. They would have to present action plans and report on their effects which would be periodically assessed by peer review. Should they abuse this discretion in the judgement of their peers in the Council, more centralized sanctions and enforcement procedures would still be available as a 'fleet in being'. 'Moreover, opportunities for policy learning could be greatly enhanced if Open Coordination were to be organised within subgroups of member states with roughly similar [welfare-state] institutions and policy legacies' (Scharpf, 2002: 665). From this perspective, EU enlargement might be seen as an opportunity rather than a threat.

Theoretical implications

Our final comments take us back to the Preface and the implications of seeing the main focus of industrial relations as governance. First is the need for a multi-disciplinary approach. Evidently, no one discipline has the armoury to explain the impact of European integration on industrial relations. The developments described here can be explained in terms of neither a purely economic nor a solely political perspective. European integration has its origins in both the economic and – inspired by the 'European idea' of Monnet and Schuman – the political.

Key economic actors such as MNCs are also political actors. The complex interaction between market and political forces has given rise to a multi-level system of industrial relations, which is mediating their impact as well as being continually influenced by them.

Concerning the association between markets and industrial relations systems first raised by Commons (1909/1968), the development of EMU has had important 'spillover' effects, helping to produce a framework for a European industrial relations system. A single European market has also brought homogenizing tendencies, most evidently amongst large MNCs with internationally integrated operations. Industrial relations systems do not automatically follow the market, however: the political matters. The experience of the EU confirms a feature too often taken for granted in discussions of the development of national systems. A single market does not produce a vertically integrated industrial relations system unless there is a parallel political authority, which is willing and able to support the development of multi-employer collective bargaining. The observation equally applies to the accession countries of central eastern Europe.

Our second point concerns research methods and the importance of a multi-method approach. In comments on a summary version of our work, Visser (2003: 194) criticizes us for relying on case studies; he also laments the poverty of methods used in industrial relations more generally, by which he appears to mean the lack of sophisticated, multivariate analysis of quantitative survey data. We would be among the last to decry the survey method, having been intimately involved in pioneering its use in industrial relations. There are two great dangers of the 'quantitative turn' in industrial relations research, however, which have wider application. One, which Marshall (1890) warned about more than a century ago, is that the measurable tends to crowd out the immeasurable. The result is that analysis of the formal tends to be prioritized at the expense of the informal. Visser himself is vulnerable here, when he argues that our findings are not reflected in the figures for union representation or collective bargaining coverage across EU countries. Such data may tell us many things, but they have little to say about the functions and process of collective bargaining, for which they are essentially an 'institutional shell', let alone the causes and effects of European integration. An exclusive concern with the quantitative is as one-eyed as that which draws only on the qualitative. Understanding evolving developments involving complex, unpredictable processes needs in-depth qualitative methods, the results of which can be checked with appropriate quantitative data, as Chapters 9 and 10 have attempted to do. Furthermore, as our use of wages and working time data there have demonstrated, advanced econometrics is not always needed to tease out some of the most obvious messages.

The other danger is the reification of processes for the purpose of measurement. An illustration comes from the macro-level centralization–decentralization debate, where coordination has become a mantra. As Sako (1997: 40) writes, however, few commentators have gone beyond the use of 'simple three point scales' and 'stylized facts'. More lamentably, few have attempted to define what they mean by coordination. The result is a false impression of developments. As Chapter 9 argued, there has been convergence in the rates of change in wages and labour costs across member states, but this can hardly be said to be the result of any formal process of coordination. Rather it largely arises from the informal processes of isomorphism that European integration has been encouraging. Especially important is the 'Europe learning from Europe' (Teague, 2001: 23) that European integration is encouraging. Take for example the negotiation of social pacts. EMU provided an initial stimulus for their negotiation, yet as important was the European Commission's encouragement of social dialogue and its example of developing an all-round view of policy making (on wages, employment, social protection, fiscal and macroeconomic policies). So too was the momentum built up as the phenomenon spread across countries. Learning is also taking place at the sector level, trade union cross-border bargaining coordination activity for example, and at the company level, as the discussion of MNCs below emphasizes.

Our third point is closely related. Industrial relations requires a multi-level perspective. The need for an analytical perspective sensitive to the articulation between 'top-down' and 'bottom-up' developments has been a constant theme. A more or less exclusive concern with the national level will inevitably exaggerate the impression of cross-national diversity. EU countries continue to be characterized by considerable variety in their formal institutions and institutional frameworks (Traxler *et al.*, 2001: 289), reflecting member states' opposition to 'the recreation of internal sovereignty at the international level' (Streeck, 1996: 313). Yet, at sector and company levels, there is much more that is common, embracing developments in process, such as the negotiation of PECs, and outcomes, such as working time arrangements. Multi-speed Europeanization is promoting growing diversity within national systems. Factors such as industrial structure, product market integration, industrial relations traditions and union organization underpin *sector* and *company* variation from a 'bottom-up' perspective. Factors such as state traditions, national business systems and the legal framework of industrial relations, alongside the extent of pre-existing economic integration with other economies, give *country* variation from a 'bottom-up' perspective. These in turn shape the extent to which the emerging 'top-down' framework is utilized and built on. Moreover, the multi-level governance system that the EU is producing means that the national systems are less and less islands unto themselves. They can no longer be understood, and therefore studied, without taking into account the wider European dimension. Neither can the European level be fully comprehended without attention being paid to developments at the national cross-sector, sector and company levels.

In illuminating the above country-, sector- and company-level variations, the methodological strengths and enormous potential of comparative analysis are underscored. Our approach and findings lend further weight to recent cross-country research at the sector and company levels questioning the prevailing assumption in comparative analysis, confirmed by Hollingsworth and Streeck's (1994) influential study, that country should be accorded prior analytical status (Katz and Darbishire, 2000; Locke, 1995; MacDuffie, 1995). Taking a multi-level perspective shifts the emphasis towards revealing the interaction of country-, sector- and company-specific influences in which there is no evident hierarchy of levels. It also underlines the interdependency of convergence and divergence processes. Sector- and company-specific factors loom as large as the country-specific national frameworks that have traditionally been placed at the centre of analysis. Of note is the robustness of the design of our principal research project (see the Appendix) in supporting this conclusion, which – like Katz and Darbishire's (2000) – is simultaneously cross-country and cross-sector. A prospective comparative agenda would include new analysis at the inter-regional level of the impact of regional economic integration in different parts of the world on the development of industrial relations within and across the countries concerned.

Within this overall framework, greater attention needs to be given to the level at which the employment relationship originates. Traditionally neglected in the continental industrial relations literature, it is no longer adequate to assume that the firm is an arena where the actors largely implement the terms of agreements concluded at higher levels. It is even less acceptable to see the business organization as a 'black box' where passive agents react in predetermined and 'rational' ways to changes in the external environment, as economics still so often assumes. The significance of the firm also goes beyond the pressure group activity with which it tends to be most closely identified in political science. The decisions taken within the firm and, above all, within MNCs have had and continue to have a profound effect on European integration. Indeed, contrary to the accepted wisdom that 'formal integration' precedes 'informal integration' (Wallace, 1990), the opposite proposition appears equally valid. Not only have MNCs played a key role in promoting a single European market with a single currency. Developments within MNCs have also been crucial in shaping much of the form that such integration has taken. It is their use of benchmarking that has provided the model for the OMC which is at the heart of the EU decision-making process. It is their resort to coordinated devolution of managerial responsibilities that has set the pattern for handling the problem of heteronomy and autonomy, i.e. through 'subsidiarity'. It is MNCs' combining of benchmarking with coordinated devolution, as applied to local negotiations across countries, which has alerted trade unions to the possibilities for themselves.

MNCs are also key agents in industrial relations. Prominent has been their role in promoting decentralization as a vehicle for greater flexibility. In turn, this decentralization is encouraging the further development of 'internal' (organization) labour markets that are to a considerable extent insulated from the 'external' labour market. In Teague and Grahl's (1992: 38) words:

> The scope offered by internal markets for relatively independent personnel policies is seen as an increasingly important aspect of company strategy while a new awareness of the value of firm-specific labour as a relatively fixed resource has encouraged the new managerial disciplines of human resource management.

The development of these 'internal' labour markets tends to impede rather than encourage the labour mobility that is held necessary to correct any labour market imbalances. Pressure to reduce labour costs is likely to lead to a reduction in employment rather than wages. In creating their own 'transnational social space' (Morgan *et al.*, 2001) in which country of origin and country of location influences interact, MNCs have also been generating significant isomorphic pressures. These are both direct, in the form of the elaboration and/or transfer of similar policies and practices across countries, and indirect, in the form of institutional response. The EWCs' Directive is a notable instance, triggering the creation of transnational institutional mechanisms which in turn have the potential to prompt further direct effects. Looking to the future, the decisions that MNCs take – for example, to remain party to multi-employer collective bargaining arrangements – will be key in determining the direction of industrial relations.

The firm also needs to be situated in its context. This means the sector as well as the national institutional nexus. The sector can be conceived of as operating at three levels (Smith *et al.*, 1990), each of which has a national *and* cross-national dimension. The first, the 'objective conditions', comprise the immediate market structures, product as well as labour, to which management in the workplace must refer, together with technology, which is a major influence on the nature and organization of work. The second, the 'cognitive area', is where ideas about 'accepted' or 'best' practice are generated, reflecting shared understandings. The third, the 'collaborative network', underlines that the sector, irrespective of the level of collective bargaining, offers a wide range of opportunities, formal as well as informal, to acquire and diffuse the information and experience that goes to make up these shared understandings. A major challenge is to develop a more differentiated typology of sectors. The established distinctions between internationally exposed and sheltered, and trading and non-trading, continue to be useful. But a finer-grained differentation is needed. The form of international exposure, for example, typically differs between manufacturing sectors – where it is final and intermediate products which move across borders – and the transportation sectors – where labour as well as products tend to cross frontiers. It is different again in services, where for many, but not all, products the place of production coincides with the point of consumption. Important in generating differences amongst manufacturing, or service, sectors are variables such as operating time and operating predictability, which are so important in differentiating sector working time arrangements.

Fourth, are implications for debates over structure and agency. This study confirms that both market and institutional structures are important in enabling and constraining action. Concerning institutional structures, Scharpf's (2000a: 224) 'path-dependent constraints of existing policy legacies' have been shown to be especially salient. As Streeck (1999) has come to recognize, the tried and trusted give legitimacy; a consideration Chapter 5 found was integral to the emergence of national social pacts. Social actors rely not only on what and who they know; but also on what they think they can influence – explaining why, seemingly illogically, they continue to place their faith in established national institutions as opposed to fashioning EU-level counterparts. The creation of such would have threatened their room for manoeuvre and added further uncertainty.

Convergence in the rate of increase in wages and (declining) levels of unit labour costs may lead some to conclude that institutions no longer matter. Yet industrial relations, to repeat an earlier point, is about far more than wage and cost outcomes. Multi-employer bargaining's deep embeddedness, coupled with its advantage in helping to ensure inclusive coverage, helps to explain both its promotion by the EU – in the form of the Maastricht social policy process – and by national governments – in the form of social pacts – as the most effective way of handling the implications of EMU. At another level, differences in the nature of multi-employer bargaining from one country to another help to explain differences in the nature and extent of company bargaining – whether, in the language of Chapters 6 and 7, such bargaining is supplementary or semi-autonomous. The institutions of employment regulation, which have been the bread-and-butter issues of the study of industrial relations, really do matter. Moreover, they do so for positive and not negative reasons, in that rather than standing in the way of economic adjustment (Bean *et al.*, 1998) they can be mobilized to facilitate its progress in ways which minimize social upheaval.

Institutions are not 'iron cages', however, and there have been notable changes that could not have been anticipated if path dependency was as powerful as some analysts (see Chapter 1) have implied. National social pacts in several countries are but one example. Such changes in direction provide evidence of the importance of the processes of 'patching up' and 'transposition' identified by Visser and Hemerijck (1997) that enable actors to break out of the constraints of path dependency, especially at times of crisis or particular points of conjuncture such as EMU. An example of 'patching up', i.e. modifying existing institutions and processes, is the increasing flexibility built into multi-employer agreements. The clearest example of 'transposition', i.e. the putting to a different use of institutions established for a particular purpose, is collective bargaining. In most EU countries collective bargaining was seen primarily as a vehicle for improving on the legal status of employees, but in recent years has added a wider range of functions as Chapter 3 established. The preferences and courses of action decided on by the parties matter.

Finally there is the case for seeing the main focus of industrial relations as governance. Such an approach has two main strengths, which this study has demonstrated. The first is that it helps to illuminate the key concerns of industrial relations, offering the best balance in terms of parsimony and complexity. It is multi-disciplinary and multi-level. It is inclusive in the sense that it embraces both the individual and the collective aspects of industrial relations and yet it does not seek to explain all facets of work and employment. A governance perspective, in our view, makes it possible for industrial relations to continue to make a unique contribution to understanding contemporary developments in the world of work and their outcomes.

The second strength is that, while much of the approach is similar to that which has been developed in political analysis, there are also some lessons with wider application reflecting the arena of industrial relations. Notable here are the relationships between private and public arrangements, formal and informal institutions, and 'top-down' and 'bottom-up' developments, together with the importance of conflicts of interest, uncertainty and how they are dealt with by negotiation. European industrial relations is a system of multi-level governance in the making. Equally, a governance perspective is central to the remaking of industrial relations.

Appendix: The Research Base

The books draws on the analytical and empirical findings of three projects undertaken between 1998 and 2002: a study of 'Emerging Boundaries of European Collective Bargaining at Sector and Enterprise Levels' funded under the UK Economic and Research Council's 'One Europe or Several?' programme (Award No. L213252040) (2000–2002); and investigations of 'The Impact of EMU on Industrial Relations at Sector and Company Levels' (1999–2000) and 'Handling Restructuring: Collective Agreements on Employment and Competitiveness' (1998–2000) commissioned by the European Foundation for the Improvement of Living and Working Conditions. Each of the studies comprised interlinked sector- and company-level elements, and in their design they were each cross-national and cross-sectoral within a single study. The focus on the company as well as the sector entails the 'firm in sector' approach (Kenis, 1992; Smith *et al.*, 1990). The company is a basic unit of decision making and has too often been overlooked in reviews of industrial relations developments, including those surrounding the implications of European integration (Sisson *et al.*, 1999). Abstracted from its sector, however, the company is shorn of its context. The sector has a powerful influence on the market structure and institutions to which management has to relate, as well as being important in shaping ideas about 'accepted' and 'best' practice. The cross-national design of the three studies enables the equally salient influence of the country context on organizational responses to be captured as well. Furthermore, the dynamics between the market structure, institutional and wider influences stemming from respective sector and country contexts in shaping industrial relations developments can be explored.

Emerging boundaries of European collective bargaining

Through an in-depth study of employers and trade unions at European level, in four European countries – Belgium, Germany, Italy and the UK – and focusing on two sectors – metalworking and financial services – the project investigated emerging forms of European-level collective bargaining and cross-border dimensions to national and local negotiations in a context of growing decentralization within national bargaining arrangements. The cross-national and cross-sectoral design of the research reflected the emergent strand of comparative industrial relations analysis that underlines the interdependency between the simultaneous processes of increased differentiation at sector and company levels within national systems and increased convergence at these levels across borders (Katz and Darbishire, 2000). This design enabled the relative weight of country- and sector-specific effects on developments in collective bargaining arrangements, and the prevailing methodological assumption that the former dominates the latter (Hollingsworth and Streeck, 1994), to be explored. By also addressing the supranational level, the design enabled the linkages between European-level developments and those at sector and country levels to be investigated.

The countries were selected to reflect differences in size of economy and integration with other EU economies, as well as different systems of industrial relations. Belgium, Germany and Italy are part of the Euro zone, whilst the UK has remained outside. Economic interdependence between Belgium and Germany far exceeds that between either country and Italy. The collective bargaining systems of Belgium, Germany and Italy represent (differing) instances of 'organized decentralization' (Traxler, 1995; Traxler *et al.*, 2001). The UK, where sector-level collective bargaining has all but disappeared, is the main instance of 'disorganized decentralization' amongst the EU-15.

The rationale for the choice of the two sectors was that they provide contrasts in terms of market structures, production organization, and institutional structures. The criteria for selecting the company case studies, one in each sector in Belgium, Germany and Italy and two in each sector in the UK, was that each company should be international in the scale of its operations and, where sector-level bargaining remains entrenched, a leading player within its respective employers' association.

Metalworking is a key manufacturing sector in each of the countries, long open to international competition. It is increasingly dominated by MNCs which in some parts of the sector are internationally-integrated manufacturers. As for industrial relations, sector agreements remain influential in Belgium, Germany and Italy, although strongly-organized trade unions and works councils have an established tradition of negotiating at company-level, within and beyond the scope of sector agreements. Company-level is the sole level of bargaining in the UK. Financial services are also significant to the economy of all four countries. Investment banking is already characterized by globally organized operations. Retail banking, however, remains a largely domestic affair with some sharp contrasts in market structure between EU countries. In insurance, cross-border operations are more widespread than in retail banking. Both sub-sectors are undergoing major changes in technologies and products. Banking and insurance are covered by separate sector collective agreements in Belgium, Germany and Italy. Company-level negotiations are more recent in origin than in metalworking but now constitute the only level of bargaining in the UK. Elsewhere they are becoming more widespread, within the frame of the sector agreement.

The field research in the two sectors involved two phases at, respectively, sector and company levels, comprising in-depth interviews with key actors and collection of relevant documentation. Where there were different collective bargaining arrangements for blue- and white-collar workers, the research focused on those for the larger workforce group. At the sector level, a comprehensive programme of interviews was undertaken over a six-month period between late 2000 and early 2001, with senior officials of *all* major employers' organizations and trade unions in the two sectors at EU-level and in the four countries and, where appropriate, at inter-sector level also. None of the employer and trade union organizations approached declined an interview, and a total of 43 interviews were undertaken in this first phase. The officials interviewed were typically the head of, respectively, the industrial relations, the collective bargaining or the European departments of employers' and trade union organizations. The organizations involved are listed in Table A1.

At company level, access was negotiated to ten leading multinational companies in the two sectors and four countries. Because sector-level respondents

Table A1   List of sector organizations interviewed

	Employers' organizations	Trade unions
Belgium		
Metalworking	Agoria	FGTB-Metallos CSC-Metal
Banking	Association Belges des Banques	CNE – finance sector SECTA – finance sector
Germany		
Metalworking	Gesamtmetall	IG-Metall (Head office; NordRhein Westfalen district)
Banking	AGV des privaten Bankgewerbes	DAG HBV
Italy		
Metalworking	Federmeccanica (Assolombardo)	Fiom-CGIL Fim-CISL Uilm-UIL
Banking	ABI (banking)	Fisac-CGIL Fiba-CISL
UK		
Metalworking	EEF	AEEU TGWU
Banking	Leading company representatives in British Banking Association	UNIFI MSF
EU level/Cross-border level		
Metalworking	WEM (West European Metalworking employers)	European Metalworkers' Federation Belgium, Netherlands, NordRhein Westfalen metal working unions regional cooperation network
Banking	European Banking Federation	UNI-Europa Finance section

indicated that within financial services banking tended to lead collective bargaining developments, the company case studies were focused on banks. Each of the case companies is a leading multinational with large-scale operations in the country concerned. In Belgium, Germany and Italy, the companies are either the leading or one of a leading group of companies within their respective employers' association; they are therefore influential in shaping developments in their sector agreement.

The case studies were undertaken over a nine-month period from Autumn 2001. Interviews were conducted with senior managers and employee (trade union or works council) representatives at group level, and at the Italian metalworking MNC and the four UK case studies with similar respondents in two of the main business streams or divisions. Between four and seven interviews were conducted in each company. In total, 49 company-level respondents were interviewed, comprising 29 senior managers and 20 trade union or works council representatives. The sensitivity of the issues discussed necessitated giving each of the companies an assurance of anonymity in publishing findings. Summary details of the ownership, size, business activity, internationalization and industrial relations of the ten MNCs are given in Table A2.

The sector- and company-level field research in Belgium, Germany and Italy was undertaken with the involvement of partner institutes, respectively IST in Louvain, IAAEG in Trier and IRES Lombardia in Milan. The assistance of the partner institutes in identifying the appropriate respondents, setting up interviews and subsequently conducting them with one of the research team, proved most valuable. The result was a high level of cooperation: all the sector-level employer and trade union organizations approached agreed to participate and high-profile MNCs were recruited for the case studies. Methodologically, the 'co-interviewing' method (Rainbird, 1996) enabled the research to benefit from the comparative insights which derive from interviewers operating within different national frames of reference.

The impact of EMU on industrial relations: a sectoral and company view

This European Foundation project built on two commissioned literature reviews on the impact of EMU on industrial relations (Pochet *et al.*, 1999; Sisson *et al.*, 1999) which had identified a lack of attention to EMU's implications at sector and company level. The focus of the study was threefold: the practicalities of introducing the Euro; the implications of EMU for processes of industrial relations, including pressures for greater 'Europeanization' and challenges to national systems; and EMU's implications for the wage and employment outcomes of these processes. Three sectors were chosen as the basis of the comparison: automotive (manufacturing and components), finance (banking and insurance) and road haulage. Each plays a significant role in the economies of most EU countries, being a substantial employer. Each is characterized by different market structures, technologies and institutional arrangements.

The field research was concentrated in six countries: Finland, France, Germany, the Netherlands, Spain and the UK. The six countries gave a regional spread across the EU, represent economies of differing sizes and differing degrees of international exposure, as well as comprising differing industrial relations systems. The UK represented an EU member state which has not joined the single currency but which is a significant base and host to multinational companies. In Finland and Germany, sector collective agreements are generally applicable to companies within the sector. In France, sector agreements increasingly only have approximate relevance to what is subsequently concluded at company level. In the Netherlands, large companies in some sectors, including parts of metalworking

Table A2 Summary information on the case companies

			Metalworking		
	Belmetal	Germetal	Italmetal	Britmetal1	Britmetal2
Country (Parent company location if different)	Belgium (US)	Germany	Italy	UK	UK (US)
No. of employees	Worldwide: > 50,000 Europe: 20,000 Belgium: 5,000	Worldwide: > 150,000 Europe: 145,000 Germany: 90,000	Worldwide: > 200,000 Europe: 155,000 Italy: 110,000	Worldwide: > 40,000 Europe: 22,000 UK: 16,000	Worldwide: > 200,000 Europe: 85,000 UK: 10,000
Business segment	Automotive – mobile machinery and engines	Automotive components; industrial components	Automotive – cars, trucks and mobile machinery	Aerospace and marine equipment	Automotive – cars, light commercial vehicles
Market position	One of six producers dominating European market.	One of the leading automotive component suppliers in Europe.	One of the leading manufacturers in Europe in each segment.	One of the leading manufacturers in a world wide market.	One of the leading manufacturers in Europe in both segments.
Internationalization of production	Manufacturing operations in 10 European countries. Plants manufacture for pan-European market. Some internal competition. (Extensive US operation.)	Manufacturing operations in 19 European countries. Cross-border integration of production and market servicing within business units. (Substantial US operation.)	Manufacturing operations in 8 European countries. Cross-border integration of production and market servicing within segments. (Substantial US operation in mobile machinery.)	Manufacturing operations in 3 European countries. Cross-border sourcing of in-house components. (Substantial US operation.)	Manufacturing operations in 10 European countries. Cross-border integration of production and market servicing. (Extensive US operation.)
Employer's association role	Influential, represented on negotiating committee.	Influential, central role in sector negotiations in key region.	Influential, leading role in sector negotiations.	Influential, represented on industrial relations policy committee.	Non-member.
Collective bargaining arrangements	Three-year company agreements with trade unions under derogation from sector agreement.	Sector agreement applied to virtually all the workforce. Company agreements with central and local works councils.	Sector agreement applied to all the workforce. Central company and local site agreements with unions.	Single-employer bargaining: a mixture of geographical area and site collective agreements.	Single-employer bargaining: company and local agreements.
EWC (date of establishment)	Yes (1996, revised 1999)	Yes (1998)	Yes (1996, revised 2001)	No (EWC being set up at time of field research)	Yes (1996)

Table A2 Continued

		Banking			
	Belbank	Gerbank	Italbank	Britbank1	Britbank2
Country (Parent company location if different)	Belgium	Germany	Italy	UK	UK
No. of employees	Worldwide: > 60,000 Europe: 55,000 Belgium: 20,000	Worldwide: > 80,000 Europe: 70,000 Germany: 45,000	Worldwide: > 60,000 Europe: 60,000 Italy: 40,000	Worldwide: > 120,000 Europe: 75,000 UK: 50,000	Worldwide: > 80,000 Europe: > 60,000 UK: 60,000
Business segment	Retail, commercial and investment banking; insurance	Retail, commercial and investment banking	Retail and commercial banking	Retail, commercial and investment banking	Retail, commercial and investment banking; insurance
Market position	One of the three large banks in Belgium.	One of four large private banks in Germany.	One of the six large banks in Italy	One of the four large banks in the UK	One of the four large banks in the UK
Internationalization of activities	Banking activities concentrated in Benelux and France. Some cross-border integration of back-office operations.	Retail and commercial activities focused on Germany but retail networks in 5 other European countries. Some cross-border integration of back-office operations. Investment banking in Germany, UK and US.	Retail and commercial activities focused on Italy but retail networks in 4 east European countries.	Retail and commercial operations in each of the main global regions, with those in Europe focused on the UK. Extensive retail banking network in France, with more limited retail operations in four other European countries.	Focus on retail, commercial and insurance activities in UK. Limited presence elsewhere in Europe.
Employer's association role	Influential, leading role on negotiating committee.	Influential, central role in sector negotiations.	Influential, central role in sector negotiations	Employers' association disbanded in late 1980s. Influential in banking business association.	Employers' association disbanded in late 1980s. Influential in banking business association.
Collective bargaining arrangements	Sector agreements applied to all the workforce. Company agreements with trade unions.	Sector agreements not applied to all the workforce. Company agreements with central works councils.	Sector agreements applied to all the workforce. Company negotiations with trade unions.	Central company agreement.	Central company agreement for all banking activities; separate arrangements for insurance businesses
EWC (date of establishment)	Yes (1996, revised 2000)	Yes (1996)	No.	Yes (1996)	Yes (2000)

and – subsequent to the field research – banking, have their own company agreements. Sector-level bargaining is the exception rather than the rule in the UK and is only partial in its coverage of different sectors in Spain.

The sector- and company-based research was undertaken by local researchers in each country on the basis of common templates. Methods included examination of relevant documentation and published materials, together with interviews with representatives of employers' associations and trade unions at sector level. In the automotive and finance sectors, company-level interviews with management and employee representatives (trade union or works council) were secured in every case. In road haulage, where a number of the small companies that make up the overwhelming majority were included, several companies did not have employee representatives. The interviews were undertaken over the summer and autumn of 1999, as was the writing of the national reports.

In total, 54 company cases (three in each sector in each of the six countries) were completed. The company cases focused on firms which were cross-border in their reach, either because they were multinational – which in most instances was the case – or because they were internationally exposed national companies, with substantial export or cross-border transactions. Summary information on the employment size, product market, ownership and internationalization and industrial relations of the 54 companies can be found in Sisson and Marginson (2000).

Handling restructuring: collective agreements on employment and competitiveness

In this European Foundation project, two sets of data were involved. The first was information from the EIRO-Online records summarized by Zagelmeyer (2000) dealing with collective agreements on employment and competitiveness, or so-called 'pacts for employment and competitiveness' (PECs). These records included both the specific reviews of PECs undertaken by each of the 16 national EIRO centres in 1997 and any subsequent entries referring to agreements covering competitiveness and employment. The observation period ran from 1997 until early 1999 and, altogether, embraced more than 300 records.

The second set of data came from national reports commissioned from major research centres during 1998. Eleven EU member states were included reflecting size and/or known developments in the area: Austria, Denmark, Germany, Finland, France, Ireland, Italy, the Netherlands, Spain, Sweden and the UK. As well as producing up-to-date overviews of the national trends and developments in their countries, correspondents were asked to supply three to five case studies for each country, which would be written to a common format and fulfil two main objectives:

- to provide sufficient data on the themes and issues to write an authoritative and up-to-date review of experience of PECs;
- to offer the general reader an accessible, stand-alone account of what is involved in negotiating specific arrangements linking employment to competitiveness.

In selecting the case studies, national correspondents were asked to use their professional judgement taking into account two main considerations:

- *significance*: the country's social partners would generally regard the selected case studies as typical of any general trend and/or as setting such a trend;
- *sector*: the selected case studies would come from a range of sectors, both manufacturing and services.

Case studies could be based on secondary sources where the coverage was adequate to cover the issues outlined above. National correspondents were nonetheless required to obtain up-to-date views on the PEC from representatives of each of the relevant social partners. If the case study was to be based on primary sources, interviews were to be held with representatives of each of the main social partners involved. In total, more than 50 case studies were produced, some focusing on sector-level but the majority on company-level arrangements, details of which are summarized in Sisson and Artiles (2000).

References

Adnett, N. (1995) 'Social dumping and European economic integration', *Journal of European Social Policy*, 5(1), 2–12.

Arrowsmith, J. (2002) 'The struggle of working time in nineteenth- and twentieth-century Britain', *Historical Studies in Industrial Relations*, 13, 1–35.

Arrowsmith, J., Marginson, P. and Sisson, K. (2003) 'Externalisation and internalisation of collective bargaining in Europe: variation in the role of large companies', *Industrielle Beziehungen*, 10(3), 363–92.

Arrowsmith, J. and Sisson, K. (1999) 'Pay and working time: towards organisation-based systems?', *British Journal of Industrial Relations*, 37(1), 51–75.

Arrowsmith, J. and Sisson, K. (2001) 'International competition and pay, working time and employment: exploring the processes of adjustment', *Industrial Relations Journal*, 32(2), 136–53.

Arrowsmith, J., Sisson, K. and Marginson, P. (2004) 'What can "benchmarking" offer the open method of co-ordination?', *European Journal of Public Policy*, 11(2), 311–28.

Arrowsmith, J., Sisson, K. and Schmidt, W. (2001) 'Decentralization *and* internationalization? The significance of the sector within European industrial relations', *Comparative Labor Law and Policy Journal*, 21(3), 577–89.

Artiles, A.M. and Alós-Moner, R. (1999) 'Collective bargaining on employment and competitiveness. National overview'. Spanish report on collective bargaining on employment and competitiveness for the European Foundation for the Improvement of Living and Working Conditions.

Atamer, T. (1993) 'Stratégies d'européanisation dans les industries multidomestiques', *Revue française de gestion*, mars-avril-mai, 95–105.

Atkinson, A. (1996) 'Reflections on social protection and the European Economic and Monetary Union', in J. Pacolet (ed.), *Social Protection and the European Economic and Monetary Union*. Aldershot: Avebury, 291–7.

Atkinson, A. (2002) 'Reassessing the fundamentals: social inclusion and the European Union', *Journal of Common Market Studies*, 40(4), 625–43.

Bach, S. and Sisson, K. (2000) 'Personnel management in perspective', in S. Bach and K. Sisson (eds), *Personnel Management*. Oxford: Blackwell, 3–42.

Barnard, C and Deakin, S. (2000) 'In search of coherence: social policy, the single market and fundamental rights', *Industrial Relations Journal*, 31(4), 331–45.

Barrell, R. and Pain, N. (1997) 'The growth of foreign direct investment in Europe', *National Institute Economic Review*, 160 (February), 63–75.

Bartlett, C. and Ghoshal, S. (1992) *Managing Across Borders: the Transnational Solution*. London: Century Business.

Batstone, E. (1978) 'Arm's length bargaining: industrial relations in a French company'. Unpublished manuscript.

Bean, C., Bentolila, S., Bertola, G. and Dolado, J. (1998) *Social Europe: One for All?* London: Centre for Economic Policy Research.

Begg, I. (2002) 'EMU and employment – social models in the EMU: convergence? co-existence? The role of economic and social actors', ESRC One Europe or Several?, Working Paper 42/02. Brighton: University of Sussex.

Biagi, M. (2000) 'The impact of European employment strategy on the role of labour law and industrial relations', *The International Journal of Comparative Labour Law and Industrial Relations*, 16(2), 155–73.

Bispinck, R. and Schulten, T. (2000) 'Alliance for jobs – is Germany following the path of "competitive corporatism"?', in G. Fajertag and P. Pochet (eds), *Social Pacts in Europe – New Dynamics*. Brussels: ETUI, 187–288.

Bloch-London, C., Daniel, C., Estrade, M. and Orain, R. (n.d.) 'La NAF6TT: Une nomenclature d'activité adpatée à l'étude de l'organisation du temps du travail' Note. DARES, Ministère de l'emploi et de la solidarité, Paris.

Boeri, T. and Brücker, H. (2001) 'Eastern enlargement and EU-labour markets', IZA Discussion Paper No. 256, Bonn.

Boldt, P. (1998) 'EMU and the labour market: the Finnish case', in T. Kauppinen (ed.), *The Impact of EMU on Industrial Relations in European Union*. Helsinki: Finnish Industrial Relations Association, 62–71.

Bordogna, L. and Cella, G.-P. (1999) 'Admission, exclusion, correction: the changing role of the state in industrial relations', *Transfer*, 5(1–2), 14–33.

Borrás, S. and Jacobsson, K. (2003) 'The Open coordination method and the new governance patterns in the EU'. Paper presented to 'Workshop on the Open Method of Coordination and Economic Governance in the European Union', Minda de Gunzburg Center for European Studies, Harvard University, 28 April.

Bosch, G. (2001) 'Working time: from redistribution to modernisation', in P. Auer (ed.), *Changing Labour Markets in Europe: the Role of Institutions and Policies*. Geneva: International Labour Office.

Bouget, D. (1998) 'Social policy in the EMU area: between a dream and a nightmare', *Transfer*, 4(1), 67–87.

Brown, W. and Sisson, K. (1975) 'The use of comparisons in workplace wage determination', *British Journal of Industrial Relations*, 13(1), 23–53.

Brown, W. and Walsh, J. (1991) 'Pay determination in Britain in the 1980s: the anatomy of decentralisation', *Oxford Review of Economic Policy*, 7(1), 44–59.

Brown, W. and Walsh, J. (1994) 'Managing pay in Britain', in K. Sisson (ed.), *Personnel Management*, 2nd edn. Oxford: Blackwell, 437–64.

Buckley, P. and Castro, F. (2001) 'A survey-based investigation of the determinants of FDI in Portugal', in J. Taggart, M. Berry and M. McDermott (eds), *Multinationals in a New Era*. Basingstoke: Palgrave, 226–58.

Buiges, P. (1993) 'Evaluation des concentrations: entreprises et pouvoirs publics face à face', *Economie internationale*, 55, 91–108.

Calmfors, L. and Driffill, J. (1988) 'Bargaining structure, corporatism and macro-economic performance', *Economic Policy*, 6, 13–61.

Caprile, M. and Llorens, C. (2000) 'Outsourcing and industrial relations in motor manufacturing', *European Industrial Relations Observatory On-line*, Ref: TN0008201S.

Cardani, A. (1998) 'The monetary union and the single market: challenges and opportunities', in P. Pochet and B. Van Hercke (eds), *Social Challenges of Economic and Monetary Union*. Brussels: European Interuniversity Press.

Carley, M. (2001) *Bargaining at European Level? Joint Texts Negotiated by European Works Councils*. Luxembourg: Office for Official Publications of the European Communities.

Carley, M. (2002a) 'European-level bargaining in action?', *Transfer*, 8(4), 646–53.

Carley, M. (2002b) *Industrial Relations in the EU Member States and Candidate Countries*. Luxembourg: European Foundation for the Improvement of Living and Working Conditions/Office for Official Publications of the European Communities.

Carley, M. and Marginson, P. (2000) *Negotiating European Works Councils: a Comparative Study of Article 6 and Article 13 Agreements*. Luxembourg: Office for Official Publications of the European Communities.

Casey, B., Metcalf, H. and Millward, N. (1997) *Employers' Use of Flexible Labour*. London: Policy Studies Institute.

Chouraqui, A. (1998) 'From heteronomy towards regulated autonomy: Participation in the heart of new Regulatory Arrangements'. Paper presented at the 11th IIRA World Congress, Bologna, 22–6 September.

Chouraqui, A. and O'Kelly, K. (2001) 'A questioning of the European social model. A challenged balance between regulation and deregulation'. Paper for the 6th IIRA European Congress Oslo, 25–9 June.

Coller, X. (1996) 'Managing flexibility in the food industry: a cross-national comparative case study in European MNCs', *European Journal of Industrial Relations*, 2(2), 153–72.

Coller, X. and Marginson, P. (1998) 'Transnational management influence over changing employment practice: a case from the food industry', *Industrial Relations Journal*, 29(1), 4–17.

Commons, J. (1909/1968) 'American shoemakers 1648–1895: A sketch of industrial evolution', *Quarterly Journal of Economics*, 24, 38–83, reprinted in 1968 in R.L. Rowan and H.R. Northrup (eds), *Readings in Labor Economics and Labor Relations*. Homewood, IL: Irwin, 60–76.

Cooke, W. and Noble, D. (1998) 'Industrial relations systems and US foreign direct investment abroad', *British Journal of Industrial Relations*, 36(4), 581–609.

Crouch, C. (1993) *Industrial Relations and European State Traditions*. Oxford: Clarendon Press.

Cully, M., Woodland, S., O'Reilly, A. and Dix, G. (1999) *Britain at Work*. London: Routledge.

Delbridge, R., Lowe, J. and Oliver, N. (1995) 'The process of benchmarking. A study from the automotive industry', *International Journal of Operations and Production Management*, 15(4), 50–62.

Dicken, P. (1998) *Global Shift: Transforming the World Economy*. London: Paul Chapman.

DiMaggio, P. and Powell, W. (1983) 'The iron cage revisited: institutional isomorphism and collective rationality in organizational fields', *American Sociological Review*, 48, 161–73.

Dølvik, J. (1997) *Redrawing the Boundaries of Solidarity?*, ARENA Report No. 5. Oslo: University Press.

Dølvik, J. (1999) *An Emerging Island? ETUC, Social Dialogue and the Europeanisation of the Trade Unions in the 1990s*. Brussels: ETUI.

Dølvik, J. (2000) 'Economic and Monetary Union: implications for industrial relations and collective bargaining in Europe'. ETUI Discussion and Working Paper, DWP 2000.01.04. Brussels: ETUI.

Dølvik, J. (ed.) (2001a) *At your Service? Comparative Perspectives on Employment and Labour Relations in the European Private Sector Services*. Berne/Oxford: Peter Lang.

Dølvik, J. (2001b) 'Industrial relations in EMU: re-nationalization and Europeanisation – two sides of the same coin?' Paper presented at the 6th IIRA European Congress, Oslo, 25–9 June.

Dølvik, J. and Martin, A. (2000) 'A spanner in the works and oil on troubled waters – the divergent fates of social pacts in Sweden and Norway', in G. Fajertag and P. Pochet (eds), *Social Pacts in Europe – New Dynamics*. Brussels: ETUI, 279–320.

Dufresne, A. (2002) 'Wage co-ordination in Europe: roots and routes', in P. Pochet (ed.), *Wage Policy in the Eurozone*. Brussels: Peter Lang, 79–110.

Dunlop, J. (1958) *Industrial Relations Systems*. New York: Holt.

Ebbinghaus, B. (1999) 'Does a European Social Model exist and can it survive?', in G. Huemer, M. Mesch and F. Traxler (eds) (1999), *The Role of Employers Associations and Labour Unions in the EMU*. Aldershot: Ashgate, 1–26.

Ebbinghaus, B. and Hassel, A. (1998) 'The role of tripartite concertation in the reform of the welfare state', *Transfer*, 5(1–2), 64–81.

Ebbinghaus, B. and Hassel, A. (2000) 'From means to ends: linking wage moderation and social policy reform', in G. Fajertag and P. Pochet (eds), *Social Pacts in Europe – new Dynamics*. Brussels: ETUI.

Ebbinghaus, B. and Visser, J. (1999) 'When institutions matters: union growth and decline in western Europe, 1950–1995', *European Sociological Review*, 15(1), 135–58.

Ebbinghaus, B. and Visser, J. (2000) *Trade Unions in Western Europe since 1945*. London: Macmillan.

Edwards, P. (1992) 'La recherche comparative en relations industrielles: l'apport de la tradition ethnographique', *Relations Industrielles*, 47(3), 411–36.

Edwards, P. (2003) 'The future of industrial relations', in P. Ackers and A. Wilkinson (eds), *Understanding Work and Employment*. Oxford: OUP, 337–58.

Edwards, T. (1998) 'Multinationals, labour management and the process of reverse diffusion', *International Journal of Human Resource Management*, 9(4), 698–709.

Edwards, T. (1999) 'Cross-border mergers and acquisitions: the implications for labour', *Transfer*, 5(3), 320–43.

Edwards, T. (2002) 'Corporate governance systems and the nature of industrial restructuring', *European Industrial Relations Observatory On-line*, Ref: TN0209101S.

Edwards, T. (2004) 'Multinational companies and the diffusion of HRM practices', in A.-W. Harzing and J. Van Ruysselveldt (eds), *International Human Resource Management*, 2nd edn. London: Sage, 389–410.

Edwards, T., Rees, C. and Coller, X. (1999) 'Structure, politics and the diffusion of employment practice in multinationals', *European Journal of Industrial Relations*, 5(3), 286–306.

Eichener, V. (1997) 'Effective European problem-solving: lessons from the regulation of occupational safety and environmental protection', *Journal of European Public Policy*, 4, 591–609.

Eichengreen, B. and Wyplosz, C. (1998) 'The Stability Pact: more than a minor nuisance?', in D. Begg, J. Von Hagen, C. Wyplosz and K. F. Zimmerman (eds), *EMU: Prospects and Challenges for the Euro*. Special issue of *Economic Policy*. Oxford: Blackwell.

EIRO (1997a) 'The Renault Case and the Future of Social Europe', *EIRObserver Update* 2/97, 2–3.

EIRO (1997b) 'Opening clauses increase in branch-level collective agreements', *European Industrial Relations Observatory On-line*, Ref: DE9709229F.

EIRO (1997c) 'New proposals for a reform of collective bargaining in metalworking', *European Industrial Relations Observatory On-line*, Ref: DE9712240F.

EIRO (1998a) 'Agreement signed on reducing labour costs and managing redundancies in banking', *European Industrial Relations Observatory On-line*, Ref: IT98033221F.

EIRO (1998b) 'Parliament intervenes to end major conflict', *European Industrial Relations Observatory On-line*, Ref: DK9805168F.

EIRO (2000) 'Lisbon Council agrees employment targets', *European Industrial Relations Observatory On-line*, Ref: EU0004241F.

EIRO (2001) 'WSI survey examines decentralisation of bargaining in 1999–2000', *European Industrial Relations Observatory On-line*, Ref: DE0103212F.

EIRO (2002a) 'Government issues assessment of 35-hour week legislation', *European Industrial Relations Observatory On-line*, Ref: FR0210106F.

EIRO (2002b) 'Pay developments – annual update 2001', *European Industrial Relations Observatory On-line*, Ref: 0202102U.

EIRO (2002c) 'Working time developments – annual update 2001', *European Industrial Relations Observatory On-line*, Ref: 0202103U.

EIRO (2002d) 'IG Metall debates "manifesto for the future"', *European Industrial Relations Observatory On-line*, Ref: DE0206205F.

EIRO (2002e) 'Industrial relations in the EU, Japan and USA', *European Industrial Relations Observatory On-line*, Ref: TN0212101F.

EIRO (2002f) 'New study analyses development of employers' associations', *European Industrial Relations Observatory On-line*, Ref: DE021202F.

EIRO (2002g) 'National tripartite agreement signed on 2003 wage increase recommendations and minimum wage', *European Industrial Relations Observatory On-line*, Ref: HU0212015F.

EIRO (2003a) 'New collective agreements signed in banking', *European Industrial Relations Observatory On-line*, Ref: DE0301202N.

EIRO (2003b) 'New agreements introduce "individual options" for employees', *European Industrial Relations Observatory On-line*, Ref: DK0302102F.

EIRO (2003c) 'Dispute in banking', *European Industrial Relations Observatory On-line*, Ref: BE0303301N.

EIRO (2003d) 'EU-level developments in 2002', *European Industrial Relations Observatory On-line*, Ref: EU0303101F.

EIRO (2003e) 'Metalworking agreement signed without Fiom-Cgil', *European Industrial Relations Observatory On-line*, Ref: IT0305204F.

EIRO (2003f) 'Employers' organisations demand more flexible industry-wide agreements', *European Industrial Relations Observatory On-line*, Ref: DE0307107F.

EIRO (2003g) 'EU-level social partners negotiate joint text on restructuring', *European Industrial Relations Observatory On-line*, Ref: EU0307203F.

EIRO (2003h) 'Draft EU Constitution presented to the Thessaloniki Council', *European Industrial Relations Observatory On-line*, Ref: EU0307204F.

EIRO (2003i) 'Social partners sign pact for development', *European Industrial Relations Observatory On-line*, Ref: IT0307105F.

EIRO (2003j) 'European social dialogue launched in shipbuilding', *European Industrial Relations Observatory On-line*, Ref: EU0311203N.

Elmuti, D. and Kathawala, Y. (1997) 'An overview of benchmarking process: a tool for continuous improvement and competitive advantage', *Benchmarking for Quality Management and Technology*, 4(4), 229–43.

EMF (2001) 'Report on the European co-ordination rule', EMF Collective Bargaining Conference, Oslo, 20–21 June.

Erickson, C. and Kuruvilla, S. (1994) 'Labor costs and the social dumping debate in the European Union', *Industrial and Labor Relations Review*, 48(1), 28–47.

Esping-Andersen, G. (1990) *The Three Worlds of Welfare Capitalism*. Princeton: Princeton University Press.

ETUC (2001) *Luxembourg Process: ETUC Employment 'Fiches' (June 2001)*. Brussels: European Trade Union Confederation.

ETUI (2002) 'Multinationals having a European Works Council Agreement' http://www.etuc.org/etui/databases/EWCNov02.pdf.

ETUI (2003) *Benchmarking Working Europe 2003*. Brussels: European Trade Union Institute.

Euro-FIET/LRD (1999) 'Collective bargaining in Euroland'. A Euro-FIET issues paper prepared in collaboration with the Labour Research Department. Geneva: Euro-FIET.

European Commission (1993) White Paper on *Growth, Competitiveness and Employment*. Luxembourg: Office for the Official Publications of the European Communities.

European Commission (1995) 'Medium-term Social Action Programme, 1995–1997', *Social Europe*. Vol. 1.

European Commission (1997) Green Paper, *Partnership for a New Organisation of Work*. Bulletin of the European Union. Supplement 4/97. Luxembourg: Office for the Official Publications of the European Communities.

European Commission (1998a) Euro 1999 Report on Progress Towards Convergence and the Recommendation with a view to the Transition to the First Stage of Economic and Monetary Union. Part I: Recommendation. Luxembourg: Office for the Official Publications of the European Communities.

European Commission (1998b) *Managing Change. Final Report of the High Level Group on Economic and Social Implications of Industrial Change*. Luxembourg: Office for the Official Publications of the European Communities.

European Commission (2000) *Industrial Relations in Europe 2000*. Luxembourg: Office for the Official Publications of the European Communities.

European Commission (2001a) *Promoting a European Framework for Corporate Social Responsibility*. Green paper. Luxembourg: Office for the Official Publications of the European Communities.

European Commission (2001b) *Employment in Europe 2001*. Luxembourg: Office for the Official Publications of the European Communities.

European Commission (2001c) *Enhancing Democracy: A White Paper on Governance in the European Union*. Brussels. Available from <http://europa. eu.int/comm/governance/index_en.htm>.

European Commission (2002a) *Industrial Relations in Europe 2002. Recent Trends and Prospects*. Luxembourg: Office for the Official Publications of the European Communities.

European Commission (2002b) *Report of the High Level Group on Industrial Relations and Change in the European Union*. Luxembourg: Office for the Official Publications of the European Communities.

European Commission (2002c) *Employment in Europe 2002*. Luxembourg: Office for the Official Publications of the European Communities.

European Commission (2002d) Directorate General for Employment and Social Affairs. *Social Agenda*. Issue No. 1, April. Luxembourg: Office for the Official Publications of the European Communities.

European Commission (2003a) *Employment in Europe 2003*. DG Employment and Social Affairs. Brussels: European Commission.

European Commission (2003b) '2003 Employment Guidelines and Recommendations' http://europa.eu.int/comm/employment_social/employment_strategy/newees_en.htm.

European Foundation for the Improvement of Living and Working Conditions (2001) *Third European Survey on Working Conditions*. Luxembourg: Office for the Official Publications of the European Communities.

Eurostat (1991) *Labour Force Survey 1990*. Luxembourg: Office for the Official Publications of the European Communities.

Eurostat (1999) *Services in Europe – Data 1995–1997*. Luxembourg: Office for the Official Publications of the European Communities.

Eurostat (2001) *Labour Force Survey 2000*. Luxembourg: Office for the Official Publications of the European Communities.

Eurostat (2003) 'Labour costs survey 2000', *Statistics in Focus*, Population and Social Conditions, Theme 3 – 18/2003 Catalogue No. KS-NK-03-018-EN-N Eurostat.

EWCB (2000) 'Codes of corporate conduct and industrial relations – part one', *European Works Councils Bulletin*, Issue 27 (May/June), 11–16.

EWCB (2001) 'Vauxhall job cuts controversy continues', *European Works Councils Bulletin*, Issue 32 (March/April), p. 2.

EWCB (2002) 'Global agreements – an update', *European Works Councils Bulletin*, Issue 39 (May/June), 7–12.

EWCB (2003) 'Fiat EWC calls European day of action', *European Works Councils Bulletin*, Issue 43 (Jan/Feb), p. 3.

Fajertag, G. (ed.) (2000) *Collective Bargaining in Europe 1998–1999*. Brussels: ETUI.

Fajertag, G. (ed.) (2002) *Collective Bargaining in Europe 2001*. Brussels: ETUI.

Fajertag, G. and Pochet, P. (eds) (1997) *Social Pacts in Europe*. Brussels: ETUI.

Fajertag, G. and Pochet, P. (2000) 'A new era for social pacts in Europe', in G. Fajertag and P. Pochet (eds), *Social Pacts in Europe – New Dynamics*. Brussels: ETUI, 9–40.

Falkner, G. (1996) 'European Works Councils and the Maastricht Social Agreement: towards a new policy style?', *Journal of European Public Policy*, 3(2), 192–208.

Falkner, G. (1998) *EU Social Policy in the 1990s*. London: Routledge.

Falkner, G. (2003) 'The interprofessional social dialogue at European level: past and future', in B. Keller and H.-W. Platzer (eds), *Industrial Relations and European Integration*. Aldershot: Ashgate, 11–29.

Ferner, A. (1994) 'The state as employer', in R. Hyman and A. Ferner (eds), *New Frontiers in European Industrial Relations*. Oxford: Blackwell, 52–79.

Ferner, A. (1997) 'Multinationals, "relocation" and employment in Europe' in J. Gual (ed.), *Job Creation: the Role of Labour Market Institutions*. Aldershot: Edward Elgar, 165–96.

Ferner, A. and Hyman, R. (1992) 'Introduction: industrial relations in the New Europe: seventeen types of ambiguity', in A. Ferner and R. Hyman (eds), *Industrial Relations in the New Europe*. Blackwell: Oxford, xvi–xlix.

Ferner, A. and Hyman, R. (1998) 'Introduction: towards European industrial relations?', in A. Ferner and R. Hyman (eds), *Changing Industrial Relations in Europe*. Oxford: Blackwell, xi–xxvi.

Ferner, A. and Quintanilla, J. (1998) 'Multinationals, national identity and the management of HRM: "Anglo-Saxonization" and its limits', *International Journal of Human Resource Management*, 9(4), 710–31.

Ferrera, M., Hemerijck, A. and Rhodes, M. (2000) 'The future of social Europe: recasting work and welfare in the new economy'. Report for the Portuguese Presidency of the European Union.

Financial Times (2002) 'Swedes could reject euro, says union body', *Financial Times*, 4 November.

Flanders, A. (1970) *Management and Union: the Theory and Reform of Industrial Relations*. London: Faber.

Flassbeck, H. (1999) 'Employment stability and efficiency. Strategic essentials of European economic policy' (www.flassback.de/Publikationen/Ausgehlte_Veroffentlichungen/Strategi.pdf).

Foden, D. (1998) 'Trade union proposals towards EMU', *Transfer*, 4(1), 88–114.

Frege, C. and Kelly, J. (2003) 'Union revitalisation strategies in comparative perspective', *European Journal of Industrial Relations*, 9(1), 7–24.

Freyssinet, J and Michon, F. (2003). 'Overtime in Europe', *European Industrial Relations Observatory On-line*, Ref: TN0302101S.

Gilman, M. and Marginson, P. (2002) 'Negotiating European Works Councils: contours of constrained choice', *Industrial Relations Journal*, 33(1), 36–51.

Goetschy, J. (1998) 'France: the limits of reform', in A. Ferner and R. Hyman (eds), *Changing Industrial Relations in Europe*. Oxford: Blackwell, 357–94.

Goetschy, J. (1999) 'The European Employment strategy: genesis and development', *European Journal of Industrial Relations*, 5(2), 117–37.

Goetschy, J. (2000) 'The European Union and National Social Pacts: employment and social protection put to the test of joint regulation', in G. Fajertag and P. Pochet (eds), *Social Pacts in Europe – New Dynamics*. Brussels: ETUI, 41–60.

Goetschy, J. (2001) 'The European employment strategy from Amsterdam to Stockholm', *Industrial Relations Journal*, 32(5), 401–18.

Goetschy, J. (2003) 'The European employment strategy and the open method of co-ordination: lessons and perspectives', *Transfer*, 9(2), 281–301.

Gollbach, J. and Schulten, T. (2000) 'Cross-border collective bargaining networks in Europe', *European Journal of Industrial Relations*, 6(2), 161–79.

Grote, J.R. and Schmitter, P. (1998) 'The renaissance of national corporatism: unintended side-effect of European Economic and Monetary Union or calculated response to the absence of European social policy?', *Transfer*, 5(1–2), 34–63.

Haas, E. (1964) *Beyond the Nation State: Functionalism and International Organisation*. Stanford: University Press.

Hall, M. (1992) 'Behind the European Works Councils Directive: the European Commission's legislative strategy', *British Journal of Industrial Relations*, 30(4), 547–66.

Hall, M. (1994) 'Industrial relations and the social dimension of European integration', in R. Hyman and A. Ferner (eds), *New Frontiers in European Industrial Relations*. Oxford: Blackwell, 281–311.

Hall, M., Hoffmann, A., Marginson, P. and Müller, T. (2003) 'National influences on European Works Councils in UK- and US-based companies', *Human Resource Management Journal*, 13(4), 75–92.

Hall, P. and Soskice, D. (2001) 'An introduction to varieties of capitalism', in P. Hall and D. Soskice (eds), *Varieties of Capitalism: the Institutional Foundations of Comparative Advantage*. Oxford: Oxford University Press, 1–68.

Hancké, B. (2000) 'European Works Councils and industrial restructuring in the European motor industry', *European Journal of Industrial Relations*, 6(1), 35–59.

Hancké, B. (2002) 'The political economy of wage-setting in the Eurozone' in P. Pochet (ed.), *Wage Policy in the Eurozone*. Brussels: PIE-Peter Lang S.A, 131–48.

Hank, R. (2000) *Das Ende der Gleichheit oder Warum der Kapitalismus mehr Wettbewerb braucht*, Frankfurt a.M.

Hassel, A. (1999) 'The erosion of the German industrial relations system', *British Journal of Industrial Relations*, 37(3), 484–505.

Hassel, A. (2002a) 'The erosion continues: reply', *British Journal of Industrial Relations*, 40(2), 309–17.

Hassel, A. (2002b) 'A new going rate? Co-ordinated wage bargaining in Europe', in P. Pochet (ed.), *Wage Policy in the Eurozone*. Brussels: PIE-Peter Lang S.A, 149–73.

Hassel, A. and Rehder, B. (2001) 'Institutional change in the German wage bargaining system – the role of big companies' MPIfG Working Paper 01/9 Cologne: Max-Planck-Institut für Gesellschaftsforschung.

Hassel, A. and Schulten, T. (1998) 'Globalization and the future of central collective bargaining', *Economy and Society*, 27(4), 486–522.

Hastings, M. (1997) *Managing the Management Tools*. London: Institute of Management.

Hay, C. (2000) 'Contemporary capitalism, globalization, regionalization and the persistence of national variation', *Review of International Studies*, 26(4), 509–31.

Hay, C. (2002a) 'Common trajectories, variable paces, divergent outcomes? Models of European capitalism under conditions of complex economic interdependence'. Paper presented at the biannual Conference of Europeanists, Chicago, 14–16 March.

Hay, C. (2002b) 'Globalisation, regionalisation and the future of the welfare state'. Paper presented at the University of Bristol, 20 March.

Hay, C. (2002c) *Political Analysis: a Critical Introduction*. Basingstoke: Palgrave.

Hay, C. and Rosamond, B. (2000) 'Globalization, European integration and the discursive construction of economic imperatives'. Paper prepared for the Second Annual Conference of the ESRC 'One Europe or Several?' programme, University of Sussex, 21–2 September.

Hemerijck, A., van der Meer, M. and Visser, J. (2000) 'Innovation through co-ordination – two decades of social pacts in the Netherlands', in G. Fajertag and P. Pochet (eds), *Social Pacts in Europe – New Dynamics*. Brussels: ETUI, 257–78.

Hirst, P. and Thompson, G. (1996) *Globalization in Question*, 1st edn. Cambridge: Polity.

Hirst, P. and Thompson, G. (1999) *Globalization in Question*, 2nd edn. Cambridge: Polity.

HM Treasury (2003) 'UK membership of the single currency: an assessment of the five economic tests', *HM Treasury*, Cm 5776.

Hodson, D. and Maher, I. (2001) 'The open method as a new mode of governance', *Journal of Common Market Studies*, 39(4), 719–46.

Hoffman, J, Hoffman, R., Kirton-Darling, J. and Rampeltshammer, L. (2002) *The Europeanization of Industrial Relations in a Global Perspective: a Literature Review*. Luxembourg: European Foundation for the Improvement of Living and Working Conditions/Office for Official Publications of the European Communities.

Hoffmann, R. (1998) Book review of O. Jacoby and P. Pochet (eds), *A Common Currency Area – a Fragmented Area for Wages, Transfer*, 4(1), 144–6.

Hoffmann, R. and Mermet, E. (2001) 'European trade union strategies on Europeanisation of collective bargaining', in T. Schulten and R. Bispinck (eds), *Collective Bargaining under the Euro*. Brussels: ETUI/EMF, 37–60.

Hollingsworth, J. and Streeck, W. (1994) 'Countries and Sectors', in J. Hollingsworth, P. Schmitter and W. Streeck (eds), *Governing Capitalist Economies*. Oxford: Oxford University Press, 270–300.

Hooghe, L. and Marks, G. (2002) 'Types of multi-level governance'. Department of Political Science, University of North Carolina. Mimeo.

Hornung-Draus, R. (2001) 'Between e-economy, Euro and enlargement: Where are employer organisations in Europe beading?' Plenary paper presented to the 6th IIRA European Congress, Oslo, 25–9 June.

Huiskamp, R. and Looise, J. (2000) *Competitive consensus: the process of organised decentralisation in Dutch labour relations*, unpublished paper.

Hyman, R. (1994) 'Changing trade union identities and strategies', in R. Hyman and A. Ferner (eds), *New Frontiers in European Industrial Relations*. Oxford: Blackwell, 108–39.

Hyman, R. (2001) 'The Europeanisation – or the erosion – of industrial relations?', *Industrial Relations Journal*, 32(4), 280–94.

IMF (1998) *World Economic Outlook*. New York: IMF.

IRS (1999) 'Benchmarking best practice', *IRS Management Review 14*. London: IRS Eclipse.

Iversen, T. (1999) *Contested Economic Institutions*. Cambridge: Cambridge University Press.

Jacobi, O. (1998) 'Contours of a European collective bargaining system', *Transfer*, 4(2), 299–309.

Jacobs, A. and Ojeda Avilés, A. (1999) 'The European Social Dialogue: some legal issues', in B. Bercusson, T. Blanke, N. Bruun, A. Jacobs, A. Ojeda Avilés, B. Veneziani and S. Clauewaert (eds), *A Legal Framework for European Industrial Relations*. Brussels: ETUI.

Jörgensen, H. (2000) 'From deregulation to regulation – neo corporatism and its contribution to a theory of co-ordinated labour market regulation'. Paper presented to the 12th IIRA World Congress, Tokyo, 29 May to 2 June.

Jörgensen, H. (2001) 'Regulatory practices and contractualisation of relationships – Cooperative adaptation as policy alternative illustrated by examples from Danish labour market policy'. Paper presented to the 6th IIRA European Congress, Oslo, 25–9 June.

Katz, H. (1993) 'The decentralization of collective bargaining: a literature review and comparative analysis', *Industrial and Labor Relations Review*, 47(1), 3–22.

Katz, H and Darbishire, O. (2000) *Converging Divergencies*. Ithaca, NY: ILR Press.

Kaufman, B. (2001) 'Paradigms and strategic choices for industrial relations: the importance of getting Commons right'. Institute of Personnel and Employment Relations, Georgia State University. Mimeo.

Kauppinen, T. (ed.) (1998) *The Impact of EMU on Industrial Relations in the European Union*. Helsinki: Finnish Industrial Relations Association.

Kauppinen, T. (2001) 'Industrial relations in the 24 hour society', Paper presented to the 6th IIRA European Congress, Oslo, 25–9 June.

Keep, E. and Rainbird, H. (2000) 'Towards the learning organization?', in S. Bach and K. Sisson (eds), *Personnel Management*. Oxford: Blackwell, 173–94.

Keller, B. (2000) 'The emergence of regional systems of employment regulation: the case of the European Union'. Paper presented to the 12th IIRA World Congress, Tokyo, 29 May to 2 June.

Keller, B. (2001) 'The Employment Chapter of the Amsterdam Treaty. Towards a new European Employment Policy?' Paper for the 6th IIRA European Congress Oslo, 25–9 June.

Keller, B. (2003) 'Social dialogues at sectoral level', in B. Keller and H.-W. Platzer (eds), *Industrial Relations and European Integration*. Aldershot: Ashgate, 30–57.

Keller, B. and Bansbach, M. (2000) 'Social dialogues: an interim report on recent results and prospects', *Industrial Relations Journal*, 31(4), 291–307.

Keller, B. and Platzer, H.-W. (eds) (2003) *Industrial Relations and European Integration*. Aldershot: Ashgate.

Keller, B. and Sörries, B. (1999) 'Sectoral social dialogues: new opportunities or more impasses?', *Industrial Relations Journal*, 30(4), 330–44.

Kelly, J. (1998) *Rethinking Industrial Relations*. London: Routledge.

Kenner, J. (1995) 'EC labour law: the softly, softly approach', *International Journal of Comparative Labour Law and Industrial Relations*, 11(3), 307–27.

Kenis, P. (1992) *The Social Construction of an Industry: a World of Chemical Fibres*. Frankfurt and Boulder, CO: Campus Verlag/Westview Press.

Kerr, C., Dunlop, J.T., Harbison, F. and Meyers, C. (1960) *Industrialism and Industrial Man*. Cambridge, MA: Harvard University Press.

Kirton-Darling, J. and Clauwaert, S. (2003) 'European social dialogue: an instrument in the Europeanisation of industrial relations', *Transfer*, 9(2), 247–64.

Kittel, B. (2002) 'EMU, EU Enlargement, and the European Social Model: trends, challenges and questions', MPIfG Working Paper 02/1, February. Cologne: Max-Planck Institut für Gessellschaftforschung.

Knill, C. and Lehmkuhl, D. (1999) 'How Europe matters: different mechanisms of Europeanization', *European Integration online Papers (EIoP)*, 3(7).

Kohl, H., Lecher, W. and Platzer, H.-W. (2000) *Labour Relations in East-Central Europe between Transformation and EU Membership*. Bonn: Friederich Ebert Stiftung.

Kollewe, K. and Kuhlmann, R. (2003) 'Creating a more dynamic European social dialogue by strengthening the sectoral dimension', *Transfer*, 9(2), 265–80.

Korczynski, M. (1997) 'Centralisation of collective bargaining in a decade of decentralisation', *Industrial Relations Journal*, 28(1), 14–26.

Kozul-Wright, R. and Rowthorn, R. (1998) 'Spoilt for choice? Multinational corporations and the geography of international production', *Oxford Review of Economic Policy*, 14(2), 74–92.

Lane, C. (1989) *Management and Labour in Europe*. Aldershot: Edward Elgar.

Le Queux, S. and Fajertag, G. (2001) 'Towards Europeanisation of collective bargaining? Insights from the European chemical industry', *European Journal of Industrial Relations*, 7(2), 117–36.

Lecher, W., Nagel, B., Platzer, H.-W., Fulton, L., Jaich, R., Rehfeldt, U., Rüb, S., Telljohann, V. and Weiner, K.-P. (1999) *The Establishment of European Works Councils*. Aldershot: Gower.

Lecher, W. and Rüb, S. (1999) 'The constitution of European Works Councils', *European Journal of Industrial Relations*, 5(1), 7–25.

Lecher, W., Platzer, H.-W., Rüb, S. and Weiner, K.-P. (2001) *European Works Councils: Developments, Types, Networking*. Aldershot: Gower.

Leftwich, A. (1984) 'On the politics of politics', in A. Leftwich (ed.) *What is Politics?* Oxford: Blackwell, 1–18.

Legge, K. (1995) *Human Resource Management: Rhetorics and Realities*. Basingstoke: Macmillan.

Lehndorff, S. (1998) 'From "collective" to "individual" reductions in working time? Trends and experience with working time in the European Union', *Transfer*, 4(4), 598–620.

Leisink, P. (2002) 'The European sectoral social dialogue and the graphical industry', *European Journal of Industrial Relations*, 8(1), 101–17.

Léonard, E. (2001) 'Industrial relations and the regulation of employment in Europe', *European Journal of Industrial Relations*, 7(1), 27–47.

Levinson, C. (1972) *International Trade Unionism*. London: Allen and Unwin.

Levinson, H. (1966) *Determining Forces in Collective Wage Bargaining*. New York: John Wiley.

Lilja, K. and Tainio, R. (1996) 'The nature of the typical Finnish firm', in R. Whitley and P. Kristensen (eds), *The Changing European Firm: Limits to Convergence*. London: Routledge, 159–91.

Lind, J. (2000) 'Recent issues on the Social Pact in Denmark', in G. Fajertag and P. Pochet (eds), *Social Pacts in Europe – New Dynamics*. Brussels: ETUI, 135–60.

Locke, R. (1995) 'The transformation of industrial relations? A cross-national review', in K. Wever and L. Turner (eds), *The Comparative Political Economy of Industrial Relations*. Madison: IRRA, 9–30.

Macaire, S. and Rehfeldt, U. (2001) 'Industrial relations aspects of mergers and takeovers', *European Industrial Relations Observatory On-line*, Ref: TN0102410S.

MacDuffie, J. (1995) 'International trends in work organization in the auto industry', in K. Wever and L. Turner (eds), *The Comparative Political Economy of Industrial Relations*. Madison: IRRA, 71–114.

Majone, G. (ed.) (1996) *Regulating Europe*. London: Routledge.

Marginson, P. (2000a) 'The Eurocompany and Euro industrial relations', *European Journal of Industrial Relations*, 6(1), 9–34.

Marginson, P. (2000b) 'Multinational companies: innovators or adaptors?', in H. Rainbird (ed.), *Training in the Workplace*. Basingstoke: Macmillan, 81–100.

Marginson, P. (2001) 'The implications of EMU for collective bargaining in the British engineering sector', in T. Schulten and R. Bispinck (eds), *Collective Bargaining under the Euro*. Brussels: ETUI/EMF, 285–302.

Marginson, P., Armstrong, P., Edwards, P. and Purcell, J. with Hubbard, N. (1993) *The Control of Industrial Relations in Large Companies*. Warwick Papers in Industrial Relations, 45. Coventry: IRRU, University of Warwick.

Marginson, P., Armstrong, P., Edwards, P. and Purcell, J. (1995) 'Extending beyond borders: multinational companies and the international management of labour', *International Journal of Human Resource Management*, 6(3), 702–19.

Marginson, P., Gilman, M., Jacobi, O. and Krieger, H. (1998) *Negotiating European Works Councils: an Analysis of Agreements under Article 13*. Luxembourg: Office for Official Publications of the European Communities.

Marginson, P., Hall, M., Hoffmann, A. and Müller, T. (2004) 'The impact of European Works Councils on management decision-making in UK- and US-based multinationals', *British Journal of Industrial Relations* 42 (2), 209–33.

Marginson, P. and Schulten, T. (1999) 'The "Europeanisation" of Collective Bargaining', *European Industrial Relations Observatory On-line*, Ref: TN9907201S.

Marginson, P. and Sisson, K. (1994) 'The structure of transnational capital in Europe: the emerging Euro-company and its implications for industrial relations', in R. Hyman and A. Ferner (eds), *New Frontiers in European Industrial Relations*. Oxford: Blackwell, 15–51.

Marginson, P. and Sisson, K. (1996) 'Multinational companies and the future of collective bargaining: a review of the research issues', *European Journal of Industrial Relations*, 2(2), 173–97.

Marginson, P. and Sisson, K. (1998) 'European collective bargaining: a virtual prospect?', *Journal of Common Market Studies*, 36(4), 505–28.

Marginson, P. and Sisson, K. (2002) 'European integration and industrial relations: a case of convergence and divergence?', *Journal of Common Market Studies*, 40(4), 671–92.

Marginson, P., Sisson, K. and Arrowsmith, J. (2003) 'Between decentralisation and Europeanisation: sectoral bargaining in four countries and two sectors', *European Journal of Industrial Relations*, 9(2), 163–87.

Marsden, D. (1999) *A Theory of Employment Systems: Micro-Foundations of Societal Diversity*. Oxford: Oxford University Press.

Marshall, A. (1890) *Principles of Economics*, 9th edn. London: Macmillan.

Martin, A. (1996) 'European institutions and the Europeanization of trade unions: support or seduction?', European Trade Union Institute Discussion and Working Papers, DWP 96.04.1.

Martin, A. (1999) 'Wage bargaining under EMU: Europeanisation, re-nationalisation or Americanisation?', European Trade Union Institute Discussion and Working Papers, DWP 99.01.03.

Martin, A. (2001) 'Labour market structures and macroeconomic performance in Europe and the US'. Paper presented at the 6th IIRA European congress, Oslo, 25–9 June.

Martin, G. and Beaumont, P. (1998) 'Diffusing "best practice" in multinational firms: prospects, practice and contestation', *International Journal of Human Resource Management*, 9(4), 672–95.

Martin, P. (1998) 'Europe boldly goes', *The Financial Times*, 28 March.

Maurice, M., Sellier, F. and Silvestre, J.J. (1986) *The Social Foundations of Industrial Power: a Comparison of France and Germany*. Cambridge, MA: MIT Press.

Mayer, M. and Whittington, R. (1996) 'The survival of the European holding company', in R. Whitley and P. Kristensen (eds), *The Changing European Firm: Limits to Convergence*. London: Routledge, 87–109.

McWilliams, D. (1992) *Will the Single European Market cause European Wage Levels to Converge?* London: London Economics.

Meardi, G. (2002) 'The Trojan Horse for the Americanisation of Europe? Polish industrial relations towards the EU', *European Journal of Industrial Relations*, 8(1), 77–99.

Meardi, G. (2003) 'Foreign direct investment in Central Eastern Europe and industrial relations'. Paper presented at the 13th IIRA World Congress, Berlin, 8–13 September.

Mendez, A. (1994) 'L'internationalization comme processus de création de ressources: diversité et cohérence des trajectories d'entreprises'. PhD Thesis, Université d'Aix Marseille II, September.

Mériaux, O. (1999) 'Négocier l'emploi et la compétitivité: le cas d'Air France *"Accord Pour un Développement Partagé" du Personnel au sol – 13 janvier 1999'*. French report on collective bargaining on employment and competitiveness for the European Foundation for the Improvement of Living and Working Conditions.

Mermet, E. (2001) 'Annual report on the co-ordination of collective bargaining in Europe: 2001'. Prepared for ETUC Executive Committee, 9 December.

Mermet, E. and Clarke, P. (2002) 'Third annual report on the co-ordination of collective bargaining in Europe: 2002'. Prepared for ETUC Executive Committee, 19 November.

Milner, M. (2002) 'A pact, yes. But not a stable one', *Guardian*, 13 August.

Molina, O. and Rhodes, M. (2002) 'Corporatism: the past, present and future of a concept', *Annual Review of Political Science*, 5, 305–31.

Moravcsik, A. (1993) 'Preferences and power in the European Community: a liberal intergovernmentalist approach', *Journal of Common Market Studies*, 31(4), 473–524.

Morgan, G., Kristensen, P. and Whitley, R. (eds) (2001) *Organising Internationally: Restructuring Firms and Markets in the Global Economy*. Oxford: Oxford University Press.

Moseley, H. (1990) 'The social dimension of European integration', *International Labour Review*, 129(2), 147–64.

Mueller, F. (1994) 'Societal effect, organizational effect and globalization', *Organization Studies*, 15(3), 407–20.

Mueller, F. (1996) 'National stakeholders in the global contest for corporate investment', *European Journal of Industrial Relations*, 2(3), 345–68.

Mueller, F. and Purcell, J. (1992) 'The Europeanization of manufacturing and the decentralization of bargaining', *International Journal of Human Resource Management*, 3(1), 15–24.

Müller, T. and Platzer, H.-W. (2003) 'European Works Councils', in B. Keller and H.-W. Platzer (eds), *Industrial Relations and European Integration*. Aldershot: Ashgate, 58–84.

Münchau, W. (1998) 'Europe's big opportunity' (The case for EMU), *The Financial Times*, 23 March.

Mundell, R. (1961) 'A theory of optimum currency areas', *American Economic Review*, 51(4), 657–65.

Neave, G. (1988) 'On the cultivation of quality, efficiency and enterprise; an overview of recent trends in higher education in Western Europe, 1986–1988'. *European Journal of Education*, 23(1–2), 7–23.

Negrelli, S. (2000) 'Social pacts in Italy and Europe: similar strategies and structures; different models and national stories', in G. Fajertag and P. Pochet (eds), *Social Pacts in Europe – New Dynamics*. Brussels: ETUI, 85–112.

Nollert, M. (2000) 'Lobbying for a Europe of big business: the European Roundtable of Industrialists', in V. Bornschier (ed.), *State-building in Europe: the Revitalisation of Western European Integration*. Cambridge: Cambridge University Press, 187–209.

Obstfeld, M. and Peri, G. (1998) 'Regional non-adjustment and fiscal policy', in D. Begg, J. Von Hagen, C. Wyplosz, and K.F. Zimmerman (eds), *EMU: Prospects and Challenges for the Euro*. Special issue of *Economic Policy*. Oxford: Blackwell.

O'Donnell, R. (2001) 'Towards post-corporatist concertation in Europe?', in H. Wallace (ed.) *Interlocking Dimensions of European Integration*. Basingstoke: Palgrave.

OECD (1994) *The OECD Jobs Study*. Paris: OECD.

Olsen, J. (2001) 'Organizing European institutions of governance ... a prelude to an institutionalized account of political integration', in H. Wallace (ed.), *Interlocking Dimensions of European Integration*. Basingstoke: Palgrave, 323–54.

Pain, N. (1997) 'Continental drift: European integration and the location of UK foreign direct investment', *The Manchester School Supplement*, 65, 94–117.

Pakashlati, J. (1998) 'EMU and social protection in the European Union', in P. Pochet and B. Van Hercke (eds), *Social Challenges of Economic and Monetary Union*. Brussels: European Interuniversity Press.

Peters, T. and Waterman, R. (1982) *In Search of Excellence*. New York: Harper & Row.

Pizzorno, A. (1978) 'Political exchange and collective identity in industrial conflict', in C. Crouch and A. Pizzorno (eds), *The Resurgence of Class Conflict in Western Europe since 1968, Vol. 2. Comparative Analyses*. London: Macmillan.

Pochet, P. (1998) 'The social consequences of EMU: an overview of national debates', in P. Pochet and B. VanHercke (eds), *Social Challenges of Economic and Monetary Union*. Brussels: European Interuniversity Press.

Pochet, P. (ed.) (2002) *Wage Policy in the Eurozone*. Brussels: PIE-Peter Lang S.A.

Pochet, P., Beine, M., de Decker, C., Kabatusuila, F., Vanherk, B. and Lamby, P. (1999) *Economic and Monetary Union, Employment, Social Conditions and Social Benefit: a Literature Survey*. Dublin: European Foundation for the Improvement of Living and Working conditions.

Pochet, P. and Fajertag, G. (2001) 'Social pacts in the Euro aftermath'. Paper presented at the 6th IIRA European Congress Oslo, 25–9 June.

Porter, M. (ed.) (1986) *Competition in Global Industries*. Boston, MA: Harvard University Press.

Pulignano, V. (2000) 'Il mercato in fabbrica: terziarizzazioni e relazioni industriali tra retorica e realtà', *Studi Organizzativi*, 3, 105–29.

Purcell, J. (1993) 'The end of institutional industrial relations', *Political Quarterly*, 64(1), 6–23.

Rainbird, H. (1996) 'Negotiating a research agenda for comparisons of vocational training', in L. Hantrais and S. Mangen (eds), *Cross-National Research Methods in the Social Sciences*. London: Pinter, 109–19.

Ramsay, H. (1995) 'Le Défi Européen', in A. Amin and J. Tomaney (eds), *Behind the Myth of the European Union*. London: Routledge, 174–97.

Reder, M. and Ulman, L. (1993) 'Unions and Unification' in L. Ulman, B. Eichengreen and W.T. Dickens (eds), *Labor and an Integrated Europe*. Washington DC: The Brookings Institute.

Regalia, I. (1995) *Humanise Work and Increase Profitability? Direct Participation in Organizational Change Viewed by the Social Partners in Europe*. Luxembourg: Office for the Official Publications of the European Communities.

Regalia, I. and Regini, M. (1998) 'Italy: the dual character of industrial relations', in A. Ferner and R. Hyman (eds), *Changing Industrial Relations in Europe*. Oxford: Blackwell, 459–503.

Rhodes, M. (1995) 'A regulatory conundrum: industrial relations and the social dimension', in S. Leibfried and R. Pierson (eds), *European Social Policy: Between Fragmentation and Integration*. Washington DC: Brookings Institution.

Rhodes, M. (1997) 'The welfare state: internal challenges, external constraints' in M. Rhodes, P. Heywood and V. Wright (eds), *Development in West European Politics*. Basingstoke: Macmillan, 57–74.

Rhodes, M. (1998) 'Globalisation, labour markets and welfare states: a future of "competitive corporatism"?' in Rhodes, M. and Mény, Y. (eds), *The Future of European Welfare*. Basingstoke: Macmillan.

Rhodes, M. (2003) National 'Pacts' and EU Governance in Social Policy and the Labour Market, in Zeitlin, J. and Trubeck, D. (eds.), *Governing Work and Welfare in the New Economy: European and American Experiments*. Oxford: Oxford University Press, 129–57.

Richardson, G. (1972) 'The organisation of industry', *Economic Journal*, 82(4), 883–96.

Richardson, K. (2000) 'Big Business and the European Agenda'. *Working Papers in Contemporary European Studies*. University of Sussex; Sussex European Institute.

Rivest, C. (1996) 'Voluntary European Works Councils', *European Journal of Industrial Relations*, 2(2), 235–53.

Rogers, J. and Streeck, W. (eds) (1995) *Works Councils*. Chicago: Chicago University Press.

Rosamond, B. (2000) *Theories of European Integration*. Basingstoke: Palgrave – now Palgrave Macmillan.

Rosamond, B. (2001) 'Functions, levels and European governance', in H. Wallace (ed) *Interlooking Dimensions of European Integration*. Basingstoke: Palgrave, 68–86.

Ross, A. (1948) *Trade Union Wage Policy*. Berkeley: University of California Press.

Rubery, J. and Grimshaw, D. (2002) *The Organization of Employment: An international perspective*. Basingstoke: Palgrave – now Palgrave Macmillan.

Rugman, A. (2000) *The End of Globalization*. London: Random House.

Runciman, W. (1966) *Relative Deprivation and Social Justice*. London: Routledge.

Ruigrok, W. and van Tulder, R. (1995) *The Logic of International Restructuring*. London: Routledge.

Sadowski, D. and Jacobi, O. (eds) (1991) *Employers' Associations in Europe: Policy and Organisation*. Baden-Baden: Nomos Verlagsgesellschaft.

Sako, M. (1997) 'Wage bargaining in Japan: Why employers and unions value industry-level coordination', *Centre for Economic Performance Discussion Paper No. 334*. London: Centre for Economic Performance.

Sarfati, H. (2001) 'Labour market vs. social protection – what challenges for the social actors in Europe?' Paper presented to the 6th IIRA European Congress, Oslo, 25–9 June.

Scharpf, F. (1988) 'The Joint-Decision Trap: lessons from German federalism and European integration', *Public Administration*, 66, 239–78.

Scharpf, F. (2000a) 'The viability of advanced welfare states in the international economy: vulnerabilities and options', *Journal of European Public Policy*, 7(2), 190–228.

Scharpf, F. (2000b) 'Institutions in comparative policy research' MPIFG working paper 00/3, March. Cologne: Max-Planck Institut für Gessellschaftsforschung.

Scharpf, F. (2002) 'The European Social Model: coping with the challenges of diversity', *Journal of Common Market Studies*, 40(4), 645–70.

Schmitt, M. and Sadowski, D. (2001) 'The international transfer of HRM/IR practices within MNCs'. Paper presented at the International Conference on Multinational Companies and HRM, De Montfort University, Leicester, 12–14 July.

Schmitter, P. and Grote, J. (1997) 'The Corporatist Sisyphus: past, present and future', European University Institute SPS Working Paper, No. 97/4.

Schulten, T. (1996) 'European Works Councils: prospects for a new system of European industrial relations', *European Journal of Industrial Relations*, 2(3), 303–24.

Schulten, T. (1998) 'Collective bargaining in the metal industry under the conditions of the European Monetary Union', in T. Kauppinen (ed.), *The Impact of EMU on Industrial Relations in the European Union*. Helsinki: Finnish Industrial Relations Association, 207–24.

Schulten, T. (2001) 'The European Metalworkers' Federation approach to a European co-ordination of collective bargaining: experiences, problems and prospects', in T. Schulten and R. Bispinck (eds), *Collective Bargaining under the Euro*. Brussels: ETUI, 303–32.

Schulten, T. (2002) 'A European solidaristic wage policy?', *European Journal of Industrial Relations*, 8(2), 173–96.

Schulten, T. (2003) 'Europeanisation of collective bargaining: trade union initiatives for the transnational co-ordination of collective bargaining', in B. Keller and H.-W. Platzer (eds), *Industrial Relations and European Integration*. Aldershot: Ashgate, 112–36.

Schulten, T. and Stückler, A. (2000) 'Wage policy and EMU', *European Industrial Relations Observatory On-line*, Ref: TN0007201S.

Sciarra, S. (1995) 'Social values and multiple sources of European social law', *European Law Journal*, 1(1), 60–83.

Seltzer, G. (1951) 'Pattern bargaining and the United Steelworkers', *Journal of Political Economy*, 59(4), 319–31.

Sisson, K. (1987) *The Management of Collective Bargaining: an International Comparison*. Oxford: Blackwell.

Sisson, K. (1991) 'Employers' organisations and industrial relations: the significance of the strategies of large companies', in D. Sadowski and O. Jacobi (eds), *Employers' Associations in Europe: Policy and Organisation*. Baden-Baden: Nomos Verlagsgesellschaft.

Sisson, K. (2001a) 'Pacts for employment and competitveness: an opportunity to reflect on the role and practice of collective bargaining', *Transfer*, 7(4), 600–15.

Sisson, K. (2001b) 'Structural and economic changes affecting industrial relations: global trends rather than globalization?', Paper presented at the 6th IIRA European Congress, Oslo 25–29 June.

Sisson, K., Arrowsmith, J., Gilman, M. and Hall, M. (1999) *EMU and the Implications for Industrial Relations: a Select Bibliographic Review*. Dublin: European Foundation for the Improvement of Living and Working Conditions.

Sisson, K., Arrowsmith, J. and Marginson, P. (2003) 'All benchmarkers now? Benchmarking and the Europeanisation of industrial relations', *Industrial Relations Journal*, 34(1), 15–31.

Sisson, K. and Artiles, A.M. (2000) *Handling Restructuring: a Study of Collective Agreements on Employment and Competitiveness*. Luxembourg: Office for the Official Publications of the European Communities.

Sisson, K. and Marginson, P. (2000) *The Impact of Economic and Monetary Union on Industrial Relations: a Sectoral and Company View*. Luxembourg: Office for Official Publications of the European Communities.

Sisson, K. and Marginson, P. (2002) 'Co-ordinated bargaining: a process for our times?', *British Journal of Industrial Relations*, 40(2), 197–220.

Smith, C., Child, J. and Rowlinson, M. (1990) *Reshaping Work: the Cadbury Experience*. Cambridge: Cambridge University Press.

Soskice, D. (1990) 'Wage determination: the changing role of institutions in advanced industrialised countries', *Oxford Review of Economic Policy*, 6(4), 36–61.

Soskice, D. and Iversen, T. (1998) 'Multiple wage-bargaining systems in the single European currency area', *Oxford Review of Economic Policy*, 14(3), 110–24.

Spyropoulos, G. (2002) 'Le droit du travail à la recherche de nouveaux objectifs', *Droit Social*, 4 (April), 391–402.

Storey, J. (1992) *Developments in the Management of Human Resources*. Oxford: Blackwell.

Strange, S. (1997) 'The future of global capitalism; or, will divergence persist forever?', in C. Crouch and W. Streeck (eds), *Political Economy of Modern Capitalism: Mapping Convergence and Diversity*. London: Sage.

Streeck, W. (1992) 'National diversity, regime competition and institutional deadlock: problems in forming a European industrial relations system', *Journal of Public Policy*, 12, 301–30.

Streeck, W. (1995) 'Neo-voluntarism: a new European policy regime', *European Law Journal*, 1(1), 31–59.

Streeck, W. (1996) 'Public power beyond the nation-state: the case of the European Community', in R. Boyer and D. Drache (eds), *States Against Markets: the Limits of Globalisation*. London: Routledge, 299–315.

Streeck, W. (1997) 'Neither European nor Works Councils: a reply to Paul Knutsen', *Economic and Industrial Democracy*, 18(2), 325–37.

Streeck, W. (1998) 'The internationalization of industrial relations in Europe: prospects and problems', *Politics and Society*, 26(4), 429–59.

Streeck, W. (1999) 'Competitive Solidarity: Rethinking the "European Social Model"', MPIfG Working Paper 99/8, September. Cologne: Max-Planck Institut für Gesellschaftforschung.

Streeck, W. and Vitols, S. (1993) 'European Works Councils: between statutory enactment and voluntary adoption', WZB Discussion Paper FS I 93–312, Berlin: Wissenschaftszentrum Berlin für Sozialforschung.

Supiot, A. (ed.) (1999) *Au-delà de l'emploi. Transformations du travail et devenir du droit du travail en Europe*. Paris: Flammarion.

Supiot, A. (2000) 'The dogmatic foundations of the market', *Industrial Law Journal*, 29(4), 321–46.

Swenson, P. and Pontusson, J. (2000) 'The Swedish employer offensive against centralised wage bargaining', in T. Iversen, J. Pontusson and D. Soskice (eds), *Unions, Employers and Central Banks*. Cambridge: Cambridge University Press, 77–106.

Taylor, R. (1999) 'Blair "rejects" partnership with unions and employers', *Financial Times*, 7 July.

Teague, P. (1999a) *Economic Citizenship in the European Union: Employment Relations in the New Europe*. London: Routledge.

Teague, P. (1999b) 'Reshaping employment regimes in Europe: policy shifts alongside boundary change', *Journal of Public Policy*, 19(1), 38–72.

Teague, P. (2000) 'Macroeconomic constraints, social learning and pay bargaining in Europe', *British Journal of Industrial Relations*, 38(3), 429–53.

Teague, P. (2001) 'Deliberate governance and EU social policy', *European Journal of Industrial Relations*, 7(1), 7–26.

Teague, P. and Grahl, J. (1992) *1992 – the Big Market: the Future of the European Community*. London: Lawrence and Wishart.

Thelen, C. (2001) 'Varieties of labour politics in the developed democracies', in P. Hall and D. Soskice (eds), *Varieties of Capitalism: the Institutional Foundations of Comparative Advantage*. Oxford: Oxford University Press.

Thörnqvist, C. (1999) 'The decentralisation of industrial relations: the Swedish case in comparative perspective', *European Journal of Industrial Relations*, 5(1), 71–87.

Tinbergen, J. (1965) *International Economic Integration*, 2nd edn. Amsterdam: Elsevier.

Traxler, F. (1995) 'Farewell to labour market associations? Organised versus disorganised decentralization as a map for industrial relations', in C. Crouch and F. Traxler (eds), *Organised Industrial Relations in Europe: What Future?* Aldershot: Avebury.

Traxler, F. (1996) 'European trade union policy and collective bargaining', *Transfer*, 2(2), 287–97.

Traxler, F. (1997) 'The logic of social pacts', in G. Fajertag and P. Pochet (eds), *Social Pacts in Europe*. Brussels: ETUI.

Traxler, F. (1998a) 'Collective bargaining in the OECD: developments, preconditions and effects', *European Journal of Industrial Relations*, 4(2), 207–26.

Traxler, F. (1998b) 'Austria: still the country of corporatism', in A. Ferner and R. Hyman (eds), *Changing Industrial Relations in Europe*. Oxford: Blackwell, 239–61.

Traxler, F. (1999) 'Wage-setting institutions and European Monetary Union', in G. Huemer, M. Mesch and F. Traxler (eds), *The Role of Employer Associations and Labour Unions in the EMU*. Aldershot: Ashgate, 115–36.

Traxler, F. (2000a) 'Employers and employer organization in Europe: membership strength, density and representativeness', *Industrial Relations Journal*, 31(4), 308–16.

Traxler, F. (2000b) 'National pacts and wage regulation in Europe: a comparative analysis', in G. Fajertag and P. Pochet (eds), *Social Pacts in Europe – New Dynamics* Brussels: ETUI, 401–18.

Traxler, F. (2003) 'Bargaining, state regulation and the trajectories of industrial relations', *European Journal of Industrial Relations*, 9(2), 141–61.

Traxler, F. and Behrens, M. (2002) 'Collective bargaining coverage and extension procedures', *European Industrial Relations Observatory On-line*, Ref: TN0212102S.

Traxler, F., Blaschke, S. and Kittel, B. (2001) *National Labour Relations in Internationalized Markets*. Oxford: Oxford University Press.

Traxler, F. and Mermet, E. (2003) 'Co-ordination of collective bargaining: the case of Europe', *Transfer*, 9(2), 229–46.

Treu, T. (2001) Presentation during the closing ceremony, 6th IIRA European Congress, Oslo, 25–9 June.

Tronti, L. (1998) 'Benchmarking labour market performances and practices', *Labour*, 12(3), 489–513.

Tsebelis, G (1999) 'Approaches to the study of European politics', *ECSA Review*, 12(2), 4–6.

UIMM (Union des Industries Métallurgiques et Minières) (1968) *Année Métallurgique*. Paris: UIMM.

Ulman, L. (1974) 'Connective bargaining and competitive bargaining', *Scottish Journal of Political Economy*, 21(2), 97–109.

UNICE (1999) *Releasing Europe's Employment Potential: Companies' Views on European Social Policy Beyond 2000*. Brussels: UNICE.

UNI-Europa (2000) *Pay Benchmarking and the Euro – How Should Uni-Europa Respond?* Geneva: UNI-Europa.

United Nations (2000) 'Cross-border mergers and acquisitions and development', *World Investment Report 2000*. Geneva: UNCTAD.

United Nations (2002) 'Export competitiveness', *World Investment Report 2002*. Geneva: UNCTAD.

van de Meer, M. (2001) 'From Taylor-made to tailor-made'. Paper presented at the Conference of the Netherlands HRM Network, Nijmegen, 15 November.

Van Ruysseveldt, J. and Visser, J. (1996) 'Contestation and state intervention forever? Industrial relations in France', in J. Van Ruysseveldt and J. Visser (eds), *Industrial Relations in Europe*. London: Sage, 82–123.

Van Tulder, R., van den Berghe, D. and Muller, A. (2001) *Erasmus (S)coreboard of Core Companies: the World's Largest Firms and Internationalization*. Rotterdam: Rotterdam School of Management.

Venturini, P. (1998) 'The prospects for European social policy: some reflections', in P. Pochet and B. VanHercke (eds), *Social Challenges of Economic and Monetary Union* Brussels: European Interuniversity Press, 103–16.

Verdun, A. (1996) 'An asymmetrical Economic and Monetary Union in the EU', *Journal of European Integration*, 20(1), 60–81.

Vilrokx, J. and Van Leemput, J. (1998) 'Belgium: the great transformation', in A. Ferner and R. Hyman (eds), *Changing Industrial Relations in Europe*. Oxford: Blackwell, 315–47.

Visser, J. (1998) 'The Netherlands: the return of responsive corporatism', in A. Ferner and R. Hyman (eds), *Changing Industrial Relations in Europe*. Oxford: Blackwell, 283–314.

Visser, J. (1999) 'Societal support for social dialogue' in G. Huemer, M. Mesch and F. Traxler (eds), *The Role of Employers' Associations and Labour in the EMU*. Aldershot: Ashgate, 85–114.

Visser, J. (2003) 'Convergent divergence or divergent convergence? A comment on Marginson and Sisson', in J. Weiler, I. Begg and J. Peterson (eds), *Integration in an Expanding European Union: Reassessing the Fundamentals*. Oxford: Blackwell, 191–5.

Visser, J. and Hemerijck, A. (1997) *'A Dutch Miracle': Job Growth, Welfare Reform and Corporatism in the Netherlands*. Amsterdam: Amsterdam University Press.

Vitols, S. (2003) *Management Cultures in Europe: European Works Councils and Human Resource Management in Multinational Enterprises*. Final Report of a Study Commissioned by the Forum Mitbestimmung und Unternehmen, Wissenschaftszentrum, Berlin.

Waddington, J. (2001) 'Articulating trade union organisation for the New Europe', *Industrial Relations Journal*, 32(5), 449–63.

Waddington, J. (2003) 'What do representatives think of the practices of European Works Councils?', *European Journal of Industrial Relations*, 9(3), 303–25.

Waddington, J. and Kerckhofs, P. (2003) 'European Works Councils: what is the current state of play?', *Transfer*, 9(2), 322–39.

Wallace, H. (2001) 'The changing politics of the EU: an overview', *Journal of Common Market Studies*, 39(4), 581–94.

Wallace, W. (1990) 'Introduction: the dynamics of European integration' in W. Wallace (ed.), *The Dynamics of European Integration*. London: Pinter.

Walton, R. and McKersie, R. (1965) *A Behavioral Theory of Labor Negotiations*. New York: McGraw-Hill.

Webb, S. and Webb, B. (1902) *Industrial Democracy* 4th impression. London: Longmans.

Wedderburn, Lord W. (1997) 'Consultation and collective bargaining in Europe: success or ideology?', *Industrial Law Journal*, 26(1), 1–34.

Weiss, L. (1998) The *Myth of the Powerless State*. Cambridge: Polity Press.

Wendon, B. (2000) 'The Commission as image-venue entrepreneur in EU social policy', *Journal of European Public Policy*, 5(2), 339–53.

Whitley, R. (1992) *European Business Systems: Firms and Markets in their National Contexts*. London: Sage.

Whitley, R. (1996) 'The social construction of economic actors', in R. Whitley and P. Kristensen (eds), *The Changing European Firm: Limits to Convergence*. London: Routledge, 39–66.

Whittington, R. and Mayer, M. (2000) *The European Corporation: Strategy, Structure and Social Science*. Oxford: Oxford University Press.

Williamson, O. (1985) *The Economic Institutions of Capitalism: Firms, Market, Relational Contracting*. New York: Free Press.

Williamson, O. (1986) *Economic Organization*. Brighton: Wheatsheaf.

Windolf, P. (1989) 'Productivity coalitions and the future of European corporatism', *Industrial Relations*, 28(1), 1–20.

Zagelmeyer, S. (2000) *Innovative Agreements on Employment and Competitiveness in the European Union and Norway*. Luxembourg: Office for the Official Publications of the European Communities.

Index